Qualitative
Data Analysis

Edition 3

Matthew B. Miles ■ A. Michael Huberman ■ Johnny Saldaña
Arizona State University

Qualitative Data Analysis

A Methods Sourcebook

Edition 3

SAGE

Los Angeles | London | New Delhi
Singapore | Washington DC

Los Angeles | London | New Delhi
Singapore | Washington DC

FOR INFORMATION:

SAGE Publications, Inc.
2455 Teller Road
Thousand Oaks, California 91320
E-mail: order@sagepub.com

SAGE Publications Ltd.
1 Oliver's Yard
55 City Road
London EC1Y 1SP
United Kingdom

SAGE Publications India Pvt. Ltd.
B 1/I 1 Mohan Cooperative Industrial Area
Mathura Road, New Delhi 110 044
India

SAGE Publications Asia-Pacific Pte. Ltd.
3 Church Street
#10-04 Samsung Hub
Singapore 049483

Acquisitions Editor: Helen Salmon
Editorial Assistant: Kaitlin Perry
Assistant Editor: Kalie Koscielak
Production Editor: Laura Barrett
Copy Editor: QuADS Prepress (P) Ltd.
Typesetter: C&M Digitals (P) Ltd.
Proofreader: Theresa Kay
Indexer: Will Ragsdale
Cover Designer: Janet Kiesel
Marketing Manager: Nicole Elliott
Permissions Editor: Adele Hutchinson

First and Second Edition Copyright © 1994 by Matthew B. Miles and A. Michael Huberman

Third Edition Copyright © 2014 SAGE Publications, Inc.

Printed in the United States of America

Library of Congress Cataloging-in-Publication Data

Miles, Matthew B.
Qualitative data analysis: a methods sourcebook / Matthew B. Miles, A. Michael Huberman, Johnny Saldaña, Arizona State University. — Third edition.

pages. cm
Includes bibliographical references and index.

ISBN 978-1-4522-5787-7 (pbk. : alk. paper)

1. Social sciences—Research. 2. Education—Research. I. Huberman, A. M. II. Saldaña, Johnny. III. Title.

H62.M437 2014
001.4'2—dc23   2013002036

This book is printed on acid-free paper.

14 15 16 17 10 9 8 7 6 5 4 3 2

Brief Table of Contents

List of Displays   xiii

Preface to the Third Edition by Johnny Saldaña   xvii

Acknowledgments From the Second Edition
by Matthew B. Miles and A. Michael Huberman   xxi

About the Authors   xxiii

Part One – The Substantive Start 1

Chapter 1 - Introduction   3

Chapter 2 - Research Design and Management   17

Chapter 3 - Ethical Issues in Analysis   55

Chapter 4 - Fundamentals of Qualitative Data Analysis   69

Part Two – Displaying the Data 105

Chapter 5 - Designing Matrix and Network Displays   107

Chapter 6 - Methods of Exploring   121

Chapter 7 - Methods of Describing   161

Chapter 8 - Methods of Ordering   193

Chapter 9 - Methods of Explaining   221

Chapter 10 - Methods of Predicting   255

Part Three – Making Good Sense 273

Chapter 11 - Drawing and Verifying Conclusions   275

Chapter 12 - Writing About Qualitative Research   323

Chapter 13 - Closure   339

Appendix – An Annotated Bibliography of Qualitative Research Resources   345

References   363

Author Index   369

Subject Index   373

Contents

List of Displays   xiii

Preface to the Third Edition by Johnny Saldaña   xvii

Acknowledgments From the Second Edition
by Matthew B. Miles and A. Michael Huberman   xxi

About the Authors   xxiii

Part One – The Substantive Start 1

Chapter 1 - Introduction 3

The Purpose of This Book   4
The Nature of This Book   5
    Audiences   5
    Approach   6
Our Orientation   6
Genres of Qualitative Research   8
An Approach to Qualitative Data Analysis   9
    Analytic Methods: Some Common Features   10
The Nature of Qualitative Data   10
    General Nature   10
    Strengths of Qualitative Data   11
Our View of Qualitative Data Analysis   12
    Data Condensation   12
    Data Display   12
    Drawing and Verifying Conclusions   13
Suggestions for Readers   15
    Students and Other Novice Researchers   15
    Experienced Researchers   15
    Teachers of Qualitative Research Methods Courses   16
Closure and Transition   16

Chapter 2 - Research Design and Management 17

Introduction   18
Tight Versus Loose Designs: Some Trade-Offs   19
Building a Conceptual Framework   20
    Description and Rationale   20
    Examples   21
    Advice   25

Formulating Research Questions   25

    Description and Rationale   25

    Example   26

    Advice   27

Defining the Case   28

    Description and Rationale   28

    Examples   28

    Advice   30

Sampling: Bounding the Collection of Data   30

    Description and Rationale   30

    Key Features of Qualitative Sampling   31

    General Sampling Strategies   32

    Within-Case Sampling   33

    Multiple-Case Sampling   33

    Example   34

    Advice   36

Instrumentation   37

    Description and Rationale   37

    Example   40

    Advice   42

Linking Qualitative and Quantitative Data   42

    Approaches to Mixed-Methods Designs   43

Management Issues Bearing on Analysis   45

    Computer and Software Use   46

    Data Management   50

    Staffing and Time Planning   52

Closure and Transition   53

Note   53

Chapter 3 - Ethical Issues in Analysis 55

Introduction   56

Agreements With Study Participants   56

Ethical Issues   58

    Worthiness of the Project   59

    Competence   59

    Informed Consent   59

    Benefits, Costs, and Reciprocity   60

    Harm and Risk   61

    Honesty and Trust   62

    Privacy, Confidentiality, and Anonymity   62

    Intervention and Advocacy   64

    Research Integrity and Quality   64

    Ownership of Data and Conclusions   65

    Use and Misuse of Results   66

Conflicts, Dilemmas, and Trade-Offs   66

Closure and Transition   68

Chapter 4 - Fundamentals of Qualitative Data Analysis.......... 69

Introduction 70
    Data Processing and Preparation 71
First-Cycle Codes and Coding 71
    Description 71
    Applications 73
    First-Cycle Coding Examples 73
    Creating Codes 81
    Revising Codes 82
    Structure and Unity in Code Lists 82
    Definitions of Codes 84
    Levels of Coding Detail 85
Second Cycle Coding: Pattern Codes 86
    Description 86
    Applications 86
    Examples 86
    From Codes to Patterns 89
    Coding Advice 93
Jottings 93
Analytic Memoing 95
    Description and Rationale 95
    Examples 96
    On Visual Data 98
    Memoing Advice 99
Assertions and Propositions 99
Within-Case and Cross-Case Analysis 100
    Purposes of Cross-Case Analysis 101
    A Key Distinction: Variables Versus Cases 101
    Strategies for Cross-Case Analysis 102
Closure and Transition 104

Part Two – Displaying the Data.......... 105

Chapter 5 - Designing Matrix and Network Displays............107

Introduction 108
Display Format Options 109
    Matrices 109
    Networks 111
Timing of Display Design 112
Formatting the Matrix Template 113
Entering Matrix and Network Data 115
Making Inferences and Drawing Conclusions From
    Matrices and Networks 117
The Methods Profiles 118
Closure and Transition 119

Chapter 6 - Methods of Exploring 121

Introduction	122
Exploring Fieldwork in Progress	122
Data Accounting Log	122
Contact Summary Form	124
Case Analysis Meeting	128
Interim Case Summary	131
Partially Ordered Meta-Matrix	135
Explanatory Effects Matrix	140
Exploring Variables	142
Checklist Matrix	142
Content-Analytic Summary Table	148
Contrast Table	150
Two-Variable Case-Ordered Matrix	152
Exploring Reports in Progress	154
Pre-structured Case	154
Sequential Analyses	157
Closure and Transition	159

Chapter 7 - Methods of Describing 161

Introduction	162
Describing Participants	162
Role-Ordered Matrix	162
Context Chart	167
Describing Variability	170
Construct Table	171
Conceptually Clustered Matrix	173
Folk Taxonomy	179
Describing Action	182
Vignettes	182
Poetic Display	185
Cognitive Maps	187
Closure and Transition	192

Chapter 8 - Methods of Ordering 193

Introduction	194
Ordering by Time	194
Event-Listing Matrix	194
Growth Gradient	198
Time-Ordered Matrix	202
Ordering Processes	206
Decision Modeling	206
Event-State Network	209
Composite Sequence Analysis	211

Ordering by Cases   214

    Case-Ordered Descriptive Meta-Matrix   214

Closure and Transition   220

Chapter 9 - Methods of Explaining **221**

Introduction   222

Explaining Interrelationship   223

    Variable-by-Variable Matrix   223

Explaining Change   228

    Effects Matrix   228

    Case Dynamics Matrix   231

Explaining Causation   234

    Causal Chains   235

    Causal Network: Within-Case Analysis   236

    Causal Network: Cross-Case Analysis   247

Closure and Transition   253

Chapter 10 - Methods of Predicting **255**

Introduction   256

Methods of Predicting   256

    Making and Testing Predictions   256

    Prediction-Outcome-Consequences Matrix   262

    Causal-Prediction Models   266

Closure and Transition   272

Part Three – Making Good Sense 273

Chapter 11 - Drawing and Verifying Conclusions. 275

Introduction   276

Tactics for Generating Meaning   277

    1. Noting Patterns, Themes   277

    2. Seeing Plausibility   278

    3. Clustering   279

    4. Making Metaphors   280

    5. Counting   282

    6. Making Contrasts/Comparisons   284

    7. Partitioning Variables   285

    8. Subsuming Particulars Into the General   285

    9. Factoring   286

    10. Noting the Relations Between Variables   287

    11. Finding Intervening Variables   289

    12. Building a Logical Chain of Evidence   290

    13. Making Conceptual/Theoretical Coherence   292

Tactics for Testing or Confirming Findings   293

    1. Checking for Representativeness   295

2. Checking for Researcher Effects   296

3. Triangulating   299

4. Weighting the Evidence   300

5. Checking the Meaning of Outliers   301

6. Using Extreme Cases   302

7. Following Up Surprises   303

8. Looking for Negative Evidence   304

9. Making If-Then Tests   304

10. Ruling Out Spurious Relations   305

11. Replicating a Finding   307

12. Checking Out Rival Explanations   308

13. Getting Feedback From Participants   309

Standards for the Quality of Conclusions   310

Objectivity/Confirmability   311

Reliability/Dependability/Auditability   312

Internal Validity/Credibility/Authenticity   312

External Validity/Transferability/Fittingness   314

Utilization/Application/Action Orientation   314

Analytic Documentation   315

The Problem   315

Illustration   317

Closure and Transition   322

Chapter 12 - Writing About Qualitative Research **323**

Introduction   324

Audiences and Effects   325

The Reader and the Writer   325

Types of Effects   326

Voices, Genres, and Stances   327

Writing Example   328

Formats and Structures   332

Traditional Presentation Modes   333

Progressive Presentation Modes   334

On Theses and Dissertations   335

Closure and Transition   337

Chapter 13 - Closure **339**

Qualitative Analysis at a Glance   339

Reflections   341

Final Advice   343

Appendix – An Annotated Bibliography of
Qualitative Research Resources   345

References   363

Author Index   369

Subject Index   373

List of Displays

Display 1.1   Components of Data Analysis: Interactive Model   14

Display 2.1   A First-Draft Conceptual Framework for a Case Study Teacher and the Influences on Her Practice   22

Display 2.2   Major Influences on a Language Arts Teacher's Practice   23

Display 2.3   Conceptual Framework for a Multicase "School Improvement" Field Study, Initial Version   24

Display 2.4   General and Specific Research Questions Relating to the Adoption Decision (School Improvement Study)   27

Display 2.5   The Case as the Unit of Analysis   29

Display 2.6   Prior Instrumentation: Key Decision Factors   38

Display 2.7   Excerpts From Interview Guide, School Improvement Study   41

Display 2.8   Illustrative Designs Linking Qualitative and Quantitative Data   44

Display 2.9   Uses of Computer Software in Qualitative Studies   46

Display 2.10   An Excel Spread Sheet With Qualitative and Quantitative Data   47

Display 2.11   An NVivo 10 Screen Shot of a Coded Digital Video Interview   48

Display 2.12   A Model of Lifelong Confidence From High School Speech and Theatre   49

Display 2.13   What to Store, Retrieve From, and Retain   51

Display 3.1   Questions for Agreement With Study Participants   57

Display 4.1   Illustration of a Start List of Codes   82

Display 4.2   Definitions of Selected Codes From Display 4.1 (Excerpts)   85

Display 4.3   Smoking Cessation Patterns at Months 1 and 6   92

Display 4.4   A Model of Smoking Cessation Loss Transformation   92

Display 4.5   Interview Transcript With Jottings   95

Display 5.1   Effects Matrix: Assistance Location and Types (Masepa Case)   110

Display 5.2   A Network Model of "Lifelong Impact" From High School Speech Participation   111

Display 5.3   A QDA Miner 4 3-D Map of a Codes Network   113

Display 6.1   Data Accounting Log   123

Display 6.2   Contact Summary Form: Illustration (Excerpts)   125

Display 6.3   Contact Summary Form: Illustration With Coded Themes (Excerpt)   127

Display 6.4   Case Analysis Meeting Form   128

Display 6.5   Case Analysis Form: Exhibit With Data   130

Display 6.6   Summary-Aided Approach to Analysis   131

Display 6.7   Interim Case Summary Outline: Illustration   132

Display 6.8   Data Accounting Sheet: Abstract Example   135

Display 6.9   Case-Level Display for Partially Ordered Meta-Matrix (Format)   135

Display 6.10   Case-Level Display for Partially Ordered Meta-Matrix: Users' Second Year of Implementation at Lido   137

Display 6.11   Partially Ordered Meta-Matrix: User Feelings/Concerns and Other Variables (Format)   138

Display 6.12   Partially Ordered Meta-Matrix: User Feelings/Concerns and Other Variables (Lido Data)   138

Display 6.13   Time-Ordered Meta-Matrix (Format)   139

Display 6.14   Summary Table: Individual and Institutional Concerns During Later Implementation   139

Display 6.15   Explanatory Effects Matrix: Ongoing Assistance   141

Display 6.16   Checklist Matrix: Conditions Supporting Preparedness at Smithson School, Banestown Case   143

Display 6.17   Checklist Matrix on Preparedness (Alternative Format 1)   147

Display 6.18   Checklist Matrix on Preparedness (Alternative Format 2)   147

Display 6.19   Checklist Matrix on Preparedness (Alternative Format 3)   148

Display 6.20   Content-Analytic Summary Table: The Content of Organization Changes   149

Display 6.21   Contrast Table: Exemplary Cases Showing Different Degrees of User Change   151

Display 6.22   Two-Variable Case-Ordered Matrix: Relationships Between User Practice Stabilization and Local Continuation   153

Display 6.23   Pre-structured Case Outline: Abbreviated Version   155

Display 6.24   Traditional Analysis Sequence Compared With Pre-structured Case   157

Display 7.1   Role-Ordered Matrix: First Reactions to the Innovation   164

Display 7.2   Context Chart for Tindale East High School and District   168

Display 7.3	Lifelong Impact: Variability of Influence	171
Display 7.4	Conceptually Clustered Matrix: Motives and Attitudes (Format)	174
Display 7.5	Conceptually Clustered Matrix: Motives and Attitudes of Users, Nonusers, and Administrators at Masepa	176
Display 7.6	A Folk Taxonomy of the Ways Children Oppress Each Other	180
Display 7.7	A Cognitive Map of One Person's Housecleaning Process	188
Display 8.1	Event Listing, Banestown Case	195
Display 8.2	Event History of a Case Study	199
Display 8.3	Growth Gradient for ECRI Innovation, Masepa Case	200
Display 8.4	Time-Ordered Matrix: Changes in the CARED Innovation (a Work Experience Program)	202
Display 8.5	Summary Table for Verifying and Interpreting Time-Ordered Matrix: Changes in the CARED Innovation	205
Display 8.6	One Person's Decision Model for Saving Money	206
Display 8.7	Event–State Network, Banestown Case (Excerpt)	210
Display 8.8	Composite Sequence Analysis: Career Trajectory Data for 11 Cases (Huberman, 1989)	212
Display 8.9	Case-Ordered Meta-Matrix: Format for Student Impact Data	214
Display 8.10	Case-Ordered Descriptive Meta-Matrix (Excerpt): Program Objectives and Student Impact (Direct, Meta-Level, and Side Effects)	216
Display 8.11	Case-Ordered Effects Matrix Template	219
Display 9.1	Variable-by-Variable Matrix: Coping Strategies and Problems, by Case	224
Display 9.2	Summary Table: Typical Consequences of Coping, by Case	227
Display 9.3	Effects Matrix: Organizational Changes After Implementation of the ECRI Program	229
Display 9.4	Case Dynamics Matrix: The IPA Innovation as a Force for Organizational Change in the District and Its Schools	232
Display 9.5	Causal Chain: Illustration	235
Display 9.6	Causal Chain: Illustration	236
Display 9.7	Causal Fragment: Mastery of a New Educational Practice	237
Display 9.8	Excerpt From a Causal Network: Perry-Parkdale School	240

Display 9.9	Excerpt From an Event–State Network: Perry-Parkdale School	240
Display 9.10	List of Antecedent, Mediating, and Outcome Variables: School Improvement Study	241
Display 9.11	Causal Network for Perry-Parkdale CARED Program	244
Display 9.12	Narrative for Causal Network: Perry-Parkdale CARED Program	246
Display 9.13	Subnetwork: Variable Streams Leading to High Job Mobility, Perry-Parkdale Case	248
Display 9.14	Subnetwork for Job Mobility, Calston Case	250
Display 9.15	Subnetwork for Job Mobility, Banestown Case	251
Display 9.16	Subnetwork for Job Mobility, Plummet Case	252
Display 10.1	Prediction Feedback Form	257
Display 10.2	Factors Supporting "Institutionalization" Prediction	259
Display 10.3	Factors Working Against "Institutionalization" Prediction	260
Display 10.4	Filled-Out Response Form From Case Informant for "Institutionalization" Prediction	261
Display 10.5	Predictor-Outcome-Consequences Matrix: Antecedents and Consequences of Assistance	264
Display 10.6	Causal-Prediction Model Tracing User Practice Changes	267
Display 10.7	Predictor-Outcome Matrix: Predictors of Magnitude of User Practice Change	269
Display 11.1	Reasons Given for Adoption by Users	283
Display 11.2	Two-Variable Relationship	289
Display 11.3	Two-Variable Relationship With Intervening Variables	290
Display 11.4	Example of a Chain of Evidence Supporting an Observed Outcome	291
Display 11.5	Possible Explanation of a Spurious Relationship	306
Display 11.6	Display for Testing Explanations in Display 11.5	306
Display 11.7	Qualitative Analysis Documentation Form	318
Display 11.8	Code List for Analysis Operations	320
Display 13.1	Overview of Qualitative Data Analysis Processes	340

Preface to the Third Edition

Johnny Saldaña

This new edition of Matthew B. Miles and A. Michael Huberman's classic 1994 text, *Qualitative Data Analysis: An Expanded Sourcebook*, updates and streamlines the late authors' unique work for a new generation of qualitative researchers as well as for the dedicated followers of their methods over the past three decades. I have been honored to join them, in spirit, as the third author of this revised text.

To this day, qualitative data analysis seems to remain a somewhat mysterious and elusive process for newcomers to the field. This is due in part to the wide variety of genres, methodologies, and methods available to researchers, making it sometimes difficult to choose the "best" ones for the particular study in hand. In addition, qualitative research has a solid foundation of analytic traditions but no current standardization of practice—there is no official qualitative executive board out there mandating exactly how analysis must be conducted. Ours is "designer research," customized to the particular goals and needs of the enterprise and interpreted through each researcher's unique analytic lens and filter. Books on research methods can no longer require; they can only recommend.

This book offers its readers practical guidance in recommended methods for assembling and analyzing primarily text-based data. *Qualitative Data Analysis: A Methods Sourcebook* is designed for researchers in virtually all fields and disciplines that honor what their human participants have to say, treasure the products and artifacts they create, and respect the complexity of social action as it happens all around us. It is intended for students in graduate degree programs who are learning how to investigate the human condition through qualitative research coursework and for established scholars and practitioners continuing their professional development by reading the literature on current methods.

A Note on This Revision

For this third edition, SAGE Publications charged me to maintain the general spirit and integrity of the core contents of Miles and Huberman's (1994) authoritative work, while making their text more accessible and relevant to contemporary researchers. I have added information on the newer computing technology and software available today, and reorganized and streamlined the original authors' classic methods. Readers familiar with the previous edition will notice that in this edition I have re-envisioned the primary display chapters, not organizing them by within-case and cross-case divisions but by Miles and Huberman's five primary purposes of display: to explore, describe, order, explain, and predict. I have reduced the number of displays from the second edition and, when possible, reformatted them using mainstream software. SAGE Publications' art production staff have redrawn many of the original figures.

I have also added selected coverage of additional genres of qualitative inquiry, such as narrative inquiry, autoethnography, mixed methods, and arts-based research, that have emerged prominently over the past 20 years. I have smoothed down the second edition's semiquantitative edges to align and harmonize the original authors' approach with that of current qualitative inquirers. And I have brought my own analytic signature to the text, respecting some of the original authors' traditions while adapting others into a newer, evolving research culture. Overall, I have scaled back the impressive, if sometimes overwhelming, size of Miles and Huberman's original work to present and re-present their insightful analytic methods in a more focused and useful manner.

In certain problematic sections of the second edition, I struggled with deciding whether to delete, maintain, or revise the text. Since my charge as third coauthor was to *adapt* Miles and Huberman's work, not to write my own book on qualitative data analysis, I have respected the original authors' contributions to the field by maintaining the conceptual approaches and most of the analytic methods of their book. Nevertheless, I have, without guilt, mercilessly deleted most of its early references, second-source displays, duplicate and overextended discussions, and some more convoluted sections.

I have brought my own working knowledge of the book's second edition into my revision efforts because, as a student, I was enrolled in two courses where Miles and Huberman's text was required reading. This revision is based on what I wish the book had offered me as a novice to qualitative research and what I believe today's graduate students need from a textbook on qualitative data analysis. My reorganizing decisions are based on pedagogical knowledge of how most university graduate students learn and on how I personally prefer to teach: progressing in a highly organized, systematic way, one building block at a time, toward a spiraled, cumulative synthesis—a process I'm almost certain Miles and Huberman would have appreciated and found compatible with their own approach.

I also brought my knowledge of Miles and Huberman's book to my work as author of SAGE Publications' *The Coding Manual for Qualitative Researchers* (Saldaña, 2013), in which I included a few of their coding and analysis methods. And I incorporated some of *The Coding Manual*'s content into this book, further integrating the three coauthors' work. In addition, I supplemented a few of the original authors' display methods and discussions with examples from my own research projects and incorporated *The Coding Manual*'s method profile structure (Description, Applications, Example, Analysis, Notes) into this revision.

Finally, as the third coauthor of this edition, I have been in the position, both privileged and awkward, of "speaking" for the late Miles and Huberman. When I am in agreement with their original premises and assertions, I deliberately use "we" in writing, as I do when making some informed assumptions that my own opinions would be similar to theirs. Occasionally, when our opinions seem to diverge, subtly or greatly, I specify whose belief is being discussed.

Acknowledgments

I am honored that Helen Salmon, acquisitions editor of SAGE Publications' College Division, commissioned me to adapt Miles and Huberman's text for its third edition. Her editorial assistant Kaitlin Perry was a tremendous resource for manuscript and display preparation. I also thank Laura Barrett, Kalie Koscielak, Judith Newlin, Nicole Elliott, and Janet Kiesel of SAGE Publications for their production work on this book.

Betty Miles offered me not only her support but also her keen eye and editorial prowess for this revision. My initial contact with SAGE began with their London office editor, Patrick Brindle, who encouraged me to develop *The Coding Manual for Qualitative Researchers*, and for his welcoming invitation I am truly grateful.

My own qualitative research methods professors at Arizona State University significantly influenced my growth as a scholar and writer. I am indebted to Tom Barone, Mary Lee Smith, Amira De la Garza, and Sarah J. Tracy for their life-changing impact on my academic career. Coleman A. Jennings from The University of Texas at Austin served as my graduate school artistic mentor; Lin Wright from Arizona State University started me as an assistant professor on my research trajectory; and Mitch Allen, Joe Norris, Laura A. McCammon, Matt Omasta, and Angie Hines are my research colleagues and loyal supporters. I also extend thanks to my long-distance mentors, Harry F. Wolcott, Norman K. Denzin, and Yvonna S. Lincoln, for their insightful writings, wisdom, and guidance.

In the second edition of *Qualitative Data Analysis*, Miles and Huberman thanked a large number of individuals and organizations. Their contributions continue to enrich this revised edition of the book, and they have my gratitude as well. For this particular edition, I also thank Oxford University Press for their permission to reprint selected excerpts from my text *Fundamentals of Qualitative Research* (Saldaña, 2011b); *Teachers College Record* and Taylor & Francis for article excerpt permissions; and Normand Péladeau of Provalis Research/QDA Miner and Katie Desmond of QSR International/ NVivo for their permission to use qualitative data analysis software screenshots.

My final thanks go to Matthew B. Miles and A. Michael Huberman themselves. To my knowledge, I never met them or heard them speak at professional conferences, but their data-analytic methods, which I learned intimately in my qualitative research courses, have been part of my work ever since. I always strive to meet their rigorous standards, and I frequently quote their now classic advice to "think display." I owe much of my career trajectory to the legacy of scholars before me whose methods books and articles helped shape my own ways of working as a qualitative researcher and data analyst. Miles and Huberman are two of those esteemed scholars, and I am honored to be connected with them in this new way. I hope that this third edition of their book pays proper tribute and homage to their significant level of scholarship.

Publisher's Acknowledgments

SAGE Publications and Johnny Saldaña are grateful for feedback on the draft manuscript of the third edition from the following reviewers: James H. Banning of Colorado State University–Fort Collins, Carolyn M. Garcia of the University of Minnesota, Madelyn Iris of Northwestern University, Mary Madden of The University of Maine–Orono, Sharon M. Ravitch of the University of Pennsylvania, Patricia Somers of The University of Texas–Austin, and Mildred E. Warner of Cornell University.

Acknowledgments From the Second Edition

Matthew B. Miles and A. Michael Huberman

The first edition of this book grew out of our (Miles and Huberman's) experience in two linked research projects. One, beginning in 1978, was the field study component of the Study of Dissemination Efforts Supporting School Improvement (Department of Education Contract 300-78-0527), led by David P. Crandall of The Network, Inc. We are indebted to him for his steady encouragement and support, and that of Ann Bezdek Weinheimer, project officer from the Office of Planning, Budgeting and Evaluation.

In the field study itself, Beverly Loy Taylor and Jo Ann Goldberg were strong colleagues; their fieldwork and case study analysis, along with ours, led to Volume 4 of the DESSI final report, *People, Policies, and Practices: Examining the Chain of School Improvement*, later published as *Innovation Up Close* (Huberman & Miles, 1984).

The second project, "The Realities of School Improvement Programs: Analysis of Qualitative Data" (NIE grant G-81-001-8), gave us the opportunity to develop our methodological ideas further and to write the first edition of this book. Rolf Lehming, of the Program on Dissemination and Improvement of Practice, was our project officer; we valued his sustained interest and advice.

The ideas in the first edition—and indeed in this one—do not necessarily reflect the views or policies of the Department of Education. But we remain grateful for its sponsorship of these studies.

In the past 10 years, many people have contributed to our understanding of qualitative data analysis and to the development of the second edition. We have experimented in the company of colleagues with studies that expanded, tested, and refined the methods described in the first edition. We are indebted to Ann Lieberman, Ellen Saxl, Myrna Cooper, Vernay Mitchell, and Sharon Piety-Jacobs, who joined Miles in a study (1983–1985) of school "change agents"; to the late Eleanor Farrar, Karen Seashore Louis, Sheila Rosenblum, and Tony Cipollone, in a study with Miles (1985–1989) of urban high school reform; to Per Dalin, Adriaan Verspoor, Ray Chesterfield, Hallvard Kuløy, Tekle Ayano, Mumtaz Jahan, and Carlos Rojas, whom we assisted in a World Bank study (1988–1992) of educational reform in Bangladesh, Ethiopia, and Colombia; to Marie-Madeleine Grounauer and Gianreto Pini, Huberman's associates in a teachers' life cycle study (1982–1986); and to Monica Gather-Thurler and Erwin Beck, associates in Huberman's study of research use (1984–1988).

As always, the process of teaching from the book taught us a great deal. There are too many participants to list, but we were fortunate to have led an extended series of seminars at the universities of Nijmegen and Utrecht (strong thanks to Rein van der Vegt) and at many other universities as well: Geneva, Zürich, Paris, Dijon, Leuven, Göteborg, Montreal, Toronto, Queen's, Utah, Monash, Melbourne, and Adelaide.

During 1990–1991, we sent an informal survey to a wide range of people engaged in qualitative research, asking for collegial advice and examples of their work. Our warm thanks to the 126 researchers who responded; they provided a wide range of ideas, papers, advice, and cautions that were immensely helpful. Many of these colleagues are quoted or cited in this book. Grants supporting the extensive retrieval and synthesis work for this edition came to us from the John D. and Catherine T. MacArthur Foundation, where Peter Gerber provided thoughtful support, and from SAGE Publications. Sara Miller McCune and David McCune of SAGE took a keen interest in the project. We are grateful for the active, intelligent guidance that our editor, Mitch Allen, provided throughout the work.

We owe a very special debt to Carolyn Riehl. Her ability to locate and extract interesting ideas—both substantive and methodological—from a wide range of qualitative studies is remarkable. She was a strong third colleague during our extended period of retrieval and ordering.

Drafts of this edition were reviewed by many people: Our warm thanks for the thoughtful advice of Martha Ann Carey, Rick Ginsberg, David Marsh, Joseph Maxwell, Betty Miles, Renata Tesch, Harry Wolcott, and an anonymous Sage reviewer. As with the first edition, we are grateful to each other for the energy, stimulation, and productivity of our work in a demanding enterprise.

M. B. M.

A. M. H.

About the Authors

Matthew B. Miles, a social psychologist, had a career-long interest in strategies for educational reform. His work focused on planned change in education, group and organizational studies, and the dissemination and implementation of research findings. His first major research project was a 4-year study of six new, innovative public schools.

A. Michael Huberman's long-term interests were in scientific epistemology, and adult cognition and knowledge use. His work focused on education policy, school reform, and the practical translation of research knowledge into effective school practice. His first extensive project was a 4-year study of an experimental elementary school's implementation of Piagetian theories in classroom practice.

Johnny Saldaña, a theatre educator, has explored qualitative research methodologies ranging from coding to ethnodrama. His work focuses on young people's and adults' participation in, and transformation through, the arts. His first qualitative research project was a 2½-year ethnography of a beginning teacher's experiences at an inner-city fine arts magnet school.

Miles and Huberman collaborated for many years on studies of the dissemination of educational innovations and school improvement. In the course of a multisite study sponsored by the National Institute of Education, they began a study of the procedures they were using to analyze data, which provided the intellectual stimulus and the content of much of this book. Miles and Huberman led seminars based on the book in the United States, Canada, Western Europe, and Australia.

Miles and Huberman's work together and with other colleagues included the study of school change agents, innovation in urban high schools, the social architecture of schools, teachers' life cycles, the use of scientific knowledge in vocational education, and educational reform in Bangladesh, Ethiopia, New Zealand, and Colombia.

Saldaña's studies have included child audience responses to theatre, teachers' perceptions of achievement standards, a survey of adults reflecting on their high school experiences, longitudinal qualitative research methodology, and arts-based research methodologies, including ethnodramatic and ethnotheatrical play production. Johnny Saldaña is the Evelyn Smith Professor of Theatre at Arizona State University and the author of Sage Publications' *The Coding Manual for Qualitative Researchers*.

Part
1

Chapter 1 - Introduction

Chapter 2 - Research Design and Management

Chapter 3 - Ethical Issues in Analysis

Chapter 4 - Fundamentals of Qualitative Data Analysis

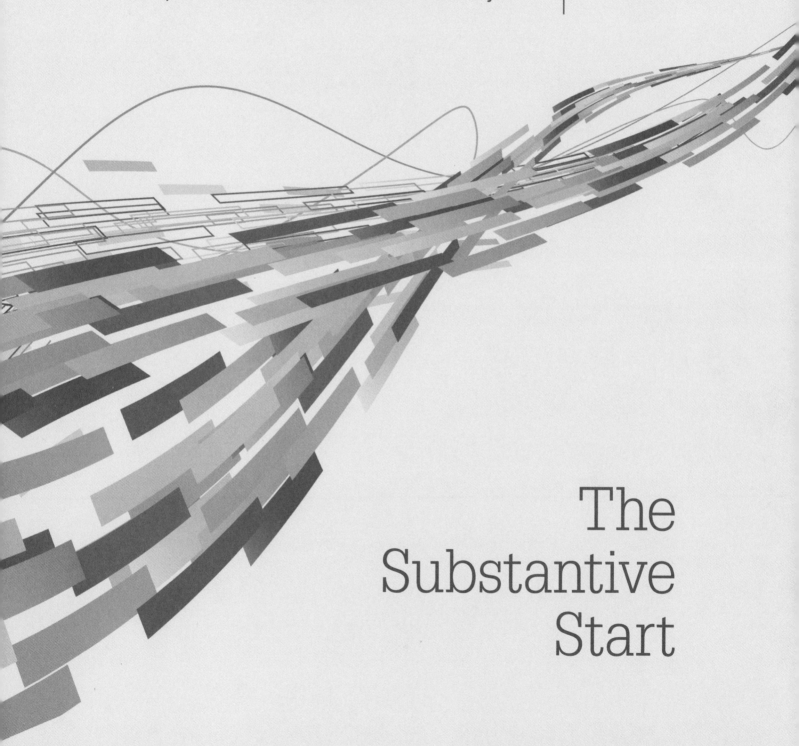

The
Substantive
Start

Introduction

Chapter Summary

This chapter introduces the reader to the coauthors' perspectives about the nature, goals, and selected genres of qualitative research, and the interconnected components of qualitative data analysis. We offer recommended guidance for the various audiences of this book and establish the parameters of what we will cover in the text.

Contents

The Purpose of This Book
The Nature of This Book
    Audiences
    Approach
Our Orientation
Genres of Qualitative Research
An Approach to Qualitative Data Analysis
    Analytic Methods: Some Common Features
The Nature of Qualitative Data
    General Nature
    Strengths of Qualitative Data

Our View of Qualitative Data Analysis
    Data Condensation
    Data Display
    Drawing and Verifying Conclusions
Suggestions for Readers
    Students and Other Novice Researchers
    Experienced Researchers
    Teachers of Qualitative Research Methods Courses
Closure and Transition

The Purpose of This Book

We wrote this book to address a need faced by researchers in all fields of the human sciences. Put simply, how can we draw valid and trustworthy meaning from qualitative data, and what methods of analysis can we use that are practical and will get us knowledge that we and others can rely on?

Qualitative data are a source of well-grounded, rich descriptions and explanations of human processes. With qualitative data, one can preserve chronological flow, see which events led to which consequences, and derive fruitful explanations. Then, too, good qualitative data are more likely to lead to serendipitous findings and to new integrations; they help researchers get beyond initial conceptions and generate or revise conceptual frameworks. Finally, the findings from well-analyzed qualitative studies have a quality of "undeniability." Words, especially organized into incidents or stories, have a concrete, vivid, and meaningful flavor that often proves far more convincing to a reader—another researcher, a policymaker, or a practitioner—than pages of summarized numbers.

The expansion of qualitative inquiry from the 1970s onward has been phenomenal. There are now numerous handbooks (e.g., Denzin & Lincoln's, 2012, *The SAGE Handbook of Qualitative Research*; Gubrium, Holstein, Marvasti, & McKinney's, 2012, *The SAGE Handbook of Interview Research*), exemplary textbooks (Charmaz's, 2006, *Constructing Grounded Theory*; Creswell's, 2013, *Qualitative Inquiry and Research Design*), prestigious peer-reviewed journals (*Qualitative Inquiry*, *Qualitative Health Research*), online newsletters and forums (SAGE Publications' Methodspace, *The Qualitative Report*), annual conferences (International Congress for Qualitative Inquiry, International Institute for Qualitative Methodology), and qualitative special-interest groups in several major professional associations (American Educational Research Association).

Yet, in the flurry of this activity, we should be mindful of some pervasive issues that have not gone away. These issues include the labor intensiveness (and extensiveness over months or years) of data collection, frequent data overload, researcher integrity, the time demands of processing and coding data, the adequacy of sampling when only a few cases can be managed, the generalizability of findings, the credibility and quality of conclusions, and their utility in the world of policy and action.

Although many researchers, from graduate students writing their dissertations to experienced researchers, work alone on their projects and often focus on single cases, qualitative work is becoming more complex. Increasingly, we see mixed-methods studies that combine qualitative and quantitative inquiry, carried out by research teams working with comparable data collection and analysis methods. And exciting new approaches to qualitative inquiry draw their inspiration from poetry, dramatic literature, visual art, and other creative genres to present and represent social life in fresh, evocative ways.

Some qualitative researchers still consider analysis to be an art form and insist on intuitive approaches to it. We are left with the researcher telling us of categories and patterns drawn from the welter of field data, in ways that are irreducible or even incommunicable. We do not really know how the researcher got from 1,000 pages of field notes and transcriptions to the final conclusions, as sprinkled with vivid illustrations as they may be.

This book is written in the belief that, as qualitative researchers, we need to keep sharing our *craft*—that is, the explicit, systematic methods we use to draw conclusions. We need methods that are credible, dependable, and replicable in *qualitative* terms. That is the need our book addresses.

The Nature of This Book

This is a practical methods sourcebook for all researchers who make use of qualitative data. But it is not intended as a comprehensive text; we do not address matters such as how to gain entry into a site, how to write field notes, or how to facilitate participant interviews. We want to share our experiences and those of other colleagues in the design and use of *qualitative data analysis methods*. Strong emphasis is placed on data displays—matrices and networks—that go beyond ordinary narrative text. Each method of data display and analysis is described and illustrated in detail, with practical suggestions for the researcher's use and adaptation with accessible software and basic programs.

Audiences

This book is for practicing researchers in all fields whose work, whether basic or applied, involves actual qualitative data analysis issues.

An important subset of that audience is the *beginning researcher*—a graduate student or early-career faculty member—working with qualitative data. We have encountered many students who launch into qualitative dissertations or research projects who sometimes feel overwhelmed and undertrained. With them in mind, we keep the language accessible and supportive, and we offer suggestions for using the book in qualitative research methods courses.

Another audience is *staff specialists and managers*, who rely on qualitative information as a routine part of their work and who need practical methods for making the best use of it.

Many examples used in the book are drawn from educational research, both ours and others'. We also include relevant discussion for other disciplines—health care, anthropology, sociology, psychology, business, political science, public administration, program evaluation, the arts, library science, organizational studies, criminology, human communication, family studies, and policy research—to underline that the methods are generic, not field limited.

Some of the methods reported here grew out of multiple case studies of organizations carried out by a research team. But do not despair if you are working alone, your study has just one case, or you are focusing at the individual or small-group level. There are many relevant examples for you, along with targeted advice.

Approach

This is a sourcebook, not a comprehensive handbook. We have tried to bring together a serviceable set of resources to encourage their use and, above all, to stimulate their further development, testing, and refinement. We also tend to be pragmatic. We believe that any method that works—that will produce clear, verifiable, and credible meanings from a set of qualitative data—has utility, regardless of its origins.

This book is about *doing analysis*. We cover questions of research design and data collection only as they bear on analysis and only glancingly address matters such as access to field sites and trust building with participants. Others have dealt with these issues repeatedly and well; we cite their work along the way and refer you to the Appendix's annotated bibliography for more information.

We have taken as concrete and direct an approach as possible, staying close to the reader's elbow and serving as a helpful guide through uneven territory. Although in each chapter we aim to provide a coherent intellectual frame for specific methods, we always emphasize hands-on work with actual data. For each of the methods outlined, we give specific examples with enough detail so that the reader can see how things work, can try the method, and, most important, can revise the method in future work.

These methods are manageable and straightforward, though some displays may, at first, appear daunting. Don't let them intimidate you; they are *examples*, not standards of practice. They do not necessarily require prolonged training or a specialized vocabulary. We can add that the experience of inventing analysis methods and of using/adapting those of others has been a productive one. The strongest message of this book is not that these particular methods should be applied scrupulously but that the creation, testing, and revision of simple, practical, and effective analysis methods remain the highest priority for qualitative researchers.

Finally, this book was written to share the experimentation, dialogue, and learning that good qualitative data analysis requires. We remain convinced that concrete, sharable methods do indeed belong to all of us. In the past few decades, we've found that refining and developing analysis methods on new projects had a clear payoff; also, our confidence in our findings was greater, and credibility for our research, practice, and policy audiences was enhanced. We hope that our experiences will be helpful to our colleagues, as theirs has been to us.

Our Orientation

It is worthwhile, we think, for researchers to make their preferences clear. To know how a researcher construes the shape of the social world and aims to give us a credible account of it is to know our conversational partner.

We label ourselves *pragmatic realists*. We believe that social phenomena exist not only in the mind but also in the world—and that some reasonably stable relationships can be found among the idiosyncratic messiness of life. There are regularities and sequences that link together phenomena. From these patterns, we can derive the constructs that underlie individual and social life. The fact that most of those constructs are invisible to the human eye does not make them invalid. After all, we all are surrounded by lawful physical mechanisms of which we're, at most, remotely aware.

Human relationships and societies have unique peculiarities and inconsistencies that make a realist approach to understanding them more complex—but not impossible. Unlike researchers in physics, we must contend with the institutions, structures, practices, and conventions that people reproduce and transform. Human meanings and intentions are worked out within the frameworks of these social structures—structures that are invisible but nonetheless real. In other words, social phenomena, such as language, decisions, conflicts, and hierarchies, exist in the world and exert strong influences over human activities because people construe them in common ways. Things that are believed become real and can be inquired into.

We agree with interpretivists who point out that knowledge is a social and historical product and that "facts" come to us laden with theory. We affirm the existence and importance of the subjective, the phenomenological, and the meaning making at the center of social life. Our goal is to register and transcend these processes by making assertions and building theories to account for a real world that is both bounded and perceptually laden—and to test these assertions and theories in our various disciplines.

Our tests do not use the deductive logic of classical positivism. Rather, our explanations flow from an account of how differing structures produced the events we observed. We want to account for events, rather than simply document their sequence. We look for an individual or a social process, a mechanism, or a structure at the core of events that can be captured to provide a causal description of the most likely forces at work.

The paradigms for conducting social research are always shifting beneath our feet. Our view is that sharing more about our craft is essential and that it is possible to develop practical methods for judging the goodness of our conclusions. We may face the risk of formalization when we dissect and reassemble the analytic procedures used by qualitative researchers, but not a large one. To us, research is actually more a craft (and sometimes, an art) than a slavish adherence to methodological rules. No study conforms exactly to a standard methodology; each one calls for the researcher to bend the methodology to the uniqueness of the setting or case. At the least, we need to find out what qualitative researchers actually *do* when they assemble and analyze data from the field.

Readers looking at the methods in this sourcebook will find them to be orderly ones, with a good degree of formalization. Many colleagues prefer more relaxed and open-ended voyages through their data, and we wish them well. We have opted for thoroughness and explicitness in this book, not just because it suits us but because vague descriptions are of little practical use to others. Note, however, that some techniques in this book call for metaphorical thinking, creative representations, and even free associations. And the overall structure of the text allows for some techniques to be used and others to be left aside. We advise you to look behind any apparent formalism and seek out what will be *useful* in your own work.

Genres of Qualitative Research

Qualitative research may be conducted in dozens of ways, many with long traditions behind them. To do them all justice is impossible here. For our purposes, the questions are as follows: What do selected genres (types) of qualitative research have to say about *analysis*? And can we see some common themes and practices?

Saldaña (2011b) describes more than 20 different qualitative research genres out of many more available to investigators, ranging from well-established traditions such as ethnography, grounded theory, phenomenology, case study, and content analysis to more progressive genres of qualitative research, such as poetic inquiry, narrative inquiry, ethnodrama, autoethnography, and duoethnography.

Each approach (several of these will be discussed later) will generally employ particular forms of analysis with their data. Grounded theory, for example, uses a series of cumulative coding cycles and reflective analytic memoing to develop major categories for theory generation. Phenomenology tends to look at data thematically to extract essences and essentials of participant meanings. Mixed-methods research integrates both qualitative and quantitative data and analyses for a more multidimensional approach to inquiry. Poetic inquiry, narrative inquiry, and ethnodrama adopt and adapt the conventions of fictional literature to render nonfictional participant experiences in poetic, prosaic, and dramatic forms, as opposed to the traditional and conventional formats of scholarly/academic writing.

The primary methodology of social anthropology—ethnography—stays close to the naturalist form of inquiry: that is, (a) extended contact within a given community; (b) concern for mundane, day-to-day events as well as for unusual ones; (c) direct or indirect participation in local activities, with particular care given to the description of local particularities; (d) a focus on individuals' perspectives and interpretations of their world; (e) relatively little pre-structured instrumentation, but often a wider use of audio and video recordings; and (f) more purposeful observation than in other research traditions.

Ethnographic methods tend toward the descriptive. The analysis task is to reach across multiple data sources and to condense them. Of course, in deciding what to leave in, what to highlight, what to report first and last, what to interconnect, and what main ideas are important, analytic choices are being made continuously.

Genres such as content analysis, conversation analysis, and discourse analysis pay meticulous attention to the nuances and embedded meanings of literally every single word in a data corpus as part of their analytic processes, while genres such as visual arts–based research and photovoice place primacy on the power of the image to represent human experience. Oral history documents the past, while action research envisions and works for a better future. Autoethnography examines the self, while duoethnography examines the self in relationship with another—who is also examining one's self.

The purpose of this section is not to describe every single genre of qualitative research available to you but to focus on some common features that occur in most genres of qualitative inquiry. We list some of them here, aware that some exemplars are missing:

- Qualitative research is conducted through intense and/or prolonged contact with participants in a naturalistic setting to investigate the everyday and/or exceptional lives of individuals, groups, societies, and organizations.

- The researcher's role is to gain a holistic (systemic, encompassing, and integrated) overview of the context under study: its social arrangement, its ways of working, and its explicit and implicit rules.

- Relatively little standardized instrumentation is used. The researcher himself or herself is essentially the main instrument in the study.

- The researcher attempts to capture data on the perceptions of local participants from the inside through a process of deep attentiveness, of empathetic understanding, and of suspending or bracketing preconceptions about the topics under discussion.

- Most of the analysis is done with words. The words can be assembled, subclustered, or broken into segments. They can be reorganized to permit the researcher to compare, contrast, analyze, and construct patterns out of them.

- Reading through these empirical materials (i.e., data), the researcher may construct certain themes and patterns that can be reviewed with participants.

- The main task is to describe the ways people in particular settings come to understand, account for, take action, and otherwise manage their day-to-day situations.

- Many interpretations of this material are possible, but some are more compelling for theoretical reasons or on grounds of credibility and trustworthiness.

These features may be more relevant for naturalistic studies, but they are configured and used differently in any particular research tradition.

An Approach to Qualitative Data Analysis

When you've been doing qualitative research as long as we have, the genres start to blur. As pragmatic realists, we no longer adhere slavishly to one school of thought, or practice solely within the boundaries of one particular philosophical approach. The data-analytic methods and techniques we've employed over the past few decades have been "a little bit of this and a little bit of that," used on an "as needed" basis. This is not to suggest that we were being improvisationally foolhardy as we figured out what to do next. On the contrary, we have been quite deliberate and diligent in our analytic methodologies and work.

Over time, the methods included in this book have become almost signature works—the "Miles and Huberman" way of analyzing qualitative data. But if you ask established qualitative researchers to describe Miles and Huberman's methods, you'll hear diverse opinions, ranging from positive descriptors such as "systematic," "rigorous," and "authoritative" to negative descriptors such as "old fashioned," "confusing," and (a personal favorite) "positivists in sheep's clothing." Add Saldaña as a new coauthor to the third edition of this text, and the evolution of these methods continues.

The three of us do not subscribe to any one particular genre of qualitative research—we are "shamelessly eclectic," as the popular saying goes. But our analytic sequence depicted throughout the book is probably closest to ethnographic methods, with some borrowed techniques from grounded theory. It moves from one inductive inference to another by selectively collecting data, comparing and contrasting this material in the quest for patterns or regularities, seeking out more data to support or qualify these emerging clusters, and then gradually drawing inferences from the links between other new data segments and the cumulative set of conceptualizations.

Analytic Methods: Some Common Features

We've observed features that recur in many approaches to qualitative analysis. On the face of it, there may be some irreconcilable pairs—for example, the quest for lawful relationships (social anthropology) versus the search for essences—that may not transcend individuals and that lend themselves to multiple compelling interpretations (phenomenology). Still, some analytic practices may be used across different qualitative research types. Here is a fairly classic set of analytic moves arranged in sequence:

- Assigning codes or themes to a set of field notes, interview transcripts, or documents
- Sorting and sifting through these coded materials to identify similar phrases, relationships between variables, patterns, themes, categories, distinct differences between subgroups, and common sequences
- Isolating these patterns and processes, and commonalities and differences, and taking them out to the field in the next wave of data collection
- Noting reflections or other remarks in jottings, journals, and analytic memos
- Gradually elaborating a small set of assertions, propositions, and generalizations that cover the consistencies discerned in the database
- Comparing those generalizations with a formalized body of knowledge in the form of constructs or theories

The analytic challenge for all qualitative researchers is finding coherent descriptions and explanations that still include all of the gaps, inconsistencies, and contradictions inherent in personal and social life. The risk is in forcing the logic, the order, and the plausibility that constitute theory making on the uneven, sometimes random, nature of social life.

We'll return to recurring features such as these, while acknowledging the desirable diversity of analytic approaches now in use. Next, however, we need to take a step back to ask, "What kind of data are we actually faced with in qualitative studies?"

The Nature of Qualitative Data

General Nature

In this book, we focus primarily on data in the form of words—that is, language in the form of extended text. Qualitative data also can appear as still or moving images, but we do not deal with these forms extensively (see the Appendix for recommended titles and guidance for visual data).

The words we collect and analyze are based on *observations, interviews, documents,* and *artifacts.* These data collection activities typically are carried out in close proximity to a local setting for a sustained period of time. Such data are not usually immediately accessible for analysis but require some type of processing: Raw field notes need to be expanded and typed up, audio recordings need to be transcribed and corrected, and photographs need to be documented and analyzed.

But the words we attach to fieldwork experiences are inevitably framed by our implicit concepts, and the processing of field notes is itself problematic. The words we choose to document what we see and hear in the field can never truly be "objective"; they can only be *our interpretation* of what we experience. Similarly, transcription of audio recordings can be done in many ways that will produce rather different texts. And the influence of the researcher's personal *values, attitudes,* and *beliefs* from and toward fieldwork is not unavoidable.

To put it another way, qualitative data are not so much about behavior as they are about *actions* (which carry with them intentions and meanings and lead to consequences). Some actions are relatively straightforward; others involve "impression management"—how people want others, including the researcher, to see them. Furthermore, those actions always occur in specific situations within a social and historical context, which deeply influence how they are interpreted by both insiders and the researcher as outsider.

Thus, the apparent simplicity of qualitative data masks a good deal of complexity, requiring plenty of care and self-awareness on the part of the researcher.

Strengths of Qualitative Data

One major feature of well-collected qualitative data is that they focus on *naturally occurring, ordinary events in natural settings,* so that we have a strong handle on what "real life" is like. That confidence is buttressed by *local groundedness,* the fact that the data were collected in close proximity to a specific situation. The emphasis is on a specific *case,* a focused and bounded phenomenon embedded in its context. The influences of the local context are not stripped away but are taken into account. The possibility for understanding latent, underlying, or nonobvious issues is strong.

Another feature of qualitative data is their *richness and holism,* with strong potential for revealing complexity; such data provide "thick descriptions" (Geertz, 1973) that are vivid, are nested in a real context, and have a ring of truth that has a strong impact on the reader.

Furthermore, the fact that such data are typically collected over a *sustained period* makes them powerful for studying any process (including history); we can go far beyond snapshots of "what?" or "how many?" to just how and why things happen as they do—and even *assess causation* as it actually plays out in a particular setting. And the inherent *flexibility* of qualitative studies (data collection times and methods can vary as a study proceeds) gives further confidence that we really understand what is going on.

Qualitative data, with their emphasis on people's lived experiences, are fundamentally well suited for locating the *meanings* people place on the events, processes, and structures of their lives and for connecting these meanings to the *social world* around them.

We make three other claims for the power of qualitative data, to which we will return in later chapters. They often have been advocated as the best strategy for discovery, for exploring a new area, and for *developing hypotheses*. In addition, we underline their strong potential for *testing hypotheses*, seeing whether specific predictions hold up. Finally, qualitative data are useful when one needs to supplement, validate, or illuminate *quantitative* data gathered from the same setting.

The strengths of qualitative data rest centrally on the competence with which their analysis is carried out. What do we mean by analysis?

Our View of Qualitative Data Analysis

We see analysis as three concurrent flows of activity: (1) data condensation, (2) data display, and (3) conclusion drawing/verification. We will explore each of these components in more depth as we proceed through the book. For now, we make only some overall comments.

Data Condensation

Data condensation refers to the process of selecting, focusing, simplifying, abstracting, and/or transforming the data that appear in the full corpus (body) of written-up field notes, interview transcripts, documents, and other empirical materials. By condensing, we're making data *stronger*. (We stay away from *data reduction* as a term because that implies we're weakening or losing something in the process.)

As we see it, data condensation occurs continuously throughout the life of any qualitatively oriented project. Even before the data are actually collected, anticipatory data condensation is occurring as the researcher decides (often without full awareness) which conceptual framework, which cases, which research questions, and which data collection approaches to choose. As data collection proceeds, further episodes of data condensation occur: writing summaries, coding, developing themes, generating categories, and writing analytic memos. The data condensing/transforming process continues after the fieldwork is over, until a final report is completed.

Data condensation is not something separate from analysis. It is a *part* of analysis. The researcher's decisions—which data chunks to code and which to pull out, which category labels best summarize a number of chunks, which evolving story to tell—*are all analytic choices*. Data condensation is a form of analysis that sharpens, sorts, focuses, discards, and organizes data in such a way that "final" conclusions can be drawn and verified.

By data condensation, we do *not* necessarily mean quantification. Qualitative data can be transformed in many ways: through selection, through summary or paraphrase, through being subsumed in a larger pattern, and so on. Occasionally, it may be helpful to convert the data into *magnitudes* (e.g., the analyst decides that the program being looked at has a "high" or "low" degree of effectiveness), but this is not always necessary.

Data Display

The second major flow of analysis activity is data display. Generically, a *display* is an organized, compressed assembly of information that allows conclusion drawing and action. In daily life, displays vary from gasoline gauges to newspapers to Facebook status updates. Looking at displays helps us understand what is happening and to do something—either analyze further or take action—based on that understanding.

The most frequent form of display for qualitative data in the past has been *extended text*. As we will note later, text (in the form of, say, 1,000 pages of field notes) is terribly cumbersome. It is dispersed, sequential rather than simultaneous, poorly structured, and extremely bulky. Using only extended text, a researcher may find it easy to jump to hasty, partial, and unfounded conclusions. Humans are not very powerful as processors of large amounts of information. Extended text overloads our information-processing capabilities and preys on our tendencies to find simplifying patterns. Or we drastically overweight vivid information, such as the exciting event that jumps out of page 124 of the field notes after a long, "boring" passage. Pages 89 through 123 may be ignored, and the criteria for weighting and selecting may never be questioned.

In the course of our work, we have become convinced that good displays are a major avenue to robust qualitative analysis. The displays discussed and illustrated in this book include many types of matrices, graphs, charts, and networks. All are designed to assemble organized information into an immediately accessible, compact form so that the analyst can see what is happening and either draw justified conclusions or move on to the next step of analysis that the display suggests may be useful.

As with data condensation, the creation and use of displays is not separate from analysis—it is a *part* of analysis. Designing displays—deciding on the rows and columns of a matrix for qualitative data and deciding which data, in which form, should be entered in the cells—are analytic activities. (Note that designing displays also has clear *data condensation* implications.)

In this book, we advocate more systematic, powerful displays and urge a more inventive, self-conscious, and iterative stance toward their generation and use. As we've coined in our previous writings, "You know what you display."

Drawing and Verifying Conclusions

The third stream of analysis activity is conclusion drawing and verification. From the start of data collection, the qualitative analyst interprets what things mean by noting patterns, explanations, causal flows, and propositions. The competent researcher holds these conclusions lightly, maintaining openness and skepticism, but the conclusions are still there, vague at first, then increasingly explicit and grounded. "Final" conclusions may not appear until data collection is over, depending on the size of the corpus of field notes; the coding, storage, and retrieval methods used; the sophistication of the researcher; and any necessary deadlines to be met.

Conclusion drawing, in our view, is only half of a Gemini configuration. Conclusions are also *verified* as the analyst proceeds. Verification may be as brief as a fleeting second thought crossing the analyst's mind during writing, with a short excursion back to the field notes; or it may be thorough and elaborate, with lengthy argumentation and review among colleagues to develop "intersubjective consensus" or with extensive efforts to replicate a finding in another data set. The meanings emerging from the data have to be tested for their plausibility, their sturdiness, their confirmability—that is, their validity. Otherwise, we are left with interesting stories about what happened but of unknown truth and utility.

We have presented these three streams—data condensation, data display, and conclusion drawing/verification—as interwoven before, during, and after data collection in parallel form, to make up the general domain called "analysis." The three streams can also be represented as shown in Display 1.1—our first network display. In this view, the three types of analysis activity and the activity of data collection itself form an interactive, cyclical process. The researcher steadily moves among these four nodes during data collection and then shuttles among condensing, displaying, and conclusion drawing/verifying for the remainder of the study.

The coding of data, for example (*data condensation*), leads to new ideas on what should go into a matrix (*data display*). Entering the data requires further data condensation. As the matrix fills up, preliminary *conclusions* are drawn, but they lead to the decision, for example, to add another column to the matrix to *test* the conclusion.

In this view, qualitative data analysis is a continuous, iterative enterprise. Issues of data condensation, display, and conclusion drawing/verification come into play successively as analysis episodes follow each other. Such a process is actually no more complex, conceptually speaking, than the analysis modes quantitative researchers use. Like their qualitative colleagues, they must be preoccupied with data condensation (calculating means, standard deviations), with display (correlation tables, regression printouts), and with conclusion drawing/verification (significance levels, experimental/control group differences). But their activities are carried out through well-defined, familiar methods; are guided by canons; and are usually more sequential than iterative or cyclical. Qualitative researchers are in a more fluid and more humanistic position.

Thus, as we've suggested, qualitative analysis needs to be well documented as a process—mainly to help us learn. We need to understand more clearly just what is going on when we analyze data, in order to reflect, refine our methods, and make them more generally usable by others.

Display 1.1

Components of Data Analysis: Interactive Model

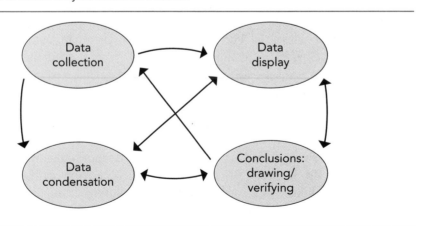

Source: Miles, M. B., & Huberman, A. M. (1994). *Qualitative data analysis: An expanded sourcebook* (2nd ed.). Thousand Oaks, CA: Sage Publications.

Suggestions for Readers

Recommendations for what a reader should do with any particular book are often presumptuous, mistaken, or both. Authors have no control over who reads their books or what readers may find useful. Nevertheless, we offer a few suggestions for different types of users.

Students and Other Novice Researchers

We give some direct advice here, keeping in mind that you will often be working alone, usually on a single case, and may be feeling worried about the quality of your study—dissertation or not.

1. *This book* focuses on *analysis*. Use other, introductory books to help with the basics of fieldwork (see the Appendix for recommended titles and resources).

2. Learn by doing. Use your own study (whether it is in the planning stage or under way) as a vehicle and apply it to relevant methods in each chapter.

3. Compensate for the problem of having to work alone by finding someone to be a critical friend or mentor to respond to your work as you proceed.

4. Keep an informal log or journal of what you are running up against. This tactic will help your learning and will be useful when you write up your study.

5. Don't worry about the jargon-like names of particular displays; the issue is what a display can do for you.

6. The biggest enemy of your learning is the gnawing worry that you're not "doing it right." Dissertation work tends to encourage that. But any given analytic problem can be approached in many useful ways. Creativity—that is, inventing your way out of a problem—is definitely the better stance.

Experienced Researchers

This is a sourcebook. Colleagues have told us that they have used it in several ways:

1. *Browsing:* The book contains a wide range of material, so simply exploring it in an unstructured way can be fruitful.

2. *Problem solving:* Anyone opening the book comes to it with more or less specifically defined problems in doing qualitative data analysis. The index has been designed to be "problem sensitive" to permit easy access to appropriate sections of the book. The Contents can also be used in this way.

3. *"A to Z":* Some readers prefer to go through a book sequentially, from start to finish. We have organized the book so that it makes sense that way.

4. *Operational use:* For readers conducting an ongoing qualitative research project, either alone or with colleagues, it's useful to read particular sections focusing on upcoming analysis tasks (e.g., the formation of research questions, coding, time-ordered displays), then discuss them with available colleagues, and finally plan

the next steps in the project, revising the methods outlined here or developing new ones.

5. *Research consulting:* The book can be used by people with an advisory or consulting role in the start-up and ongoing life of research projects. Assuming good problem identification, a research consultant can work with the client in either a problem-solving or a direct-training mode to aid in thoughtful project design and coping with early problems.

Teachers of Qualitative Research Methods Courses

Some colleagues have used this book as a primary text, others as a supplementary one. In either case, our advice is to engage students in active data collection and analysis. The book is not designed to be helpful in the type of methods course that is "about" qualitative research and provides no direct experience in doing it. Actual data are needed.

For each topic, we have used a learning approach like this, carried out by individuals or working pairs, who stay together throughout a workshop:

1. *Introductory* lecture and/or reading to clarify the main conceptual points of the section

2. A brief learning task (e.g., drawing a conceptual framework, coding a data excerpt, designing a matrix template, drawing a network, interpreting a filled-out matrix, or writing an initial analysis)

3. Comparing the products of individuals or pairs, drawing generalizations, and discussing future applications of the method

The same general principles apply when the book is used in a semester-long course, although the coverage will be deeper. Interim exercises focusing on actual research tasks, critiqued in class, are particularly productive. Active, reflective self-documentation through personal logs or journals is also beneficial.

Closure and Transition

This Introduction provided some brief groundwork for the rest of the book. Analysis is doing, so let's proceed in the next chapter to preparatory research design decisions that will later play important roles in analytic work.

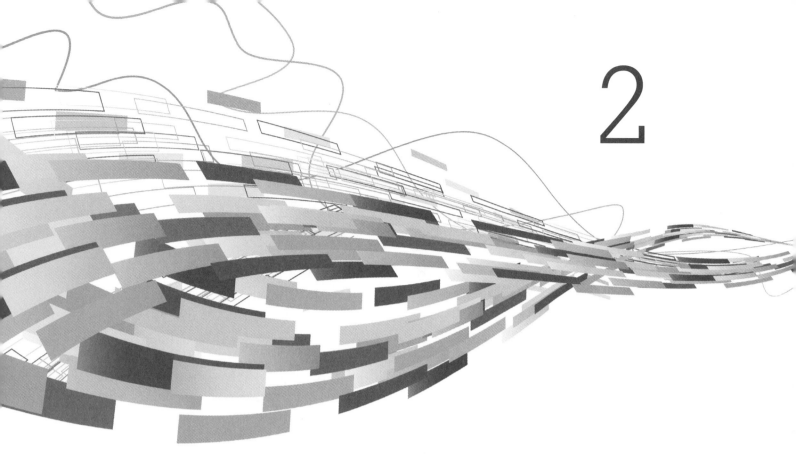

Research Design and Management

Chapter Summary

This chapter describes the initial and technical matters involved in qualitative research design. Such core topics include conceptual frameworks, research questions, sampling, instrumentation, consideration of mixed methods, and data management with computers and software.

Contents

Introduction
Tight Versus Loose Designs: Some Trade-Offs
Building a Conceptual Framework
    Description and Rationale
    Examples
    Advice
Formulating Research Questions
    Description and Rationale

    Example

    Advice

  Defining the Case

    Description and Rationale

    Examples

    Advice

  Sampling: Bounding the Collection of Data

    Description and Rationale

    Key Features of Qualitative Sampling

    General Sampling Strategies

    Within-Case Sampling

    Multiple-Case Sampling

    Example

    Advice

  Instrumentation

    Description and Rationale

    Example

    Advice

  Linking Qualitative and Quantitative Data

    Approaches to Mixed-Methods Designs

  Management Issues Bearing on Analysis

    Computer and Software Use

    Data Management

    Staffing and Time Planning

  Closure and Transition

  Note

Introduction

At the proposal stage and in the early planning and start-up stages of a qualitative research project, many design decisions get made—some explicitly and precisely, others implicitly, some unknowingly, and still others by default. The qualitative researcher begins to focus on the study's issues, the participants to be observed, the data to be collected, and how these data will be managed and analyzed.

This book is about analysis, but we also need to discuss research design. Study design decisions can, in a real sense, be seen as analytic—a sort of *anticipatory data condensation*—because they affect later analysis by ruling out certain variables and relationships and attending to others; they prefigure your analytic moves. Some design decisions are mainly conceptual: the conceptual framework and research questions, sampling, case definition, instrumentation, and the nature of the data to be collected. Others, though they appear in the guise of management issues, are equally focusing: how data will be stored, organized, and processed and what computer software may be used to support the work.

We cannot deal thoroughly here with qualitative research design; see the Appendix for recommended titles on the subject. In this chapter, we discuss the *analytic issues* that arise as a study is focused and organized. We provide specific examples but want to emphasize that these issues must be dealt with uniquely and flexibly in any particular study. Someone else's qualitative research design is not always replicable by others. And initial design decisions nearly always lead to a redesign.

Tight Versus Loose Designs: Some Trade-Offs

Prior to fieldwork, how much shape should a qualitative research design have? Any researcher, no matter how unstructured or inductive, comes to fieldwork with *some* orienting ideas. A sociologist may focus on families or organizations and, through those lenses and filters, will look for data marked by discipline-specific concepts such as "the 5 *rs*": roles, relationships, rules, routines, and rituals. If that researcher looks at closets or lunchrooms, it is not with the eyes of an architect or a cook but with an interest in what the room and its contents have to say about the patterns shared by the people using it. A psychologist would orient differently toward the same phenomena, focusing perhaps on motivations, anxieties, and interpersonal communication dynamics.

Some qualitative researchers keep pre-structured designs to a minimum. They consider social processes to be too complex, too relative, too elusive, or too fluid to be approached with explicit conceptual frames or standard instruments. They prefer a more loosely structured, emergent, inductively grounded approach for gathering data: Their conceptual frameworks will tend to emerge from the field during the course of the study; the important research questions will become clear only gradually; meaningful settings and participants will not be selected prior to fieldwork but only after initial orientation to the field site.

Highly inductive, loosely designed studies make good sense when experienced researchers have plenty of time and are exploring unfamiliar cultures, understudied phenomena, or very complex social processes. But if you're new to qualitative studies and are looking at a better understood phenomenon within a familiar culture or subculture, a loose, inductive design may be a waste of time. Months of fieldwork and voluminous case studies may yield only a few banalities.

Tighter designs are a wiser course for researchers working with well-delineated constructs. In fact, we should remember that qualitative research can be outright confirmatory—that is, can seek to test or further explicate a conceptualization. Tighter designs also provide clarity and focus for beginning researchers worried about procedures and overload.

So a case can be made for tight, pre-structured qualitative designs and for loose, emergent ones. Much of qualitative research lies between these two extremes. But how pre-structured should a qualitative research design be? It depends on the time available, how much already is known about the phenomena under study, the instruments already available, and the analysis that will be made.

The looser the initial design, the less selective the collection of data; *everything* looks important at the outset if you are waiting for the key concepts or regularities to emerge from the case, and that wait can take a long time. The researcher, submerged in data, will need months to sort it out. You may have that kind of time if you're doing a dissertation or are funded by a long-term grant, but most projects are time constrained.

Second, fieldwork may well involve multiple-case research rather than single-case studies. If different field-workers are operating inductively, with no common framework or instrumentation, they are bound to end up with the double dilemma of data overload and lack of comparability across cases.

Then, too, we should not forget why we are out in the field in the first place: to describe and analyze a pattern of interrelationships. Starting with them (deductively) and getting gradually to them (inductively) are both possible. In the life of a conceptualization, we need both approaches—and may well need them from several field researchers—to pull a mass of facts and findings into a wide-ranging, coherent set of generalizations.

Finally, as researchers, we do have background knowledge. We see and decipher details, complexities, and subtleties that would elude a less knowledgeable observer. We know some of the questions to ask, which incidents to attend to closely, and how our theoretical interests are embodied in the field. Not to "lead" with your conceptual strength can be simply self-defeating.

Clearly, trade-offs are involved here. In multiple-case research, for example, the looser the initial framework, the more each researcher can be receptive to local idiosyncrasies—but cross-case comparability will be hard to get, and the costs and the information load will be colossal. Tightly coordinated designs face the opposite dilemma: They yield more economical, comparable, and potentially generalizable findings, but they are less case sensitive and may entail bending data out of contextual shape to answer a cross-case analytic question. Whether you choose one end of the continuum or the other for your particular study must be your decision. But a midway point between the extremes is yet another position, and perhaps the one most qualitative researchers take.

Building a Conceptual Framework

Description and Rationale

A conceptual framework explains, either graphically or in narrative form, the main things to be studied—the key factors, variables, or constructs—and the presumed interrelationships among them. Frameworks can be simple or elaborate, commonsensical or theory driven, descriptive or causal.

Conceptual frameworks are simply the current version of the researcher's map of the territory being investigated. As the explorer's knowledge of the terrain improves, the map becomes correspondingly more differentiated and integrated. Thus, conceptual frameworks are developed at the beginning of a study and evolve as the study progresses.

A conceptual framework forces you to be selective—to decide which variables are most important, which relationships are likely to be most meaningful, and, as a consequence, what information should be collected and analyzed—at least at the outset. If multiple researchers are involved, the framework helps them study the same phenomenon in ways that will permit an eventual cross-case analysis.

Theory building relies on a few general constructs that subsume a mountain of particulars. Constructs such as *culture*, *social intelligence*, and *identity* are the labels we put on intellectual "bins" containing many discrete actions, states, variables, categories, processes, and events. Any researcher, no matter how inductive in approach, knows which bins are likely to be in play in the study and what is likely to be in them. Bins come from theory, from personal experience, and (often) from the general objectives of the study envisioned. Setting out bins, naming them, and getting clearer about their interrelationships help lead you toward a conceptual framework.

Examples

A conceptual framework first specifies who and what will (and will not) be studied. Display 2.1 is a *first-cut*, *first-draft* attempt at listing, in graphic form, the myriad influences on a single classroom teacher.

This illustration identifies the people (State School Superintendent, District Reading Specialists, etc.) and the "things" or official documents/policies (State Mandated Textbooks, District Standards and Curriculum, etc.) the researcher identified as influential on a classroom teacher's instructional practices with her students. There is a general clustering of *who*s and *what*s by level, state, district, and local, and an implied hierarchy of supervision/authority and distribution of power from top to bottom.

We see here the focusing function of a conceptual framework. Some, not all, social actors in this long list are going to be studied, along with some, not all, aspects of their activity. For example, the researcher may be unable, due to accessibility, to directly interview the State School Superintendent or State School Board Members. But he can certainly access public documents and records of their official business from published minutes of state school board meetings. Once all permissions have been obtained, the Language Arts Teacher herself will be interviewed several times and observed teaching in several of her classrooms. Documents such as her lesson plans and samples of graded student work will be reviewed. Only some relationships in this conceptual framework will be explored, certain kinds of processes documented, and certain analyses made—at least at the outset.

Now for a slightly more complex (read "messy") conceptual framework using some of the same aspects of this study as they evolved.

Display 2.2 includes the exact same bins and labels as Display 2.1, but their arrangement and the arrows of influence are different. There is less symmetry (support that the network reflects the "asymmetrical" social world we live in), a new hierarchy, and a different set of interrelationships.

The researcher got to this display after spending some time observing and interviewing the Language Arts Teacher. State Standards and Testing were the primary factors that influenced both her practice and the students' classroom experiences. Of all the players from Display 2.1 that were hierarchically listed, some were actually quite peripheral *according to the perspective of the Language Arts Teacher*; these are listed at the bottom of the display, with dashed arrows toward the major bins suggesting minimal influence.

The other three major factors the researcher learned and interpreted as most salient were the teacher's School Principal, and her "obsession" with raising the school's standardized test scores; the District In-Service Teacher Education Workshops (which the teacher praised and found "extremely useful for me and my kids"); and the State Mandated Textbooks (which heavily emphasized writing over literature appreciation for language arts).

A First-Draft Conceptual Framework for a Case Study Teacher and the Influences on Her Practice

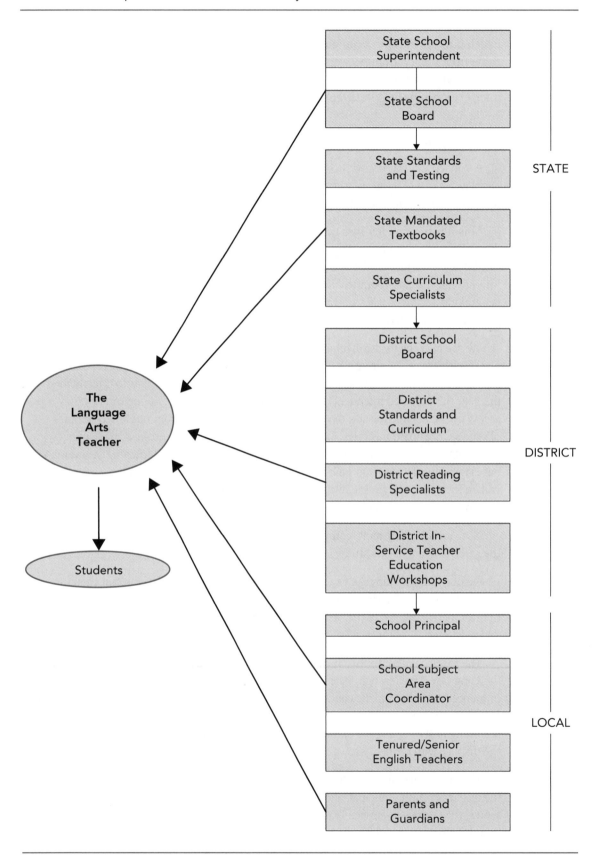

A display such as this might be considered partly confirmatory if the researcher is able to visit other Language Arts teachers within the same school and within other schools outside the district to determine if their spheres of influence also include the same factors. A *working hypothesis* for field testing that the researcher developed after studying and analyzing this display is this: *The mandates of education manifest themselves primarily as prescriptive products imposed on educators and their students.* Overall, what Display 2.2 illustrates is that conceptual frameworks *evolve* as a study continues and the bigger picture becomes clearer.

On our continuum from exploratory to confirmatory designs, Display 2.1 is closer to the exploratory end and Display 2.2 to the more confirmatory one. Let's have a look at an entirely new study with a conceptual framework about midway between the exploratory–confirmatory continuum (see Display 2.3).

This framework is of particular interest in that it lays out the "school improvement study"[1] from which we (Miles and Huberman) draw many of our subsequent displays (see also Huberman & Miles, 1983, 1984). Take some time to review the display to see how all the pieces fit together and to see what leads to what as we've laid out the directional arrows. This is our initial conceptual framework of how we felt an educational program innovation was going to unfold throughout a number of school sites across time.

Rather than bins of people and documents, we labeled our bins as *events* (e.g., "Prior history with innovations"), *settings* (e.g., "Community, district office"), *processes*

Display 2.2

Major Influences on a Language Arts Teacher's Practice

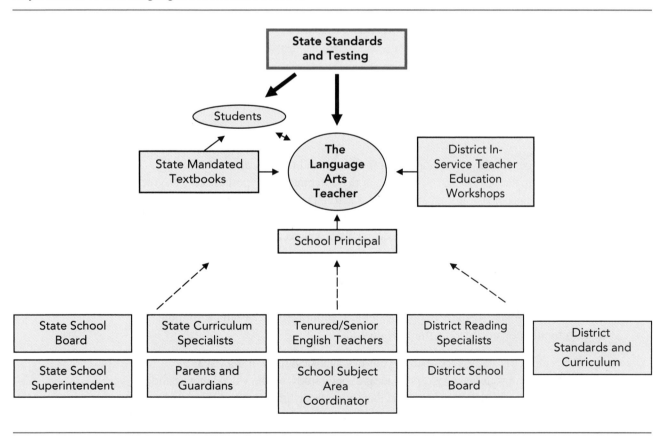

Conceptual Framework for a Multicase "School Improvement" Field Study, Initial Version

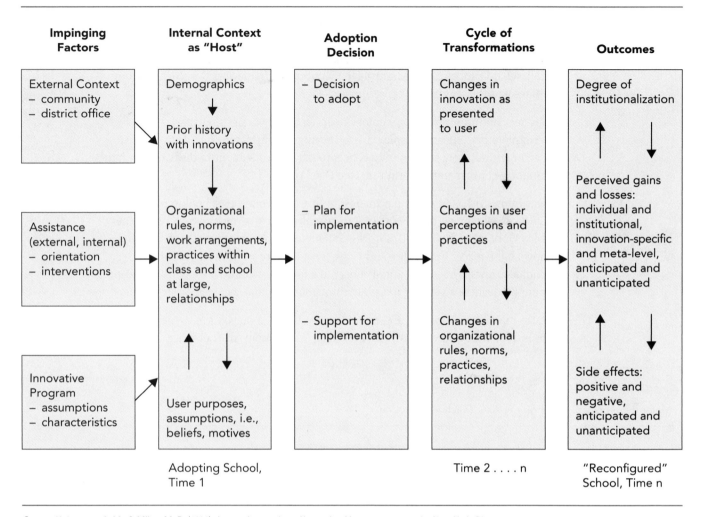

| Impinging Factors | Internal Context as "Host" | Adoption Decision | Cycle of Transformations | Outcomes |

Source: Huberman, A. M., & Miles, M. B. (1984). *Innovation up close: How school improvement works.* New York: Plenum.

(e.g., "Changes in user perceptions and practices"), and *theoretical constructs* (e.g., "Organizational rules, norms . . ."). Some of the outcomes are hypothesized ("Degree of institutionalization"), but most are open-ended ("Perceived gains and losses"). The directional arrows follow the time flow, but some bets still are being made that most assistance comes early and that reciprocal changes will occur among the innovation, its users, and the organization.

This is a very general brief. It is also a brief that can change en route, as this conceptual framework did. As qualitative researchers collect data, they revise their frameworks—make them more precise, replace empirically weak bins with more meaningful ones, and reconfigure relationships.

The conceptual framework, then, is your first analytic *display*. It is a visual representation of your main conceptual ideas about a study and how they interact and interplay with each other. We do not feel that there are any prescriptive differences between an ethnography's and a phenomenology's mapping of people and processes, for example. But always remember that conceptual frameworks tell a story of some kind. They are evolving, one-page representations of your research in progress, comparable to the storyboards of filmmakers, who first draw on paper what they will eventually document on digital video.

Advice

Here are some suggestions that summarize and extend what has been reviewed in this section:

1. Conceptual frameworks are best done graphically rather than in text. Having to get the entire framework on a single page obliges you to specify the bins that hold the discrete phenomena, map likely interrelationships, divide variables that are conceptually or functionally distinct, and work with all of the information at once.

2. Expect to do several versions, right from the outset. There are probably as many ways of representing the main variables as there are variables to represent, but some—typically, later cuts—are more elegant than others.

3. If your study has more than one researcher, have each field researcher do a cut at a framework early on and then compare the several versions. This procedure will show, literally, where everyone's head is. It usually leads to an explication of contentious or foggy areas that otherwise would have surfaced later on.

4. Avoid the no-risk framework—that is, one that defines variables at a very global level and has two-directional arrows everywhere. This avoidance amounts essentially to making no focusing decisions and is little better than the strategy of going indiscriminately into the field to see what the site has to tell. However, you can begin with an omnibus or generic framework as a way of getting to a more selective and specific one.

5. Prior theorizing and empirical research are, of course, important inputs. It helps to lay out your own orienting frame and then map onto it the variables and relationships from the literature available, to see where the overlaps, contradictions, qualifications, and refinements are.

For an extended discussion of conceptual frameworks and how they influence and affect all aspects of research, see Ravitch and Riggan (2012).

Formulating Research Questions

Description and Rationale

Research questions represent the facets of inquiry that the researcher most wants to explore. Research questions may be general or particular, descriptive or explanatory. The formulation of research questions may precede, follow, or happen concurrently with the development of a conceptual framework. They also may be formulated at the outset or later on and may be refined or reformulated during the course of fieldwork.

It is a direct step from conceptual framework to research questions. If I have a bin labeled "State Mandated Textbooks," as in Display 2.1, with an arrow from that bin directed toward "The Language Arts Teacher," I am implicitly asking myself some questions about how textbooks influence a teacher's practice (e.g., *In what ways do state-mandated language arts textbooks shape the language arts teacher's curriculum?*). If I have a two-way arrow between "The Language Arts Teacher" and "Students," as in

Display 2.2, my question has to do with the reciprocal interrelationship between them and the interpersonal dynamics of education (e.g., *What kinds of teaching–learning methods best prepare students for state-mandated testing in language arts?*).

If my conceptual framework is more constrained, so are my questions. In Display 2.2, the "District School Board" has little, if any, influence and affect on the teacher. There may be one research question about the Board to verify its inconsequential impact, but not much time or effort will be spent in pursuing this minimal factor.

What do these questions do for me? They tell me what I want to know most or first; my collection of data will be more focused. I am also beginning to make some implicit sampling decisions. I will look only at *some* actors in *some* contexts dealing with *some* issues. The questions also begin to point me toward data-gathering devices—observations, interviews, document collection, or even questionnaires. Finally, the research questions begin to operationalize the conceptual framework and make the initial theoretical assumptions even more explicit.

As another example, take the problem of understanding police work (van Maanen, 1979). If you use an inductive approach, you explore open-endedly all facets of police work. But there are so many that you can't look at them all. And where will you study them? You can't look everywhere. And when? If you delay that decision for a few months until you've spent some time, say at the precinct station, that simply reflects two tacit sampling decisions (start at the precinct house, then recheck after a while).

Suppose the implicit research question was "How do arrests and bookings work?" That choice immediately excludes many other issues and leads to *sampling and instrumentation* choices (e.g., using observation rather than official documents; selection of different kinds of suspects, crimes, styles of apprehending suspects, and types of officers). These sampling and instrumentation decisions, often inexplicit, are actually focusing the settings, actors, processes, and events to be studied. In sum, the research questions, implicit or explicit, also suggest the possible types of analyses.

A conceptual framework's display shows researchers' preferred bins and relational arrows as they map and carve up social phenomena. They use these explicitly or implicitly to decide which questions are most important and how they should get the answers. We believe that better research happens when you make your framework (and associated choices of research questions, cases, sampling, and instrumentation) explicit, rather than claiming inductive purity.

Example

Our (Miles and Huberman's) school improvement study shows how a conceptual framework hooks up with the formulation of research questions. Look back at Display 2.3, where the main variable sets of the study were laid out. Look at the third column, labeled "Adoption Decision." Its component parts are listed inside the bin: the decision to adopt, the plan for implementation, and support for the implementation. The task, then, is to decide what you want to find out about these topics. The procedure we used was to cluster specific research questions under more general ones, as shown in Display 2.4.

Notice the choices being made within each topical area. For example, in the first two areas, the main things we want to know about the decision to adopt are who was involved, how the decision was actually made, and how important this project was relative to others. All of the questions seem to be functional rather than theoretical or descriptive—they have to do with getting something done.

Display 2.4

General and Special Research Questions Relating to the Adoption Decision
(School Improvement Study)

How was the adoption decision made?

    Who was involved (e.g., principal, users, central office people, school board, outside agencies)?

    How was the decision made (top-down, persuasive, consultative, collegial-participative, or delegated styles)?

How much priority and centrality did the new program have at the time of the adoption decision?

    How much support and commitment was there from administrators?

    How important was it for teachers, seen in relation to their routine, "ordinary" activities, and any other innovations that were being contemplated or attempted?

    Realistically, how large did it loom in the scheme of things?

    Was it a one-time event or one of a series?

What were the components of the original plan for implementation?

    Thesse might have included front-end training, monitoring and debugging/troubleshooting unexpected problems, and ongoing support.

    How precise and elaborate was this plan?

    Were people satisfied with it at the time?

    Did it deal with all of the problems anticipated?

Were the requisite conditions for implementation ensured before it began?

    These might have included commitment, understanding, materials and equipment, skills, time allocation, and organizational backup.

    Were any important conditions seen as missing? Which were most missing?

Source: Miles, M. B., & Huberman, A. M. (1994). *Qualitative data analysis: An expanded sourcebook* (2nd ed.). Thousand Oaks, CA: Sage Publications.

Also notice that, conceptually, more is afoot than we saw in the conceptual framework. The "requisite conditions" in the fourth section of questions indicate that the researchers have some a priori (determined beforehand) notions about which factors make for the greatest preparedness.

When such a research question gets operationalized, an attempt will be made to determine whether these conditions were present or absent at the various field sites and whether that made any difference in the execution of the project. This is an example of how research questions feed directly into data collection. Of course, field researchers will be attentive to other, as yet undreamed of, requisite conditions, and the idea of requisite conditions may not be retained throughout the study.

Advice

1. Even if you are in a highly inductive mode, it is a good idea to start with some general research questions. They allow you to get clear about what, in the general domain, is of most interest. They make the implicit explicit, without necessarily freezing or limiting your vision.

2. If you are foggy about your priorities or about the ways they can be framed, begin with a foggy research question and then try to defog it. Most research questions do not come out right on the first cut, no matter how experienced the researcher or how clear the domain of study.

3. Formulating more than a dozen or so general research questions is looking for trouble. You can easily lose the forest for the trees and fragment the collection of data. Having a large number of questions makes it harder to see emergent links across different parts of the database and to integrate findings. As we saw in Display 2.4, a solution to research question proliferation is the use of major questions, each with subquestions, for clarity and specificity. It also helps to consider whether there is a key question, the "thing you *really* want to know."

4. It is sometimes easier to generate a conceptual framework *after* you've made a list of research questions. You look at the list for common themes, common constructs, implicit or explicit relationships, and so on, and then begin to map out the underlying framework joining these pieces. Some researchers operate best in this mode.

5. In a multiple-case study, be sure all field-workers understand each question and see its importance. Multiple-case studies have to be more explicit, so that several researchers can be aligned as they collect information in the field. Unclear questions or different understandings can make for noncomparable data across cases.

6. Once the list of research questions is generated and honed, look it over to ensure that each question is, in fact, researchable. Delete those questions that you or your participants have no real means of answering, or you of measuring (qualitatively or quantitatively).

7. Keep the research questions in hand, and review them during fieldwork. This closeness will focus data collection; you will think twice before noting down what participants have for lunch or where they park their cars. Unless something has an obvious, direct, or potentially important link to a research question, it should not fatten your field notes.

Defining the Case

Description and Rationale

Qualitative researchers often struggle with the questions of "what my case is" and "where my case leaves off." Abstractly, we can define a *case* as a phenomenon of some sort occurring in a bounded context. The case is, in effect, your unit of analysis. Studies may be of just one case or of several. Display 2.5 shows this graphically: There is a focus or "heart" of the study, and a somewhat indeterminate boundary defines the edge of the case: what will not be studied.

Examples

What are some examples of cases? Sometimes the "phenomenon" may be an *individual* in a defined context, as suggested by Displays 2.1 and 2.2: a Language Arts teacher and her series of classes with junior-level high school students during an 18-week spring semester—the same semester her students will take a state-mandated

Display 2.5

The Case as the Unit of Analysis

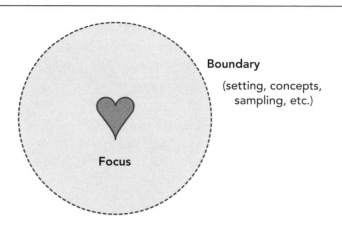

Source: Miles, M. B., & Huberman, A. M. (1994). *Qualitative data analysis: An expanded sourcebook* (2nd ed.). Thousand Oaks, CA: Sage Publications.

standardized "high-stakes" test in language arts. Note that the "heart" here is the teacher. The boundary defines her students and school site as the major contexts. The researcher will not, for example, interview the teacher's mother or visit the child care facility where the teacher leaves her own child during workdays. The bounding is also by time: No information will be gathered after the spring semester ends in 18 weeks and the standardized test scores have been reported.

We can also expect that the boundary will be defined further by *sampling* operations, which we'll discuss later. For example, this researcher will not be interviewing the school guidance counselor, only the principal and, if pertinent, other language arts teachers.

A case may also be defined by

- a role (school principal, CEO, nurse supervisor),

- a small group (African American men in an inner-city neighborhood, a college-level rock band, a breast cancer survivor support group),

- an organization (a nursery school, a computer chip manufacturing company, the American Sociological Association),

- space and environment (a mall for adolescents to "hang out," visitors at the Vietnam Veterans Memorial Mall in Washington D.C., nighttime foot traffic along the Las Vegas Strip),

- a community or settlement (the French Quarter of New Orleans, a village in Tanzania, the Tenderloin District of San Francisco),

- episodes or encounters (voting for the first time, a "one night stand," bullying incidents on an elementary school playground),

- an event (a search committee meeting, a high school graduation ceremony, New Year's Eve in New York City's Time Square),

- a period of time (a day in the life of a fire fighter, spring break, how customers use their time between ordering food from a server and having it delivered to their table),

- a process (grocery shopping and meal preparation, organizing and managing an international conference, the adoption and implementation of an innovational education program in a school district),

- a culture or subculture (female African Americans in academia, Los Angeles drag queens, "skater dudes"), or

- a nation (Greece during the period of its 21st-century economic crisis, America during the 2012 presidential election cycle).

Single cases are the stuff of much qualitative research and can be very vivid and illuminating, especially if they are chosen to be "critical," extreme or unique, or "revelatory," as Yin (2009) suggests. But the cases may not be monolithic. Yin further points out that cases may have subcases embedded within them. A case study of a school may contain cases of specific classrooms; a case study of a hospital ward may have cases of specific doctor–patient relationships within it.

We suggest that multiple cases offer the researcher an even deeper understanding of the processes and outcomes of cases, the chance to test (not just develop) hypotheses, and a good picture of locally grounded causation. The question of just which cases to include in a sample is discussed below.

A comment on notation: We sometimes prefer—and use here and there in this book—the word *site* because it reminds us that a "case" always occurs in a specified social and physical *setting*; we cannot study individual cases devoid of their context in the way a quantitative researcher often does.

Advice

1. Start intuitively, but remember the focus and build outward. Think of who and what you will *not* be studying as a way to firm up the boundaries.

2. Define the case as early as you can during a study. Given a starting conceptual framework and research questions, it pays to get a bit stern about who and what you are defining as a case; that will help clarify further both the framework and the questions.

3. Remember that sampling will define the case(s) further.

4. Attend to several dimensions of the case: its *conceptual* nature, its *social size*, its *physical* location, and its *temporal* extent.

Sampling: Bounding the Collection of Data

Description and Rationale

Sampling involves decisions not only about which people to observe and/or interview but also about settings, events, and social processes. Multiple-case studies also demand clear choices about which types of cases to include. Qualitative studies call for continuous refocusing and redrawing of study parameters during fieldwork, but some initial selection still is required. A conceptual framework and research questions can help set the foci and boundaries for sampling decisions.

Sampling may look easy. Much of qualitative research examines a single "case"—some phenomenon embedded in a single social setting. But settings have subsettings (schools have classrooms, classrooms have cliques, cliques have individuals), so deciding where to look is not easy. And as much as you might want to, you cannot study everyone everywhere doing everything. Your choices—whom to look at or talk with, where, when, about what, and why—place limits on the conclusions you can draw and on how confident you and others feel about them. Sampling is crucial for later analysis.

Within any case, social phenomena proliferate (science lessons, teachers' questioning techniques, student unruliness, use of innovations); they, too, must be sampled. And the question of multiple-case sampling adds another layer of complexity. How do we manage it all? We discuss some general principles and suggest useful references for detailed help.

Key Features of Qualitative Sampling

Qualitative researchers usually work with *small* samples of people, nested in their context and studied in-depth—unlike quantitative researchers, who aim for larger numbers of context-stripped cases and seek statistical significance.

Qualitative samples tend to be *purposive* rather than random. Samples in qualitative studies are usually not wholly prespecified but can evolve once fieldwork begins. The initial choices of participants lead you to similar and different ones; observing one class of events invites comparison with another; and understanding one key relationship in the setting reveals facets to be studied in others. This is conceptually driven sequential sampling.

Sampling in qualitative research involves two actions that sometimes pull in different directions. First, you need to set *boundaries*: to define aspects of your case(s) that you can study within the limits of your time and means, that connect directly to your research questions, and that probably will include examples of what you want to study. Second, at the same time, you need to create a conceptual *frame* to help you uncover, confirm, or qualify the basic processes or constructs that undergird your study. Display 2.2 suggests that the frame of this study is primarily about the pressures and consequences of state-mandated testing on a language arts teacher and her students.

Qualitative sampling is often decidedly *theory driven*, either "up front" or progressively, as in a grounded theory mode. Suppose that you were studying how adolescents develop friendships and that you could only manage to look at one high school. At first, that seems very limited. But if you chose a site according to relevant theory, you might choose one that has a wide range and diversity of students in terms of gender, race/ethnicity, socioeconomic class, sexual orientation, religious background, and so on. This will enable you to test the theory that friendships become more selective—that is, discriminating—when multiple choices are available to adolescents. And you would sample *within* each class (freshman, sophomore, junior, senior) for certain developmentally expected processes such as clique formation, orientation of the newcomer, use of technology for friendship maintenance, and so on. You might also find that certain events, such as lunchtime and organized extracurricular sports and arts activities, were unusually rich with socialization actions, and then you would sample more carefully for these. Sampling like this, both within and across cases, puts flesh on the bones of general constructs and their relationships. We can see generic processes; our generalizations are not to "all adolescents" but to existing or new theories of how friendship development works.

General Sampling Strategies

Erickson (1986) suggests a generic, funneling sampling sequence, working from the outside in to the core of a setting. For example, in studying schools, he would begin with the school community (census data, a walk around the neighborhood) and then enter the school and the classroom, staying several days to get a sense of the frequency and occurrence of different events. From there, the focus would tighten: specific events, times, and locations. Periodically, however, Erickson would follow lines of influence into the surrounding environment to test the typicality of what was found in a given classroom and to get a better fix on external influences and determinants.

There is a wide range of sampling strategies available to qualitative researchers (Patton, 2002, 2008), within a complex case or across cases. They can be selected ahead of time or can evolve during early data collection. It is impossible to prescribe which sampling strategies go best with each type of study, for there are too many unique conditions within each project (specific research questions, specific sites and cases, etc.). But you should be able to provide to your readers justification for why you selected certain types of sampling over others.

Random sampling is a gold standard of quantitative research but is used quite minimally in qualitative research because random sampling can sometimes deal you a biased hand. Our sampling tends to be more *strategic* and *purposive* because we are focusing on a case's unique contexts. Admittedly, there are times when we select a case to study because it is accessible to us geographically and immediately—a form of *convenience* sampling.

How do sampling strategies affect analysis? *Maximum variation sampling*, for example, involves looking for outlier cases to see whether the main patterns still hold, while *homogeneous sampling* focuses on people with similar demographic or social characteristics. The *critical case* is the instance that "proves" or exemplifies the main findings. Searching deliberately for *confirming and disconfirming cases*, *extreme or deviant cases*, and *typical cases* serves to increase confidence in conclusions. Some strategies benefit inductive, theory-building analysis (e.g., *opportunistic* or *snowball sampling*). *Politically important cases* are "salient" participants who may need to be included (or excluded) because they connect with politically sensitive issues anticipated in the analysis.

Other strategies can be used for selection of participants prior to data collection. For example, Goetz and LeCompte (1984) offer (a) *comprehensive sampling*— examining every case, instance, or element in a given population; (b) *quota selection*— identifying the major subgroups and then taking an arbitrary number from each; (c) *reputational case selection*—instances chosen on the recommendation of an expert or key participant; and (d) *comparable case selection*—selecting individuals, sites, and groups on the same relevant characteristics over time (a replication strategy). Most of these strategies will increase confidence in analytic findings on the grounds of representativeness.

The sampling strategies we've been discussing can be applied both within and across cases. Let's turn to some of the core issues in each of these domains.

Within-Case Sampling

Quantitative researchers usually think of cases as individual persons. They draw a sample of persons and then collect comparable "data points" from each one. By contrast, a qualitative case may range widely in definition from individuals to roles, groups, organizations, processes, and cultures. But even when the case is an individual, the qualitative researcher has many within-case sampling decisions: Which *activities*, *processes*, *events*, *times*, *locations*, and *role partners* will I sample?

Within-case sampling is almost always *nested*—for example, studying children within classrooms within schools within neighborhoods, with regular movement up and down that ladder. For a cardiovascular bypass patient, we might want to sample his diet and exercise activities; the processes of understanding, taking in, and acting on medical advice; events such as admission and discharge interviews; time periods, including prehospitalization, hospitalization, and posthospitalization (once every 2 weeks); locations, including the recovery room, the ward, and the patient's home; and role partners, including the patient's physician, ward nurses, dietitian, and spouse.

A second major point is that such sampling should be *theoretically* driven—whether the theory is prespecified or emerges as you go, as in traditional grounded theory's "theoretical sampling." Choices of participants, episodes, and interactions should be driven by a conceptual question, not by a concern for representativeness. To get to the construct, such as *negotiation*, we need to see different instances of it, at different moments, in different places, with different people. The prime concern is with the *conditions* under which the construct or theory operates, not with the generalization of the findings to other settings.

The third point is that within-case sampling has an *iterative* or "rolling" quality, working in progressive waves as the study progresses. Sampling is investigative; we are cerebral detectives, ferreting out answers to our research questions. We observe, talk to people, and pick up artifacts and documents. That leads us to new samples of participants and observations, new documents. At each step along the evidential trail, we are making sampling decisions to clarify the main patterns, see contrasts, identify exceptions or discrepant instances, and uncover negative instances—where the pattern does not hold. Our analytic conclusions depend deeply on the within-case sampling choices we made.

So within-case sampling helps us see a local configuration in some depth. What can adding cases do for us, and how do we create a sample of cases?

Multiple-Case Sampling

Multiple-case sampling adds *confidence* to findings. By looking at a range of similar and contrasting cases, we can understand a single-case finding, grounding it by specifying *how* and *where* and, if possible, *why* it carries on as it does. We can strengthen the precision, validity, stability, and trustworthiness of the findings. In other words, we are following a *replication* strategy (Yin, 2009). If a finding holds in one setting and, given its profile, also holds in a comparable setting but does not in a contrasting case, the finding is more robust.

With multiple-case studies, does the issue of *generalizability* change? Essentially, no. We are generalizing from one case to the next on the basis of a match to the underlying theory, not to a larger universe. The choice of cases usually is made on *conceptual* grounds, not on representative grounds. The cases often are arrayed on a continuum (e.g., highly gifted to underachieving pupils), with few exemplars of each, or they are contrasted (e.g., assertive and passive adolescents). Other, unique properties may be added (e.g., some assertive adolescents are from cities, some from rural areas). Because case study researchers examine intact settings in such minute detail, they know all too well that each setting has a few properties it shares with *many* others, some properties it shares with *some* others, and some properties it shares with *no* others. Nevertheless, the multiple-case sampling gives us confidence that our emerging theory is generic, because we have seen it work out—and not work out—in predictable ways.

How many cases should a multiple-case study have? This question is not answerable on statistical grounds, of course. We have to deal with the issue conceptually: How many cases, and in what kind of sampling frame, would give us confidence in our analytic generalizations? It also depends on how rich and complex the within-case sampling is. With high complexity, a study with more than 10 cases or so can become unwieldy. There are too many data to scan visually and too many permutations to account for. And the problems of practical and intellectual coordination among multiple researchers get very large once you are a staff of more than five people. Still, we've seen multiple-case studies in the 20s and 30s; the price is usually thinner data.

If we were forced to recommend a specific number, we would suggest five richly researched cases as a minimum for multiple-case sampling adequacy. (We have read outstanding qualitative studies that compared just two, three, and four cases, but their authors did not assert any generalizability.)

Example

Suppose we wanted to deal with "police work." This example has no orienting conceptual frame but rather a general perspective on social processes, notably how people literally "make sense" of their habitual surroundings. The decision to explore this perspective by studying the arrest and booking of suspects in a single precinct is a good example of a sampling choice. You could ask, "How are laws interpreted by people enforcing them in face-to-face situations?" and then select police officers as a sample of such people. Or you can move right away from the general domain to sampling *events* and *processes* and ask, "How do police officers interpret laws when arresting and booking suspects?"

However you proceed, the sampling parameters are partially set by the conceptual framework and the research questions: police work, rule interpreting, arrests, and booking. There is still room for choices within each dimension of the study, but the universe is now far more bounded and focused. To get a sense of a minimal set of initial sampling choices within this universe, let's list some options:

Sampling Parameters	Possible Choices
Settings	Precinct station, squad car, scene of the crime, suspect's residence or hangout
Actors/participants	Police officers with different characteristics (e.g., rank, seniority, experience, race/ethnicity, beliefs, education) and suspects with different attributes (age, race/ethnicity, beliefs, education, type of offense)
Events	Arrests, bookings, possibly pursuits of suspects, and post hoc justifications of booking to others
Processes	Making the arrest, doing the booking, relating to suspects, interpreting laws, justifying laws, generally negotiating law enforcement within the precinct

The researcher may have to touch most or all of these bases to get the research question well answered. The first base usually is the setting—say, the precinct station. From there, several options emerge:

1. Start with the precinct station, one kind of police officer, all bookings during the working day, and all instances of the social interactions around "legal" and "illegal" behavior that occur.

2. Start with the precinct station and all types of officers, bookings, and justifications for the booking.

3. Start with one officer, and follow the officer through several episodes of pursuits, arrests, bookings, and justifications for them.

4. Start with a booking at the precinct station, and then reconstitute the prior events.

An ethnographer setting out to "hang around" a precinct is continuously making sampling decisions about what to observe, whom to talk with, what to ask, what to write down, and whether to stay in one room or another. And these choices, in turn, are determined by the questions being asked and the perspective—implicit or explicit—that determines why these questions, and not others, are being asked.

Questions of practicality also face us. There is a finite amount of time, with variable access to different actors and events, and an abundance of logistical problems. Being selective calls for some restraint in the classes of data you go after. Here we might suggest some guidelines. For example, useful data would (a) identify *new leads* of importance, (b) *extend* the area of information, (c) *relate* or bridge the already existing elements, (d) reinforce the main *trends*, (e) account for *other information* already in hand, (f) exemplify or provide more evidence for an *important theme*, and (g) *qualify or refute* existing information.

Finally, sampling means just that: taking a smaller chunk of a larger universe. If I begin with a well-developed conceptualization, I can focus on one precinct station and one kind of police officer making one kind of booking; if my conceptualization stands up, I can make statements about bookings that may apply to other officers and other precincts. But to test and verify those claims and to establish their *analytic generality*, I have to move on to several other precinct stations with similar and contrasting characteristics. Here again, the main goal is to strengthen the conceptual validity of the study, but the procedure also helps determine the conditions under which the findings hold.

Key processes can be identified at the outset or gradually—often via pattern codes, analytic memos, and interim summaries (to be described in later chapters). Being explicit about processes and collecting comparable data on them will foster cross-case comparability and give you easier access to the core underlying constructs as you get deeper into data collection.

Advice

1. If you're new to qualitative research, rest assured that there is never enough time to do any study. So taking the tack "I'll start somewhere and take it from there" is asking for trouble. It is probably a good idea to start with a fallback sample of participants and subsettings: the things you have to cover in light of what you know at that point. That sample will change later but less than you may think.

2. Just thinking in sampling-frame terms is good for your study's health. If you are talking with one kind of participant, you need to consider why this kind of participant is important and, from there, who else should be interviewed or observed.

3. In complex cases, remember that you are sampling people to get at the characteristics of settings, events, and processes. This means watching out for an overreliance on talk or on observation of participants while neglecting sampling for key events, interactions in different settings, and episodes embodying the emerging patterns in the study. The sampling choices at the start of the study may not be the most pertinent or data-rich ones. A systematic review can sharpen the early and late choices.

4. In qualitative research, as well as in survey research, there is a danger of sampling too narrowly. Go to the meatiest, most study-relevant sources. But it is also important to work a bit at the peripheries—to talk to people who are not central to the phenomenon but are neighbors to it, to people no longer actively involved, to dissidents and renegades and eccentrics. Spending a day in the adjoining village, school, neighborhood, or clinic is also worth the time, even if you don't see the sense at that point. You may learn a lot and obtain contrasting and comparative information that may help you understand the phenomenon at hand by "decentering" yourself from a particular way of viewing your other cases.

5. Spend some time on checking whether your sampling frame is feasible. Be sure the time is there, the resources are there, the requisite access to people and places is ensured, and the conditions are right for doing a careful job. Plan to study a bit less, rather than more, and "bank" the extra time. If you are done, the time is yours for a wider or deeper pass at the field.

6. Three kinds of instances have great payoff. The first is the apparently "typical" or "representative" instance. If you can find it, try to find another one. The second is the "negative" or "disconfirming" instance; it gives you both the limits of your conclusions and the point of greatest variation. The third is the "exceptional"

or "discrepant" instance. This instance will allow you to qualify your findings and to specify the variations or contingencies in the main patterns observed. Going deliberately after negative and atypical instances is also healthy in itself; it may force you to clarify your concepts, and it may tell you that you indeed have sampled too narrowly.

7. Apply some criteria to your first and later sampling plans. Here's a checklist, summarizing what we've said and naming some underlying issues:

- Is the sampling *relevant* to your conceptual frame and research questions?

- Will the phenomena you are interested in *appear*? In principle, *can* they appear?

- Does your plan enhance the *generalizability* of your findings, if relevant, either through conceptual power or through representativeness?

- Can *believable* descriptions and explanations be produced, ones that are true to real life?

- Is the sampling plan *feasible* in terms of time, money, access to people, and your own work style?

- Is the sampling plan *ethical*, in terms of issues such as informed consent, the potential benefits and risks, and the relationship with participants (see the next chapter)?

Instrumentation

Description and Rationale

Instrumentation comprises specific methods for collecting data: They may be focused on qualitatively or quantitatively organized information and may be loosely to tightly structured. Note that the term *instrumentation* may mean little more than some shorthand devices for observing and recording events. But note, too, that even when the instrumentation is an open-ended interview or fieldwork observation, some technical choices must be made: Will notes be taken? Of what sort? Will the transaction be audio- or video-recorded? Transcribed?

We've been emphasizing that conceptual frameworks, research questions, and sampling plans have a focusing role within a study. They give some direction to the researcher, before and during fieldwork, by clarifying what he or she wants to find out from whom and why. Knowing what you want to find out, at least initially, leads to the question of *how* you will get that information. That question, in turn, constrains the analyses you can do. If I want to find out how suspects are arrested and booked, I may decide to *interview* the people associated with this activity (police officers, suspects, and attorneys), *observe* bookings, and collect arrest-relevant *documents* (e.g., regulations, interrogation transcripts). If permitted, I may also take pictures of bookings or record them digitally. But how much of this instrumentation has to be designed prior to going out to the field? And how much structure should such instruments have?

Kvale and Brinkmann (2009) point out that during an open-ended interview much interpretation occurs along the way. The person describing his or her "life world" discovers new relationships and patterns during the interview; the researcher who occasionally summarizes or reflects what has been heard is, in fact, condensing and interpreting the flow of meaning. Data are not being collected but rather coauthored. (Yet note that the same things may be happening even when the interview question is much more structured and focused.)

How much preplanning and structuring of instrumentation is desirable? There are several possible answers: "little" (i.e., hardly any prior instrumentation) to "a lot" (of prior instrumentation, well structured) to "it depends" (on the nature of the study). Each view has supporting arguments; let's review them in capsule form (Display 2.6 is a summary of some of the main issues in deciding on the appropriate amount of front-end instrumentation).

Arguments for Little Prior Instrumentation

1. Predesigned and structured instruments blind the researcher to the site. If the most important phenomena or underlying constructs at work in the field are not in the instruments, they will be overlooked or misrepresented.

2. Prior instrumentation is usually stripped of context for purposes of universality, uniformity, and comparability. But qualitative research lives and breathes

Display 2.6

Prior Instrumentation: Key Decision Factors

Little Prior Instrumentation	"It Depends"	A Lot of Prior Instrumentation
Rich context description needed		Context less crucial
Concepts inductively grounded in local meanings		Concepts defined ahead by researcher
Exploratory, inductive		Confirmatory, theory-driven
Descriptive intent		Explanatory intent
"Basic" research emphasis		Applied, evaluation or policy emphasis
Single case		Multiple cases
Comparability not too important		Comparability important
Simple, manageable, single-level case		Complex, multilevel, overloading case
Generalizing not a concern		Generalizability/representativeness important
Need to avoid researcher impact		Researcher impact of less concern
Qualitative only, free-standing study		Multimethod study, quantitative included

Source: Miles, M. B., & Huberman, A. M. (1994). *Qualitative data analysis: An expanded sourcebook* (2nd ed.). Thousand Oaks, CA: Sage Publications.

through seeing the context; it is the particularities that produce the generalities, not the reverse.

3. Many qualitative studies involve single cases with few people involved. Who needs questionnaires, observation schedules, or tests—whose usual function is to yield economical, comparable, and parametric distributions for large samples?

4. The lion's share of fieldwork consists of taking field notes, recording events (conversations, meetings), and picking up things (documents, products, artifacts). *Instrumentation* is a misnomer. Some orienting questions, some headings for observations, and a rough-and-ready document analysis form are all you need at the start—perhaps all you will ever need during the course of the study.

Arguments for a Lot of Prior Instrumentation

1. If you know what you are after, there is no reason not to plan in advance how to collect the information.

2. If interview schedules or observation schedules are not focused, too much superfluous information will be collected. An overload of data will compromise the efficiency and power of the analysis.

3. Using the same instruments as in prior studies is the only way we can converse across studies. Otherwise, the work will be noncomparable, except in a very global way. We need common instruments to build theory, to improve explanations or predictions, and to make recommendations about practice.

4. A biased or uninformed researcher will ask partial questions, take selective notes, make unreliable observations, and skew information. The data will be invalid and unreliable. Using validated instruments well is the best guarantee of dependable and meaningful findings.

Arguments for "It Depends"

1. If you are running an *exploratory*, largely descriptive study, you do not really know the parameters or dynamics of a social setting. So heavy initial instrumentation or closed-ended devices are inappropriate. If, however, you are doing a *confirmatory* study, with relatively focused research questions and a well-bounded sample of persons, events, and processes, then well-structured instrument designs are the logical choice. Within a given study, there can be both exploratory and confirmatory aspects that call for differential front-end structure, or there can be exploratory and confirmatory *times*, with exploration often called for at the outset and confirmation near the end.

2. A *single-case* study calls for less front-end preparation than does a *multiple-case* study. The latter is looking forward to cross-case comparison, which requires some standardization of instruments so that findings can be laid side by side in the course of analysis. Similarly, a *freestanding* study has fewer constraints than a *multimethod* study. A *basic* study often needs less advance organizing than an

applied, *evaluation*, or *policy* study. In the latter cases, the focus is tighter and the instrumentation more closely keyed to the variables of interest.

3. Much depends on the *case definition* and levels of analysis expected. A researcher studying classroom climate in an elementary school might choose to look intensively in 3 of the building's 35 classrooms and so probably would be right to start with a looser, orienting set of instruments. If, however, an attempt is made to say something about how classroom climate issues are embedded in the working culture of the building as a whole, a more standardized, validated instrument—a teacher survey or a group interview schedule—may also be required.

We think that there is wisdom in all three stances toward front-end instrumentation and its degree of structure. Figure out first what kind of study you are doing and what kind of instruments you are likely to need at different moments within that study, and then go to work on the ones needed at the outset. But in all cases, as we have argued, the amount and type of instrumentation should be a function of your conceptual focus, research questions, and sampling criteria. If not, the tail is likely to be wagging the dog, and later analysis will suffer.

Example

How can front-end instrument design be driven in different ways by a study's scope and focus? We give an example, showing a mix of predesigned and open-ended instrumentation that follows the implications of a conceptual framework and research questions, without locking in too tightly. Back to the school improvement study.

This is a multiple-case (N = 12) study, and the phenomenon under study is moderately well (but not fully) understood from prior research. Both of these points suggest that some front-end instruments are likely to be called for. One important research question in the study was this: *In which ways did people redefine, reorganize, or reinvent the new program to use it successfully?*

Looking back at Display 2.3, we can see that the question derives from the fourth bin, "Cycle of Transformations," and within that bin, from the first variable cluster, "Changes in innovation as presented to user." Previous empirical research and cognitive and social-psychological theory both led us to the idea that people will adapt or reinvent practices while using them.

The *sampling* decisions are straightforward. The question addresses teachers in particular, and to get the answer, we will have to observe or interview them or, ideally, do both. We should sample events such as the teacher's first encounter with the innovation and processes such as assessing its strong and weak points and making changes in it to fit one's practice.

Let's look at the interview component of the **instrumentation**. We developed a semistructured interview guide. Each field researcher was closely familiar with the guide but had the latitude to use a personally congenial way of asking and sequencing the questions and to segment them appropriately for different respondents.

The guide was designed after the field work had begun. An initial wave of site visits had been conducted to get a sense of the context, the participants, and how the school improvement process seemed to be working locally. From that knowledge, we went for a deeper and broader understanding.

Display 2.7

Excerpts From Interview Guide, School Improvement Study

33. Probably you have a certain idea of how _____ looks to you now, but keep thinking back to how it first looked to you then, just before students came. How did it seem to you then?

    Probes:

    ___ Clearly connected, differentiated vs. unconnected, confusing

    ___ Clear how to start vs. awesome, difficult

    ___ Complex (many parts) vs. simple and straightforward

    ___ Prescriptive and rigid vs. flexible and manipulatable

34. What parts of aspects seemed ready to use, things you thought would work out OK?

35. What parts or aspects seemed not worked out, not ready for use?

36. Could you describe what you actually did during that week or so before you started using _____ with students?

    Probes:

    ___ Reading

    ___ Preparing materials

    ___ Plannning

    ___ Talking (with whom, about what)

    ___ Training

. . . .

40. Did you make any changes in the standard format for the program before you started using it with students? What kind of changes with things you thought might not work, things you didn't like, things you couldn't do in this school?

    Probes:

    ___ Things dropped

    ___ Things added, created

    ___ Things revised

Source: Miles, M. B., & Huberman, A. M. (1994). *Qualitative data analysis: An expanded sourcebook* (2nd ed.). Thousand Oaks, CA: Sage Publications.

Now to dip into the guide near the point where the research question will be explored (see Display 2.7). The interviewer begins by taking the participant back to the time just before he or she was to use the innovation with students, asking for detailed context—what was happening, who the colleagues were, and what feelings they had.

Questions 33 through 36 move forward through time, asking how the innovation looked, its ready or unready parts, and what the teacher was doing to prepare for its use. Question 40 comes directly to the research question, assessing the pre-use changes made in the innovation. The probes can be handled in various ways: as aids to help the interviewer flesh out the question, as prompts for items the participant may have overlooked, or as subquestions derived from previous research. Later in the interview, the same question recurs as the interviewer evokes the teacher's retrospective views of early and later use, then moves into the present ("What changes are you making now?") and the future ("What changes are you considering?").

Advice

Simply thinking in instrument design terms from the outset strengthens data collection as you go. If you regularly ask, "Given that research question, how can I get an answer?" it will sharpen *sampling* decisions (I have to observe/interview this class of people, these events, those processes), help clarify *concepts*, and help set *priorities* for actual data collection. You also will learn the skills of redesigning instrumentation as new questions, new subsamples, and new lines of inquiry develop.

People and settings in field studies can be observed more than once. Not everything is riding on the single interview or observation. In qualitative research, there is nearly always a second chance. So front-end instrumentation can be revised—in fact, should be revised. You learn how to ask a question in the site's terms and to look with new eyes at something that began to emerge during the first visit. Instrumentation can be modified steadily to explore new leads, address a revised research question, or interview a new class of participants.

In qualitative research, issues of instrument validity and reliability ride largely on the skills of the researcher. Essentially, a *person* is observing, interviewing, and recording, while modifying the observation, interviewing, and recording devices from one field visit to the next. Thus, you need to ask about yourself and your colleagues: How valid and reliable is this *person* likely to be as an information-gathering instrument? To us, some markers of a good qualitative researcher-as-instrument are

- good familiarity with the phenomenon and the setting under study;
- a multidisciplinary approach, as opposed to a narrow grounding or focus in a single discipline;
- good investigative skills, the ability to draw people out, and meticulous attention to detail;
- being comfortable, resilient, and nonjudgmental with participants in the setting; and
- a heightened sense of empathetic engagement, balanced with a heightened sense of objective awareness.

Although unfamiliarity with the phenomenon or setting allows for a fertile decentering, it also can lead to relatively naive, easily misled, and easily distracted fieldwork, along with the collection of far too much data. On balance, we believe that a savvy practitioner is often a better research instrument in a qualitative study: sharper, more refined, more attentive, people-friendly, worldly-wise, and quicker to hone in on core processes and meanings about the case.

Linking Qualitative and Quantitative Data

We have to face the fact that numbers and words are *both* needed if we are to understand the world. The question is not whether the two sorts of data and associated methods can be linked during study design but whether it should be done, how it will be done, and for what purposes.

Both types of data can be productive for descriptive, exploratory, inductive, and opening-up purposes. And both can be productive for explanatory, confirmatory, and hypothesis-testing purposes. For example, the careful measurement, generalizable samples, experimental control, and statistical tools of good quantitative studies are precious assets. When they are combined with the up-close, deep, credible understanding of complex real-world contexts that characterize good qualitative studies, we have a very powerful mix.

Looked at the other way, qualitative data can help the quantitative side of a study during design by aiding in conceptual development and instrumentation. They can help during data collection by making access and data collection easier. During analysis, they can help by validating, interpreting, clarifying, and illustrating quantitative findings, as well as through strengthening and revising theory.

Mixed methods is a genre of inquiry that has been gaining ground in several research circles. Whether you choose to employ some form of quantitative component in your qualitative study is both an epistemological and a methodological decision that should be driven by your study's needs—not by the desire to be trendy. The reasons cited most often for mixing both genres are (a) to provide analytic texture to your work, (b) to compensate for the deficiencies of one genre with the strengths of another, and (c) to modify or strengthen the analytic findings when the results of each genre support, corroborate, or contradict each other.

There is, of course, a long and well-developed tradition of dealing quantitatively with qualitative data: content analysis, where the issue is one of counting the frequency and sequencing of particular words, phrases, or concepts found in the data. In multicase studies, it is possible to rank cases and to benefit from the availability of nonparametric statistical techniques for contrasting them. Also note the tradition of using quantitative information in anthropological fieldwork; Bernard (2011) includes a helpful compilation of methods.

Approaches to Mixed-Methods Designs

We see the qualitative–quantitative linkage at three levels. The first is the "quantitizing" level, where qualitative information can be either counted directly (say, the number of times a doctor interrupts a patient during an interview) or converted into magnitudes of ranks or scales (e.g., in this teacher's classroom, "moderate" rather than "low" mastery of a specific innovation has occurred). The second level is that of linkage between distinct data types, where qualitative information (say, from an open-ended interview) is compared with numerical data (say, from a survey the same person filled out).

The third is that of the overall study design, such as the multimethod approaches sketched in Display 2.8 or more complex ones; all may involve combinations of case study, survey, experiments, and unobtrusive-measure studies.

In Design 1, fieldwork involves steady, integrated collection of both quantitative and qualitative data, as needed to understand the case at hand.

Design 2 shows a multiwave survey, conducted in parallel with continuous fieldwork. The first survey wave may draw attention to things the field-worker should look for, the next fieldwork findings may lead to revisions in Wave 2 of the survey, and so on.

Design 3 alternates the two kinds of data collection, beginning with exploratory fieldwork and leading to the development of quantitative instrumentation, such as

Display 2.8

Illustrative Designs Linking Qualitative and Quantitative Data

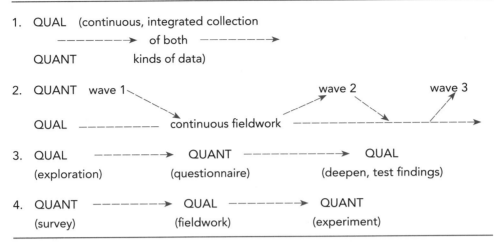

Source: Miles, M. B., & Huberman, A. M. (1994). *Qualitative data analysis: An expanded sourcebook* (2nd ed.). Thousand Oaks, CA: Sage Publications.

a questionnaire. The questionnaire findings can be further developed and tested systematically with the next round of qualitative work.

Design 4 shows another, alternating style: An initial survey helps point the field-worker to phenomena of importance; the field-worker moves to develop a close-up, strong conceptual understanding of how things work; and a quantitative experiment is designed to test some of the resulting, perhaps competing, hypotheses.

Here are some examples of various mixed-methods designs.

The Quantitizing Level

During our school improvement study, we gradually became aware of the importance of job mobility and looked at people in our sites who had changed jobs (moving up, out, sideways, or down). It proved helpful to know how many people had moved (75, for 12 sites), how many of these had moved because of their experience with the innovation (83%), and how many were actually upward moves (35%).

We also converted some interview data into rating scales or *magnitudes*: the degree of pressure teachers felt to adopt an innovation, their satisfaction with the assistance they received, or the "roughness" or "smoothness" of the implementation. Because our cases were schools, not individuals, this conversion involved examining interviews from different people, checking the degree of agreement, and arriving at a site-level rating. Three- to five-point scales seemed the easiest and most reliable: for example,

- 5 = *high*, 4 = *moderate/high*, 3 = *moderate*, 2 = *moderate/low*, 1 = *low*
- 5 = *smooth*, 4 = *mostly smooth*, 3 = *mixed*, 2 = *rough*, 1 = *very rough*

In the displays and analysis, we aimed to keep numbers or magnitudes like these closely associated with the words from which we drew the judgment and to keep the words associated with the context.

Linking Data Types

Kell (1990) studied the effects of computers on classroom teaching and learning. The research team repeatedly visited classrooms in six school districts over a school year, doing interviews with teachers and administrators and making systematic classroom observations. They also asked teachers to complete two different standardized questionnaires at three times during the year, covering their theoretical orientation to reading and their concerns about the adoption and use of innovations. Thus, the two data types were closely linked, and they permitted Kell to study the changes occurring over the whole school year.

Multimethod Designs

McCammon, Saldaña, Hines, and Omasta (2012) received e-mail survey responses from 234 participants about their high school arts experiences. The survey asked for demographic information (e.g., gender, year of high school graduation, state[s] of high school attendance) and ratings to a series of prompts (4 = *strongly agree*, 3 = *agree*, 2 = *disagree*, 1 = *strongly disagree*) and provided space for an open-ended qualitative commentary to the prompts. The demographic information provided descriptive statistics such as percentages, the ratings provided means and other statistics for various *t* tests, and the open-ended survey responses were qualitatively coded and analyzed.

This multimethod design enabled us to compare means between various groupings (e.g., between men and women) and apply a two-tailed *t* test to discern any significant statistical differences ($p < .05$), followed by a qualitative comparison of codes. After a few initial queries, we observed *paradigmatic corroboration*: In other words, the lower and more significant the *p* level, the more qualitative differences seemed to appear between groups; conversely, when the *p* level was moderate or high, the fewer the qualitative differences we could detect between the groups. This phenomenon in our own data harmonized with mixed-methodological analytic theory (Tashakkori & Teddlie, 2003) and guided our decisions about whether quantitative results merited qualitative follow-up and inquiry.

Overall, consider whether your study can benefit from a quantitative aspect or component. Think *purposes* and think ahead: In light of my research questions and the audiences for my study report, will qualitative information be enough or should it be complemented by a numerical data set of some kind?

Also remember that, during study design, you are setting up the social system of the project. If you are a lone researcher, can you manage both sorts of information? What technical support might you need? We advise finding and using a mentor who can advise you, critique products, and provide a supportive, different perspective. If you are part of a research team, what will be the consequences of a specific division of labor? In our experience, for example, keeping qualitative and quantitative researchers separate can feed negative comparisons, stereotyping, and sterile arguments about "which data you trust more."

Management Issues Bearing on Analysis

How a qualitative study is managed from Day 1 strongly influences the kinds of analyses that can be done, and how easily. Qualitative studies, especially those done by the lone researcher or the novice graduate student, can be notorious for their vulnerability to poor study management. Kvale and Brinkmann (2009) point out in their entertaining analysis of the naive question "How shall I find a method to analyze the 1,000 pages of interview transcripts I have collected?" that the first answer is "Never conduct interview research in such a way that you find yourself in a situation where you ask such a question" (pp. 189–190).

We make no pretense of being exhaustive on issues of study management but want to point to a series of issues and associated design decisions with strong implications for analysis. We illustrate along the way with brief examples and give advice, largely from our own experience and the lore of colleagues.

We deal with three topics in turn: (1) the use of computers and software, (2) data management, and (3) staffing/time planning.

Computer and Software Use

It is taken for granted that you need a good desktop or laptop computer to conduct qualitative research. Handwritten or dictated field notes, along with audio recordings, must be converted into analyzable text, which then needs to be condensed, displayed, and used to draw and verify conclusions. It's also fair to say that the researcher who does not use software beyond programs such as Microsoft Word will be hampered in comparison with those who do. Display 2.9 lists some of the most common and frequent tasks qualitative researchers will conduct on a desktop or laptop computer.

Display 2.9

Uses of Computer Software in Qualitative Studies

1. Making notes in the field
2. Writing up or transcribing field notes
3. Editing: correcting, extending or revising field notes
4. Coding: attaching key words or tags to segments of text to permit later retrieval
5. Storage: keeping text in an organized database
6. Search and retrieval: locating relevant segments of text and making them available for inspection
7. Data "linking": connecting relevant data segmens with each other, forming categories, clusters or networks of information
8. Analytic memoing: writing reflective commentaries on some aspect of the data, as a basis for deeper analysis
9. Content analysis: counting frequencies, sequence or locations of words and phrases
10. Data display: placing selected data in a condensed, organized format, such as a matrix of network, for inspection
11. Conclusion drawing and verification: aiding the analyst to interpret displayed data and to test or confirm findings
12. Theory building: developing systematic, conceptually coherent explanations of findings; testing hypotheses
13. Graphic mapping: creating diagrams that depict findings or theories
14. Preparing interim and final reports

Source: Miles, M. B., & Huberman, A. M. (1994). *Qualitative data analysis: An expanded sourcebook* (2nd ed.). Thousand Oaks, CA: Sage Publications.

"What software is best?" cannot be answered meaningfully. You have to get specific about the kind of database you are building in your project and about the kind of analysis you will be doing. Microsoft Word and Excel (or comparable programs) are bare minimum requirements. Word includes many layout features and enables you to easily construct complex tables for displays. Excel is most useful for building simple matrices and especially for holding qualitative survey data and taking quantitative data through selected statistical calculations and tests—a boon for mixed-methods studies (see Display 2.10).

As for CAQDAS (Computer Assisted Qualitative Data Analysis Software), there are multiple options available, varying in complexity, cost, and functions available. These programs' websites provide online tutorials or demonstration software/manual downloads of their most current versions:

- AnSWR: www.cdc.gov/hiv/topics/surveillance/resources/software/answr
- ATLAS.ti: www.atlasti.com
- CAT (Coding Analysis Toolkit): cat.ucsur.pitt.edu/
- Dedoose: www.dedoose.com
- DiscoverText: www.discovertext.com
- HyperRESEARCH: www.researchware.com
- MAXQDA: www.maxqda.com
- NVivo: www.qsrinternational.com
- QDA Miner: www.provalisresearch.com
- Qualrus: www.qualrus.com
- Transana: www.transana.org (for audio and video data materials)
- Weft QDA: www.pressure.to/qda/

Display 2.10

An Excel Spread Sheet With Qualitative and Quantitative Data

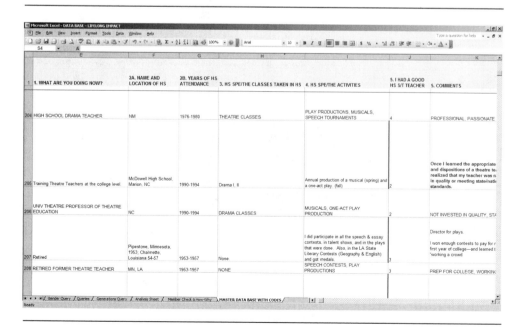

Selected CAQDAS programs, such as AnSWR and Weft QDA, are free of charge. Online-only programs like Wordle (www.wordle.net) employ basic content-analytic functions yet display results in intriguing visual arrays.

We do not recommend one program over others, and you may find that the scope of your study is so small that a CAQDAS program may not even be needed. But this software is indispensable for longitudinal, large-scale, or multisite studies and studies with digital photographs and video data (see Display 2.11). You should select one that seems compatible with your research needs and personal ways of working (or one that permits multiple-user access for team research projects).

CAQDAS is first and foremost an excellent way to store and maintain your data corpus. Selected programs can visually display which code you've assigned to which chunk of data through clear, at-a-glance graphics. Their search and retrieval functions permit rapid access to construct categories and allow you to test your hunches, hypotheses, and queries; they also keep records of these operations for analytic documentation. Some programs also feature quantitative/statistical capabilities for mixed-methods studies, and more sophisticated CAQDAS packages can construct semantic networks or displays with nodes and lines that suggest interrelationships between data chunks. Saldaña has found the CAQDAS modeling features for network display drawing most helpful and much easier to use than the time-consuming artwork features of text-based programs. Display 2.12 (from McCammon et al., 2012, p. 14) illustrates a complex model of interacting variables leading to participant confidence from participating in high school speech and theatre classes and activities. The model was drawn originally with NVivo 8 software.

Display 2.11

An NVivo 10 Screen Shot of a Coded Digital Video Interview

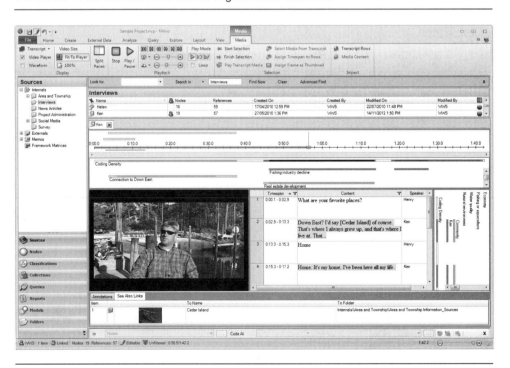

Source: Courtesy of QSR International, www.qsrinternational.com.

Display 2.12

A Model of Lifelong Confidence From High School Speech and Theatre

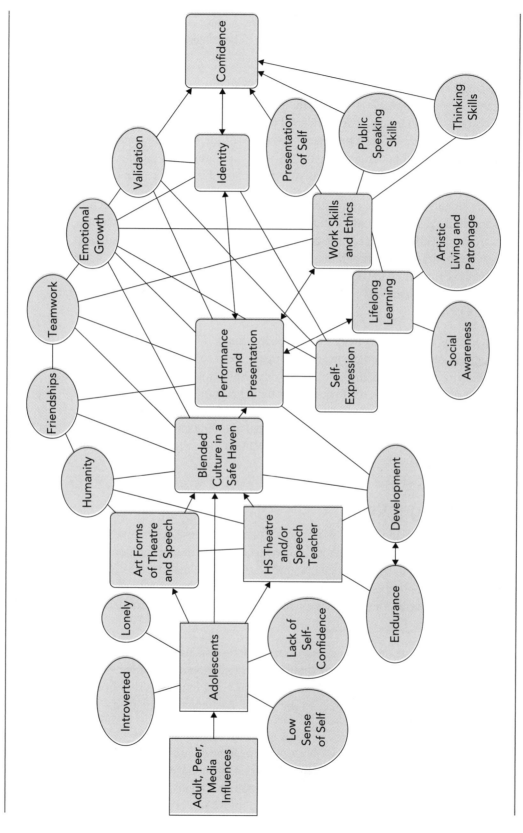

Source: McCammon, L., Saldaña, J., Hines, A., & Omasta, M. (2012). Lifelong impact: Adult perceptions of their high school speech and/or theatre participation. Youth Theatre Journal 26(1), 2–25.

There is still ongoing debate within the field about the utility of these software programs for data *analysis*. CAQDAS does not automatically analyze qualitative data for the user, but these programs do enable selective monitor display of data and your assigned codes in multiple configurations for researcher review and *analytic thinking* about their various assemblages and meanings.

No single software program can do everything well. You may end up with several programs, each with specific strengths, rather than with one all-purpose package. Some CAQDAS programs include wonderful features to support analyses, but there is a steep learning curve for most programs. Invest your time wisely, and spend it more on analyzing data and not on figuring out a software program's operations and syntax. Think critically about what you need as your projects and research career evolve.

Work initially at a level of computer literacy that is comfortable for you, technically speaking, and extend your understanding with the help of friends whose computer skills are stronger than yours. Although tutorials supplied with programs can help, the best way to learn a new program is to use it on real tasks, with a mentor for consultation. Allow time in your study design for learning new software. See the Appendix for recommended titles in print to supplement the use of basic text programs and CAQDAS.

CAQDAS is a fast-moving field. Expect the information here to become outdated as programs are refined and new programs appear. Refer to Bazeley (2007), Friese (2012), Lewins and Silver (2007), and Richards (2009) for accompanying literature on and practical guidance with the major commercial programs. Also, see Hahn (2008) for qualitative data management and analysis with Microsoft Office software. Many CAQDAS programs are discussed and reviewed at an online forum for users: http://caqdas.soc.surrey.ac.uk/. More about CAQDAS will be discussed throughout the later chapters.

Data Management

The idea of data management is familiar to quantitative researchers; they have been taught to think in terms of systematic data sets, codebooks, documentation of defined variables, records of analyses carried out, and so on. Data management is just as—perhaps even more—important for qualitative researchers. Typically, large amounts of data come from several sources, cases, or sites and sometime include numerical data sets as well.

The main issues are ensuring (a) high-quality, accessible data; (b) documentation of just what analyses have been carried out; and (c) retention of data and associated analyses after the study is complete. Many questions are at hand, but they boil down to these: What do I need to anticipate in the way of data management needs? How thorough do I need to be?

Display 2.13 presents an ideal wish list of needs to be included in the data that are managed in a project and retained after the project. Do you have to set all this up, use it all, and keep it all? No. Will you be better off if you think about these possibilities and their relative importance during the design of the study? Yes. Is it easier to do it with the right software? Yes, two or three times easier. Some CAQDAS programs automatically generate and store material of this sort as you go along. But you will also need a well-organized physical place for storage and retrieval of raw field notes, audio and related

Display 2.13

What to Store, Retrieve From, and Retain

1. Raw material: field notes, recordings, site documents

2. Partially processed data: write-ups, transcriptions, initial version, and subsequent corrected, "cleaned," "commented-on" versions

3. Coded data: write-ups with specific codes attached

4. The coding scheme or codebook, in its successive iterations

5. Memos or other analytic material: the researcher's reflections on the conceptual meaning of the data

6. Search and retrieval records: information showing which coded chunks or data segments the researcher looked for during analysis, and the retrieved material; records of links made among segments

7. Data displays: matrices or networks used to display retrieved information, along with the associated analytic text. Revised versions of these

8. Analysis episodes: documentation of what you did, step by step, to assemble the displays and write the analytic text

9. Report text: successive drafts of what is written on the design, methods, and findings of the study

10. General chronological log or documentation of data collection and analysis work

11. Index of all of the above material

Source: Miles, M. B., & Huberman, A. M. (1994). *Qualitative data analysis: An expanded sourcebook* (2nd ed.). Thousand Oaks, CA: Sage Publications.

media, edited hard copies, and so on. Preliminary organization is key, yet expect to revise and extend your data management system as you go. Institutional review boards (discussed further in Chapter 3) may also impose particular requirements for data management, such as the use of pseudonyms and secure storage, to ensure participant anonymity and confidentiality.

Some researchers prefer to keep each form and unit of data as a separate computer file, but in categorized folders. For example, a folder labeled "Interviews" contains the files "Interview 1—Janice," "Interview 2—Janice," and so on. Others prefer to label folders by case or site, with appropriate subfolders, such as a folder named "Janice Data" with subfolders of "Interviews," "Participant Observation," "Photos," and so on.

Saldaña recommends a single master document for a one-person, short term, qualitative case study. All the data get placed in one "working" file (with the original and complete data sets in separate backup files) and eventually get condensed and transformed into the final report. Interview excerpts, after condensation, are available as participant quotes for the final report. Related chunks of data get cut-and-pasted together as a form of instantaneous categorization.

Remember that most research data are irreplaceable. If they are lost, erased, vandalized, or damaged, you are out of luck. ***Back up all of your work.*** And you can never be too obsessive about careful data management for

- complex, multicase, multiresearcher, multimethod projects that get chaotic in a hurry if they are not well planned;

- high-stakes projects where much is riding on the results and your field is waiting for well-defended answers;

- projects you believe are crucial or even definitive; and

- projects for which you expect or are seeking an external audit.

Staffing and Time Planning

Qualitative studies are chronically called "labor intensive," but the details are rarely provided. Here, too, we rely on our experience and that of colleagues.

Who will do the work, and how much time will it take? These innocent questions mask more complexity than you often expect. We've said that lone researchers, new or experienced, should find a critical friend, partner, mentor, or colleague who can supply alternative perspectives, support, and protection from bias. In studies that have more than one staff member, there will always be a diversity of experiences, backgrounds, and skills.

That complexity means that the social system of the project needs attention; it will not develop automatically. It is crucial to build strong relationships with research partners or within larger staffs. We've found it useful, for example, to devote plenty of the initial time to work on core issues (the conceptual framework, research questions, sampling) and to more general maintenance issues, such as hopes for and worries about the project, reports of "what else is happening in my life," and procedural guidelines for joint work. Research teams are not built in a day. Take time deliberately for the start-up of the relationship between you and your research partner, or the functioning of the research team.

One other rule of thumb we've found useful: Avoid sharp senior–junior divisions of labor, such as having juniors do the fieldwork and the seniors do the analysis and writing. Senior people need to be directly involved in data collection in order to have a concrete feel of what the field setting is like. You cannot be a principal investigator in a field study without spending time in the field. Junior people will function poorly as "hired hands." Both need to be actively and mutually engaged in thinking about the project and the meaning of emergent findings.

At the start, people rarely have all the skills they need for a study. Allow for learning time on issues such as fluency with new software, use of a new coding method, or drawing data displays. The time estimates we use look something like this: For each day of fieldwork, expect to spend

- 2 or 3 days processing field notes (writing them up, correcting, etc.) if audio or video recordings are being transcribed, the multiple may run from 4 to 8, depending on the fineness of detail and the transcriber's familiarity with the content;

- 1 or 2 days coding (depending on the fineness and complexity of the evolving scheme); and

- 1 or 2 days completing displays and writing (depending on the number and type of displays).

These are multipliers for a single case. In a multiple-case study, you (a) multiply by the number of cases, (b) consider what cross-case analyses will be carried out and what the within-case and cross-case reports will look like, and (c) make a total-days estimation.

Closure and Transition

We've looked at substantive moves that serve to focus the collection of data and condensing it. These moves include systematic *conceptual frameworks* of variables or concepts and their interrelationships, *research questions* that further define the inquiry, defining the core and parameters of a study through *case definition*, planning for within-case and multiple-case *sampling*, and creating *instrumentation*. All these moves serve both to constrain and to support analysis. All can be done inductively and developmentally in advance of data collection. Designs may be tight or loose. Such choices depend on not only your preferred research style but also the study's topic and goals, available theory, and the researcher's familiarity with the settings being studied.

Added design issues that make a big difference in analysis include how qualitative data may be linked with quantitative information from the same setting, and a series of nuts-and-bolts management issues. Careful decisions about which computer software to use for what purposes need to be made. A systematic plan for data management—storage and retrieval of everything from raw data to final study reports—is equally important. Building good colleague and staff relationships is essential, as is initial and recurring time planning.

In the next chapter, we will examine the more human dimensions of fieldwork and analysis through the perspectives of the participants and our ethical obligations to them.

Note

1.   When we (Miles and Huberman) had the chance to collaborate on a major field study, we leaped at it. The project was a study of the dissemination of educational innovations carried out during 1979–1983. Many of the examples in this text come from that study. (More detailed information appears in the first and second editions of this book.)

The study was nested in a larger study of school improvement, covering 145 school buildings and nearly 4,000 people throughout the United States involved in the implementation of educational innovations. Joined by two colleagues, Beverly Loy Taylor and Jo Anne Goldberg, we repeatedly visited a stratified sample of 12 field sites across the country throughout the 1979–1980 school year, with follow-up contacts the next year to verify the main findings.

The volume of data collected included 440 interviews, 85 observations, some 259 documents, and 2,713 pages of transcribed field notes. Interview and observation notes were dictated and transcribed. We developed a common set of data displays and, for each of the 12 field sites, used them to draw conclusions, resulting in a case report ranging from 70 to 140 pages, with a common format. Our subsequent cross-case analysis was built from the appropriate sections of the 12 case reports. In a second multiple-case field study, we replicated many of the techniques for collecting, condensing, and analyzing qualitative data from the school improvement study, finding that they "traveled" quite well.

In the course of the cross-case analysis, we began another study, sponsored by the National Institute of Education. The task was to document the procedures we used for analyses, from the initial coding of site-level notes to the more explanatory cross-case analyses. Each analysis fed into a detailed self-documentation form; this exercise provided many of the illustrations and rules of thumb in the present book. We learned a great deal through teaching seminars in the United States, Canada, Western Europe, and Australia. The generic issues of qualitative data analysis become clearer as they are confronted not only across researchers but across cultures.

3

Ethical Issues in Analysis

Chapter Summary

This chapter surveys ethical matters and dilemmas that may be faced by researchers during fieldwork. Questions are posed to consider issues such as participant consent, benefits, risk, confidentiality, and data ownership.

Contents

Introduction
Agreements With Study Participants
Ethical Issues
    Worthiness of the Project
    Competence
    Informed Consent
    Benefits, Costs, and Reciprocity
    Harm and Risk
    Honesty and Trust

Privacy, Confidentiality, and Anonymity
Intervention and Advocacy
Research Integrity and Quality
Ownership of Data and Conclusions
Use and Misuse of Results
Conflicts, Dilemmas, and Trade-Offs
Closure and Transition

Introduction

We cannot focus only on the quality of the knowledge we are producing, as if its truth were all that counts. We must also consider the potential "wrongness" of our actions as qualitative researchers in relation to the people whose lives we are studying, to our colleagues, and to those who sponsor our work. All researchers must be guided by the classic principle of humane conduct: *First, do no harm*.

Any responsible qualitative researcher ponders moral and ethical questions such as the following: Is my project really worth doing? Am I exploiting people with my research? Do the respondents have a right to see my report? What good is anonymity if people and their colleagues can easily recognize themselves in my report? When they do, might it hurt or damage them in some way? What do I do if I observe harmful actions during my fieldwork? Who owns the data, and who owns the report?

The qualitative literature is full of rueful testimony on such questions, peppered with sentences beginning with "I never expected . . ." and "If I had only known that . . ." and "I only later realized that . . ." We need to attend to the ethics of what we are doing before, during, and after a study.

We cannot begin to deal with all ethical issues, but we do hope to cut across some of the problems involved and raise as much ethical consciousness as we can. In this chapter, we describe agreements with participants and specific issues that often arise in qualitative research, exploring their implications for analysis. We then examine some of the conflicts, dilemmas, and trade-offs involved and conclude with some general advice.

Agreements With Study Participants

Usually, study participants and researchers need to reach some explicit agreements about shared expectations. Our intent here is to examine the analysis-related aspects of agreements made with those whose daily lives are being examined. The main issue is what explicit expectations we want to build with study participants that will maintain and improve the quality of our conclusions.

We might think first of a "meta-agreement": Are we contemplating an equal-status, *polyvocal* model, in which researchers and participants are jointly telling their stories? Or are we heading for a *collaborative* or *participatory action research* model, in which researchers join forces with people facing a problem in their community to help them study and resolve it? Or will it be a more *traditional* model that differentiates researchers from participants, on whom the research is conducted? The first two models imply more shared control over the design and conduct of the project than does the last.

Whatever the basic relationship implied in such a meta-agreement, some matters need to be clarified with participants at the outset. (It's important to remember that these matters may not be fully understood on both sides until the study unfolds.) Display 3.1 presents issues that might be considered as the elements of an initial set of expectations. Many different agreements can be reached. We comment on the implications of some for doing analysis.

Data collection agreements (see Question 2 in Figure 3.1) that include active involvement of participants, such as journal writing, are threatened when such participation is coerced, even gently (see Question 3). Such agreements also tend to move the study in the direction of shared study design and steering (Question 4).

Vagueness about confidentiality (Question 5), as when a researcher voluntarily or involuntarily passes on a participant's comments to another, often has "drying up" or distorting effects on subsequent data collection; relationships may get strained, and subsequent analyses may be biased.

The same goes for anonymity (Question 6). An individual, group, or organization not assured in advance of nonidentifiability in study reports may provide biased data (self-censored, defensive, and rosy) if it is believed that an accurate, identifiable account would jeopardize some interest. In any case, anonymity of individuals is difficult or impossible to assure when a case study of a group or organization is read by its members. (An alternative agreement is to use real names from the outset; under these circumstances, individuals only provide information they regard as public or nondamaging. This, too, has its conclusion-narrowing aspects.)

Display 3.1

Questions for Agreement With Study Participants

1. How much time and effort will be involved?
2. What kind of data collection is involved (e.g., observation, interviewing, journal writing, life histories)?
3. Is participation voluntary?
4. Who will design and steer the study?
5. Will material from participants be treated confidentially?
6. Will participants' anonymity be maintained?
7. Who will produce descriptive and explanatory products?
8. Will participants review and critique interim and final products?
9. What benefits will accrue to both participants and researchers?

Source: Miles, M. B., & Huberman, A. M. (1994). *Qualitative data analysis: An expanded sourcebook* (2nd ed.). Thousand Oaks, CA: Sage Publications.

A typical agreement is that researchers will produce the products of the study (Question 7). This agreement rests on the traditional assumption that well-prepared researchers will get good data and will draw well-founded conclusions. In some models, however, expertise resides in participants as much as in researchers. The collaborative or participatory action research model implies that participant expertise is developed through the researcher's facilitation during the process—for example, in community-based projects. In either case, issues of "goodness of analysis" are just as pressing as in the traditional model (see Chapter 11).

Study products are sometimes fed back to participants (Question 8) as a way of providing member checks on the accuracy of descriptions, explanations, and interpretations. Agreements can vary: Does an individual see material about his or her case before others do? Can an individual or group censor or veto material, or even block publication? Or is the agreement only that errors of fact will be corrected and alternative interpretations will be included in footnotes? Such agreements can improve the quality of both the data and the final conclusions, but they also can result in truncated or distorted conclusions if someone has been given, and exercises, the right of censorship.

Researchers usually benefit (Question 9) from their studies through insights, recognition, promotion, new grants, and consulting. That is why they keep on researching. Participants' benefits are often posed quite vaguely at the start: "the chance to reflect," "clarifying ideas," "learning what others are doing." Advance agreements that mention assistance (as in collaborative research), consultation or training, joint authorship, or shared royalties as expected benefits may improve the quality of the data and the conclusions. If the benefits do not materialize, data and conclusion quality may suffer.

We offer these final pieces of advice on agreements with study participants:

1. Be clear in your mind what you want your agreement with participants to be like. Commit it to paper as a vehicle for discussion with them while negotiating entry and access. Once the agreement is clear, a copy of a summary of the study and its ground rules is helpful for a study that has multiple participants.

2. Incorporate in data collection plans an explicit procedure for logging participants' understanding (or misunderstanding) of agreements, including any threats to data or conclusion quality that you see.

3. Researchers held to their institutional review board (IRB) regulations may have specific requirements imposed on them that affect researcher–participant relationships, agreements, and data collection protocols.

Ethical Issues

Most professions have well-defined codes of ethics, which include guidelines ranging from research participants' rights to inappropriate forms of researcher–participant relationships. Organizations subject to an IRB or comparable overseeing agency also mandate guidelines for securing permissions, maintaining confidentiality, working with minors, and other legal matters. But fieldwork and its accompanying dilemmas are often quite unpredictable and site specific. Plus, research questions, instrumentation, and sampling all may evolve over the course of a qualitative study, making the IRB's requirements for these details to be precisely specified *before* a study begins nearly impossible to comply with. Nevertheless, some planning and forethought are necessary for application and review.

We now outline some specific ethical matters and issues for reflection.

Worthiness of the Project

Ask yourself: Is my contemplated study worth doing? Will it contribute in some significant way to a domain broader than my funding, my publication opportunities, and my career? And is it congruent with values important to me?

Implications for Analysis

In general, a study that is only opportunistic, without a larger significance or real meaning to you, is likely to be pursued in a shallow way, with less care devoted to design, data collection, and analysis. The report will be written to "look good" rather than to be right. Initial conclusions may not be questioned; follow-up analyses with rival hypotheses may be rare. There's nothing wrong with taking on a commissioned research project for personal income. But if you slant your findings to accommodate and please your funders, you become complicit and dishonest.

Competence

Ask yourself: Do I (and my colleagues) have the expertise to carry out a study of good quality? Or (because researchers, both novice and experienced ones, are always exploring things they do not quite know how to do) am I prepared to study and be supervised, trained, and consulted with? Is such help available?

Implications for Analysis

Unacknowledged (or not understood) incompetence is, we think, responsible for a certain pattern of analytic weakness in qualitative studies: accumulation of large amounts of poorly collected, unanalyzed data and drawing superficial and hasty conclusions as deadlines loom. This picture often occurs when lone researchers fail to seek help from friends, colleagues, or mentors. Graduate students often understand their own inexperience but sometimes cannot get support and help from their teachers or dissertation supervisors. That is research malpractice.

Informed Consent

Ask yourself: Do the people I am studying have full information about what the study will involve? Is their consent to participate freely given—fully voluntary and uncoerced? Does a hierarchy of consent (e.g., children, parents, teachers, administrators) affect such decisions?

IRB regulations are strict but thorough when it comes to recruiting voluntary participants, informing them about the study's goals, and assuring them of their rights throughout the project. Research with minors or other vulnerable populations (e.g., prisoners, pregnant women) includes additional guidelines for permissions processes, such as securing parental consent and children's assent.

Be an open book with your project; this will help develop a sense of trust between you and the setting's individuals. Also, acknowledge that participants are doing the researcher a great favor by volunteering to be part of the study. Respect their gifts of time, insight, and privacy, for the root meaning of "data" is not something that is collected but something that is *given*. If children and adolescents are part of the mix, they too have a say in the matter. There are only extremely rare occasions when covert research and deceit are necessary for the integrity of a research project's goals (e.g., investigating the social processes of humans engaged in illegal activity). If you have something to hide from participants, it better be for a good reason.

Implications for Analysis

Weak consent usually leads to poor data. Respondents will try to protect themselves in a mistrusted relationship or one formed with the researcher by superiors only. Ambiguity about the later stages of analysis also can be damaging to study quality and to the interests of people in the case. If you plan to use "member checks" to verify or deepen conclusions, that expectation and specific procedures need to be clear as the study proceeds. Securing a participant's permission is not a single hurdle to be jumped; dialogue and ongoing renegotiation are needed throughout the study.

Benefits, Costs, and Reciprocity

Ask yourself: What do participants have to invest in time, energy, or financial resources? What will each party to the study gain from having taken part? Is the balance equitable?

As we suggested earlier, researchers are often "paid" in one way or another. They usually enjoy their work and learn from it, they may get a dissertation out of it, and their papers, articles, and books not only contribute to their fields but also can bring them recognition, royalties, new funding, and career advancement.

Study participants have a somewhat different set of benefits: They get to be listened to, they may gain insight or learning, they may improve their personal practice, a program or policy they are involved with may be strengthened, and they may get help in taking effective action on some recurring problem. But study participants rarely share in publication, and they usually don't become famous. Most don't get paid for their research contributions.

The question of costs and who bears them is important. The researcher's time is repaid—usually not fully—in cash or a class grade or dissertation approval. Research participants normally must take time from or beyond whatever else they are doing and are usually not recompensed. The local organization may well have added costs (e.g., for teacher substitutes).

Implications for Analysis

Study participants' concern about the inequity of benefits and costs serves to jeopardize access and thin out data. But we are always moved and amazed when people do keep talking to us thoughtfully, inviting us into their lives day after day, when the benefits to them seem so slim, so intangible, and often so delayed.

Researchers vary in their perspectives about monetarily compensating their participants (e.g., offering a gift card or a token $20.00 for each hour of interview time). Some feel that the offer of money may unduly influence participants' responses to become more favorable and positive than they really think. Other researchers feel that working-class professionals, such as teachers and social workers, deserve some type of financial compensation for their valuable time and opinions. This is an issue to be resolved by each individual researcher and his or her particular project.

Researchers traffic in *understanding*. Most study participants are preoccupied with *action*—how to work and live better. It can be argued that if you approach your analytic work with a deeper sense of its action implications, your understanding will be deeper—and the benefits to participants more equitable.

Harm and Risk

Ask yourself: What might this study do to hurt the people involved? How likely is it that such harm will occur?

Harm to participants can come in many varieties: from blows to self-esteem or "looking bad" to others, to threats to one's interests, position, or advancement in the organization, to loss of funding for a program, and so on, up to being sued or arrested. The information from a qualitative study is never value-free, and it may have negative consequences.

Harm cuts both ways. We like the story told by a *New York Times* reporter who asked a drug dealer if he really felt comfortable about talking frankly. The dealer said cheerfully, "Sure. If I don't like what you write, I'll kill you." As researchers, we have occasionally been threatened with litigation and with warnings to intervene with our funding agency when a draft report was seen as threatening a key interest.

Sieber (1992) points out that it's important to think of varying vulnerability to harm. More vulnerable persons (and institutions) include those who are publically visible, lack resources or autonomy, are stigmatized, are weakened or institutionalized, cannot speak for themselves, are involved in illegal acts, or are too closely associated with those studied.

Setting risk levels for potential harm is very difficult—perhaps impossible—in qualitative studies. It's wise to assume that the chances of some type of harm are better than others and to consider in advance ways of reducing that likelihood.

Implications for Analysis

As with inequitable benefits and costs, if harm is expected, access and data quality may suffer. The prospect of immediately impending harm—which well may occur when reports are made to local participants, sponsors, or funding agencies—can lead to pressure on you to revise or delete conclusions or to self-censor them in advance.

Honesty and Trust

Ask yourself: What's my relationship with the people I'm studying? Am I telling the truth? Do we trust each other?

Most qualitative researchers are unlikely to lie, cheat, or steal in the course of their work. But broken promises are not unknown. And some researchers have reported deceiving respondents about the true nature of the inquiry (as in some participant observation studies such as Humphreys' [1970] study of homosexuals, where he posed as a "watch queen" lookout inside public toilets).

Typically, dishonesty is more subtle. The field-worker may project a "fake persona" (the friendly listener or the would-be insider) to gain knowledge or access. At some levels, as van Maanen (1979) notes, whenever the field-worker works to "penetrate fronts," symbolic violence is being done: "People are, to a degree, coaxed, persuaded, pushed, pressured, and sometimes almost blackmailed into providing information to the researcher that they might otherwise prefer to shield" (p. 545). There are always individually drawn moral limits to this violence: A researcher may decide not to push on a delicate matter, or to leave an embarrassing scene. Nevertheless, the question of just how coercive and unauthentic relationships with respondents are cannot be ignored, or be defined away by the pious stipulation that "my relationship is fully honest."

Implications for Analysis

If people feel betrayed by you when they read a report, it becomes almost impossible for them to accept it as a reasonable interpretation of what happened, because of their natural defensiveness when "the truth hurts," as it well may, and their feelings of anger at having been misled. Deceptiveness and broken promises—especially if benefits and costs have been inequitable or harm has occurred—will make any continuation of the inquiry problematic. We will have wronged not only our respondents but also our colleagues.

We will not pretend to have any easy or foolproof answers for this slippery category of ethical dilemmas. All we can pass along is some classic advice: When in doubt, tell the truth.

Privacy, Confidentiality, and Anonymity

Ask yourself: In what ways will the study intrude, come closer to people than they want? How will information be guarded? How identifiable are the individuals and organizations studied?

Sieber (1992) makes these helpful distinctions among three terms, which often are confused or used interchangeably in research practice:

- *Privacy:* control over others' access to oneself and associated information or preservation of boundaries against giving protected information or receiving unwanted information

- *Confidentiality:* agreements with a person or organization about what will be done (and may not be done) with their data—may include legal constraints

- *Anonymity:* lack of identifiers, information that would indicate which individuals or organizations provided which data

As Sieber notes, issues of privacy are often subtle and misunderstood by the researcher, surfacing only when there are unexpected reluctances, an outpouring of information beyond what the person meant to say, or a confidence overheard by others. Privacy is, in part, about secrecy.

Confidentiality and anonymity are usually promised—sometimes very superficially—in initial agreements with respondents. For example, unless the researcher explains very clearly what a fed-back case will look like, people may not realize that they will *not* be anonymous at all to other people within the setting who read the case.

Issues of privacy, confidentiality, and anonymity take a completely new turn when visual media such as digital photos and video are used in data collection and reporting. Individuals and groups still need to have control over how they are depicted, and can resist privacy invasions (e.g., by vetoing specific pictures or sequences), but the possibility of anonymity is almost surely gone, even with facial-blur or digital tiling effects.

Implications for Analysis

When you realize that privacy has been threatened, new analytic moves (e.g., data from other sources) may be needed to protect data quality. If privacy has, in fact, been breached, questions of the report's impact when it is fed back to respondents become central; can the information involved be connected with an identifiable person?

Using member checks to verify or extend interpretations and conclusions helps with anonymity problems, particularly if you begin with the most vulnerable respondents before moving in a wider circle; they usually (though not always) can spot information that would identify them and thus threaten their interests.

The basic problem of identifiability when the case is a complex site must be considered before and during report preparation. Local people nearly always can tell (or will assume) who is being depicted. You may need to err on the side of protecting anonymity, if it has been promised, and to rely on dialogue and negotiation for corrective action before the report is finalized.

Explicit confidentiality agreements about where raw data and analyses will be stored, and who will have access to them, probably enhance data quality by increasing trust. However, courts have not normally treated social science researchers' data as a legally privileged communication. If a case is brought to litigation, your documents and other data could become "un-confidential" evidence.

Intervention and Advocacy

Ask yourself: What do I do when I see harmful, illegal, or wrongful behavior on the part of others during a study? Should I speak for anyone's interests besides my own? If so, whose interests do I advocate?

Take, for example, the vivid instance of police brutality witnessed by van Maanen (1983) and written up in his field notes. Although he did not assist the police, he did not protest or intervene either. He thus protected the police by default and avoided supporting the victim. Later, in a suit brought by police officers against a newspaper, van Maanen opted to protect the interests of the patrolmen by refusing to release his field notes.

Ethical choices are not always so dramatic, but they are still there when we see indifferent teachers, medical malpractice, abused children, or evidence of misspent funds—and do or don't report them. Ethical choices are also present when we study people who are breaking the law as we study them: drug dealers and users, corrupt agency heads, prostitutes and their pimps and customers, violent gangs, embezzlers, and so on. It is important to know more about deviance; but are we somehow condoning it by our neutral, noncondemning presence?

Implications for Analysis

A situation in which you have "dirty hands"—cannot evade doing wrong to one party or another—is personally anguishing. And no matter how it is resolved, it skews your understanding and personal values system. If you decide to withhold knowledge in favor of continued access, then not only your public reports but also your conceptualization and explanatory theories may become lopsided.

Research Integrity and Quality

Ask yourself: Is my study being conducted carefully, thoughtfully, and correctly in terms of some reasonable set of standards or established practices?

"On-the-job training" for a student of qualitative research is part of the learning curve; there will be some expected stumbling and gaffes along the way. But a student's teacher/supervisor should ensure that there has been sufficient preparation for independent fieldwork, and constant communication and monitoring throughout the process to better guarantee a quality experience for all concerned.

As for the findings, if we provide a set of conclusions based on sloppy (or even fraudulent) work and claim their validity, then we are being dishonest with our sponsors, colleagues, supervisors, participants, and anyone else who reads and trusts our reports.

Outright scientific fraud is rare, but it does occur when the stakes are high (funding, primacy of discovery, career advancement). It would be naive to expect that a qualitative study could never be faked.

Far more common, as noted in Adler's (1991) report of a conference on integrity in behavioral science research, is "poor science": sloppy data recording; insufficient, selective, or misleading reporting of findings; unwillingness to share or retain data; undisclosed conflicts of interest; and inappropriate citation.

Implications for Analysis

In Chapter 11, we will acknowledge the difficulties of assessing the quality of qualitative studies and suggest a series of tactics for enhancing the goodness of any particular study: its confirmability, dependability, credibility, and potential transferability to other settings. A student should run his or her data and analyses in progress past a supervisor, mentor, or peers for periodic "reality checks."

The practical implication here is that if you have not attended to the issue of goodness criteria in your study, you are on shaky intellectual ground. It is not just that we must somehow please our critical colleague audiences; the deeper issue is avoiding self-delusion. After that, we can turn to the task of being honest with our readers about how we did the study and what worried us about its quality. Without such methodological frankness, we run the risk of reporting "knowledge that ain't so."

As for fraud, the truth eventually will come out, though it may take as long as the decades before Cyril Burt's famous results on the intelligence similarity of separated twins were detected as faked. We should concentrate on not lying to *ourselves*.

Ownership of Data and Conclusions

Ask yourself: Who owns my field notes and analyses: me, my organization, my participants, or my funders? And once my reports are written, who controls their distribution?

The issue of confidentiality requires being clear about who can have access to the data. Most researchers consider their data and analyses as belonging to them and, in the absence of some form of litigation, consider themselves to be responsible for safeguarding their confidentiality, preserving anonymity, and making the data available to others for auditing, reanalyses, secondary analyses, and replications. But the issues here are not that simple. For example, the Freedom of Information Act in the United States permits public access to fieldwork data from federally funded projects. IRBs may require that a project's data records be destroyed/erased within a specified period of time.

The control of report diffusion is also a crucial issue. Some participants may vehemently object to an unpublished report's depiction of them and threaten to block its publication through legal means. Funding agencies, too, may exert this right; at the 1993 meeting of the American Educational Research Association, there were at least two instances of a government agency refusing to allow a public report of completed research: In one, it appeared that the agency saw the release of the findings as politically unwise; in the other, the agency's "internal review had not been completed."

Implications for Analysis

Make certain that all ownership agreements are specified in writing before data are collected. There are potential risks to respondents if the data fall into the wrong hands, so you need to think carefully about how others can access your database and how confidentiality and anonymity can be maintained.

In our experience, nothing seems to hit a researcher harder than the realization that some person, group, or organization may block the dissemination of months or years of research effort. Freedom of scholarly inquiry is a strong value, as are the values of career advancement, recognition, and funding. Researchers can easily become obsessed about this. You need to be clear about the political context of your work and to guard against agreeing too easily to others' veto efforts or to altering important substantive aspects as a way of ensuring publication or continued funding.

Use and Misuse of Results

Ask yourself: Do I have an obligation to help my findings to be used appropriately? What if they are used harmfully or wrongly? Who am I trying to help, specifically? Do I have the right to change my participants' values, attitudes, and beliefs? Is consciousness raising without action support enough?

Examples of misuse of study findings are not hard to find. Findings may be misinterpreted (deliberately or not) and used to support wrong policies (e.g., student test score differences as a justification for tracking or special program placement). Or the findings, correctly understood, can be used by organizations the researcher deplores (e.g., by conservative political action committees). We may have discovered something that the participants may not realize (e.g., a program that has adverse rather than positive effects) and attempt to "change the system," when the system feels that it's not our place or right to interfere with its established ways of working. A participant may share an opinion or perspective that you find disturbing during an interview, and you may be tempted to debate the issue rather than to listen and learn more. Knowledge is not exactly power. Rather, the use of our knowledge raises our awareness of—and enmeshes us in—the power relationships in the world we have been studying.

Implications for Analysis

On any given project, it probably pays to be as clear as possible from the start just how committed you are to supporting the use of your findings (and/or to warding off misuse from various quarters). Check your findings regularly with the people you're researching to discuss the broader implications and ramifications. Accept the fact that not everyone thinks and feels the same way you do and that you have an obligation in your analysis to acknowledge the multiplicity of perspectives you encounter. Your write-up should also clearly specify how you envision your findings being used by others, especially for policy and practice.

Conflicts, Dilemmas, and Trade-Offs

The infamous long-term study of syphilis patients begun in 1932 at the Tuskegee Institute exemplifies the dilemma of *scientific understanding versus individual rights*, which in this case was resolved in a particularly inhumane and destructive way. The scientific purpose was understanding the long-term course of syphilis, and it was given priority. African American men in the study were left without treatment and were not informed of the availability of penicillin (in 1943) as an effective treatment. The study was not terminated until 1972, by which time most of the participants had died. At a less tragic level, this dilemma appears in studies where we do not intervene in harmful situations for fear of jeopardizing our access (and thus perhaps our future scientific understanding). A positive outcome of this atrocity was the composition of ethical principles and guidelines for research involving human participants—The Belmont Report.

The more typical qualitative research experience is also full of dilemmas. For example, there is often a conflict between the demands of *validity versus avoiding harm*. One of us once studied a school where the new principal, a bit shaky on the job, received regular consultation from an experienced ex-principal—who was called by some staff members as "the principal's babysitter." During feedback of a report draft, several respondents said, "You don't need to put that in," acknowledging tacitly that it would damage the principal's self-esteem. But when the phrase was excised, readers did not know that the staff believed their principal needed a "babysitter" *and* was a decent man who did not deserve to be hurt—or that they were, perhaps, asking the researcher to collude with them in keeping their feelings from the principal.

Another dilemma appears when the use of results is considered: *detached inquiry versus help*. In any given situation, we can define our role as that of "understanding" what is going on and providing "help" only vaguely, in the long-term future when the fieldwork is over and the report appears. That stance defines our actual assistance to respondents in solving the problems they face. If, on the other hand, we choose to make helping our priority, we risk becoming co-opted and forfeiting our intellectual independence.

There is also the dilemma of *help giving versus confidentiality*. It's ordinarily quite difficult to assist (or get assistance for) a respondent you have discovered to be in need (let's say, a new teacher who is floundering unassisted), without breaching the agreement that no one else will have access to what the person told you.

Freedom of inquiry versus political advantage represents another dilemma. Most researchers opt for the first and are distressed when their findings are blocked. Yet suppose you were strongly committed to the improvement of early-childhood education at a point when legislators were about to reauthorize an important national program. And let's suppose that your data (like some in the 1990s) were fairly pessimistic about that program's effects. Might you want to temper the "whole truth" a bit by saying that the findings were only partial or methodologically flawed?

This list of dilemmas is illustrative; it certainly is not exhaustive. And more often than not, multiple dilemmas will be in play. Many of the accounts we've read of ethical dilemmas in qualitative studies describe "compromises," "trade-offs," "balances," and "unhappy choices." If ethical issues and their resolutions were clear-cut, life would be simple. But we have to keep thinking and talking about ethical dilemmas, weighing how we and our respondents are choosing one side or the other.

We offer these final pieces of advice on ethics in qualitative studies:

Anticipation: Most of the specific issues raised above can benefit from advance thinking during the early stages of project design. Do not delude yourself that they can be pre-resolved, but thinking them through—perhaps running through the issues as a sort of checklist—can help you avoid problems later.

Third parties: Because ethical issues often tend to be masked by our taken-for-granted assumptions, beliefs, and values, engaging a trusted third party can be very helpful in bringing them to our attention. Such a person can raise unheeded issues, suggest alternate viewpoints, help surface tacit assumptions, be an advocate for respondents, or serve as a mediator between participants and researchers when there are unresolved problems.

Regular checking and renegotiation: The evolution of any qualitative study normally involves some twists and turns that no one fully anticipated, even with the best of goodwill. Initial agreements and working procedures almost always need updates. In our experience, agreement revision is quite typical as issues of feedback, member checks, and reporting come into focus. It's useful from the start to create the expectation that agreements may need renegotiation and that "recheck" meetings can be called at any point by either researchers or respondents.

Closure and Transition

We've examined a series of specific ethical issues, ranging from early matters (the project's worthiness, your own competence, informed consent, and anticipated benefits and costs) to those occurring as a project develops (harm and risk, your relationship with respondents, privacy/confidentiality/anonymity, and intervention) and those that are prominent later (research quality, data ownership, and use of results). All have implications for analysis and the quality of conclusions. Dealing with ethical issues effectively involves heightened awareness, negotiation, and making trade-offs among ethical dilemmas, rather than the application of foolproof rules.

In the next chapter, we will present some fundamental principles of qualitative data analysis, before venturing into methods of display in Part Two.

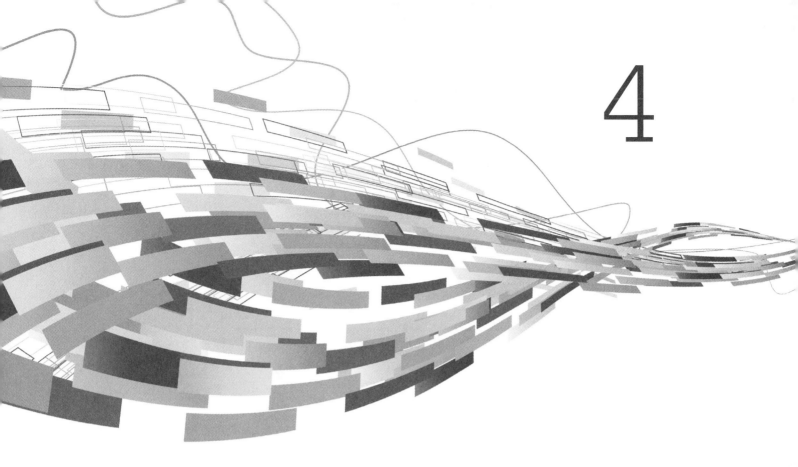

Fundamentals of Qualitative Data Analysis

Chapter Summary

This chapter reviews fundamental approaches to qualitative data analysis, with a particular focus on coding data segments for category, theme, and pattern development. Other analytic strategies include jottings, memos, and the formulation of assertions and propositions. Within-case and cross-case analysis are then compared for their unique advantages and contributions to the research enterprise.

Contents

Introduction
    Data Processing and Preparation
First Cycle Codes and Coding
    Description
    Applications

    First Cycle Coding Examples

    Creating Codes

    Revising Codes

    Structure and Unity in Code Lists

    Definitions of Codes

    Levels of Coding Detail

  Second Cycle Coding: Pattern Codes

    Description

    Applications

    Examples

    From Codes to Patterns

    Coding Advice

  Jottings

  Analytic Memoing

    Description and Rationale

    Examples

    On Visual Data

    Memoing Advice

  Assertions and Propositions

  Within-Case and Cross-Case Analysis

    Purposes of Cross-Case Analysis

    A Key Distinction: Variables Versus Cases

    Strategies for Cross-Case Analysis

  Closure and Transition

Introduction

In this chapter, we describe fundamental methods for qualitative data analysis while data collection progresses. They help organize data for later, deeper analyses, such as those using the displays described in Chapters 6 through 10.

Some qualitative researchers put primary energy into data collection for weeks, months, or even years and then retire from the field to "work over their notes." We believe this is a big mistake. It rules out the possibility of collecting new data to fill in gaps or to test new hypotheses that emerge during analysis. It discourages the formulation of rival hypotheses that question a field-worker's routine assumptions. And it makes analysis into a giant, sometimes overwhelming, task that frustrates the researcher and reduces the quality of the work produced.

We strongly advise analysis concurrent with data collection. It helps the field-worker cycle back and forth between thinking about the existing data and generating strategies for collecting new, often better, data. It can be a healthy corrective for built-in blind spots. It makes analysis an ongoing, lively enterprise that contributes to the energizing process of fieldwork. Furthermore, early analysis permits the production of interim reports, which are required in most evaluation and policy studies. So we advise interweaving data collection and analysis from the very start.

Data Processing and Preparation

For the methods in this and the following chapters, we assume that the field-worker has collected information in the form of handwritten or typed field notes, audio or video recordings of interviews or other events in the field setting, and documents or other print/digital artifacts. In all cases, we are focusing on words as the basic form in which the data are found. Photographs can be part of the data corpus, but they are best analyzed through memoing (discussed later).

We further assume that the basic, raw data (scribbled field notes, recordings) must be processed before they are available for analysis. Field notes must be converted into expanded write-ups, either typed directly or transcribed from dictation. A write-up is an intelligible product for anyone, not just for the field-worker. It can be read, edited for accuracy, commented on, coded, and analyzed using several of the methods we later describe.

Raw field notes may contain private abbreviations. They are also sketchy. Field notes taken during an interview usually contain a fraction of the actual content. But a formal write-up usually will add back some of the missing content because the raw field notes, when reviewed, stimulate the field-worker to remember things that happened at that time that are not in the notes.

Direct recordings of field events also must be processed in some way. For example, the field-worker listens to or watches the recording, makes notes, selects excerpts, and, if applicable, makes judgments or ratings. More typically, the recording is transcribed into text. This process, however, is fraught with slippage; it is dependent on the knowledge and skill of the transcribing person. Note, too, that transcripts can be done at different levels of detail, from the "uhs," "ers," pauses, word emphases, mispronunciations, and incomplete sentences of an apparently incoherent speaker to a smooth, apparently straightforward summary of the main ideas presented by a fluent participant.

So we are focusing on *words* as the basic medium and are assuming that the words involved have been refined from raw notes or recordings into a text that is clear to the reader or analyst. Note, however, that this text may be condensed and simplified considerably from the raw events.

Now, on to the methods. We begin with First Cycle coding, then Second Cycle or *Pattern codes* and the process of deriving even more general themes through *jottings* and *analytic memoing*. We then discuss *assertion and proposition development* and conclude this chapter with a section on *within-case* and *cross-case analysis*. Our presentation here addresses only the fundamentals of analysis; Chapters 5 to 10 include additional methods and specific examples.

First Cycle Codes and Coding

Description

Codes are labels that assign symbolic meaning to the descriptive or inferential information compiled during a study. Codes usually are attached to data "chunks" of varying size and can take the form of a straightforward, descriptive label or a more evocative and complex one (e.g., a metaphor). Saldaña (2013) defines a code as

> most often a word or short phrase that symbolically assigns a summative, salient, essence-capturing, and/or evocative attribute for a portion of language-based or visual data. The data can consist of interview transcripts, participant observation field notes, journals, documents, drawings, artifacts, photographs, video, Internet sites, e-mail correspondence, literature, and so on. The portion of data to be coded during First Cycle coding processes can range in magnitude from a single word to a full paragraph to an entire page of text to a stream of moving images. In Second Cycle coding processes, the portions coded can be the exact same units, longer passages of text, analytic memos about the data, and even a reconfiguration of the codes themselves developed thus far. Charmaz (2001) describes coding as the "critical link" between data collection and their explanation of meaning. . . . In qualitative data analysis, a code is a researcher-generated construct that symbolizes and thus attributes interpreted meaning to each individual datum for later purposes of pattern detection, categorization, theory building, and other analytic processes. Just as a title represents and captures a book, film, or poem's primary content and essence, so does a code represent and capture a datum's primary content and essence. (pp. 3–4)

In other words, coding *is* analysis. Some research methodologists believe that coding is merely technical, preparatory work for higher level thinking about the study. But we believe that coding is deep reflection about and, thus, deep analysis and interpretation of the data's meanings.

Codes are primarily, but not exclusively, used to retrieve and categorize similar data chunks so the researcher can quickly find, pull out, and cluster the segments relating to a particular research question, hypothesis, construct, or theme. Clustering and the display of condensed chunks then set the stage for further analysis and drawing conclusions.

For example, let's assume you were interested, as we were in the school improvement study, in the reasons why a new educational practice is adopted. You might begin by asking participants why they or others decided to try the practice. A piece of the formatted field notes might look like this:

> I asked the principal what the need for the new program was, and he responded that the students coming into the 9th grade were two years below grade level and that the old curriculum was ineffective. Through testing (the Nelson Reading Test) it was determined that students were growing academically only 5 or 6 months during the 10-month school year.

Assuming that you found it possible to apply a single summarizing notation or code to this chunk, it might be MOTIVATION (other codes could be applicable). That code would appear capitalized in the right-hand margin beside the segment (the left-hand margin might be used for a *jotting*, explained later):

[1] MOTIVATION

[1] I asked the principal what the need for the new program was, and he responded that the students coming into the 9th grade were two years below grade level and that the old curriculum was ineffective. Through testing (the Nelson Reading Test) it was determined that students were growing academically only 5 or 6 months during the 10-month school year.

Other chunks of field notes or interview transcripts that also relate to MOTIVATION would receive the same code.

Applications

As soon as the field researcher begins to compile information, challenges appear. A big one comes from the multiplicity of data sources and forms. Some information comes from structured or informal observations. More, if not most, comes from interviewing. There are also everyday or special documents, archival records, and physical artifacts. In some studies, there can be information from questionnaires and surveys, videos, or statistical records.

All of this information piles up geometrically. In the early stages of a study, most of it looks promising. But if you don't know what matters more, everything matters. You may never have the time to condense and order, much less to analyze and write up, all of this material. That's why we think that conceptual frameworks and research questions are the best defense against overload. They also reflect a point we made earlier: that data collection is inescapably a *selective* process and that you cannot and do not "get it all," even though you might think you can.

But selectivity does not, in itself, resolve the problem of overload. In fact, you need roughly three to five times as much time for processing and ordering the data as the time you needed to collect it. Just one substantive week at a field site often can result in something like hundreds of pages of typed-up field notes, interview transcripts, documents, and ancillary materials. Codes are *prompts* or *triggers* for deeper reflection on the data's meanings. Coding is thus a *data condensation* task that enables you to retrieve the most meaningful material, to assemble chunks of data that go together, and to further condense the bulk into readily analyzable units.

Coding is also a *heuristic*—a method of discovery. You determine the code for a chunk of data by careful reading and reflection on its core content or meaning. This gives you intimate, interpretive familiarity with every datum in the corpus.

Codes are first assigned to data chunks to detect reoccurring patterns. From these patterns, similar codes are clustered together to create a smaller number of categories or *Pattern codes*. The interrelationships of the categories with each other then are constructed to develop higher level analytic meanings for assertion, proposition, hypothesis, and/or theory development.

First Cycle Coding Examples

Saldaña (2013) divides coding into two major stages: First Cycle and Second Cycle coding. First Cycle coding methods are codes initially assigned to the data chunks. Second Cycle coding methods generally work with the resulting First Cycle codes themselves.

First Cycle coding methods include up to 25 different approaches, each one with a particular function or purpose. You do not need to stick with just one approach for your coding efforts; some of these can be compatibly "mixed and matched" as needed. Below is a review of some of the most pertinent ones that apply to the particular analytic approaches profiled in this book. See Saldaña's (2013) *The Coding Manual for Qualitative Researchers* for a fuller description of each method.

First, there are three *elemental methods* that serve as foundation approaches to coding: (1) Descriptive, (2) In Vivo, and (3) Process coding.

Descriptive Coding

A descriptive code assigns labels to data to summarize in a word or short phrase—most often a noun—the basic topic of a passage of qualitative data. These eventually provide an inventory of topics for indexing and categorizing, which is especially helpful for ethnographies and studies with a wide variety of data forms (field notes, interview transcripts, documents, etc.). Descriptive codes are perhaps more appropriate for social environments than social action. An example comes from field notes about a lower-middle-class neighborhood:

[1] As I walked toward the school, there was a 7-11 convenience store 1 block away, next to a small professional office building: an optometrist, podiatrist, and other medical/health-related clinics. Directly across the street was an empty lot, but next to that stood a Burger King restaurant.	[1] BUSINESSES

An analyst would extract all passages coded BUSINESSES from various field notes to compose a more detailed inventory of the case and to construct a narrative describing the business climate in the area.

In Vivo Coding

This is one of the most well-known qualitative coding methods. In Vivo coding uses words or short phrases from the participant's own language in the data record as codes. It may include folk or indigenous terms of a particular culture, subculture, or microculture to suggest the existence of the group's cultural categories (e.g., in a hospital, you may hear unique terms such as "code blue," "sharps," and "scripts"). In Vivo coding is appropriate for virtually all qualitative studies but particularly for beginning qualitative researchers learning how to code data, and studies that prioritize and honor the participant's voice. Phrases that are used repeatedly by participants are good leads; they often point to regularities or patterns in the setting. In Vivo codes are placed in quotation marks to differentiate them from researcher-generated codes. Examples are taken from a coded interview transcript about an adolescent girl's experiences with school:

I [1] hated school last year. Freshman year, it was awful, I hated it. And [2] this year's a lot better actually I, um, don't know why. I guess, over the summer I kind of [3] stopped caring about what other people thought and cared more about, just, I don't know.	[1] "HATED SCHOOL" [2] "THIS YEAR'S BETTER" [3] "STOPPED CARING"

Process Coding

This coding method uses gerunds ("-ing" words) exclusively to connote observable and conceptual action in the data. Processes also imply actions intertwined with the dynamics of time, such as things that emerge, change, occur in particular sequences, or become strategically implemented. Process coding is appropriate for virtually all qualitative studies, but particularly for grounded theory research that extracts participant action/interaction and consequences. Here is an example from an interview transcript about an adolescent girl explaining how rumors get spread:

Well, that's one problem, that [my school is] pretty small, so [1] if you say one thing to one person, and then they decide to tell two people, then those two people tell two people, and in one period everybody else knows. [2] Everybody in the entire school knows that you said whatever it was. So. . . .	[1] SPREADING RUMORS [2] KNOWING WHAT YOU SAID

Next, there are three *affective methods* that tap into the more subjective experiences we encounter with our participants: (1) Emotion, (2) Values, and (3) Evaluation coding.

Emotion Coding

Perhaps obviously, this method labels the emotions recalled and/or experienced by the participant or inferred by the researcher about the participant. Emotion coding is particularly appropriate for studies that explore intrapersonal and interpersonal participant experiences and actions. It also provides insight into the participants' perspectives, worldviews, and life conditions. Note that a participant himself or herself may sometimes label the emotion, and thus, it should be In Vivo coded in quotation marks. The following example is taken from an interview transcript about a middle-aged man complaining about one of his work colleagues:

[1] I just hated it when he got awarded with the honor. [2] I mean, we're praising mediocrity now. Never mind that what you've accomplished isn't worth squat, it's all about who you know in the good ol' boys network.	[1] "HATED IT" [2] BITTERNESS

Values Coding

This is the application of three different types of related codes onto qualitative data that reflect a participant's values, attitudes, and beliefs, representing his or her perspectives or worldview. A value (V:) is the importance we attribute to ourselves, another person, thing, or idea. An attitude (A:) is the way we think and feel about oneself, another person, thing, or idea. A belief (B:) is part of a system that includes values and attitudes, plus personal knowledge, experiences, opinions, prejudices, morals, and other interpretive perceptions of the social world. Values coding is appropriate for studies that explore cultural values, identity, intrapersonal and interpersonal participant experiences and actions in case studies, appreciative inquiry, oral history, and critical ethnography. Here is an example from an interview transcript about a female university student discussing her political beliefs:

[1] Government regulation of women's health issues has gotten out of hand. It's not about "protecting" us, it's about their need to control and dominate women [2] through covert religious ideology. White Christian men are deciding what's law and what's moral and what's, how it's supposed to be. [3] They can say, "It's *not* a war on women" all they want, but trust me—it's a war on women.	[1] B: GOVERNMENTAL CONTROL [2] B: COVERT RELIGIOUS MOTIVES [3] A: MISOGYNIST MOTIVES

Evaluation Coding

This method applies primarily nonquantitative codes onto qualitative data that assign judgments about the merit, worth, or significance of programs or policy. Evaluation coding is appropriate for policy, critical, action, organizational, and evaluation studies, particularly across multiple cases and extended periods of time. The selected coding methods profiled thus far, such as Descriptive or In Vivo codes, can be applied to or supplement Evaluation coding, but the methods are customized for specific studies. A + symbol before a code tags it as a positive evaluation. Second-order codes that follow a primary code and a colon are called *Subcodes*. The following example comes from an interview transcript about an elementary school teacher assessing an artist-in-residency program:

[1] The artist-in-residency program was pretty successful this year. [2] The arts agency did a great job at selecting qualified candidates this time around. [3] We were pretty impressed at how they integrated math and geometry with art-making without the teachers telling them to. I think they knew the score and that it was pretty important that they cover those subject areas. And they did it in a way that made it [4] interesting for the kids. For the teachers, too! We learned some things that we can integrate into our own curriculum next year.	[1] + RESIDENCY: "SUCCESSFUL" [2] + CANDIDATES: QUALIFIED [3] + CURRICULUM: INTEGRATION [4] + CURRICULUM: "INTERESTING"

One *literary and language method*, Dramaturgical coding, explores human action and interaction through strategic analysis of people's motives.

Dramaturgical Coding

This method applies the terms and conventions of character, play script, and production analysis onto qualitative data. For character, these terms include items such as participant objectives (OBJ), conflicts (CON), tactics (TAC), attitudes (ATT), emotions (EMO), and subtexts (SUB). Dramaturgical coding is appropriate for exploring intrapersonal and interpersonal participant experiences and actions in case studies, power relationships, and the processes of human motives and agency. The following example is taken from an interview transcript about a community college instructor's dilemmas with her unit's budget cuts:

[1] There was a lot of pressure this year to "do more with less." And that always [2] frustrates me, because you don't "do more with less"— you do *less with less*. So [3] if they're expecting me to do more with less money and less resources, they're not going to get it. And it's not because I'm being snotty or passive-aggressive about this; [4] it's simply that you can't squeeze blood out of a turnip. There's only so much you can do with what you have. [5] And yes, I'm spending some of my own money this year on classroom supplies because we don't have enough to last us through the end of the year. [6] That's just the way it is these days.	[1] CON: LESS RESOURCES [2] EMO: FRUSTRATION [3] TAC: RESISTANCE [4] ATT: LIMITATIONS [5] TAC: SACRIFICING [6] ATT: ACCEPTING "THE WAY IT IS"

Three *exploratory methods*—(1) holistic, (2) provisional, and (3) hypothesis coding—make preliminary or global coding assignments, based on what the researcher deductively assumes may be present in the data before they are analyzed.

Holistic Coding

This method applies a single code to a large unit of data in the corpus, rather than line-by-line coding, to capture a sense of the overall contents and the possible categories that may develop. Holistic coding is often a preparatory approach to a unit of data before a more detailed coding or categorization process through First or Second Cycle methods. The coded unit can be as small as one-half a page in length or as large as an entire completed study. Holistic coding is most applicable when the researcher has a general idea as to what to investigate in the data. Here is an example from field notes by a researcher observing how new, tenure-track faculty become oriented to academia:

[1] The chair of the committee debated whether to start on time or to wait for latecomers to join the meeting. "We all made the effort to be here at 8:00 a.m., so let's start," he said. The network meeting began with obligatory self-introductions of the 6 people seated around a large table designed to hold 12. Most attendees were newcomers to academia at the assistant professor or faculty associate level, primarily from midwest and east coast institutions. Each one appeared to be in his or her late 20s or early 30s. "You're the new guard of the college," said the chair, "and we're here to find ways to network and support each other as we begin our teaching careers."	[1] THE "NEW GUARD"

Provisional Coding

This approach begins with a "start list" of researcher-generated codes, based on what preparatory investigation suggests might appear in the data before they are collected and analyzed. Provisional codes can be revised, modified, deleted, or expanded to include new codes. This method is appropriate for qualitative studies that build on or corroborate previous research and investigations. For example, a researcher about to interview people who successfully quit smoking may develop the following Provisional codes of smoking cessation methods beforehand:

PRESCRIPTION MEDICATION

NICOTINE PATCHES

NICOTINE GUM/LOZENGES

"ELECTRONIC" CIGARETTES

PROFESSIONAL COUNSELING

PEER SUPPORT SYSTEM

"COLD TURKEY"

Hypothesis Coding

This is the application of a researcher-generated, predetermined list of codes onto qualitative data specifically to assess a researcher-generated hypothesis. The codes are developed from a theory/prediction about what will be found in the data before they have been collected or analyzed. Statistical applications, if needed, can range from simple frequency counts to more complex multivariate analyses. This method is appropriate for hypothesis testing, content analysis, and analytic induction of the qualitative data set, particularly the search for rules, causes, and explanations in the data. Hypothesis coding also can be applied midway or later in a qualitative study's data collection or analysis to confirm or disconfirm any assertions, propositions, or theories developed thus far. For example, it is hypothesized that the responses to a particular question about language issues in the United States will generate one of four answers (and thus coded responses) from participants:

RIGHT = We have the right to speak whatever language we want in America

SAME = We need to speak the same language in America: English

MORE = We need to know how to speak more than one language

NR = No Response or "I don't know"

Two *procedural methods* utilize specific rather than open-ended ways of coding data: (1) Protocol coding and (2) Causation coding.

Protocol Coding

This is the coding of qualitative data according to a preestablished, recommended, standardized, or prescribed system. The generally comprehensive list of codes and categories provided to the researcher are applied after her own data collection is completed. Some protocols also recommend using specific qualitative (and quantitative) data-analytic techniques with the coded data. Protocol coding is appropriate for qualitative studies in disciplines with previously developed and field-tested coding systems. For example, a selected list of codes from a protocol used to determine the causes of family violence include the following:

ALCOH = alcoholism or drinking

DRUG = drug use

EDUC = lack of education

MONEY = lack of money or financial problems

Causation Coding

This method extracts attributions or causal beliefs from participant data about not just how but why particular outcomes came about. The analyst searches for combinations of antecedent and mediating variables that lead toward certain pathways and attempts to map a three-part process as a CODE 1 > CODE 2 > CODE 3 sequence. Causation coding is appropriate for discerning motives, belief systems, worldviews, processes, recent histories, interrelationships, and the complexity of influences and affects on human actions and phenomena. This method may serve grounded theorists in searches for causes, conditions, contexts, and consequences. It is also appropriate for evaluating the efficacy of a particular program or as preparatory work before diagramming or modeling a process through visual means such as decision modeling and causation networks. For example, a survey respondent describes in writing what challenges she faced when she took speech classes in high school. The + symbol refers to a combination of variables that are mentioned by the participant as connected parts of the causation sequence; the > symbol means "leads to":

[1] Without a doubt, it was a fear of speaking in front of others. My ultimate career as an adult was in the field of journalism. Early fears I had about approaching strangers and speaking in front of a group of people were overcome due to involvement in speaking events. As I mentioned above, I think speech class and the events that I participated in due to taking that class, probably led directly to my choosing journalism as a career. My success in the field of journalism would have never come about without those speech classes in high school.

[1] "FEAR OF SPEAKING" > SPEAKING EVENTS + SPEECH CLASS > JOURNALISM CAREER + SUCCESS

Four *grammatical methods* play a role in the mechanics of coding: (1) Attribute coding, (2) Magnitude coding, (3) Subcoding, and (4) Simultaneous coding.

Attribute Coding

This method is the notation of basic descriptive information such as the fieldwork setting, participant characteristics or demographics, data format, and other variables of interest for qualitative and some applications of quantitative analysis. This is appropriate for virtually all qualitative studies, but particularly for those with multiple participants and sites, cross-case studies, and studies with a wide variety of data forms. Attribute coding provides essential participant information for future management, reference, and contexts for analysis and interpretation. Examples from a data set about an educational study include the following:

CASE: Martinez School

PARTICIPANT: Nancy (pseudonym)

INTERVIEW: 2 of 5

INTERVIEW TOPICS:

    Evaluation of School Day

    Salary Issues

    Principal-Teacher Relationship

    Upcoming Extracurricular Activities

    Upcoming Fundraising Project

Magnitude Coding

Magnitudes consist of supplemental alphanumeric or symbolic codes or subcodes applied to existing coded data or a category to indicate their intensity, frequency, direction, presence, or evaluative content. Magnitude codes can be qualitative, quantitative, and/or nominal indicators to enhance description. They are most appropriate for mixed methods and qualitative studies in education, social science, and health care disciplines that also support quantitative measures as evidence of outcomes. Examples used in the school improvement study include the following:

MAJOR

MODERATE

MINOR

√ √ = Yes, clearly

√ = Possibly, in part

0 = No

++ = Very effective

+ = Effective

± = Mixed

We argue that although words may be more unwieldy than numbers, they render more meaning than numbers alone and should be hung on to throughout data analysis. Converting words into numbers and then tossing away the words gets a researcher into all kinds of mischief. You are thus assuming that the chief property of the words is that there are more of some than of others. Focusing solely on numbers and quantities shifts attention from substance to arithmetic, throwing out the whole notion of their qualities or essential characteristics. A solution to this problem, as we will see in later sections and displays, is to keep words and any associated magnitudes (LOW, EFFECTIVE, √) *together* throughout the analysis.

Subcoding

A subcode is a second-order tag assigned after a primary code to detail or enrich the entry. The method is appropriate for virtually all qualitative studies, but particularly for ethnographies and content analyses, studies with multiple participants and sites, and studies with a wide variety of data forms. Subcoding is also appropriate when general code entries will later require more extensive indexing, categorizing, and subcategorizing into hierarchies or taxonomies, or for nuanced qualitative data analysis. It can be employed after an initial yet general coding scheme has been applied and the researcher realizes that the classification scheme may have been too broad, or it can be added to primary codes if particular qualities or interrelationships emerge. This example comes from a set of field notes describing a school's facilities:

[1] The school's multipurpose room functions as a cafeteria, auditorium, assembly space, meeting space, and study hall. Its portable tables with attached seating fold up easily for somewhat quick transformation and cleaning of the space.	[1] SCHOOL-MULTIPURPOSE SPACE
[2] The adjoining media center houses books, a computer lab with 26 stations, study "nooks" for small groups, and various tables and chairs. A large screen and LCD projector suspended from the ceiling make the space look like a private movie theatre.	[2] SCHOOL-MEDIA CENTER

Simultaneous Coding

This is the application of two or more different codes to a single qualitative datum, or the overlapped occurrence of two or more codes applied to sequential units of qualitative data. The method is appropriate when the data's content suggests multiple meanings (e.g., descriptively and inferentially) that necessitate and justify more than one code. An example is taken from field notes about an organizational study of a community theatre program:

[1 & 2] The board of directors struggled with ways to keep the community theatre program going for another full season. It had been a staple in the area for almost 40 years, but now faced (like many comparable programs) the end of its existence. Less financial contributions and lower box office revenue had put the theatre severely in the red. Long-time volunteers and members were thinking with their hearts more than with their heads as they claimed that the "traditions" of this program could not be ended. The board felt otherwise, for none of its members wanted the liability of debt.	[1] FINANCIAL LOSS [2] END OF TRADITION

Creating Codes

One method of creating codes is developing a provisional "start list" of codes prior to fieldwork—*Deductive* coding. That list comes from the conceptual framework, list of research questions, hypotheses, problem areas, and/or key variables that the researcher brings to the study. In our (Miles and Huberman) school improvement study, for example, we conceptualized the innovation process, in part, as one of RECIPROCAL TRANSFORMATIONS. Teachers change the characteristics of new practices. Those practices, in turn, change the teachers and modify working arrangements in the classroom, which, in turn, influence how much of the innovation can be used, and so on.

We began with a master code—TRANSFORMATION, or TRANS for short—to indicate the transformational process we had hypothesized, plus some subcodes—TRANS-USER, TRANS-CLASS (classroom changes), TRANS-ORG (organizational changes), TRANS-INN (changes in the innovation)—to mark off segments of data in each class of variables. The list was held lightly, applied to the first sets of field notes, and then examined closely for fit and utility. Quite a few codes were revised, but the conceptual orientation seemed to bear real fruit—to fit and account well for what we saw and heard.

A start list can have from a dozen or so up to 50 codes; that number can be kept surprisingly well in the analyst's short-term memory without constant reference to the full list—*if* the list has a clear structure and rationale. It is a good idea to get that list on a single sheet for easy reference. Most CAQDAS (Computer Assisted Qualitative Data Analysis Software) programs can retain these Provisional codes before data are entered into their programs.

Still other codes emerge progressively during data collection—that is, *Inductive* coding. These are better grounded empirically and are especially satisfying to the researcher who has uncovered an important local factor. They also satisfy other readers, who can see that the researcher is open to what the site has to say rather than determined to force-fit the data into preexisting codes. Most field researchers, no matter how conceptually oriented, will recognize when an a priori coding system is ill molded to the data or when a rival perspective looks more promising.

Revising Codes

For all approaches to coding, several codes will change and develop as field experience continues. Researchers with start lists know that codes will change; there is more going on out there than our initial frames have dreamed of, and few field researchers are foolish enough to avoid looking for these things.

Some codes do not work; others decay. No field material fits them, or the way they slice up the phenomenon is not the way the phenomenon appears empirically. This issue calls for doing away with the code or changing its type (e.g., transforming a noun-based Descriptive code such as COUNSELING CENTER into an action-oriented Process code such as REHABILITATING). Other codes flourish, sometimes too much so. Too many segments get the same code, thus creating the familiar problem of bulk. This problem calls for breaking down codes into subcodes.

With manual coding, revision is tedious: Every chunk you have coded before has to be relabeled. But the search-and-replace facility of your text-based software and most CAQDAS programs can accomplish this easily.

Structure and Unity in Code Lists

Whether codes are created and revised early or late is basically less important than whether they have some conceptual and structural unity. Codes should relate to one another in coherent, study-important ways; they should be part of a unified structure. Incrementally adding, removing, or reconfiguring codes is certainly permissible, so long as some sense of "belonging" is maintained.

Display 4.1 is an excerpt from a longer, structured code list: a start list of codes, keyed to research questions and (in this case) to "bins" of conceptual variables, defined precisely enough so that researchers have a common language and can be clear about whether and how a segment of data actually fits into a category such as INNOVATION PROPERTIES, ADOPTION PROCESS, and so on. The actual coded segments then provide instances of the category (in bolded font), and marginal or appended comments begin to connect different codes with larger wholes.

Display 4.1

Illustration of a Start List of Codes

CATEGORY: INNOVATION PROPERTIES	ABBREVIATION: IP-OB J
IP: OBJECTIVES	IP-OC
IP: ORGANIZATION	IP-ORG/DD, LS
IP: IMPLIED CHANGES-CLASSROOM	IP-CH/CL
IP: IMPLIED CHANGES-ORGANIZATION	IP-CH/ORG
IP: USER SALIENCE	IP-SALIENCE
IP: (INITIAL) USER ASSESSMENT	IP-SIZUP/PRE, DUR
IP: PROGRAM DEVELOPMENT (IV-C)	IP-DEV

CATEGORY: EXTERNAL CONTEXT	EC (PRE) (DUR)
EC: DEMOGRAPHICS	EC-DEM
In county, school personnel	ECCO-DEM
Out county, nonschool personnel	ECEXT-DEM
EC: ENDORSEMENT	EC-END
In county, school personnel	ECCO-END
Out county, nonschool personnel	ECEXT-END
EC: CLIMATE	EC-CLIM
In county, school personnel	ECCO-CLIM
Out county, nonschool personnel	ECEXT-CLIM
CATEGORY INTERNAL CONTEXT	**IC (PRE) (DUR)**
IC: CHARACTERISTICS	IC-CHAR
IC: NORMS AND AUTHORITY	IC-NORM
IC: INNOVATION HISTORY	IC-HIST
IC: ORGANIZATION PROCEDURES	IC-PROC
IC: INNOVATION-ORGANIZATION CONGRUENCE	IC-FIT
CATEGORY: ADOPTION PROCESS	**AP**
AP: EVENT CHRONOLOGY-OFFICIAL VERSION	AP-CHRON/PUB
AP: EVENT CHRONOLOGY-SUBTERRANEAN	AP-CHRON/PRIV
AP: INSIDE/OUTSIDE	AP-IN/OUT
AP: CENTRALITY	AP-CENT
AP: MOTIVES	AP-MOT
AP: USER FIT	AP-FIT
AP: PLAN	AP-PLAN
AP: READINESS	AP-REDI
AP: CRITICAL EVENTS	AP-CRIT
CATEGORY: SITE DYNAMICS AND TRANSFORMATIONS	**TRANS**
TRANS: EVENT CHRONOLOGY-OFFICIAL VERSION	TRANS-CHRON/PUB
TRANS: EVENT CHRONOLOGY-SUBTERRANEAN	TRANS-CHRON/PRIV
TRANS: INITIAL USER EXPERIENCE	TRANS-START
TRANS: CHANGES IN INNOVATION	TRANS-INMOD
TRANS: EFFECTS ON ORGANIZATIONAL PRACTICES	TRANS-ORG/PRAC

(Continued)

CATEGORY: SITE DYNAMICS AND TRANSFORMATIONS	TRANS
TRANS: EFFECTS ON ORGANIZATIONAL CLIMATE	TRANS-ORG/CLIM
TRANS: EFFECTS ON CLASSROOM PRACTICE	TRANS-CLASS
TRANS: EFFECTS ON USER CONSTRUCTS	TRANS-HEAD
TRANS: IMPLEMENTATION PROBLEMS	TRANS-PROBS
TRANS: CRITICAL EVENTS	TRANS-CRIT
TRANS: EXTERNAL INTERVENTIONS	TRANS-EXT
TRANS: EXPLANATIONS FOR TRANSFORMATIONS	TRANS-SIZUP
TRANS: PROGRAM PROBLEM SOLVING	TRANS-PLAN

Source: Miles, M. B., & Huberman, A. M. (1994). *Qualitative data analysis: An expanded sourcebook* (2nd ed.). Thousand Oaks, CA: Sage Publications.

An operative coding scheme is not a catalog of disjointed descriptors but rather a conceptual web, including larger meanings and their constitutive characteristics. CAQDAS is especially helpful in displaying the structure of coding schemes, either in hierarchical form or in a network.

Definitions of Codes

Whether codes are prespecified or developed along the way, clear operational definitions are indispensable so they can be applied consistently by a single researcher over time, and multiple researchers will be thinking about the same phenomena as they code. A First Cycle code can consist of a single term—for example, TRANSFORMATION—that can easily suggest different meanings to different analysts. Because codes will drive the retrieval and organization of the data for analysis, they must be precise and their meaning shared among analysts. Defining them helps on both counts. Display 4.2 is an excerpt from the full list of definitions for the codes partially shown in Display 4.1. These definitions were improved and fine-tuned as the study proceeded.

Definitions become sharper when two researchers code the same data set and discuss their initial difficulties. A disagreement shows that a definition has to be expanded or otherwise amended. Time spent on this task is not hair-splitting but reaps real rewards by bringing you to an unequivocal, common vision of what the codes mean and which blocks of data best fit which code.

Team coding not only aids definitional clarity but also is a good reliability check. Do two coders working separately agree on how big a codable block of data is? And do they use roughly the same codes for the same blocks of data? If not, they are headed for different analyses and need to reconcile their differences for more credible and trustworthy findings.

Display 4.2

Definitions of Selected Codes From Display 4.1 (Excerpts)

Site Dynamics and Transformations-TRANS

Event chronology—official version: TRANS-CHRON/PUB	Event chronology during initial and ongoing implementation, as recounted by users, administrators or other respondents.
Event chronology—subterranean version: TRANS-CHRON/PRIV	Event chronology during initial or ongoing implementation, as recounted by users, administrators or other respondents, and suggesting (a) a consensual but different scenario than the public version or (b) varying accounts of the same events.
Changes in innovation: TRANS-INMOD	Reported modifications in components of the new practice or program, on the part of teachers and administrators, during initial and ongoing implementation.
Effects on organizational practices: TRANS-ORG/PRAC	Indices of impact of new practice or program on: (a) intraorganizational planning, monitoring, and daily working arrangements (e.g., staffing, scheduling, use of resources, communication among staff) and (b) interorganizational practices (e.g., relationships with district office, school board, community, and parent groups).
Effects on classroom practice: TRANS-CLASS	Indices of impact of new practice or program on regular or routine classroom practices (instructional planning and management).
Effects on user constructs: TRANS-HEAD	Indices of effects of new practice or program on teacher and administrator perceptions, attitudes, motives, assumptions or theories of instruction, learning, or management (e.g., professional self-image, revised notions of what determines achievement or efficiency, other attitudes toward pupils, colleagues, other staff members, stance toward other innovative practices).

Source: Miles, M. B., & Huberman, A. M. (1994). *Qualitative data analysis: An expanded sourcebook* (2nd ed.). Thousand Oaks, CA: Sage Publications.

Similarly, each coder is well-advised to code the first dozen pages of field notes, once right away and again (on an uncoded copy) a few days later. How good is the internal consistency? Eventually, intra- and/or intercoder agreement should be within the 85% to 90% range, depending on the size and range of the coding scheme.

Levels of Coding Detail

How fine should coding be? That depends on the study and your goals. But more typically, codes get applied to larger units—sentences, monothematic "chunks" of sentences, or full paragraphs in the written-up field notes.

Any block of data is usually a candidate for more than one code, as illustrated above in Simultaneous coding. But if you are coding manually and the margin gets piled up with multiple codes for too many blocks, you are in for heavy sledding when the notes are reviewed for site-level analysis. This problem is not critical when computer retrieval is used. But too much Simultaneous coding suggests an unclear or incomplete vision for a coding system and, thus, research design.

Finally, not every portion of the field notes or interview transcripts must be coded. There are things such as trivial, useless data. Most field notes and selected portions of transcripts usually contain much dross—material unrelated to the research questions, either prespecified or emerging. And if done carefully, coding of later material can be more sparing.

Second Cycle Coding: Pattern Codes

Description

First Cycle coding is a way to initially summarize segments of data. Pattern coding, as a Second Cycle method, is a way of grouping those summaries into a smaller number of categories, themes, or constructs. For qualitative researchers, it's an analog to the cluster-analytic and factor-analytic devices used in statistical analysis by our quantitative colleagues.

Pattern codes are explanatory or inferential codes, ones that identify an emergent theme, configuration, or explanation. They pull together a lot of material from First Cycle coding into more meaningful and parsimonious units of analysis. They are a sort of meta-code.

Applications

For the qualitative analyst, Pattern coding has four important functions:

1. It condenses large amounts of data into a smaller number of analytic units.

2. It gets the researcher into analysis during data collection, so that later fieldwork can be more focused.

3. It helps the researcher elaborate a cognitive map—an evolving, more integrated schema for understanding local incidents and interactions.

4. For multicase studies, it lays the groundwork for cross-case analysis by surfacing common themes and directional processes.

These four functions can be clarified as we discuss how Pattern codes are generated, what they look like, and what the field researcher does with them in the course of data collection.

Examples

Generating Pattern Codes

During initial fieldwork, the researcher is looking for threads that tie together bits of data. For example, if two or three participants say independently that they "resent" a decision made by their boss, we may be onto several different phenomena—a conflict, an organizational climate factor, or a disgruntled subgroup of employees. Any of these interpretations involves chunking and sorting data (Function 1, above). For starters, is there anything else in common between these participants or in the grounds given for resenting the decision? Is there a different or opposing semantic content among participants who are *not* resentful?

These first bits of data and the review of the coded segments being pulled together are leads; they suggest important variables to check out—factors that may account for other local perceptions and behaviors (Function 2, above). Seeing the RESENTMENT data (a First Cycle Emotion code) in any of these alternative ways also helps the researcher make sense of puzzling or surprising observations. These several bits come together in an initial plot of the terrain (Function 3). Finally, if a colleague in a multicase study comes across a similar profile of resentment or, alternatively, finds no resentment of decisions at all in a place otherwise similar to the more "resentful" case, we have the first threads of cross-case comparisons (Function 4).

Patterning happens quickly because it is the way we habitually process information. The danger is getting locked too quickly into naming a pattern, assuming you understand it, and then thrusting the name onto data that fit it only poorly. The trick here is to work with loosely held chunks of meaning, to be ready to unfreeze and reconfigure them as the data shape up otherwise, to subject the most compelling themes to merciless cross-checking, and to lay aside the more tenuous ones until other participants and observations give them better empirical grounding.

Sometimes, however, the data just don't seem to toss up any overarching themes; each code looks almost distinctive. In these cases, it helps to go back to the research questions just to remind yourself of what was important and then to review the chunks bearing those codes.

In a more inductive study, it helps to look for recurring phrases (i.e., In Vivo codes) or common threads in participants' accounts or, alternatively, for internal differences that you or participants have noted. Typically, those differences will bring forth a higher level commonality.

What Pattern Codes Look Like

Pattern codes usually consist of four, often interrelated, summarizers:

1. Categories or themes
2. Causes/explanations
3. Relationships among people
4. Theoretical constructs

Below are some concrete examples of Pattern codes, in capital letters, followed by their brief definitions:

Categories or Themes

RULES: You don't "shop talk" in the staff lounge; the unspoken understanding is that social small talk to decompress is OK; complaining is also acceptable, but without generating solutions to problems.

TRAJECTORIES: The metaphor of career "trajectories"—people are using these projects to get away from some jobs and places to other ones.

Causes/Explanations

DYSFUNCTIONAL DIRECTION: Staff perceptions of and interactions with ineffective leadership influence workplace morale and effectiveness.

BEST PRACTICES: The best projects are ones that put together the best practitioners' tested recipes for success.

Relationships Among People

LEADERS' NETWORK: This is the unofficial collective of individuals seen as key leaders at their respective sites: A. Becker, P. Harrison, and V. Wales.

NEW GUARD: This represents the new, thirtyish generation of faculty members with an aggressive yet socially conscious edge to them.

Theoretical Constructs

BARGAINING: Bargaining or negotiating, most often covertly, seems to be the way decisions get made; a conflict model is a more plausible account of how actions get initiated than cooperative teamwork.

SURVIVAL: This is a defeatist, mostly negative attitude that suggests one is working on a day-to-day basis with minimal resources and support to accomplish much against sometimes overwhelming odds.

Pattern codes can emerge from repeatedly observed behaviors, actions, norms, routines, and relationships; local meanings and explanations; commonsense explanations and more conceptual ones; inferential clusters and "metaphorical" ones; and single-case and cross-case observations.

Using Pattern Codes in Analysis

It may be useful at some point to "map" the Pattern codes—that is, to lay out the component codes that got you the pattern—along with segments from the field notes. It helps to do it visually, in a network display, seeing how the components interconnect. The mapping is a new take on your conceptual framework. Although it is not hard to do this by hand, mapping by computer and CAQDAS has some powerful advantages and does this well.

Next, the most promising codes to emerge from this exercise are written up in the form of an analytic memo (see the section below) that expands on the significance of the code. This process helps the writer become less fuzzy about the emergent category, theme, construct, and so on, and gets cross-case and higher level analytic energy flowing.

Usually, a Pattern code does not get discounted but rather gets *qualified*: The conditions under which it holds are specified. For example, the RULE of "No 'shop talk' in the lounge" can be bent in cases of conflict, crisis, or socializing of new members. This clarification provides more precise parameters for the pattern and strengthens its validity.

If a general Pattern code (such as RULES) is used a good deal, it is helpful to create subcodes that explain the content and enable easy retrieval:

RULES-INDIV: Rules about individual participant behavior

RULES-PUBLIC: Rules about behavior in public settings

RULES-WORK: Rules that specify how formal work tasks are to be carried out

Also, stay open to the idea of inventing new types of Pattern codes. For example, we developed the Pattern code QU!, meaning a query about something surprising that happened in the case. Being surprised is an important event in fieldwork, and we wanted to track it in our notes. See Saldaña (2013) for additional Second Cycle coding methods, particularly those designed for grounded theory studies.

Finally, Pattern codes get checked out in the next wave of data collection. This is largely an inferential process. The analyst tries out the code on a new participant or during an observation in a similar setting, engages in **if-then** tactics, as discussed in Chapter 11 (if the pattern holds, other things will happen or won't happen), or checks out a **rival explanation**.

(The **boldface** terms refer to specific tactics of drawing and verifying conclusions, which are discussed in detail in Chapter 11. We use this convention as a way of pointing to tactics as they occur in later chapters.)

From Codes to Patterns

Your initial or First Cycle coding of data generates an array of individual codes associated with their respective data chunks. Let's take a look at a fictional and extended example of how First Cycle codes transform into Second Cycle Pattern codes and then get inserted into matrices and networks.

A selected series of codes related to the first month of withdrawal symptoms described by a participant voluntarily participating in a smoking cessation treatment program, in random order and with their First Cycle code types indicated, are as follows:

1. ANXIETY [Emotion code]
2. NERVOUSNESS [Emotion code]
3. "HURT SOMEONE BAD" [In Vivo code/Emotion code]
4. RESTLESSNESS [Emotion code]
5. DEEP BREATHING [Process code]
6. THROAT BURNING [Process code]
7. "FELT LIKE CRYING" [In Vivo code/Emotion code/Process code]
8. ANGRY [Emotion code]
9. "EATING A LOT MORE" [In Vivo code/Process code]
10. WANDERING AROUND [Process code]

11. HABITUAL MOVEMENTS [Descriptive code]

12. MEMORIES OF SMOKING [Descriptive code]

13. SMELLING NEW THINGS [Process code]

There are several ways to approach the categorizing or patterning of these 13 codes. One possible way is to pattern them by code type:

• EMOTIONS (ANXIETY, NERVOUSNESS, "HURT SOMEONE BAD," RESTLESSNESS, "FELT LIKE CRYING," ANGRY)

• PROCESSES (DEEP BREATHING, THROAT BURNING, "FELT LIKE CRYING," "EATING A LOT MORE," WANDERING AROUND, SMELLING NEW THINGS)

• DESCRIPTORS (HABITUAL MOVEMENTS, MEMORIES OF SMOKING)

Since negative and strong emotions seem to play a critical role in withdrawal symptoms from smoking, EMOTIONS as a Pattern code choice makes sense. One can even enhance the code further with the adjective NEGATIVE EMOTIONS.

The PROCESSES and DESCRIPTORS labels, however, seem to lack the "oomph" needed for a Pattern code. Recall that Pattern codes usually consist of four, often interrelated, summarizers: (1) categories or themes, (2) causes or explanations, (3) relationships among people, and (4) theoretical constructs. There are several ways of recategorizing the remaining codes, first by reassembling them into particular clusters because they seem to go together. The analyst proposes the following:

Cluster 1: DEEP BREATHING, THROAT BURNING, "EATING A LOT MORE," SMELLING NEW THINGS

Cluster 2: WANDERING AROUND, HABITUAL MOVEMENTS

Cluster 3: "FELT LIKE CRYING," MEMORIES OF SMOKING

First, what do the four codes in Cluster 1 have in common? They seem to be all upper-body functions: respiratory, sensory, and digestive. The analyst reflects on what the four codes have in common; they seem to have a PHYSICAL CHANGES theme that unifies them, and thus get that Pattern code assigned to them.

The codes of Cluster 2 (WANDERING AROUND, HABITUAL MOVEMENTS) seem to evoke a metaphoric RESTLESS JOURNEY of some sort. Cluster 3's codes ("FELT LIKE CRYING," MEMORIES OF SMOKING) suggest a conceptual Pattern code of REGRETFUL LOSS. Where did the Pattern code labels of RESTLESS JOURNEY and REGRETFUL LOSS come from? They came from the researcher's reflection on what their constituent codes seemed to have in common.

Notice that these four Pattern codes—(1) NEGATIVE EMOTIONS, (2) PHYSICAL CHANGES, (3) RESTLESS JOURNEY, and (4) REGRETFUL LOSS—are one person's analytic proposals. Other researchers reflecting on and clustering the First Cycle codes might develop different Pattern codes altogether. Thus, an important principle to note here is that Pattern coding is not always a precise science—it's primarily an interpretive act.

The researcher can now use these four Pattern codes in various ways, according to the needs of the study. Basic narrative description is one approach; and visual displays are another primary way of analyzing data in fresh perspectives.

Narrative Description

The researcher can compose a section that identifies and elaborates on the Pattern code, weaving its component First Cycle codes into the narrative and supporting it with field note data:

> Smoking withdrawal symptoms during Month 1 include a *restless journey* for the individual: "I found myself just wandering around the house, just walking from room to room because I couldn't smoke, so I didn't know what to do with myself." The ex-smoker also continues to replicate habitual movements related to smoking, such as reaching for a cigarette pack in a shirt pocket, or leaving an indoor office to go outside to smoke. These physical actions interrelate with, and may even be caused by, several of the *negative emotions* induced by nicotine withdrawal: anxiety, nervousness, and restlessness.

In this case, the story-line function of narrative enables the researcher to outline the plots of human action and how participants (or "characters") changed throughout the course of the study. Prosaic representation and presentation of our findings are essential ways to communicate to readers how the social action we witnessed and synthesized unfolded and flowed through time. But matrices and networks are other ways of representing and presenting those observations.

Matrix Display

Matrix displays will be discussed more fully in the next 6 chapters, but they are briefly described here for illustrative purposes. Matrix displays chart or table the data—including codes—for analytic purposes. They organize the vast array of condensed material into an "at-a-glance" format for reflection, verification, conclusion drawing, and other analytic acts.

Suppose that the smoking cessation study was interested in how withdrawal symptoms change across *time*. Display 4.3 charts a participant's data at 1 month and 6 months after quitting. The Pattern codes are placed in one column, and the related First Cycle codes or other data summarizers are placed in the respective columns. A simple matrix such as this enables you—and a reader of your report—to take in the salient findings of your analysis. For example, in the NEGATIVE EMOTIONS row, you can see that such phenomena decrease across a 6-month period but *anxiety* is still present, albeit in milder form. Each cell of this matrix does not have to include the kitchen sink of withdrawal symptoms, only some of the most relevant exemplars from coding and analysis.

Network Display

This particular withdrawal symptom example describes a *process*, and thus a network of how things act or transform across time (or other aspects such as relationship dynamics or organizational patterns) can be mapped (see Display 4.4). The

Display 4.3

Smoking Cessation Patterns at Months 1 and 6

Initiating Smoking Cessation Patterns	Month 1	Month 6
NEGATIVE EMOTIONS	Anxious, nervous, angry, aggressive	Occasionally anxious
PHYSICAL CHANGES	Gained 5 pounds, felt "burning" sensation in throat and lungs	On weight loss program after gaining 20 pounds, heightened sense of smell
RESTLESS JOURNEY	Wandering and habitual movements	Habitual movements
REGRETFUL LOSS	"Felt like crying," hyper-conscious of cessation	Nostalgic for smoking, "hangs around" smokers

Display 4.4

A Model of Smoking Cessation Loss Transformation

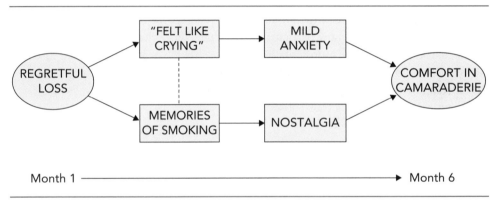

codes in matrix cells now become possible labels for bins. Lines and arrows indicate connections and flows between the clusters of action they represent.

The analyst has shown how the Pattern code REGRETFUL LOSS and its constituent codes of "FELT LIKE CRYING" and MEMORIES OF SMOKING have changed from Month 1 through Month 6. Follow-up interviews with the participant suggested that the impulse to cry was transformed through time to mild anxiety, while the deeply embedded memories of years of smoking changed into nostalgic reflection on past habits. An interesting track, however, appeared in the interview with the participant 6 months after he quit smoking:

> It's still hard, but I find myself hanging around smokers on campus whenever I can, just to smell the cigarette smoke as I smoke on my electronic cigarette. It's comforting just to hang around with smokers even though I don't smoke any more. I still feel like I'm connected to smoking in some way. And I can talk to them about my new habit and stuff. We're still partners in crime.

This interview excerpt, combined with other related coded chunks of data, led the analyst to compose the evolutionary Month 6 Pattern code COMFORT IN CAMARADERIE. The participant's ever-present mild anxiety becomes alleviated when he "hangs with" current smokers; his nostalgia for a former habit can be fed by physically placing himself among those who currently smoke.

Don't let the elegance and symmetry of the Display 4.4 network fool you into thinking that social life is always linear, balanced, and smooth flowing, and can be reduced to a few key variables. This simple example was intended to illustrate how Pattern codes can become grist for narratives, matrices, and networks, to be more fully explicated in Chapters 5 through 10.

Coding Advice

Coding is not just something you do to "get the data ready" for analysis but, as we have said several times, something that drives ongoing data collection. It is a form of early and continuing analysis. It typically leads to a reshaping of your perspective and of your instrumentation for the next round.

Remember that codes are more than a filing system. Every project needs a systematic way to store coded field data and a way to retrieve them easily during analysis. Three-ring notebooks, file folders, half-sheets of paper, index cards, sticky notes, and summaries on poster-size paper taped to a wall are "old school" but time-honored methods for qualitative data analysis. Yet, as we note, good computer software is far ahead of them when it comes to data organization and management.

Perhaps the more important point is this: The ultimate power of field research lies in the researcher's emerging map of what is happening and why. So any method that will force more differentiation and integration of that map, while remaining flexible, is a good idea. Coding, working through iterative cycles of induction and deduction to power the analysis, can accomplish these goals.

Coding can tire you; it often feels longer than it really is. So it helps to intersperse coding with jottings and analytic memos (discussed next).

Jottings

Think of a jotting (Emerson, Fretz, & Shaw, 2011) as an "analytic sticky note"—a piece of writing that could literally fit onto the space of a small square piece of paper. Adobe's .pdf document reader has this function; Microsoft Word's "Comments" feature is an equivalent. CAQDAS programs enable the user to insert "annotations" or "comments" that can be attached to particular chunks of data. If you're working on hard copy, you could use actual sticky notes, but these can get easily detached if you're not careful. So handwriting notes in the margins will suffice, and in a text file, a separate paragraph (in a different font to distinguish it from the rest of the data) will serve for jottings.

So what is a jotting, and what goes into it? A jotting holds the researcher's fleeting and emergent reflections and commentary on issues that emerge during fieldwork and especially data analysis. As you work on a project, reflections of several sorts typically swim into awareness. For example, consider the following:

- Inferences on the meaning of what a key participant was "really" saying during an exchange that seemed somehow important
- Personal reactions to some participants' remarks or actions
- What the relationship with participants feels like
- Doubts about the quality of some of the data
- Second thoughts about some of the interview questions and observation protocols
- A mental note to pursue an issue further in the next contact
- Cross-reference to material in another part of the data set
- Elaboration or clarification of a prior incident or event that now seems of possible significance

When something like any of these examples arises, it's useful to jot your mental note directly into field notes or somewhere else in the data corpus. It may or may not be fodder for a deeper analytic memo (discussed later), but at least it's in print. One convention is to distinguish the remark with italics to signal that it is of a different order from the data it comments on. Here's a field note example with a jotting:

> The administrative assistant speaks in a sincere voice over the phone: "Well, thank you so much for your help, I really appreciate it. Good-bye." Then she slams the handset into the carriage. *I find it almost amusing to hear the juxtaposition of a "professionally nice" voice followed by a hard, hang-up slam of the phone. She's probably masking a lot of on-the-job tension or frustration.*

Remarks such as these add substantial meaning to the analysis and perhaps even the write-up.

Jottings can strengthen coding by pointing to deeper or underlying issues that deserve analytic attention. Coding, as we have noted, can become tedious if you treat yourself as a sort of machine scanning the page methodically, picking out small segments of data and assigning labels to them. The sensation of being bored is usually a signal that you have ceased to think. One way of retaining mindfulness in coding is occasional jotting (see Display 4.5).

As coding proceeds, if you are alert about what you are doing, ideas and reactions to the meaning of what you are seeing will well up steadily. These ideas are important; they suggest new interpretations, leads, and connections with other parts of the data; and they usually point toward questions and issues to look into during the next wave of data collection and to ways of elaborating some of these ideas. These marginal remarks also point to important issues that a given code may be missing or blurring, suggesting revisions in the coding scheme.

Jottings in the form of reflective remarks can be added while you are writing or expanding on raw field notes. You are simultaneously aware of events in the

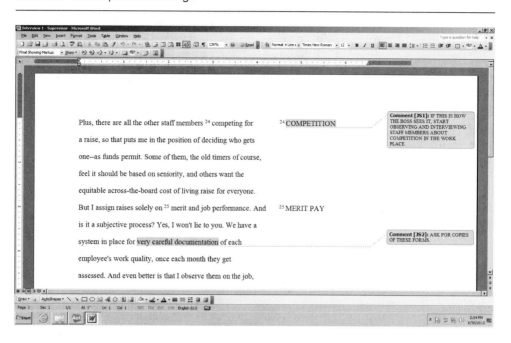

site and of your own feelings, reactions, insights, and interpretations. Bogdan and Biklen (2007) call these sections "Observer's Comments" or, in field notes, an "OC." These can be separated from the main field notes through a different font style and/ or indent:

> The committee chair recommended that they take a ten-minute break, but Carla recommended that they continue, "We've got just three more evaluations to get through, we can do that in half an hour." The chair noted, "Well, one of them's going to take a while to get through, so it would be best to come back to the task refreshed and alert." *OC: The chair gave his reason with a matter-of-fact tone of voice, but one could sense that there were a lot of sticky issues to get through with the one new candidate. Carla seems oblivious to the political infighting I've observed at other meetings, and I feel the rest of the committee wants her to stay that way.*

Marginal notes can be perceived as important "bread crumbs" that are dropped to the ground for later collection by the analyst for expansion through memoing (discussed next).

Analytic Memoing

Description and Rationale

An analytic memo is a brief or extended narrative that documents the researcher's reflections and thinking processes about the data. These are not just descriptive summaries of data but attempts to synthesize them into higher level analytic meanings.

They are first-draft self-reports, of sorts, about the study's phenomena and serve as the basis for more expanded and final reports.

Memos are typically a rapid way of capturing thoughts that occur throughout data collection, data condensation, data display, conclusion drawing, conclusion testing, and final reporting. Later in the study, however, memos can be more elaborate, especially when they piece together several strands of the data or look across multiple measures of a construct. Saldaña (2013) notes that analytic memos can be developed along the following topics:

- How you personally relate to the participants and/or the phenomenon
- Your study's research questions
- Your code choices and their operational definitions
- Emergent patterns, categories, themes, concepts, and assertions
- The possible networks (links, connections, overlaps, flows) among the codes, patterns, categories, themes, concepts, and assertions
- An emergent or related existent theory
- Any problems with the study
- Any personal or ethical dilemmas with the study
- Future directions for the study
- The analytic memos generated thus far [called "metamemos"]
- The final report for the study (pp. 49–50)

Analytic memos are primarily conceptual in intent. They don't just report data; they tie together different pieces of data into a recognizable cluster, often to show that those data are instances of a general concept. Analytic memos can also go well beyond codes and their relationships to any aspect of the study—personal, methodological, and substantive. They are one of the most useful and powerful sense-making tools at hand.

Examples

An analytic memo should be dated for reference to the analytic history and progress of your study, titled with its memo type (e.g., CODE DEFINITION, ASSERTION, THEORY, ETHICS), and subtitled with its more specific content (e.g., WHAT CASES HAVE IN COMMON, PARTICIPANT LEERINESS, AGENDA FOR NEXT SITE VISIT). Most CAQDAS programs can create and maintain memos (also called "comments" or "annotations" in selected programs), but they can also be kept as a running diary of sorts in a separate file. It is recommended that analytic memos not be embedded within field notes, transcripts, or other data but be kept as a separate document.

Here are a few examples of analytic memos from McCammon et al.'s (2012) "Lifelong Impact" study, which surveyed adults about their high school arts education experiences. This first memo documents a pattern observed by the analyst after the codes had been arranged to contrast the younger respondents with the older ones:

January 17, 2011

PATTERN: INTRINSIC AND EXTRINSIC

One of the most striking contrasts between survey respondents who graduated in the 2000s and in the 1950s-1970s is what they seem to value about the experiences. More recent graduates wrote about those intangible, intrinsic outcomes such as "camaraderie," "self-discovery," and identity, while the older generations put more stock into awards, specific roles they played, and what they've accomplished over their life course. I wonder if just being recently graduated from high school means that the memories are fresher about those internal experiences, and so it's going to be more in your head. As someone who's from the older generation, I know that I myself put a lot of stock into my own legacy, those tangible things that are evidence of what I've accomplished.

Ironically, I would have thought the older generations would have been more reflective and internal about those memories, more nostalgic, while the younger "me" generation would have valued awards, letter jackets, etc. Maybe it has something to do with human development—when you're in your late teens and early twenties, you're still trying to figure out "Who am I?" So, you're still looking within and exploring what's really important to you.

Below is an example of how a rough analytic memo was eventually transformed into a finished narrative for a final report. First the memo:

November 2, 2010

METAMEMO: ANTHROPOLOGICAL METAPHORS

It's interesting to see how this study has ties to the social sciences, and how the psychological, sociological, and anthropological disciplines have lenses to offer to the analysis. As for the anthropological, I was struck by a recent reading that used the phrase, "the mastery of sacred texts" as a condition for growing up and becoming part of the culture. In theatre and speech, the mastery of sacred texts is memorizing the script—becoming "one" with the play and taking deep ownership of a character. Theatre and religion have been long explored for their parallels, but I don't think the "rite of passage" theme through performance has been tackled (but check Victor Turner's writings on this just to be sure).

After reviewing the memos to date on major categories, labels such as "community," "tribe," and "family" appear frequently (though theatre people themselves are more likely to use the term "ensemble"—occupational term, I guess). Even better is when respondents told stories about feeling "lost" in performance—a kind of journey taken to achieve spiritual knowledge. The journeys of these participants are both internal and actual (out-of-town speech tournaments, especially)—getting lost to find yourself, leaving home to compete and either win or lose, but coming back stronger than when you left.

And now, these paragraphs from the technical report illustrate how the ideas from the memo were adapted and woven into the analytic portions of the text:

From social science perspectives (Lancy, Bock, & Gaskins, 2010), there is public expectation and prejudice, if not stigma, toward those who participate in theatre. Adolescent outcasts find their niche among a community tribe of like-minded kin. In these demarcated spaces of classrooms and performance venues, there are operant local school and national cultures of high school educational theatre programs. The adolescent cultural member assumes and adopts the ethos—the values, attitudes, and beliefs—of the social environment in which he/she participates, but with the prerequisite that the young person feels a sense of belonging in that culture. Cognitive maps for survival and safety, emotional and moral socialization, plus individual personality formation occur in these safe spaces through observation, interaction, and challenge. The rote learning and memorization of play scripts and speeches is comparable to the mastery of "sacred texts," valued as "acts of piety, discipline, personal transformation, and cultural preservation" (p. 212). These literal and community narratives contribute to identity, belonging, and expression.

The inherent demands of theatre and speech accelerate adult preparedness. There is high risk for high status. Achievement through awards, placements, and competitions harkens back to initiation rituals and rites of passage to progress toward a higher level of adulthood. Travel to another world, such as the spiritual one of performance and the spatial one of an out of town speech tournament, is comparable to the classic hero's journey in which trial must precede triumph in order to return to the tribe stronger than before. (McCammon & Saldaña, 2011, p. 103)

On Visual Data

There is much now in qualitative inquiry about the analysis of visual materials, especially since accessible and ubiquitous digital tools enable researchers to document fieldwork with ease, and the availability and amount of Internet resources proliferate daily. Good ethnographers have always documented the visual elements of social life in one way or another. It's just that the media we have nowadays permit us to archive the visual *as* images rather than just through descriptive and evocative writing.

Analyzing the visual has its own repertoire of methods (see the Appendix for recommended titles), but we do not have the space to outline them here in detail. We do, however, advocate that interpretation of what we see as still visual documentation—in a magazine, on a website, as a digital photograph, and so on—is more of a holistic venture than a systematic one. Analytic memoing of your impressions about the frozen, captured image is a more appropriate form of exploration than detailed breakdowns of components such as color, contrast, and composition. But the moving images and lengthier passages of television, film, YouTube clips, and other digital streams are more complex and might rely on more traditional content-analytic methods such as counts and categories for nuanced analysis.

Paradoxically, "A picture is worth a thousand words" must contend with "Images don't speak for themselves." You as the researcher must interpret the visual and determine whether the task merits analytic methods and strategies not applicable to language-based data. To us, the visual has *always* been a vital part of fieldwork investigation. It is simply the forms and formats—the representation and presentation—of visual data that have evolved over these decades. What's more important, we think, are the *influences and affects* of digital visual culture on our participants. And for that, we must observe and talk to them to find out how they respond and what they think and feel.

Memoing Advice

Here we draw on the recommendations of grounded theory's creators, Barney Glaser and Anselm Strauss, and Strauss's later collaborator, Juliet Corbin. Our advice is an amalgam of their experiences and ours:

1. *Prioritize memoing:* When an idea strikes, *stop* whatever else you are doing and write the memo. Don't worry about prose elegance or even grammar. Include your musings of all sorts, even the fuzzy and foggy ones. Give yourself the freedom to think; don't self-censor.

2. Memoing should begin as soon as the first field data start coming in and usually should continue right up to production of the final report. Just as codes should stabilize reasonably well by one half or two thirds of the way through data collection, the ideas raised in memos usually will start settling down then or shortly afterward, as the analyst approaches what grounded theorists call "saturation" (no significantly new explanations for data). Memoing contributes strongly to the development/revision of the coding system.

3. *Keep memos sortable:* Caption them by basic content. Like coded data, memos can be stored and retrieved using a wide variety of methods.

4. Once again, memos are about *ideas*. Simply summarizing or recounting data examples is not enough.

5. Don't necessarily standardize memo formats or types, especially in a multiple-researcher study. Memoing styles are distinctive, and memo types are as various as the imagination can reach.

6. Memo writing often provides sharp, sunlit moments of clarity or insight—little conceptual epiphanies.

Also see Saldaña (2013) for an extended chapter on analytic memo writing.

Assertions and Propositions

Coding triggers analytic thought, and memoing captures the thoughts of the analyst "writing out loud," so to say, and is important for that reason. But as a study proceeds, there is a greater need to formalize and systematize the researcher's thinking into a coherent set of explanations. One way to do that is to generate assertions and propositions, or connected sets of statements, reflecting the findings and conclusions of the study.

To us, an *assertion* is a declarative statement of summative synthesis, supported by confirming evidence from the data and revised when disconfirming evidence or discrepant cases require modification of the assertion (e.g., "The workers at Adco Incorporated were not self-motivated to achieve excellence"). A *proposition* is a statement that puts forth a conditional event—an if-then or why-because proposal that gets closer to prediction or theory (e.g., "When employees work in a dysfunctional environment, their individual workplace skills may decay from lack of motivation to achieve excellence").

Assertions and propositions are ways of summarizing and synthesizing a vast number of individual analytic observations. They are like "bullet points" of major patterns, themes, trends, and findings that you feel you can confidently put forth about your study. These points can range from descriptive, broad-brushstroke facts (e.g., "Overall, the children seemed engaged with the new, experimental learning program"), to higher level interpretations about the meanings of the study (e.g., "Experimental learning programs can be high-risk ventures for educators already demoralized by a low public opinion of their status and efficacy").

As an example, Kell (1990) conducted a multiple-case study of the effects of computers on classroom instruction. At the first analytic meeting, field researchers recorded their case-specific assertions and propositions on index cards, keyed to the research questions. The statements then were clustered thematically, and evidence was sifted for each case.

In this study, the propositions took the form of emerging hypotheses. Here are two illustrations from project data charts:

- Teachers' preferences for different software programs are greatly influenced by their theoretical orientations to reading—that is, phonics or whole-language.

- Individualized learning and self-direction, as well as cooperation and peer teaching, are promoted through computer use, and some transfer of these learning styles to other class activities may occur.

The degree of support for the proposition in each case was then rated as "strong," "qualified," "neutral," or "contradictory."

After the next wave of data collection, which attended to missing data, the propositions were revisited. For a matrix with rows showing each teacher at each site, column entries included data that supported the proposition and data that did not. As it turned out, the second proposition (above) was not supported. At the end, the propositions were tested further with other data sources (notably surveys and observations), and cases that did not fit the patterns were reexamined carefully.

Although this illustration describes proposition generation in the later stages of a study, it can be used productively much earlier—even after the first round of site visits. Keep a running list of bullet-pointed assertions and propositions as a study progresses, and revise them as fieldwork continues and evidence appears that disconfirms them. These statements in progress can also be used as a guide for next-step analysis and further data collection. Eventually, organize the bullet points into a sequential outline format and/or narrative that tells the story of your analysis.

Within-Case and Cross-Case Analysis

A primary goal of within-case analysis is to describe, understand, and explain what has happened in a single, bounded context—the "case" or site. That is the task of the traditional ethnographic researcher, whose effort is to emerge with a well-grounded sense of local reality, whether the focus is on an individual, a family, a classroom, a school, a tribe, a formal organization, a community, or even a culture as a whole.

One advantage of studying cross-case or multiple cases is to increase generalizability, reassuring yourself that the events and processes in one well-described setting are not wholly idiosyncratic. At a deeper level, the purpose is to see processes and outcomes across many cases, to understand how they are qualified by local conditions, and thus to develop more sophisticated descriptions and more powerful explanations.

Many researchers have leaned toward multiple individual cases (e.g., teachers, alcoholics, middle managers, battered women, taxi drivers). And during the past few decades, there's been a substantial growth in studies of complex settings using multicase designs, often with mixed-methods approaches and multiple research team members (Creswell, 2009; Creswell & Plano-Clark, 2011).

But developing a good cross-case analysis or synthesis is not a simple matter. Alcoholic A turns out to be quite different in personality dynamics from Alcoholic B, and they can't be easily compared, as Denzin (1993) eloquently shows us. Or suppose, for example, you have developed a good causal network explaining processes in a particular case. If you have a dozen such cases, just adding up separate variables, as in a quantitative survey approach, will destroy the local web of causality and result only in a smoothed-down set of generalizations that may not apply to any specific case in the set—let alone the others. Each case must be understood in its own terms, yet we hunger for the understanding that comparative analysis can bring.

Purposes of Cross-Case Analysis

One reason to conduct a cross-case analysis is to enhance *generalizability or transferability to other contexts*. Although it's argued that this goal is sometimes inappropriate for qualitative studies, the question does not go away. We would like to know something about the relevance or applicability of our findings to other similar settings, to transcend the particular in order to understand the general. Just adding cases is a brute-force approach that will not help. But multiple cases, adequately sampled (Are they typical? Are they diverse? Are they unusually effective or ineffective?) and analyzed carefully can help us answer the reasonable question: Do these findings apply beyond this one specific case?

A second, more fundamental reason for cross-case analysis is to deepen *understanding and explanation*. Multiple cases help the researcher find negative cases to strengthen a theory, built through examination of similarities and differences across cases. That process is much quicker and easier with multiple cases than with a single case. Multiple cases not only pin down the specific conditions under which a finding will occur but also help us form the more general categories of how those conditions may be related.

A Key Distinction: Variables Versus Cases

Our search for helpful cross-case analysis methods will be aided if we clarify two basically different approaches to inquiry.

Ragin (1987) emphasizes that a *case-oriented approach* considers the case as a whole entity—looking at configurations, associations, causes, and effects *within* the case—and only then turns to comparative analysis of a (usually limited) number of cases. We would look for underlying similarities and constant associations, compare cases with different outcomes, and begin to form more general explanations.

The *variable-oriented approach* is conceptual and theory centered from the start, casting a wide net over a (usually large) number of cases. The "building blocks" are variables and their interrelationships, rather than cases. So the details of any specific case recede behind the broad patterns found across a wide variety of cases, and little explicit case-to-case comparison is done.

As an example, *a case-oriented approach* would consist of looking at about six different families to observe how particular couples and single parents raise their children. Each parent would be interviewed to get his or her own family background, education, and so on, in addition to particular circumstances, such as ages of all family members, income, work and child care schedules, and so on. These various and richly detailed family biographical profiles would then be compared for analysis.

A *variable-oriented approach* would consist of looking at 50 families representing a diverse sample of structures (two parent, one parent, gay couple, one step-parent and one biological parent, foster parents, etc.) to observe and interview them about a predetermined set of variables included under the main category of "parent-child communication" (e.g., informal dinner conversations, directions and instructions, discipline matters, problem solving, mentorship for "growing up," bedtime stories, tone of voice, etc.).

Ragin notes that each approach has pluses and minuses. Variable-oriented analysis is good for finding probabilistic relationships among variables in a large population, but it is poor at handling the real complexities of causation or dealing with multiple subsamples; its findings are often very general, even "vacuous." Case-oriented analysis is good at finding specific, concrete, historically grounded patterns common to small sets of cases, but its findings often remain particularistic and ill suited to generalizability.

The implication is not that one or the other approach is better for qualitative data analysis. Rather, the issue is one of making deliberate choices, alternating and/or combining or integrating methods as a study proceeds. The forthcoming methods and display chapters will show how we can focus on either variables or cases, or both simultaneously as analytic needs arise.

Strategies for Cross-Case Analysis

How do qualitative researchers proceed when it comes to analyzing data from multiple cases? Here we outline several approaches (and consult the methods profiles in later chapters for more information). The goal here is to show what choices can be made as you approach the question of cross-case analysis.

Displays can help you summarize and compare findings within (and across) cases, but they also can be straitjackets. They may force the data into shapes that are superficially comparable across cases, but you actually may be comparing intrinsically different things on dimensions that turn out to be trivial. As a general rule of thumb, if the formats of within-case displays for a cross-case study are comparable, the work of the cross-case analyst is much easier.

Case-Oriented Strategies

Yin (2009) advocates a *replication* strategy: A theoretical framework is used to study one case in depth, and then successive cases are examined to see whether the pattern found matches that in previous cases. It's also useful to examine cases where the pattern is expected on a theoretical basis to be weaker or absent.

Denzin (2001) approaches the problem through *multiple exemplars*. The issue is not so much "analysis" as interpretive *synthesis*. After deconstructing prior conceptions of a particular phenomenon (e.g., the alcoholic self), you collect multiple instances (cases) and then "bracket" or isolate the relevant data passages, inspecting them carefully for essential elements or components. The elements are then rebuilt into an ordered whole and put back into the natural social context.

Many researchers approach cross-case comparison by forming *types or families*. You inspect cases in a set to see whether they fall into clusters or groups that share certain patterns or configurations. Sometimes the clusters can be ordered or sorted along some dimensions. For example, Morse and Bottorff (1992) found that 61 lactating mothers fell into four groups: (1) those who could express milk, (2) those who could not, (3) those who perceived it as easy, and (4) those who perceived it as a hassle. The meaning of the experience was fundamentally different for each type of mother.

Researchers usually assume that the cases at hand are more or less comparable, structured in similar ways. *Metasummary*, *metasynthesis*, and *meta-ethnography* (Major & Savin-Baden, 2010; Noblit & Hare, 1988; Sandelowski & Barroso, 2007) make no such assumptions. These approaches systematically *synthesize* interpretations across two or more cases, even if they were conducted by different researchers with different assumptions and different participant types.

Variable-Oriented Strategies

Researchers often look for *themes* that cut across cases. Case dynamics as such are bypassed or underplayed. For example, Pearsol (1985) looked at interviews about gender equity programs with 25 teachers. After careful inductive coding (both descriptive and interpretive), he located recurring themes, such as "concern for students," "activist view of change," and "barriers to innovation." Later, he also sorted the teachers into six types based on the configuration of the themes.

Mixed Strategies

It's possible, and usually desirable, to combine or integrate case-oriented and variable-oriented approaches. At a number of points in the forthcoming methods and display chapters, we suggest a strategy that might be called *stacking comparable cases*. You write up each of a series of cases, using a more or less standard set of variables (with leeway for uniqueness as it emerges). Then, you use matrices and other displays to analyze each case in depth. After each case is well understood (the cross-cutting variables may evolve and change during this process), you stack the case-level displays in a "meta-matrix" (which has columns and subcolumns, rows and subrows), which is then further condensed, permitting systematic comparison.

Closure and Transition

We resonate with the qualitative methodologist Robert E. Stake (1995), who muses, "Good research is not about good methods as much as it is about good thinking" (p. 19). Good thinking means to look for and find patterns in the data. Good thinking means to construct substantial categories from an array of codes. Good thinking means to transcend the localness of a particular case to find its generalizability and transferability to other contexts. Research methods are excellent tools, but they are only as good as the craftsperson who uses them.

This chapter provided an overview of analysis fundamentals for and with qualitative data. Yet it does not presume to be the definitive guide; see the Appendix for a list of additional resources. These are foundation methods for the more display-oriented strategies that follow in Part Two.

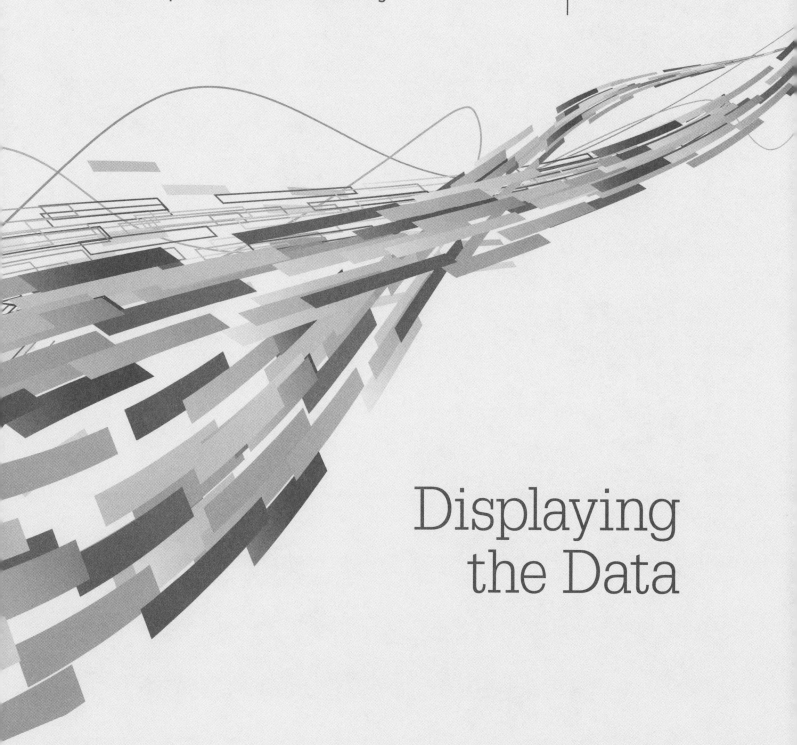

Chapter 5 - Designing Matrix and Network Displays

Chapter 6 - Methods of Exploring

Chapter 7 - Methods of Describing

Chapter 8 - Methods of Ordering

Chapter 9 - Methods of Explaining

Chapter 10 - Methods of Predicting

Part

2

Displaying
the Data

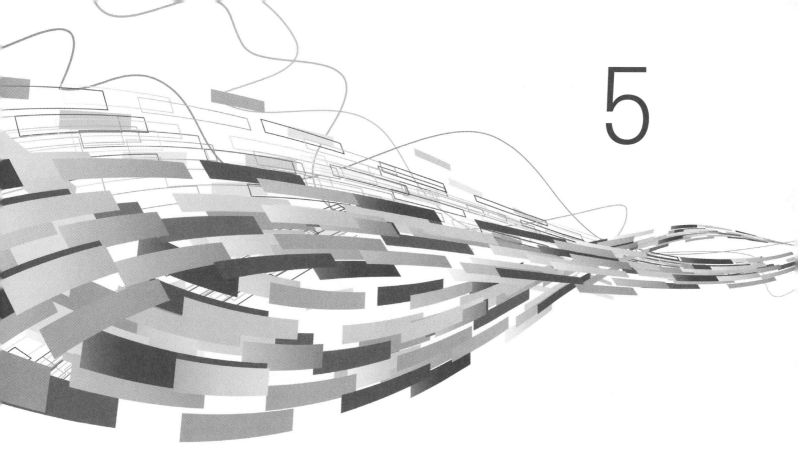

5

Designing Matrix and Network Displays

Chapter Summary

....

This chapter provides fundamental principles for the design and content of two analytic display methods: (1) matrices and (2) networks. These methods condense the major data and findings from a study to further analyze and/or to represent and present the conclusions.

Contents

....

Introduction
Display Format Options
    Matrices
    Networks
Timing of Display Design
Formatting the Matrix Template
Entering Matrix and Network Data
Making Inferences and Drawing Conclusions From Matrices and Networks
The Methods Profiles
Closure and Transition

Introduction

Lengthy, unreduced text in the form of interview transcripts, field notes, documents, and so on is cumbersome because it is dispersed over many pages and is not easy to see as a whole. It is sequential rather than simultaneous, making it difficult to look at two or three variables at once. Comparing several extended texts carefully is very difficult. It is usually poorly ordered, can get very bulky, and can make us feel monotonously overloaded. The same objections apply with even stronger force for readers of our final reports. They need, if not deserve, a concise delivery of what we analyzed. And in this highly visual culture, showing rather than telling can make a more effective and memorable impact on our audiences.

A major purpose of this text is to encourage the creation and dissemination of matrix and network displays for qualitative data. The central argument of this book is "You know what you display." Credible and trustworthy analysis requires, and is driven by, displays that are focused enough to permit a viewing of a full data set in the same location and are arranged systematically to answer the research questions at hand. A "full data set" does not, of course, mean the complete corpus of interview transcripts, field notes, documents, and so on. Rather, the condensed, distilled data presented are drawn from the full range of persons, events, and processes under study. With extended text, there can easily be "selective stacking" of the data. An organized display wards off this problem.

The idea of display is central to this book. By "display" we mean a visual format that presents information systematically so the user can draw conclusions and take needed action. Although such displays may sometimes be busy, they will never be monotonous. Most important, the chances of drawing and verifying conclusions are much greater than for extended text, because the display is arranged coherently to permit careful comparisons, detection of differences, noting of patterns and themes, seeing trends, and so on.

Quantitative researchers have software packages that can develop publishable tables, graphs, and charts. Qualitative researchers have CAQDAS programs for our unique approaches to data analysis. And even basic Microsoft Office programs such as Word and Excel are sufficient for most matrix and network displays. But the qualitative analyst has to handcraft appropriate data display formats because each project is unique. As yet, there are few familiar, agreed-on data setups among qualitative researchers, so each analyst has to adapt those of others or invent new ones. The display ideas we offer in this book are nothing more than that—*ideas*, not prescriptions, for qualitative data display.

Not everyone loves matrices and network displays—and not everyone thinks visually. But displaying your condensed data in a systematic way has immense consequences for your understanding. It requires you to think about your research questions and what portions of your data are needed to answer them; it requires you to make full analyses, ignoring no relevant information; and it focuses and organizes your information coherently. These advantages are repeated when you include displays in a final report; the reader can re-create your intellectual journey with some confidence.

Display Format Options

Deciding on and generating the format for displaying qualitative data are important first steps. Your template is a visual outline, of sorts, for the data to be filled in. Formats can be as varied as the imagination of the analyst, but the ones described in this book tend to fall into two major families:

1. *Matrices*, with defined rows and columns

2. *Networks*, a series of nodes with links (lines and arrows) between them

Data entries, however, are multiform: short blocks of text, quotes, phrases, variable labels, ratings, abbreviations, codes, categories, symbolic figures, labeled lines (dashed or solid), arrows (one way or two way), and so on.

The display format and content of the entries will depend on what you are trying to understand: a general situation, detailed chronologies, the actions of people in different roles, the interplay of variables, and so on. In other words, form follows function: Formats must always be driven by the research questions involved and your developing concepts. Formatting determines which variables will be analyzed in which ways. If a variable isn't included in the format, it won't get compared with another variable.

And it depends on how far along you are in the study and what has priority right now. The need might be for eyeballing data in an exploratory way. Or it could be for carrying out detailed analyses; for setting up data to use in another, more differentiated display; for combining parallel data for a single case; for combining data from several cases; or for reporting findings. A good format will allow all of these uses to some degree but inevitably will do some well and others less well.

Let's examine the two major families of displays with examples and illustrations.

Matrices

A matrix is essentially the "intersection" of two lists, set up as rows and columns. Let's take a look at a sample format, explaining and labeling it as we go.

Display 5.1, a table drawn with Microsoft Word software, is aimed at understanding the effects of *assistance* supplied to a school site—the Masepa Case—by various sources. This was part of a school improvement study that observed how a new project innovation was implemented. The matrix format calls for the researcher to address five related variables, to distinguish two of them according to time, to pool responses, to align some responses along an evaluative scale, and to explain the response pattern for each type of assistance source. Here, condensed information from 30 pages of field notes has been packed into a single page.

Note that the data are abstractions: There are no quotes, and generalizations and other inferential remarks appear in the last two columns. The *Longer-Run Consequences* and *Researcher Explanations* are not direct condensations of participants' remarks or of researchers' observations. Rather, for any given consequence, such as the one in the top row ("Users are helped administratively and substantively, feel obliged to do ECRI [Exemplary Center for Reading Instruction] with minor adaptations"), the researcher

Display 5.1

Effects Matrix: Assistance Location and Types (Masepa Case)

Location	User's Assessment	Types Provided	Short-Run Effects (User's 'State')	Longer-Run Consequences	Researcher Explanations
Building Administration	++ ++ − +	1. authorizes changes 2. eases schedules 3. controls fidelity 4. consults, offers solutions	1. relieves pressure, encourages 2. helps early implementation 3. feeling policed 4. feeling backed-up, substantially helped	users are helped administratively and substantively, feel obliged to do ECRI with minor adaptations	administration, authority, servicing, availability and flexibility lead to sustained, faithful implementation model
Central Office Administration	+ ++	1. promotes ECRI 2. answers building administration, trainers' requests	1. pressures non-users 2. building administrators have material, administrative support	program is perceived as supported, assisted, 'protected' by central office	central office able to push program and answer requests, yet not perceived as main actor by users
Helping Teacher	++ + ++ ++ ±	1. provides materials 2. demonstrates, models 3. answers requests 4. encourages 5. circulates, controls	1. reduces effort, increases repertoire 2. trains, facilitates use 3. problems solved rapidly 4. maintains level of effort 5. ambivalent: helped yet coerced	new, experienced users receive systematic instruction, follow-up, materials; stay with program and are careful about making changes in it	personalized in-service mechanism, with both training and assistance allows for mastery and spread of ECRI in 'faithful' format
User-Helping Teacher Meetings	++ + + +	1. comparing practices with others 2. debugging, complaining 3. learning about new parts 4. encouragement	1. encourages, regulates 2. cathartic, solves short-run problems 3. expands repertoire 4. gets through rough moments	creates reference group, gives users a voice, solves ongoing problems and lowers anxiety	multi-purpose forum which consolidates use and users, defuses opposition
Teacher-Users in Other Schools: Target Schools	+ + +	1. sharing materials 2. exchanging tips, solutions 3. comparing, encouraging	1. increases stock 2. new ideas, practices; problems solved 3. motivates, stimulates	increases commitment, regulates use (decreases deviance)	additional source of assistance, which increases as number of users grows
Trainers in Target School, Other School	++ ++ + +	1. tips for presentations 2. solution to short-term problems 3. encourages 4. serves as successful model	1. facilitates practice 2. helps expand beyond core format 3. maintains effort 4. stimulates	reliable, unthreatening backup provided in school	elaborate and effective lateral network: trainers seen as peers

Legend
++ = very effective
+ = effective
± = mixed effective
− = ineffective

Source: Miles, M. B., & Huberman, A. M. (1994). *Qualitative data analysis: An expanded sourcebook* (2nd ed.). Thousand Oaks, CA: Sage Publications.

has looked at the data segments in the three preceding columns, checked to see whether they covary in some patterned way, and drawn a second-order generalization. In this case (see the first row, first column—Building Administration), themes such as "Eases schedules," "Consults, offers solutions," "Relieves pressure, encourages," "Helps early implementation," and the *Users' Assessment* of generally positive magnitude codes all suggested the reception of help and a sense of user obligation for reasonably faithful implementation. A similar process of inductive inference occurs under *Researcher Explanations*.

Overall, the matrix is a tabular format that collects and arranges data for easy viewing in one place, permits detailed analysis, and sets the stage for later cross-case analysis with other comparable cases or sites. As the chapters progress, you'll learn how matrices can *order* data by case or time and can arrange and stack their cells in such a way as to create *meta-matrices*, which contain multiple rows within a single row and multiple columns within a single column.

Networks

A network is a collection of *nodes* or points connected by *links* or lines that display streams of participant actions, events, and processes. Networks lend themselves well to a case-oriented approach that re-creates the "plot" of events over time, as well as showing complex interrelationships between variables. They give us the kinds of narratives that tend to get chopped up analytically in matrices. They are very helpful when you want to focus on multiple variables at the same time for readily analyzable information at a glance.

Display 5.2 is a network model from McCammon et al.'s (2012) study of how high school speech classes influenced and affected adolescents and their adulthood after graduation. The network is an outline of "plot points" for an accompanying research narrative.

Display 5.2

A Network Model of "Lifelong Impact" From High School Speech Participation

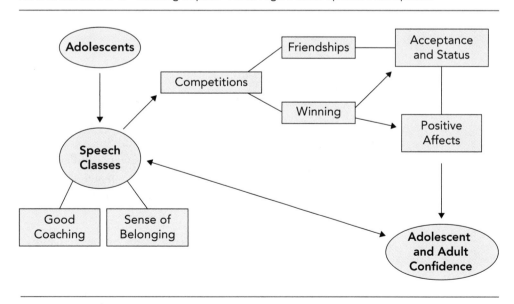

Source: Saldaña, J. (2013). *The coding manual for qualitative researchers* (2nd ed.). Thousand Oaks, CA: Sage Publications.

The proverb of this research story—the theory—suggested by the oval nodes is as follows: When *Adolescents* enroll in high school *Speech Classes*, they gain *Confidence* as an *Adolescent and Adult*. But that story line is too thin and needs to be fleshed out through an analytic narrative. The rectangular nodes attached to *Speech Classes* indicate that the classroom content must be led by a teacher who provides *Good Coaching*. Students must also feel that they are part of a classroom community through a *Sense of Belonging*.

Not all but some students from those classes participated in extracurricular speech tournaments or forensic *Competitions* (debate, extemporaneous speaking, oral interpretation of literature, etc.). Thus, a separate trajectory or stream is drawn. Respondents testified that participation in these events developed *Friendships*, a sense of *Acceptance and Status*, and thus *Positive Affects*, especially for those who reached the achievement of *Winning* at these competitive events. Regardless of whether one won or not, the respondents' stated outcome was *Confidence*—both as an *Adolescent* and later as an *Adult*.

The bidirectional arrow between *Speech Classes* and *Adolescent and Adult Confidence* suggests a cyclical or interactive effect: The more speech classes you took, the more confident you became; the more confident you became, the more likely you continued participating in speech classes and competitions.

Networks are also effective heuristics for higher level analyses such as discerning causation, analyzing longitudinal trends, and developing hypotheses and theories. They are not any easier or harder to construct than matrices—both display forms take comparable amounts of time and thought to design and assemble. Selected CAQDAS programs, however, can greatly assist with complex network construction. Display 5.3 illustrates QDA Miner 4's ability to "calculate" and assemble a three-dimensional network of codes as weighted nodes, with links suggesting interrelationship. These graphics are extremely helpful as diagnostics of data analysis in progress and as displays themselves for final reports.

See Knowlton and Phillips (2013) for a diverse collection of logic model graphic designs and the online Periodic Table of Visualization Methods for additional ideas (http://www.visual-literacy.org/periodic_table/periodic_table.html).

Timing of Display Design

When should display formats be generated? Analytic displays can be developed either during or after data collection. They can provide preliminary findings about what is happening in the case and suggest leads toward new data. Later, as fuller, more complete descriptions are at hand, these displays can supply the basic material for higher level explanations—that is, plausible reasons for why things are happening as they are.

If the format is at hand during data collection, it helps save energy by encouraging focus: You know what information you will be needing. But there are some cautions here. First, qualitative data evolve; later accounts round out, qualify, put in perspective, and disqualify the earlier ones. Analysts scout around, sleuth, and take second and third looks. So there are risks in entering the data into a set format too soon.

Display 5.3

A QDA Miner 4 3-D Map of a Codes Network

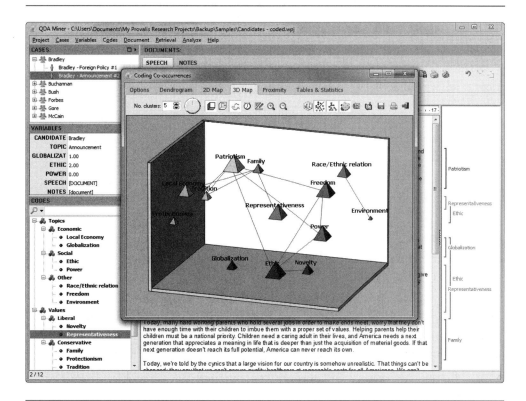

Source: Courtesy of Provalis Research, www.provalisresearch.com.

Furthermore, for any given research question or issue, you can develop many different displays (literally dozens) using the same set of variables. Each display makes somewhat different assumptions; each has trade-offs among advantages and costs. Another caution is that display formats nearly always evolve, too. The later ones are more data sensitive than the earlier ones, as things become clearer.

So our general advice is to generate rough formats early during data collection and revise them to a firmer state closer to the end of data collection, when they can be grounded more contextually and empirically. Expect to make several passes or iterations before the first format of the display is working right. Test a proposed format by entering data. Unworkable or confusing formats, or those that do not incorporate all of the relevant data, will show themselves rapidly.

Formatting the Matrix Template

There are no fixed canons for constructing a matrix. Rather, matrix construction is a creative yet systematic task that furthers your understanding of the substance and meaning of your database, even before you begin entering information. Thus, the issue is not whether you are building a "correct" matrix but whether it is a *helpful* one that will give you reasonable answers to the questions you are asking or suggest promising new ways to lay out the data to get answers. At a deeper level, the message of this book is not "Use these matrices" but "**Think display**. Adapt and invent formats that will serve you best."

Given these choices, what can we say informally about the best and easiest ways to build the templates/outlines/frameworks of matrix displays? We state these briskly, as friendly advice rather than as harsh prescription:

- Look at your *research question(s) and key variables*, and think of the data that are or will be available. Sketch the matrix outline roughly using paper and pencil.

- Get a *colleague to look at your initial format*, to help you detect the assumptions you are making and to suggest alternative ways to display your data.

- Set up the matrix template by using a *text program, database management, or CAQDAS software*. Try to make the display completely readable on your monitor screen or on one printed sheet of paper, if possible. You have to be able to see it all at once.

- Don't try to include more than a dozen or so *variables in rows or columns*; five or six is more manageable. If you are drawn to a design with larger numbers of variables, plan to cluster or partition them as meta-matrices. In effect, regroup the matrix into "streams" or adjacent "families."

- The simplest matrices are organized in two dimensions. You have a choice to move to more complexity if the data demand it by creating *partitions* for *meta-matrices*—rows within a row and/or columns within a column (to be illustrated in forthcoming chapters).

- If the matrix is an ordered one, expect to *transpose rows and columns* for a while until you have a satisfactory version. Most text-based software, database management, and CAQDAS programs can do this quite easily.

- Always stay open to the idea of *adding new rows or columns*, even late in your analysis operations.

- Keep *rows and columns fine grained* enough to accommodate meaningful differentiations in the data but not so fine as to bury you under indiscriminate detail.

- Keep in mind that any particular research question may require a *series of displays*; for example, an initial partially ordered descriptive matrix may lead to a small summary table and then to a network display. Think ahead to this possibility, but allow new matrix forms to emerge as the analysis proceeds.

Creating matrix templates is usually a matter of a few minutes; revising them as the early items of data are entered is also quick work. Virtually all CAQDAS programs can enable reformatting as data are entered and coded. The time taken to enter data into a display actually depends on the following: (a) the number of variables or dimensions in the display, (b) the number of respondents and cases, and (c) the kind and number of transformations made.

Which types of row and column headings or network bin labels are possible? The set is almost infinite, ranging from cases to variables. To illustrate, here is just a sample of types adapted from Gobo (2008), Lofland, Snow, Anderson, and Lofland (2006), and Bogdan and Biklen (2007). For concreteness, we use examples from health care settings:

Individuals:	Jane Hughes, RN, Dr. Luis Garcia
Roles:	patients, nurses, doctors, administrators
Relationships and groups:	patient–spouse, nurse–resident, intensive care unit staff, accounting department, surgical team
Settings within sites:	operating room, emergency room, cafeteria
Sites as wholes:	Good Samaritan Hospital, downtown health maintenance organization
Specific actions (what people do and say):	diagnostic questions, answers, listening, information giving, comforting
Events (marked-off happenings or occurrences):	admission, operation, discharge
Activities (regularly occurring, connected sets of actions):	grand rounds, lab tests, billing
Strategies (activities aimed toward some goal):	rehabilitation plan, nutrition counseling, radiation treatment
Meanings and perspectives (how people construe events):	patient and physician views of an HIV-positive diagnosis, the experience of labor and childbirth
Attitudes, values, and beliefs:	resentment toward physician seniority, pro-choice versus pro-life, patient anxiety
Emotions and states:	staff morale, patient fear, critical condition
Processes (ongoing flows, phases, stages, cycles, changes over time):	wound healing, convalescence, triage, decision making, social support, bereavement

Entering Matrix and Network Data

Generally, the choice of data for display entry must be driven by the particular row and column headings involved or by your definitions of network nodes and links. But these seemingly straightforward tasks are critical issues in qualitative data analysis. *The conclusions drawn from a display can never be better than the quality of the data entered.* A completed matrix or network may look coherent, plausible, and fascinating, but if the data were poorly collected in the first place or were entered in a hasty, ill-partitioned, or vague way, the conclusions are suspect. We offer some guidelines below for data entry into display formats:

- Even a dense matrix displays only a very small percentage of the available data. There is always a great deal of *selection and condensation* from the mass of field notes. Be aware of how you make that selection and how you boil the data down. You are not throwing away your field notes—you can always refer back to the full material.

- *More information is better than less:* Too thin cell entries keep you away from the meaning of the data.

- Be clear about the *forms and types of data* you want to enter: direct quotes, paraphrases, general summary judgments, ratings, and so on.

- Use codes and software *search functions* to locate key material. Entering these data is much easier with text-based software, database management, or a CAQDAS program having multiple screens; they permit you to retrieve coded chunks to one screen or region and to select/edit/condense them on another.

- Keep an explicit *record of the "decision rules"* you followed in selecting data chunks for entry (e.g., the extent of agreement among respondents or data types, the intensity of respondents' feelings, the basis for making judgments or ratings). Otherwise, you may delude yourself retrospectively, forget how you did it, or shift your decision rules during the process.

- When *data are missing, ambiguous, or were not asked for* from certain respondents, show this explicitly in the display.

- *Don't lock up your format* until later in the process. Entering data tests the adequacy, realism, and helpfulness of the display format. Keep revising it as needed.

- Be open to using *numbers, direct quantities, or judgments* in the form of ratings, scales, or magnitude codes, when applicable to the study.

- Get a *colleague to review* your display, along with your decision rules and written-up field notes, to check the procedural adequacy of your work. Such audits are time-consuming, but used selectively, they are an important check on the "confirmability" of the procedures you used.

You always have choices about the level and type of data to be entered. For example, you can include the following:

Direct quotes, extracts from written-up field notes:	"Surgeons are basically macho types—the best ones, I mean. They have to be, but they can't help it."
Summaries, paraphrases, or abstracts:	Patient advocate seems increasingly distrusted. Rules for residents' time use largely ignored.
Researcher explanations:	Patient uncertainty about diagnosis is a function of life-threatening conditions and use of denial as a buffer.
Ratings or summarized judgments:	Risk reduction behavior after cardiovascular bypass: worse, no change, improved, much improved.
Combinations of the above:	Risk reduction: improved. Diet ("I even tried broccoli"), some exercise (walks 20–30 minutes daily), and smoking (reduced, is considering using a nicotine patch).

Making Inferences and Drawing Conclusions From Matrices and Networks

The test of any display is what it helps you understand—and how trustworthy that understanding is. In the next five chapters, there will be many specific tactics for conclusion drawing and verification through the use of **boldface**. Each has its specific advantages and pitfalls, which we will discuss in Chapter 11. Here, we offer some preliminary general advice:

- It's always helpful to *start with a quick scan*—a "squint analysis" or "eyeballing" down columns and across rows and through network pathways to see what jumps out. Then, verify, revise, or disconfirm that impression through a more careful review.

- Any given display will always have *multiple tactics* used on it. The ones we have used most frequently for drawing first conclusions are **noting patterns, themes**; **making contrasts, comparisons**; **clustering**; and **counting**.

- Displays never speak for themselves—either to you or to the reader; *accompanying text is always needed*. As conclusions form in your mind, always write text explaining them. Make your conclusions explicit. The process of writing inevitably leads to reformulation, added clarity, and ideas for further analysis. Writing is itself a form of analysis.

- First conclusions drawn from a display almost always need to be *checked against written-up field notes*. If a conclusion does not ring true at the "ground level" when you try it out there, it needs revision. Look at the raw data to guard against this. Even better, check with your research colleagues and the participants themselves, when possible.

- Any early conclusion typically needs *confirmation, checking, and verification*. The most frequently used tactics we've used are as follows: **following up surprises, triangulating, making if-then tests**, and **checking out rival explanations**.

- Be sure your descriptive understanding is *clear at the individual or within-case level first* before you try to understand cross-case patterns.

- Remember that analysis usually has to *go beyond descriptive summation and reach toward explanation*. Clarify the conceptual implications of your conclusions— that is, how they tie into your or someone else's theory of social behavior. Analyses that yield verifiable but poor-meaning conclusions are of little use to anyone.

Conclusions about data displays normally appear in what we call an analytic text or narrative. Analytic narrative draws attention to the features of the displayed data and makes sense of them, knitting them together and permitting the analyst to draw conclusions and add interpretations. It also encourages a return to the field notes to consult information not in the display and to add it to the text for further clarity. Since a display does not speak for itself, analytic text does not stand alone without reference to the display.

In fact, the act of writing text as you ruminate over the meaning of a display is itself a focusing and forcing device that propels further analysis. Writing does not come after analysis; it *is* analysis, happening as the writer thinks through the meaning of data in the display. Writing is thinking, not the report of thought.

Stay open on the question of whether the display format you use for analysis should be the same display used for final reporting (the answer is often "yes"). Readers can see for themselves how conclusions were drawn, rather than being handed summarized study results to be taken on faith. Sometimes, of course, a display will be used for intermediate purposes and will not necessarily be shown to readers of the final report.

The tradition of presenting basic data is deeply ingrained in reports of quantitative data analysis, so much so that it would be unthinkable for a researcher to present conclusions without data tables or, at least, without reference to working documents containing them. We believe that the same norms should apply to qualitative researchers working within particular traditional genres of inquiry (e.g., ethnography, grounded theory, content analysis, evaluation research, etc.). Some data displays should be a normal part of reporting findings and conclusions. In some instances, of course, a summary table or a boiled-down version may suffice. Where basic matrices or networks are not presented, you owe the reader a clear explanation of the analysis methods used to get to the text. In any case, remember what the reader needs from displays. We can hardly do better than quote Tufte (1986), speaking primarily of quantitative work but with relevance for qualitative researchers:

> What we are seeking in graphic and tabular displays of information is the clear portrayal of complexity. Not the complication of the simple; rather the task of the designer is to give visual access to the subtle and the difficult—that is, the revelation of the complex. (p. 80)

As the saying goes, "Things can be complex without being complicated."

The Methods Profiles

In the next five chapters, each method profile will be presented in this format:

- *Description:* The method is briefly described with reference to its accompanying display.

- *Applications:* This section outlines the purposes of the method and its recommended uses for particular research studies or goals.

- *Example:* A study drawn from the coauthors' previous work is used to illustrate the display, its design, and data entry.

- *Analysis:* The discussion shifts to how the assembled data in the matrix or network were analyzed and interpreted by the researchers. Recommendations for reader applications are also provided.

- *Notes:* Supplemental or concluding comments about the method are offered.

The profiles vary in length, depending on the complexity of the method. They are grouped into subcategories within each chapter, when appropriate, if they share a common purpose.

We also emphasize here that the names we gave to our methods and displays were for convenient description, not for standardization. Who cares whether it is a "case-ordered descriptive meta-matrix" or a "predictor-outcome-consequences matrix"? The names may sound like jargon, but don't worry about that; the issue is how any given display works and how it can further your *understanding* of the data. All of the methods and displays can be adapted to meet the needs of any particular study. If they seem too complex, simplify; they can be modified easily for studies where the cases are a few individuals. Not every single method has to be used for every single study. Take only what is useful for your research purposes and goals. Focus on the doable while keeping as much richness as you can.

Closure and Transition

This chapter provides foundations for the next set of chapters—that is, methods of displaying and analyzing qualitative data through five modalities: (1) exploring, (2) describing, (3) ordering, (4) explaining, and (5) predicting. You're encouraged to read Chapters 6 through 10 in order, for the techniques of one strategy are generally used in the next.

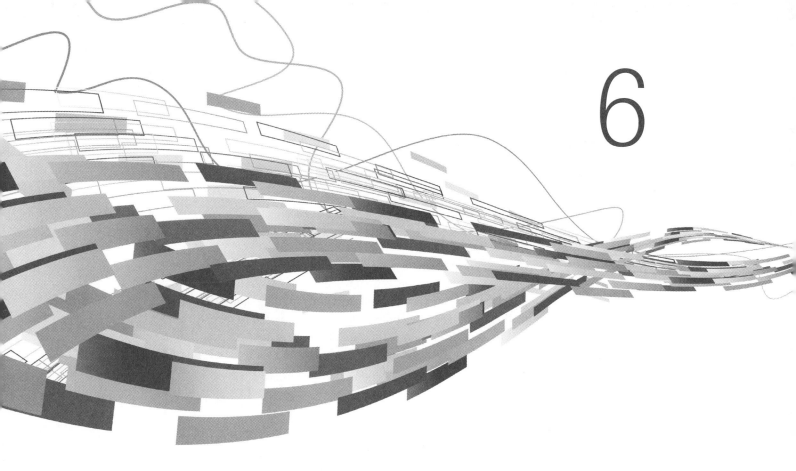

6

Methods of Exploring

Chapter Summary

This chapter profiles methods of displaying data to provide initial compilations for exploration. They are methods of documenting fieldwork in progress, exploring salient variables as they emerge, and preparing preliminary outlines for the final report.

Contents

Introduction
Exploring Fieldwork in Progress
    Data Accounting Log
    Contact Summary Form
    Case Analysis Meeting
    Interim Case Summary
    Partially Ordered Meta-Matrix
    Explanatory Effects Matrix
Exploring Variables
    Checklist Matrix
    Content-Analytic Summary Table

Contrast Table

Two-Variable Case-Ordered Matrix

Exploring Reports in Progress

Pre-structured Case

Sequential Analyses

Closure and Transition

Introduction

Theoretically, virtually everything about a research study can be exploratory in one way or another, from initial conceptualization to final write-up. But *exploratory* in this chapter refers to methods that are documentary and provisional in their analyses—"first draft" attempts, if you will, at making sense of qualitative data. Exploratory displays are not necessarily developed for final publication. They are intended as heuristics for the researcher to analyze data in progress. In the exploratory mode, it's as if we are trying to solve an unstated or ambiguous problem, which has to be framed and reframed as we go. Wolcott (1992) talks about this as the "theory first" or "theory after" approach. Both are workable.

Exploring Fieldwork in Progress describes methods to keep the researcher from getting overwhelmed by the voluminous accumulation of qualitative data. They are ways of staying ahead of the game through occasional summary and synthesis. *Exploring Variables* looks at those constituent elements of the data corpus to examine their properties, dimensions, and overall qualities. And *Exploring Reports in Progress* shows how the write-up builds over time and contributes to further studies.

Exploring Fieldwork in Progress

The *data accounting log* is a record-keeping tool for the types and quantity of data collected. A *contact summary form* is a one-page form that logs a field site visit's most salient data. The *case analysis meeting* systematically documents a research team's discussion about a study, to date. The *interim case summary* is a provisional draft of the study's fieldwork and its written report, to date.

A *partially ordered meta-matrix* is a first-draft assemblage of the most relevant data from a study into a composite display. And an *explanatory effects matrix* is the initial plotting of possible causation for more in-depth analytic explanation.

Data Accounting Log
Description

A data accounting log is a management method that simply documents on a single form when and what types of data have been collected from specific participants and sites. The analyst enters in each cell when a set of data is in hand, plus any supplemental notes (see Display 6.1).

Display 6.1

Data Accounting Log

	Carol (Teacher)	Tom (Student)	LeAnn (Principal)	Elana (Counselor)	Marci (Adm Asst)	Jake (Father)	Liz (Mother)
INTERVIEW 1	05/04/2012	05/08/2012	05/15/2012	05/17/2012	05/23/2012	05/09/2012	05/09/2012
INTERVIEW 2	05/14/2012	05/17/2012	X	inquire if a follow-up interview is possible	X	was asked but declined a 2nd interview	11/5/2012—phone interview
INTERVIEW 3	05/31/2012	X	X	X	X	X	X
PARTICIPANT OBS. 1	04/26/2012	04/26/2012	N/A	N/A	N/A	N/A	N/A
PARTICIPANT OBS. 2	4/27/2012—date of key incident	4/27/2012—date of key incident	N/A	N/A	N/A	N/A	N/A
PARTICIPANT OBS. 3	04/30/2012	04/30/2012	N/A	N/A	N/A	N/A	N/A
PARTICIPANT OBS. 4	05/01/2012	absent	N/A	N/A	N/A	N/A	N/A
PARTICIPANT OBS. 5	05/02/2012	05/02/2012	N/A	N/A	N/A	N/A	N/A
DOCUMENTS							
Lesson Plans	√	N/A	N/A	N/A	N/A	N/A	N/A
Referral Files	√—for Tom	√—has copy	√—has copy	see for access	see for access	has copy	has copy
OTHER							
Student Assignments	√—for all students	√	N/A	N/A	N/A	N/A	has copy of Tom's assignment
Standardized Test Scores	N/A	√	N/A	see for access	see for access	N/A	N/A
Transcripts	N/A	√	N/A	see for access	see for access	N/A	N/A

Applications

A data accounting log is highly recommended for all qualitative studies as good record keeping and management, particularly for those with large numbers of participants or sites. This method may look laborious, even overzealous, but it pays handsome rewards. In field research, you lose sight all too quickly of how much—and which sort of—data have been collected from different participants. Because these data are often corroborative—verifying an explanation given by others, testing an emerging hypothesis or conclusion—their absence is more than just having "missing data," as in a quantitative survey. They are the evidential bricks on which an analysis can be built.

Example

Display 6.1 illustrates a small-scale study's data accounting log, noting the key participants in the column headings and the data forms in the rows. Dates, supplemental notes, and researcher-generated confirmation marks have been entered for at-a-glance documentation of the corpus. Excel software was initially used for constructing the display.

Analysis

A scan of the form shows both the data collection in progress and, toward a study's end, the completed corpus record. Reflection on the log might suggest additional forms of data needed or that could be collected. A copy of the data accounting log can be attached to a Contact Summary Form (profiled next) and used in planning the next steps in data collection. The log can also serve as an auditor's reference or as an appendix to a technical report.

Notes

You can make a data accounting log as detailed as you need it to be. Cells can be devoted to confirming whether different participants from several cross-case sites have been asked the same particular interview question from a protocol or whether the researcher has collected sufficient forms of data to help answer a particular set of research questions.

Contact Summary Form

Description

A contact summary form is a one-page document with some focusing or summarizing questions about a particular field contact. The field-worker reviews the written-up field notes and answers each question briefly to develop an overall summary of the main points in the contact (see Display 6.2).

Applications

After a field contact (from one to several days) and the production of write-ups, there is often a need to pause and ponder, "What were the main concepts, themes, issues, and questions that I saw and heard during this contact?" Without such reflection, it is easy to get lost in a welter of detail.

The contact summary form is a rapid, practical way to do first-run data condensation without losing any of the basic information to which it refers. It captures thoughtful impressions and reflections and makes them available for further reflection and analysis not only by the field-worker but also by the other team members.

Display 6.2

Contact Summary Form: Illustration (Excerpts)

Contact type: Site: <u>Tindale</u>

    Visit   <u> X   </u>   Contact date: <u>11/28-29/79</u>

    Phone   <u>   </u>   Today's date: <u>12/28/79</u>

            (with whom)   Written by: BLT

1. <u>What were the main issues or themes that struck you in this contact?</u>

   Interplay between highly prescriptive, "teacher-proof" curriculum that is top-down imposed and the actual writing of the curriculum by the teachers themselves.

   Split between the "watchdogs" (administrators) and the "house masters" (dept. chairs & teachers) vis a vis job foci.

   District curric. coord'r as decision maker are school's acceptance of research relationship.

2. <u>Summarize the information you got (or failed to get) on each of the target questions you had for this contact.</u>

Question	Information
History of dev. of innov'n	Conceptualized by Curric. Coord'r, English Chairman & Assoc. Chairman; written by teachers in summer; revised by teachers following summer with field testing data
School's org'l structure	Principal & admin'rs responsible for discipline; dept chairs are educ'l leaders
Demographics	Racial conflicts in late 60's; 60% black stud. pop.; heavy emphasis on discipline & on keeping out non-district students slipping in from Chicago
Teacher response to innov'n	Rigid, structured, etc. at first; now, they say they like it/NEEDS EXPLORATION
Research access	Very good; only restriction: teachers not required to cooperate

3. <u>Anything else that struck you as salient, interesting, illuminating or important in this contact?</u>

   Thoroughness of the innv'n's development and training.

   Its embeddedness in the district's curriculum as planned and executed by the district curriculum coordinator.

   The initial resistance to its high prescriptiveness (as reported by users) as contrasted with their current acceptance and approval of it (again, as reported by users).

4. <u>What new (or remaining) target questions do you have in considering the next contact with this site?</u>

   How do users really perceive the innov'n? If they do indeed embrace it, what accounts for the change from early resistance?

   Nature and amount of networking among users of innov'n.

   Information on "stubborn" math teachers whose ideas weren't heard initially—who are they? Situation particulars? Resolution?

   Follow-up on English teacher Reilly's "fall from the chairmanship."

   Follow a team through a day of rotation, planning, etc.

   CONCERN: The consequences of eating school cafeteria food two days per week for the next four or five months . . .

*Source:*Miles, M. B., & Huberman, A. M. (1994). *Qualitative data analysis: An expanded sourcebook* (2nd ed.). Thousand Oaks, CA: Sage Publications.

Example

First, be clear about what you or your research team members need to know now about a particular field contact, with a write-up that may later run to dozens of pages. Which questions will get to the essence of the data set? Here are some possibilities:

- What people, events, or situations were involved?

- What were the main themes or issues in the contact?

- Which research questions and which variables in the initial framework did the contact bear on most centrally?

- What new assertions, propositions, hypotheses, speculations, or hunches about the field situations were suggested by the contact?

- Where should the field-worker place most energy during the next contact, and what kinds of information should be sought?

Questions should be arranged on a single sheet of paper (or within the one-page space limit of a text-based program), with room for the field-worker's answers. Identifying information on the case, the particular contact, the field-worker, and the date should be indicated as well.

The data on a contact summary form are essentially phrases or sentences that the field-worker considers to be an answer to the form's questions after the complete write-up of the contact has been reviewed and corrected. At this point, you have a perspective that combines immediacy with a reflective overview of what went on in the contact. You can include your own reflective remarks, as well as questions to be answered, during the next contact. Waiting until a contact's full data have been coded thoroughly and fully is probably too late. In addition, the process of coding usually adds so many subsequent thoughts about the contact that what was originally in the notes may get buried or distorted.

Display 6.2 shows excerpts from an example. Note that Questions 2 and 4 of this form indicate that the field-worker started with a focused set of "target questions." Those are useful when your time is limited. Information on each question is summarized, and new target questions are posed for the next visit. Some of these questions come from the background research questions (How do users really perceive the innovation?), and some are provoked by data collected during the visit (e.g., Follow-up on English teacher Reilly's "fall from the chairmanship").

Analysis

The filled-out contact summary form can be used in several ways:

- To guide planning for the next contact

- To reorient yourself to the contact when returning to the write-up

- To help with coordination when more than one field-worker is involved in the study

- To help with further data analysis—that is, the summary forms for a number of contacts can themselves be coded and analyzed

- To suggest new or revised codes

All of these uses are easier if the forms have been entered into a database. It is also helpful to digitally cut and paste a copy of the completed contact summary form before the first page of the write-up so it's close to the data it summarizes. We encourage doing write-ups no later than the day after a field contact.

Contact summary forms also can be used in a more systematic way by applying codes to them. An excerpted illustration appears in Display 6.3. Here, the analyst had a list of codes (called Themes or Aspects) that were applied to the Salient Points selected from the write-up. New codes were also generated.

Display 6.3

Contact Summary Form: Illustration With Coded Themes (Excerpt)

CONTACT SUMMARY

Type of contact: Mtg. <u>Principals</u>   <u>Ken's office</u>   <u>4/2/76</u>   SITE <u>Westgate</u>

               Who, what group   place   date   Coder <u>MM</u>

        Phone _____ _____ _____

              With whom, by whom place   date   Date coded <u>4/18/76</u>

       Inf. Int. _____ _____ _____

             With whom, by whom place   date

1. Pick out the most salient points in the contact. Number in order on this sheet and note page number on which point appears. Number point in text of write-up. Attach theme or aspect to each point in CAPITALS. Invent themes where no existing ones apply and asterisk those. Comment may also be included in double parentheses.

Page	Salient Points	Themes/Aspects
1	1. Staff decisions have to be made by April 30.	STAFF
1	2. Teachers will have to go out of their present grade-level assignment when they transfer.	STAFF/RESOURCE MGMT.
2	3. Teachers vary in their willingness to integrate special ed kids into their classrooms—some teachers are "a pain in the elbow."	*RESISTANCE
2	4. Ken points out that tentative teacher assignment lists got leaked from the previous meeting (implicity deplores this).	INTERNAL COMMUNIC.
2	5. Ken says, "Teachers act as if they had the right to decide who should be transferred." (would make outcry)	POWER DISTRIB.
2	6. Tacit/explicit decision: "It's our decision to make." (voiced by Ken, agreed by Ed)	POWER DISTRIB/ CONFLICT MGMT.
2	7. Principals and Ken, John, and Walker agree that Ms. Epstein is "bitch."	*STEREOTYPING
2	8. Ken decides not to tell teachers ahead of time (now) about transfers ("because then we'd have a fait accompli").	PLAN FOR PLANNING/ TIME MGMT

Source: Miles, M. B., & Huberman, A. M. (1994). *Qualitative data analysis: An expanded sourcebook* (2nd ed.). Thousand Oaks, CA: Sage Publications.

Notes

Keep contact summary forms simple. You need an instrument that makes it easy to do a rapid retrieval and synthesis of what the contact was all about. Focus on the primary concepts, questions, and issues.

Case Analysis Meeting

Description

At a case analysis meeting, the field-worker most conversant with a case meets with one or more people—a critical friend, a colleague, or coresearchers—to summarize the current status of the case. The meeting is guided by a series of prepared questions, and notes are taken on answers to the questions as the meeting progresses. Case analysis meetings can also focus on a single theme in one case or treat such a theme across several cases (see Display 6.4).

Applications

In any study that has multiple cases, the meaning of what is happening in each case tends increasingly to get lost in the welter of fieldwork, coding, and other preliminary analyses. A lone researcher or a research staff can understand quickly and economically what is happening in a case, keep himself or herself current, and develop coherent constructs to guide later analysis through case analysis meetings and summaries.

Case analysis meetings are good devices for rapid retrieval of impressions and "headnotes" and for forming preliminary descriptive and inferential generalizations. The back-and-forth interaction among colleagues helps keep the field-worker honest. Even so, care should be taken not to get locked into premature generalizations. The themes and suggestions from case analysis meetings should always be checked against events in the case, as noted in carefully coded write-ups of field notes.

Display 6.4

Case Analysis Meeting Form

Case Analysis Meeting Form	Date _____	Case _____

Recorder _____   Meeting Attendance _____

1. MAIN THEMES, IMPRESSIONS, SUMMARY STATEMENTS about what is going on in the case. Comments about the general state of the planning/implementation system.

2. EXPLANATIONS, SPECULATIONS, HYPOTHESES, PROPOSITIONS, ASSERTIONS about what is going in the case.

3. ALTERNATIVE INTERPRETATIONS, EXPLANATIONS, DISAGREEMENTS about what is going on in the case.

4. NEXT STEPS FOR DATA COLLECTION: follow-up questions, specific actions, general directions fieldwork should take.

5. Implications for REVISION, UPDATING OF CODING SCHEME.

Source: Miles, M. B., & Huberman, A. M. (1994). *Qualitative data analysis: An expanded sourcebook* (2nd ed.). Thousand Oaks, CA: Sage Publications.

If the group is bigger than three or four, it will help to have someone chairing it as well as recording it.

Example

Our (Miles and Huberman) study of the creation of new schools included six sites. We wanted to keep as current as we could on events in the planning and implementation of each new school. We were also seeking explanations and hypotheses—and we were feeling strongly that our too complex, unhelpful coding scheme needed to be revised.

We settled on the idea of a case analysis meeting that would be held for each of the six sites in rotation. To help focus the meeting, a note-taking form was needed, which appears in compressed form in Display 6.4. The actual form, of course, had its questions spread out over three or four pages to allow space for handwritten note taking. This particular example was focused on a complex case—a school—that we were following over time, but it can be adapted easily if the case is an individual or a small group.

In using the form, the meeting can begin profitably with the most involved field-workers launching a discussion of Item 1, Main Themes. Others ask questions for clarification. The recorder follows the discussion, taking notes (either by hand or on a laptop) under that heading and asking for further clarification if needed.

Often the discussion will jump forward to later questions (e.g., a theme suggests an interpretation), and the recorder should enter those data under appropriate headings. Points or items under each heading should be numbered to mark them off and aid reference to them during the discussion. If the group does not move gradually to later questions, the recorder should ask them to do so. The recorder should also summarize the notes from time to time to ensure that the discussion is being represented accurately.

Analysis

Photocopies of the notes are made for everyone, or digital copies are e-mailed to the team; they can be reviewed at the end of the meeting. Specific plans can be made (to revise codes or on how to collect new data of a certain sort), although such review and planning can be done afterward too. Display 6.5 presents some excerpts from a filled-out case analysis form for our new school study.

The field-worker had been observing the start-up of a new, open-space elementary school. In this display, we can see that the main theme was the researcher's effort to describe (Item 1) and then understand (Item 2) why the early implementation of open-space teaching was going relatively smoothly even though the advance preparation had been poor. The hypotheses and hunches in Item 2 (e.g., the "retreatability" concept, the principal–teacher relationship, or teacher professionalization) led to additional data collection plans in Item 4 (e.g., teacher interviews), as do the alternative, rival hypotheses suggested in Item 3. The notes from the case analysis meetings, as well as guiding specific next steps in data collection, can be revisited after the next round or two of data collection for confirmation/disconfirmation.

Display 6.5

Case Analysis Form: Exhibit With Data

1. MAIN THEMES, IMPRESSIONS, SUMMARY STATEMENTS about what is going on in the site.

   1. Ed (principal) efficient "technical" manager, not dealing with social system; doesn't think about it. When Ken (asst. supt.) pointed out need for Ed to work with Janet, a complaining teacher ("treat her with kid gloves . . . good luck."), Ed said, "She'll be the one needing good luck." Not supportive especialy: One teacher asked the field-worker for help, seemed reluctant when FW referred her back to Ed.

   2. Implementation of the open space approach is incredibly smooth in light of the minimal advance preparation and training. There is still a "walking on cracked eggs" feeling, though.

   3. Teachers seem cautiously willing to see how it will work out, not directly optimistic. Uncertainty, feeling unprepared. "If it doesn't work out I hope we can undo it" suggests weak commitment; is called "retreatability."

   4. Children relaxed.

   5. Teachers feel principal had no idea of what would be involved, really, in start-up.

   . . . .

2. EXPLANATIONS, SPECULATIONS, HYPOTHESES, PROPOSITIONS, ASSERTIONS about what is going on in the site.

   1. Ed's "efficiency" emphasis helps smoothness.

   2. People know who to go to for support.

   3. Many teachers were students of asst. supt. and trust him.

   4. Things aren't being imposed by outsiders.

   5. Teacher attitudes may be related to the "retreatability" concept.

   6. Principal knew teachers well enough to compose workable teams to implement the open space concept. Also sent complaining teachers to another school.

   7. Principal respects the teachers—even though during the administrative planning they were treated like cattle.

3. ALTERNATIVE EXPLANATIONS, MINORITY REPORTS, DISAGREEMENTS about what is going on in the site.

   1. Perhaps the teachers' considerable past experience and training, their professionalization makes for the smooth implementation.

   2. The size of Ed's faculty has doubled; there are many strangers. That may be increasing the uncertainty as much as the lack of preparation.

   . . . .

4. NEXT STEPS FOR DATA COLLECTION: follow-up questions, specific actions, general directions field work should take.

   1. Ask Ed about Janet, how she's adjusting. Get to know her.

   2. Need time to talk with teachers, not just observe the start-up. Teachers are probably bothered more than their "professional" surface behavior shows.

   3. Will or can Ken give the teachers technical help?

   4. What happened in yesterday's faculty meeting?

   5. We should do a careful retrieval interview with Ken and Ed about the summer work, planning decisions, etc. that preceded the start-up.

   6. Ask key people: What are your hopes for the way the school will be by Christmas? by June? What indicators would they use for good teacher collaboration? humanization of teaching?

   . . . .

5. Implications for REVISION, UPDATING OF CODING SCHEME.

   1. Consider a code for *support*.

   2. Something on teacher *commitment or ownership* of the innovation.

   3. Use a pattern for the "retreatability" idea, which seems quite key.

   4. Our codes on "planning-implementation linkage" are too complicated; need to simplify them considerably.

   . . . .

Source: Miles, M. B., & Huberman, A. M. (1994). *Qualitative data analysis: An expanded sourcebook* (2nd ed.). Thousand Oaks, CA: Sage Publications.

Don't let a field-worker's generalization or impression go unquestioned or unillustrated. The meeting allows people to entertain opposing views. The tone should be not one of arguing but one of friendly skepticism and efforts at concreteness and shared clarity. A balance should be maintained between getting a reasonable consensus and testing alternative, rival hypotheses. Summarize frequently to check understandings.

A case analysis meeting longer than 90 minutes or so begins to lose focus and bite. The frequency of such meetings depends on factors such as the number of people and cases involved and the frequency of case contacts. The rule of thumb is this: Don't let a large amount of case data pile up before holding an analysis meeting. In our school improvement project, we found it useful to hold short case analysis meetings after each site visit (which usually had taken 2 or 3 days and accumulated plenty of information).

The summaries drawn from the case analysis meetings can themselves be coded and drawn on for analysis. Display 6.6 shows how this can work.

Notes

The specific research questions for a study may also generate additional substantive issues that can go on the case analysis meeting form (e.g., What are the current outcomes of the innovation? How politically stable is the program? What are the main channels of information transfer?). Other general questions can be generated to guide case analysis meetings, such as the following:

- What is puzzling, strange, or unexpected about recent case events?
- What is the state of our rapport with various people in key roles?
- What additional analyses do we need of existing data to understand the case better?
- What is definitely not true of the case at this point?
- What probably will happen over the next few days/weeks in the case?

Interim Case Summary
Description

The interim case summary is a provisional product of varying length (5–35 pages, depending on the scope of the study) that is the first attempt to derive a coherent,

Display 6.6

Summary-Aided Approach to Analysis

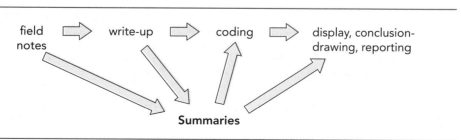

*Source:*Miles, M. B., & Huberman, A. M. (1994). *Qualitative data analysis: An expanded sourcebook* (2nd ed.). Thousand Oaks, CA: Sage Publications.

overall account of the case—a synthesis of what the researcher knows about the case and what may remain to be found out. It presents (a) a review of the findings, (b) a careful look at the quality of the data supporting them, and (c) the agenda for the next waves of data collection (see Display 6.7 for a summary outline).

The interim case summary forces the researcher to digest the materials in hand, to formulate a clearer sense of the case, and to self-critique the adequacy of the data that have been collected. This process leads to next-step data collection, planning, and usually reformulation of codes and further analysis plans.

Display 6.7

Interim Case Summary Outline: Illustration

Table of Contents

A. The Site

   1. Geography, setting

   2. Demographics of community and district

   3. Organization chart (showing key actors and their relationships)

B. Brief Chronology

   1. Adoption (includes brief description of the innovation)

   2. Planning (anything postadoption and pre-actual use with pupils)

   3. Implementation up to present

C. Current Status of Research Questions

   1. The innovation (deal with all subquestions; summarize what is currently known / if unknown, say so / if puzzles, describe them.)

   2. The school as social organization, preimplementation

   3. The adoption decision

   4. Site dynamics during implementation/transformation

   5. New configurations/outcomes

   6. Role of external and internal assistance

      (CONCLUDE THIS SECTION WITH A LIST OF UNCERTAINTIES/PUZZLES)

D. Causal Network

   1. Graphic network of variables, at this site, seen as affecting outcomes (draws on pattern codes)

   2. Discussion of network, including ties to other previous conceptual/empirical work on dissemination that seems especially salient or relevant

E. Brief Methodological Notes (how analysis was done, problems encountered, etc.; confidence in results, suggestions for next summary, etc.)

Source: Miles, M. B., & Huberman, A. M. (1994). *Qualitative data analysis: An expanded sourcebook* (2nd ed.). Thousand Oaks, CA: Sage Publications.

Applications

Typically, interim data examining is done on the run or is done for some subsets of data but not for others. You need an integrative exercise that obliges you to audit what is known and how well it is known—to collate the main findings to date, to estimate the confidence held in those findings, and to list gaps, puzzles, and data that still need to be collected. The interim case summary serves these purposes.

Whether the researcher is working alone, with occasional advisory colleague contact, or has colleagues working on other parallel cases, the interim case summary is helpful. Exchanging interim summaries with colleagues makes them up to date. And the exchange is a good occasion to subject your emerging constructs or recurrent themes to a critical review. Blind spots are usually obvious to a second reader.

Exchanging and discussing interim summaries also helps cross-case analysis. Research team members can better align their visions, argue on the basis of shared and documented instances, and resolve fuzzy or shadowy issues that need clarification for the study as a whole to move forward. Team discussion may also yield emergent explanatory variables that can be checked out rather than generated post hoc.

Strategically, the best time to compose an interim case summary is about a third of the way into fieldwork, when there are initial data to report and enough time left to atone for the gaps or weaknesses the summary has revealed. This exercise also helps you address more long-range substantive questions such as the following: What patterns and themes seem to be emerging? What is really going on in the case so far? What's the big picture?

Example

We (Miles and Huberman) have used interim summaries in several field studies. Display 6.7 presents the table of contents given to each researcher in our school improvement study as an outline for the interim case summary. Note that common formatting like this will enable cross-case comparability—which may suggest promising avenues for other analysts for their next site visits and will certainly dredge up themes and concepts that exist in more than one case.

Whether the codes have been derived directly from the research questions or evolved during early exploratory work and are more distantly connected, it makes sense to scan the write-ups, looking for the primary codes of interest, jotting down notes as you go, and then writing the summary. This process will go quite rapidly if your database is in computer files rather than only on hard copy; you can search for coded chunks, see them in context, and switch to another file to write up the themes you see emerging.

Working by hand on hard copy is slower, but sometimes a process like this seems the simplest way of synthesizing the findings to date and of becoming aware of the questions still unanswered or equivocally answered. Some analysts prefer to reread the write-ups carefully and then tackle all the research questions in one fell swoop. They then use the pattern codes to pull together the material for the summary.

Analysis

Interim summaries come in all shapes and sizes. The best ones are shapely and small—something in the order of 5 to 10 pages (but the outline shown earlier in Display 6.7 produced summaries of 25–35 pages). Summaries also can be more specialized. For example, rather than collating material for both individual research questions and overarching themes, you might do two consecutive summaries, one reviewing the research questions and, a month or so later, another tackling the larger issues that, by then, should have become clearer.

In a multicase study, be sure to allow time for individual researchers to study and discuss one another's summaries. These are usually focused and informed interactions springing from a common exercise, and they are typically more intellectual—and therefore more mind expanding—than logistically oriented staff meetings. Discussion of interim summaries is a fertile, risk-free arena for individual researchers to try out their sense of how the data—theirs and others'—are coming together and to get the analytic juices flowing.

Very brief summaries also can be produced rapidly by the case study interview method outlined in Stiegelbauer, Goldstein, and Huling (1982). One field-worker interviews another field-worker for an hour using a standard set of questions such as "How would you characterize the principal's interactions with people?" "What do you think of first when someone says _____ School?" The interviewee prepares by reviewing all the available data but leaves them aside during the interview. The transcribed interview is then edited by the interviewee, referring back to the available data as needed. This method helps the field-worker be integrative by pulling together impressions of the case and core themes that begin to appear. It is also a way to guard against the "holistic fallacy"—the assignment of a monolithic label to your case ("She's a 'traditional' teacher," "This is a 'freewheeling, innovative' school"), ignoring counterexamples and exceptions.

The most difficult part seems to be accepting the fact that interim summaries are *interim*—and likely to be incomplete, rapidly written, and fragmented. To do them well would require upward of a week, which is too much time proportionate to the yield. Do them rapidly, and then think about them with your colleagues.

Notes

In field research, you lose sight all too quickly of how much—and which sort of—data have been collected from different participants. Because these data are often corroborative—verifying an explanation given by others, testing an emerging thesis—their absence is more serious than just having "missing data," as in a quantitative survey. They are the evidential bricks on which the analysis must be built. Doing an interim case summary can be the opportunity for setting up a data accounting sheet (see Display 6.8).

The sheet simply arrays each research question by participant or group of participants. As the legend shows, the analyst checks the cell when a set of data is in hand, with the ultimate objective of filling all of the cells. At the end of coding a particular case contact, the data accounting sheet can be used in planning the next steps in data collection.

Display 6.8

Data Accounting Sheet: Abstract Example

Research Questions/ Data Sources	Background Materials			Participant Group 1					Participant Group 2, etc.			
	1	2	3	1	2	3	4	5	1	2	3	4
Q 1.1	✓	✗	✓		N.A.		N.A.	N.A.	N.A.	N.A.	✗	
Q 1.2	✗		✓	✓	✓	✗				✗		✓
Q 1.3		N.A.	✓		✗		✗	✓	✓		✗	✗
Q 2.1, etc.	N.A.	N.A.	N.A.	✗	✗							✓

Legend	blank = missing data	✓ = data complete
	✗ = incomplete data	N.A. = not applicable

Source: Miles, M. B., & Huberman, A. M. (1994). *Qualitative data analysis: An expanded sourcebook* (2nd ed.). Thousand Oaks, CA: Sage Publications.

Partially Ordered Meta-Matrix

Description

Meta-matrices are master charts assembling descriptive data from each of several cases in a standard format. The simplest form is a juxtaposition—a stacking up—of all of the single-case displays onto one large chart. The basic principle is *inclusion* of all relevant, condensed data (see Display 6.9).

From there, you usually move to *partition* the data further (divide it in new ways) and *cluster* data that fall together so that contrasts between sets of cases on variables of interest can become clearer. These partitioned and clustered meta-matrices are progressively more refined, usually requiring further transformations of case-level data into short quotes, summarizing phrases, ratings, and/or symbols (see Displays 6.11 and 6.12 for examples).

Display 6.9

Case-Level Display for Partially Ordered Meta-Matrix (Format)

Users	Feelings/ Concerns	How Innovation Looked	What Was User Doing Most?	Problems
1.				
2.				
3.				
4.				
5., etc.				

Source: Miles, M. B., & Huberman, A. M. (1994). *Qualitative data analysis: An expanded sourcebook* (2nd ed.). Thousand Oaks, CA: Sage Publications.

Applications

Cross-case analysis multiplies the data set by the number of single cases. If each case produces several hundred pages of field notes and ancillary material, no matter how well you understand things at the case level, you are faced with the specter of overload and unmanageability when you try to draw meaningful cross-case conclusions deeper than the similarities and differences.

Cross-case data need to be made comparable via common codes, common displays of commonly coded data segments, and common reporting formats for each case. Codes, displays, and reporting formats are all data-condensing devices for distilling hundreds of pages of text into workable, intellectually coherent units—that is, tables or figures and associated analytic text.

As with a single case, it's useful to start with displays that have some—but not too much—internal order. A meta-matrix is the first exploratory deep dive into cross-case analysis to see what the general territory looks like. It's also a critical one, because it will collapse the cross-case data set into partitions and clusters that may be used for subsequent analyses. Refinements in the clustering and grouping of data may be made later, but for now, you are making a commitment to a certain way of summarizing and looking at what's there, making sense of it, and trying to work out the next most likely analytic steps (which may include meta-matrices that are ordered conceptually according to key variables, by cases—such as strong to weak on some variable, or by time—such as early to late).

Example

Cross-case analysis first depends on coherent within-case information. In the example shown here, the analyst was trying to answer several questions about the experience of teachers in using a new educational practice. They are as follows:

- How did it look to the user?
- What was the user doing?
- Which feelings and concerns were paramount?
- Which problems were looming large?
- How did all of this work over a long period of time?

The empty case-level display might look like Display 6.9.

You then sort the reduced case data into the four analytic categories, user by user, in separate but commonly formatted matrices, one per case. Display 6.10 shows the display with data entered for one case, Lido School, for one time period.

Cell entries are telegraph-style phrases boiling down coded chunks from the case data. Some selection and grouping has been done, too. The analyst has selected feelings, problems, and so on according to some explicit decision rules and has clustered discrete but similar items (e.g., under Problems in the far right column, the presence of several overloading tasks equals the problem of too limited time).

Now that each cell entry includes several words/phrases, the next task is to condense these even further. You now have N case-level displays—comparable with the ones entered in Display 6.10. If there are no more than a dozen cases or so and if the

Display 6.10

Case-Level Display for Partially Ordered Meta-Matrix: Users' Second Year of Implementation at Lido

User	Feelings/ Concerns	How Innovation Looked	What Was User Doing Most?	Problems
Vance	More comfortable with style of teaching and with having kids outside	Still useful, giving good direction & helpful ideas, activities	Working through materials Giving, participating in env'l educ workshops Working with community Off-campus site work	Time too limited for tasks to be done
Drew	Concern with growing number of non-achievers in forestry/ ecology class	Too discovery-oriented for kids without biology basics; lecture style more appropriate	Adapting materials & lessons to growing non-achiever population Off-campus site work	Dealing with more non-achievers successfully
Carroll	Excitement with new activities, expanding science program	Same as first year	Working with community Giving, participating in env'l educ workshops Off-campus site work	Over-extended activity commitment

Source: Miles, M. B., & Huberman, A. M. (1994). *Qualitative data analysis: An expanded sourcebook* (2nd ed.). Thousand Oaks, CA: Sage Publications.

displays are no more complex than these examples, the data can probably all go into one composite, partially ordered meta-matrix.

The partially ordered meta-matrix will be simply a stack of the case-level charts. For example, the first two columns would appear as shown in Display 6.11.

Table construction and data entry will be relatively easy with appropriate software.

Usually you need to distill case-level cell entries somewhat as the work proceeds. Thus, for example, the filled-in chart for Lido School in Display 6.10 might appear as in Display 6.12, which shows that we are down to fewer, case-typifying words and some symbols.

Display 6.11

Partially Ordered Meta-Matrix: User Feelings/Concerns and Other Variables (Format)

Sites/Users	Feelings/Concerns	. . .
Lido School		
1.		
2.		
3.		
Masepa School		
1.		
2.		
3., etc.		

Source: Miles, M. B., & Huberman, A. M. (1994). *Qualitative data analysis: An expanded sourcebook* (2nd ed.). Thousand Oaks, CA: Sage Publications.

Display 6.12

Partially Ordered Meta-Matrix: User Feelings/Concerns and Other Variables (Lido Data)

Sites/Users	Feelings/Concerns
Lido School 1. Vance	+ Comfortable with new style, norms (lower control)
2. Drew	– Shift in target public (underachievers assigned)
3. Carroll	+ New, expanding (program, activities)

Source: Miles, M. B., & Huberman, A. M. (1994). *Qualitative data analysis: An expanded sourcebook* (2nd ed.). Thousand Oaks, CA: Sage Publications.

Feelings/Concerns have been dichotomized with positive and negative magnitude codes, and each entry has a type of feeling or concern set at about a middle range of abstraction (e.g., "comfortable," with a qualification), and often a short, category-grounding phrase (e.g., "underachievers assigned") to keep the analyst aware of what specifically was going on at this particular site.

The meta-matrix has assembled and pruned down multiple tables to one big one that has considerably condensed the original data. It lets you see all of the data in one large place. Include "just enough" words, phrases, and symbols that make summative sense to you and that prompt your ability to recall the most important features about each particular case.

Analysis

From now on, the matrices and analyses will depend more on what the data have to say and on the kinds of relationships you are most interested in. Indeed, variations of and additions to your original meta-matrices are possible. Reformatting and resorting the cells will enable you to employ the tactics of **partitioning** and **clustering** (see Chapter 11) to determine whether new analytic observations can be constructed.

Display 6.13, for example, sorts the data by the Type of Concern across each Year.

Display 6.13

Time-Ordered Meta-Matrix (Format)

Type of concern	Year 1	Year 2	Year 3	Year 4
1.				
2.				
3., etc.				

Source: Miles, M. B., & Huberman, A. M. (1994). *Qualitative data analysis: An expanded sourcebook* (2nd ed.). Thousand Oaks, CA: Sage Publications.

This matrix enables you to scan the cells for two sets of things: (1) trends—concerns that change or remain constant through time, and (2) types of concerns. Thus, the new display **partitions** the data (in this case, by time and concerns) by **clustering** the data (into different types of concerns). You may discover, for example, that types of concerns cluster into two major forms: (1) individual and (2) institutional. And you may also discover that there were more institutional than individual concerns during later implementation (tactic: **making if-then tests**).

As the next step, you could create a summary table (see Display 6.14) of individual and institutional concerns (**partitioning** the data according to some predefined variables) and see at which of the 12 cases they were considered to be primary during later implementation.

Display 6.14

Summary Table: Individual and Institutional Concerns During Later Implementation

Type of Concern/Item	School Sites at Which Item Mentioned
Individual Concerns	
Relational problems-friction among project staff	Banestown, Perry-Parkdale
Motivational problems (discouragement, "distaste" for the practice)	Calston, Lido, Masepa, Dun Hollow, Proville, Tindale
Stamina, exhaustion, excessive demands of the project	Masepa, Carson, Plummet
Institutional Concerns	
Lower institutional or district-level priority of project (with attendant lessening of rewards)	Lido, Plummet
Poor overall functioning (project as a whole, or a component)	Perry-Parkdale, Dun Hollow, Proville
Resistance, obstruction, lack of support by other staff not on project	Banestown, Perry-Parkdale, Carson
Worry whether project will "deliver" on its promises or objectives	Banestown
Continuation the following year(s)	Banestown, Calston, Lido, Perry-Parkdale, Plummet

Source: Miles, M. B., & Huberman, A. M. (1994). *Qualitative data analysis: An expanded sourcebook* (2nd ed.). Thousand Oaks, CA: Sage Publications.

During this process, you can do some empirical **clustering** within each of the two broad categories ("relational problems," "motivational problems," etc.).

Here is much useful descriptive information. For example, some school cases have multiple troubles (e.g., Banestown, Perry-Parkdale), while 3 others have only one kind (Masepa), and 2 sites of the 12 have escaped unscathed (tactic: **counting**). Also, it looks as if individual concerns are mostly nontechnical, and institutional concerns emphasize continuation (lower priority, poor functioning, delivering on promises) (tactic: **noting patterns, themes**). Such a finding leads you back to other parts of the cross-case chart to test hunches (**making if-then tests**). In this case, the hunch might be that projects with high technical mastery have just as many institutional concerns as those that do not.

Many other alternative paths may be taken from the basic, partially ordered meta-matrix to variously ordered meta-matrices. Sometimes, however, the first meta-matrices are sufficient for producing summary material for a report.

Word tables, Excel data base management, and CAQDAS applications can speed the mechanics of basic meta-matrix assembly and the processes of clustering and partitioning. But there is no real way to shortcut the *thinking* time that is needed. The process of understanding a cross-case data set, even for a few variables, is one of making gradual sense. It cannot be hurried.

Notes

Don't impose a conceptual, chronological, or other shape too quickly for a meta-matrix. Look carefully first at the multiple-case, partially ordered information. A good grounding in the first meta-matrix helps you avoid costly blind alleys later. If your cases are less complex than ours, so will your meta-matrices be. It usually takes several alternative cuts before a workable and productive set of partitions and/or clusters emerges. For more on **partitioning** and **clustering**, see Chapter 11.

Explanatory Effects Matrix

Description

An explanatory effects matrix is a broad brushstroke chart that serves as an exploratory first step to answer why certain outcomes were achieved and what caused them—either generally or specifically (see Display 6.15).

Applications

An explanatory effects matrix helps clarify a domain in *conceptual* terms; it is a useful first-cut exploration, beginning to trace back—and forward—the emerging threads of causation. The matrix helps us understand things temporally, and thus, we may get a feel for the causal mechanisms that may be involved. It is a first draft, of sorts, for further analytic work on the intricacies of explanation (to be discussed in Chapter 9).

Example

A researcher talked to users of an environmental studies program innovation, asking them from whom they had received day-to-day ongoing assistance (the conceptual domain of interest), what it actually consisted of, and what the effects (both in the short and the long run) seemed to be. The results are shown in Display 6.15. The researcher

Display 6.15

Explanatory Effects Matrix: Ongoing Assistance

Location	User's Assessment	Types Provided	Short-Run Effects ("State" of Users)	Longer-Run Consequences (Able/Unable to do)	Researcher Explanation
Superintendent	0	None	"He's going along just for the money"	Building/expansion of program on their own	Supt was a money manager not involved with programs
Bldg Admin'n Years 1-2	+	Met w/community Gave encouragement Buffered supt	"We have some help here" "We're not alone" "We'll fight our battles"	Left users more time to address program issues, students, site, buses	Admin'r supported innov. programs by providing needed help to teachers
Years 3-4	0	None	"We lost our friend"	Had to fight own battles and thus learned how	Admin'r's relative indifference probably solidified users
Developers	++	Gave ideas, help Provided framework Activity planning Positive outlook Resources	"They know their stuff" "It all makes sense" "Hey, I can do this!" "We can get equipment"	Expansion of science program to off-campus sites w/ community involvement	Dept needed money to do the program: one user needed direction and support they got both and off they went
Peer Users	+	Helped w/planning Gave ideas, sugg'ns Gave encouragement	How it could work Filled in gaps Not alone; there's help	Strong users of the off-campus program; they know how to do it	One user was experienced in this approach and brought others up to speed
Materials (Guides)	+	Overview, approach, and suggested activities in detail	This is really good stuff, well worked out, tried, useful	Good basis for development of own program	Mat'ls fulfilled their role: to stimulate & aid in development of local program

Source: Miles, M. B., & Huberman, A. M. (1994). *Qualitative data analysis: An expanded sourcebook* (2nd ed.). Thousand Oaks, CA: Sage Publications.

entered quotes and paraphrases, aiming to get at the essence of the interview material appropriate for each cell. In the last column, the researcher adds his own general explanation for each row's "story."

Analysis

The analyst scans across rows to get a sense of each one's narrative storyline. Referrals back to field notes, interviews, and other original data sources will help develop entries for the Researcher Explanation column at the far right. These cells serve not just as tracing summaries but as possible provisional hypotheses for later testing.

In Display 6.15, that tracing involves the issue of which types of assistance, from which roles, lead to which types of effect in users—and why. For example, the technical help provided by developers and the materials seems to induce clarity and legitimacy, while it may take peer and administrative support to increase actual user mastery of the new program (tactic: **making contrasts**, **comparisons**).

A look at the Researcher Explanation column shows us mostly straightforward summaries; we have not advanced the causation quest very much. It is hard to see the links between assistance types, roles, and effects more than impressionistically. Furthermore, each row is looked at one at a time as a causal sequence. It is hard to grasp the complexity of the *interactions* among rows. Thus, more detailed and thorough causation analysis usually requires other methods, such as those that will be outlined in Chapter 9.

Notes

The explanatory effects matrix is intended primarily as a heuristic for determining the *plot* or overall structure of your research story. Continued analysis may help you discover the objectives and nuanced motivations of the participant characters as the story unfolds, possibly enabling you to construct the tale's moral (i.e., its theory).

Exploring Variables

A *checklist matrix* explores the multiple dynamics of one key variable. A *content-analytic summary table* is a multicase display about a variable or dimension of interest. A *contrast table* highlights the variability of a dimension to see its extreme ranges. And a *two-variable case-ordered matrix* simultaneously explores how multiple variables relate to a selected number of cases.

Checklist Matrix
Description

A checklist matrix is a format for analyzing field data on a major variable or general domain of interest. The basic principle is that the matrix includes several components of a single, coherent variable, though it does not necessarily order the components (see Display 6.16).

Applications

Checklist matrices are good when you are exploring a new domain. If you have some rough ideas about some key variable and some first components of it, you can begin and then amplify the display as you learn more.

Sometimes qualitative researchers may need to collect comparable data from all key participants and enter them in a prespecified format. This may happen in the following situations:

- When the variable is conceptually important to the study
- When the variable can be unbundled easily into distinct indicators or components

Display 6.16

Checklist Matrix: Conditions Supporting Preparedness at Smithson School, Banestown Case

Condition	Presence of Supporting Conditions	
	For Users	**For Administrators**
Commitment	Strong - "wanted to make it work."	Weak at building level. Prime movers in central office committed; others not.
Understanding	"Basic" ("felt I could do it, but I just wasn't sure how.") for teacher. Absent for aide ("didn't understand how we were going to get all this.")	Absent at building level and among staff. Basic for 2 prime movers ("got all the help we needed from developer.") Absent for other central office staff.
Materials	Inadequate: ordered late, puzzling ("different from anything I ever used"), discarded.	N.A.
Front-end training	"Sketchy" for teacher ("it all happened so quickly"); no demo class. None for aide ("totally unprepared. I had to learn along with the children.")	Prime movers in central office had training at developer site; none for others.
Skills	Weak-adequate for teacher. "None" for aide.	One prime mover (Robeson) skilled in substance; others unskilled.
Ongoing in-service	None, except for monthly committee meeting; no substitute funds.	None
Planning, coordination time	None: both users on other tasks during day; lab tightly scheduled, no free time.	None
Provisions for debugging	None systematized: spontaneous work done by users during summer.	None
School admin. support	Adequate	N.A.
Central admin. support	Very strong on part of prime movers.	Building admin, only acting on basis of central office commitment.
Relevant prior experience	Strong and useful in both cases: had done individualized instruction, worked with low achievers. But aide no diagnostic experience.	Present and useful in central office, esp. Robeson (specialist).

Source: Miles, M. B., & Huberman, A. M. (1994). *Qualitative data analysis: An expanded sourcebook* (2nd ed.). Thousand Oaks, CA: Sage Publications.

- When you need the variable to support your findings (e.g., as a good outcome measure)

- When the study has multiple cases requiring comparability of formatting and measurement

- When you want to relate field data to survey measures of the same variable (e.g., for a mixed-methods study).

A checklist format makes data collection more systematic, enables verification, encourages comparability, and even permits simple quantification when appropriate. Checklist matrices can be formatted through programs such as Word Tables and Excel or through comparable CAQDAS features.

Example

In our (Miles and Huberman) school improvement study, "preparedness" was tied to implementation success in our conceptual framework and had strong backing in the literature. It also made good common sense that people do better those things for which they are prepared. Empirical studies had broken down preparedness to distinct components that correlated well with good project execution. In short, the variable had a lot going for it. In addition, we were studying 12 cases and needed parallel measures. We also wanted to link our findings with a large survey that had a preparedness section in its questionnaire.

We did have some doubts about the variable, though. We wondered whether the preparedness → good execution logic was too mechanistic. We also suspected that other variables could get mixed up with preparedness. For example, a highly experienced user could look well prepared, even though the technical training itself may have been dismal. And we believed that many unpredictable school-level factors could well affect project execution. So a largely individual and technical factor such as preparedness could hardly account by itself for varying degrees of successful use of the new practice. These were all things that on-site observation and interviews could capture, and we needed a display to help us sort out these matters.

The two major research questions we wanted to answer for this study are as follows:

1. What were the components of the original plan for implementation? (e.g., front-end training, monitoring and debugging/troubleshooting unexpected problems, ongoing support)

2. Were the requisite conditions for implementation assured before it began? (e.g., commitment, understanding, materials and equipment, skills, time allocation, organizational backup)

Display 6.16 is a checklist for assessing "preparedness" prior to executing a new practice. In this case, the innovation was a remedial lab program in reading, being used for the first time by a teacher and an aide. The *rows* are drawn from the various components of the implementation plan and the supporting conditions mentioned in the research questions. There is no effort to sort or order the components at this point. But we believed that preparedness might well differ for users of the new program and administrators, so the *columns* reflect that distinction. The matrix is thus partially ordered by *role*.

The cell entries include summary phrases, direct quotes, and an overall *adequacy judgment* of the condition by the analyst—evaluative words that ranged in magnitude:

- Absent/none
- Weak
- Inadequate
- Sketchy
- Basic
- Adequate
- Present
- Strong
- Very strong

The participant quotes both help justify and illuminate the rating (i.e., the magnitude code).

In sum, for a checklist matrix, the analyst reviews relevant sections of the write-ups, retrieves material by codes, forms a general judgment or rating (if needed) of the level of adequacy of the component at hand, and locates relevant and supporting quotes.

The quotes and the ratings are kept together in the cell. The idea here is that ratings only tell you how much there is of something, not what that something *means*. Brief quotes are enough to communicate and help another analyst judge, by going back to the write-ups, whether the rating is justified or not.

Be explicit about the decision rules you follow in selecting quotes and making judgments or ratings. Otherwise, colleagues or readers will be dubious about your conclusions—and you probably will come to doubt them yourself. Keep quotes and ratings together in the matrix so that their compatibility can be assessed. Some decision rules we used for data entry in Display 6.16 were as follows:

- Because there are only two users and they occupy different roles (teacher and aide), don't force a general judgment. The same applies to administrators.
- Use judgments of users and administrators if they offer them. Put them in quotes.
- Accept direct reports; do not require verification by another person.

Analysis

Now we scan down the columns of the Display 6.16 matrix and form a general idea of the level of preparedness for different components. The analytic tactic here is one of **noting patterns** or **themes** (see Chapter 11), not simply "adding up" judgments. For example, after eyeballing the data, the analyst wrote that, in part,

the image is one of solid commitment and administrative support (except for the building principal), but minimal adequacy in requisite skills and understanding of the practice, and absence of forward-looking mechanisms for training, debugging or planning.

But the display suggests a new question: What's going on here? The central office administrators were committed and had more basic understanding of the program than the users (tactic: **making comparisons**). Why didn't they help? The analyst went back to the field notes and noted,

> For Mrs. Baeurs [the administratively oriented, less skilled prime mover], all the lab teachers required were the provision of materials and initial training. . . . The teachers, she reasoned, had already done individualized work with children "so they didn't really have to do any kind of mind change." . . . At one point, however, she says, "I don't know. Maybe we got into it too fast."
>   Even Mrs. Robeson, the reading specialist, acknowledged that the teachers "didn't think they were ready," but saw few ways in which initial preparation could have been better. She also played down the size of the needed changes in teachers.

Thus, the analyst found more information: The weak, hasty training and support came about because *distant administrators minimized the actual needs of new users*. The analyst also consulted the survey data, finding that all respondents judged the list of conditions to have been "only partly in place." Administrators emphasized funds and materials; teachers had more doubts about whether there was motivation to achieve the project's purposes.

That finding, in turn, helped the analyst realize that a major missing row in the matrix was *support of other classroom teachers*, whose lack of commitment to and understanding of the lab program led to poor coordination, skepticism, and disgruntlement, which was offset only partly by their personal liking for the lab teacher and aide.

Overall, checklist matrices are effective for the systematic collection and rating of, and rumination over, a particular significant chunk of related data.

Notes

Any given research question and set of variables can have many different displays. Each has advantages and limitations. For example, Display 6.17, Checklist Matrix on Preparedness (Alternative Format 1), recasts Display 6.16 by transposing rows and columns so that we can easily follow the responses of a specific individual across all conditions, not having to lump them in one cell as in Display 6.16. Also, the analyst has clustered the conditions into two general domains: Psychosocial Conditions and the Implementation Plan. That clustering permits comparing these more easily.

Display 6.18, Checklist Matrix on Preparedness (Alternative Format 2), takes a different cut. The cell entries here are the names of *conditions*, together with the N of users or administrators reporting. An asterisk can appear beside condition names in the first row seen as "most" missing, and a number symbol beside those seen by respondents as critical for success. But note that we now have lost the data for individuals that appeared in Display 6.17. It is also much harder to track the status of any particular condition.

Display 6.19, Checklist Matrix on Preparedness (Alternative Format 3), a third possibility, de-emphasizes the differentiation among administrators and users and takes a decisive turn toward the *dynamics of conditions*—how and why they are important. It also brings in the researcher's view of the situation. We have retained the idea of

Display 6.17

Checklist Matrix on Preparedness (Alternative Format 1)

	Psycho-Social Conditions						Implementation Plan				
	Relevant Prior Experience	Commitment	Understanding	Skills	School Admin. Support	Central Admin. Support	Materials	Front-End Training	Ongoing In-Service	Planning, Coordination Time	Etc.
Users 1											
2											
Building Administrator (Principal) 1											
2											
Central Office Administrator 1											
2											
Other Central Office Staff											

Source: Miles, M. B., & Huberman, A. M. (1994). *Qualitative data analysis: An expanded sourcebook* (2nd ed.). Thousand Oaks, CA: Sage Publications.

Display 6.18

Checklist Matrix on Preparedness (Alternative Format 2)

Conditions	Users	Administrators
Missing		
Weak		
Adequate		
Strong		

Source: Miles, M. B., & Huberman, A. M. (1994). *Qualitative data analysis: An expanded sourcebook* (2nd ed.). Thousand Oaks, CA: Sage Publications.

specific examples, but we have lost identifiable individuals and the capacity to make easy comparisons between users and administrators.

The components of a checklist matrix, although they begin as unordered, may sometimes have a meaningful structure. They may fall into several clusters, as in Display 6.18, or even can be ordered by the analyst from peripheral to central, or as weak to strong.

Do not close up too rapidly on a display format, especially since the cut-and-paste functions of text-based software enable multiple variations. Try several iterations; get colleagues' ideas and reactions. Especially for exploratory work, it pays to have a column headed "Remarks," where relevant commentary of any sort can be included to aid understanding.

Checklist Matrix on Preparedness (Alternative Format 3)

Conditions	Examples[a]	How Important[b]	Why Important[c]
Commitment			
Understanding			
Materials			
Training			
etc.			

[a]Specific illustrations, marked with A or U for administrator or user, respectively.
[b]Rating: very, quite, somewhat, or not important.
[c]Explanations of reasons for importance of condition, given by respondent (A or U) or researcher (R).

Source: Miles, M. B., & Huberman, A. M. (1994). *Qualitative data analysis: An expanded sourcebook* (2nd ed.). Thousand Oaks, CA: Sage Publications.

Content-Analytic Summary Table

Description

A content-analytic summary table is a matrix display that batches or brings together all related and pertinent data from multiple cases into a single form for initial or exploratory analysis. Each cell of the matrix specifies the dimensions you are interested in (see Display 6.20).

Applications

One of the first tasks in moving from a single-case to a cross-case analysis is determining how many cases share similar characteristics. Quite simply, you take the original matrix used for the single cases and generate a meta-matrix that contains all of the condensed data. When the same characteristic appears in more than one case, this can be noted numerically next to the characteristic (e.g., "Shift in student input (5)" means that this observation occurred at five different sites).

Sometimes you may want to focus primarily on the *content* of your observations entered in a meta-matrix, without reference to which specific cases it came from. This sort of data entry deliberately drops the case identification of data to see the main trends across the cases. The aim is to be more conceptual rather than site specific.

For initial descriptive matrices, which are often large and complex because of the need to "get it all in," use content-analytic summary tables to clarify your understanding. Then, check back with the larger matrix to make sure you have not oversimplified or distorted your conclusions.

Example

Display 6.20 is an example of a content-analytic summary table from the school improvement study. We (Miles and Huberman) wanted to document two types of changes we observed: (1) transitory and (2) durable. We subdivided each type of change

Display 6.20

Content-Analytic Summary Table: The Content of Organization Changes

Type of Change	Transitory Changes		Durable Changes	
	Within the Innovation	**In the Organization**	**Within the Innovation**	**In the Organization**
Structural	Addition of project directors Evolving departments Creation and dropping of advisory committee	Change in locus of control, funding, and supervision	Shift in student input (5) Reorganization: more department interdependence Advisory committee Team teaching	Innovation itself (5): remedial lab, alt. school work experience program, English curriculum, accountability system None (5) Scheduling (4) Expansion of innovation to new users (3) Space for program (2) Creation of coordinator role Creation of management committee Creation of in-service committee Summer-school version of program added Increased team teaching Creation of helping teacher role
Procedural	Active, coercive student recruiting Leadership providing support (emotional, material) Leader "consultation" with teachers Non-users help users with testing Aides, parents help with instruction Increased community contact	Innovation lapsed, is discontinued Field testing of materials Teachers exchange books Other instruction displaced	Tighter supervision, control (2) Student "batching" Routinization of forms/procedures Charismatic leader more distant Fewer staff meetings Reduced student time in program Staff reassignment Selective use of materials	Innovation itself (5): pupil screening, referral/intake, teaming, pullout procedures More paperwork (2) Added student transportation (2) Teacher load reduction Freeing time: substitutes, early dismissal Dropping letter grades More coordination among teachers More teacher discussion of individual students Loss of teacher control over student assignment
Climate	Conflict (4): in teams between users, users-aides, departments More cohesiveness (2), pioneer spirit, esprit User resentment (2) Tension, fear, mistrust	User-non-user conflict (2) User resentment of remedial lab Ambiguity about management committee Expectations for more upward influence, violated, lower morale Resistance by principals, then support	Discouragement, burnout, loss of interest (3) Collaborative, help-giving climate (2) Cohesiveness (2) Less cohesiveness Overload Development of friendships/enmities	Resentment re. paperwork (2) Wariness about innovation More openness to innovation Norm change: flexibility, colleague-ship, el.-sec. interaction None: climate still good None: climate still bad More administrative awareness of the innovation

*Each item represents a change occurring at one site. Changes occurring in more than one site have numbers appended.

Source: Miles, M. B., & Huberman, A. M. (1994). *Qualitative data analysis: An expanded sourcebook* (2nd ed.). Thousand Oaks, CA: Sage Publications.

further into two more forms: (1) those seen within the innovation itself and (2) those observed in the organization as a whole.

Again, we subdivided our observations of transitory and durable changes even further into three types of change: (1) structural, (2) procedural, and (3) climate (referring to the social and emotional dynamics of the participants). Each cell contains relevant characteristics we observed at various school sites that were documented in our team's field notes.

Analysis

You can see at a glance the multiple-case activity in any one of the cells by noting the numbers in parentheses. You can also tell how many kinds of organizational changes are within any one type by noting the number of entries in a cell.

For example, "transitory changes in structure" within the innovation (upper-left cell) are not frequent and occur in no more than one case, while "transitory climate changes within the innovation" (two cells down) are more diverse and show recurrence across several cases (tactics: **making contrasts**, **comparisons**; **counting**).

But the picture is somewhat different for durable changes. It looks as if "durable changes in the organization" (upper cell at far right) are numerous and occurred at multiple sites. A simple eyeballing of the matrix suggests that there are many more durable than transitory changes.

This initial, exploratory assemblage of data helps you understand the structure of the data across all cases at a single glance. It suggests which characteristics, variables, interrelationships, and/or trends may be interesting for analytic follow-up.

Notes

You may, of course, attach initials or a code of some type to each data bit in the matrix that identifies the specific case or site it came from. This will allow you to track or get back to a particular case if you wish for reference and follow-up.

Contrast Table

Description

A contrast table deliberately brings together a range of representative extremes, exemplars, and/or outliers from cases into one table to explore selected variables of interest among them (see Display 6.21).

Applications

When you're trying to understand the meaning of a general variable, perhaps an important outcome for a study, and how it plays itself out across different cases, the contrast table is a useful exploratory device. It enables you to scan just a few of what may be many cases by examining a sample of the extreme ranges. Sometimes, juxtaposing the positive with the negative, or the excelling with the failing, generates analytic insights not possible from seeing a variable range or continuum of cases.

Display 6.21

Contrast Table: Exemplary Cases Showing Different Degrees of User Change

Aspects of User Change	Masepa: High Change	Burton: Low Change	Dun Hollow: Negative Change
1. Start-up discrepancy from usual practice	High discrepancy	Low discrepancy	Moderate discrepancy
2. Pervasiveness of change	High—all facets	Low—repertoire only	Low/moderate— routines and attitudes
3. Technical mastery	Slow in coming	Rapid	Slow, then rapid
4. Energy investment	Very high	Low	High, then low
5. Negative changes reported	Some	None	Many
6. Stretched— pushed beyond voluntary change	Yes—well beyond	No	Yes—at the start

Source: Miles, M. B., & Huberman, A. M. (1994). *Qualitative data analysis: An expanded sourcebook* (2nd ed.). Thousand Oaks, CA: Sage Publications.

It is important to note that you have to read through all or most cases before you know which cases are "exemplars." This process also helps you locate their attributes.

Example

Display 6.21 shows three school sites whose program changes were assessed as high, low, and negative—three extremes. These three contrasting schools are then examined for their "aspects of user change," such as technical mastery, energy investment, and so on, also researcher assessed through appropriate magnitude codes such as high, slow, rapid, high then low, and so on.

Analysis

The analyst tried to unpack the idea of how users changed as a result of trying out an innovation, choosing three representative cases and pulling out six relevant aspects of user change that he had noticed in reading case reports. The exercise aids conceptualization of what user change is composed of and how it works. For example, it looks as if the negative case, Dun Hollow, was originally more like the Masepa high-change case, and then it regressed.

Scanning the table confirms that, for the most part, magnitude codes applied to aspects of user change harmonize with and corroborate the major classification of the three sites' change as high, low, and negative. In other words, the six aspects of user change "add up" well to support the overall researcher assessment of school program change.

Contrast tables often point toward useful variables for a predictor-outcome matrix (see Chapter 10). For example, in Display 6.21, the high pervasiveness of change might be causing high amounts of user change. A new matrix configuration may confirm this.

Notes

The contrast table brings together a selected and extreme range of multiple cases for exploratory analysis. Do not rely solely on this sample as representative of other comparable cases in your study.

Two-Variable Case-Ordered Matrix

Description

A two-variable case-ordered matrix generally orders cases carefully by rows on a well-known variable, then by columns that can include several aspects of a less well-known variable(s) to explore possible interrelationships (see Display 6.22).

Applications

There are times when one portion of a research puzzle has been completed but another portion still remains a mystery. Or there are times when several cases have been initially grouped together according to some commonality but now need further analysis to see if even more commonalities exist among and between them. A two-variable case-ordered matrix can help with these two particular research needs. This method is also very useful in studying the possible interrelationships between two variables, but where the direction of causation is unknown or ambiguous.

Example

Display 6.22 illustrates 12 school cases that have been vertically classified by row according to researcher-perceived practice stabilization, ranging from high to moderate-high to moderate to low. The rows include the variable that was already investigated and "set"; the columns reflect the variables yet to be explored.

Columns 2 and 3 include additional magnitude codes (positive, mixed, high, uncertain, etc.) attributed to the cases, with Column 4 listing primary factors that may contribute to the school's likelihood of program continuance. The analyst wanted to know how "users' attitudes" and the "likelihood of continued use" may interrelate with the "prime factors."

Analysis

This display proved very rich. The analyst scanned the matrix and developed the following excerpted assertions and propositions based on tactical observations:

Were the stabilized sites more likely to continue than the poorly stabilized ones? Yes, at the extremes, but not at all in the middle range (tactic: **noting relations between variables**).

Column 2 tells us that in 7 of the 12 cases, users wanted—mostly or unequivocally—to continue (tactic: **counting**). But at only 4 of these sites were their wishes likely to be fulfilled. So positive user attitudes may enhance but do not deliver,

Display 6.22

Two-Variable Case-Ordered Matrix: Relationships Between User Practice Stabilization and Local Continuation

Extent of practice stabilization/ Cases	1. End of project year	2. Users' attitudes to continuation*	3. Likelihood of continued use* (Same level or better)	4. Prime factors contributing to high/ low likelihood of continuation
High Stabilization				
ASTORIA (E)	1	Positive	High	Project mandated Heavy local transformation for good fit
TINDALE (L)	3	Mostly positive	High	Local mandate well enforced Procedures codified User satisfaction
Moderate-High Stabilization				
CALSTON (E)	2	Mixed*	Low	Budget crisis-staff cuts, reassignments
PERRY-PARKDALE (E)	3	Mostly positive	Uncertain	Staff turnover Uncertain funding
LIDO (E)	4	Mixed+	Uncertain	Lower administrative support Lower priority (new facility now available) Users' discouragement
Moderate Stabilization				
BURTON (E)	1	Positive	High	Parts of project written into curriculum Heavy local transformation, good user fit
BANESTOWN (E)	2	Positive	Uncertain	Budget crisis Staff reduced, reassigned
MASEPA (E)	3	Mixed	High	Project mandated Strong logistical support Improved pupil performance
CARSON (L)	3	Mostly positive	High	Procedures codified, routinized Project mandated Widespread local support
PLUMMET (L)	4	Positive	Uncertain	Likely staff turnover Lower district support
Low Stabilization				
DUN HOLLOW (L)	3	Negative	Low	User + principal dissatisfaction No strong local advocate
PROVILLE (L)	4	Negative	Nil	Other central office priorities; no advocate Project discontinued User and principal dissatisfaction

*Researcher assessment, usually pooled from interview data and case report tables

+Some wanting to continue, others not

(E) = externally developed innovation

(L) = locally developed innovation

Source: Miles, M. B., & Huberman, A. M. (1994). *Qualitative data analysis: An expanded sourcebook* (2nd ed.). Thousand Oaks, CA: Sage Publications.

a high likelihood of continuation (tactic: **noting relations between variables**). On the other hand, users *not* liking the innovation look like a slightly better predictor. Still, it seems that teacher preferences are not decisive, at least when it comes to ensuring continued use at a site.

In the meatiest column, 4, the prime factors are listed in roughly estimated order of magnitude. They come directly from users' responses, pooled. Looking at *uncertain* continuation sites, it seems that we can expect less continuation when most of the people doing it or administering it do not like it, when other key actors do not support it, or when there is heavy external turbulence. If we look for one overarching contributor, it would clearly be lack of sustained *administrator support*, as seen explicitly, and through the medium of budget cuts (tactic: **factoring**).

At the five sites where continuation was highly likely, there was also explicit evidence of administrative support: administrative fiat and administrative codification. . . . So we have direct or inferred user and administrative endorsement *together* with administrative fiat—an unbeatable combination of muscle and commitment (tactics: **using extreme cases**, **noting relations between variables**).

As part of the exploratory process, this analysis also suggested some next steps: a need to unpack the various causes of stabilization more clearly and to analyze the dynamics of the institutionalization process—the next issue beyond simple "continuation."

Notes

The cut-and-paste functions of software enable you to easily explore various orders and configurations of rows and columns. If something does not strike you analytically after reviewing your initial two-variable case-ordered matrix, try a different configuration of rows or columns to see if the new arrangement generates additional connections and insights.

Exploring Reports in Progress

The *pre-structured case* is a template for successive drafts of a report. *Sequential analyses* show how successive studies build on previous ones to develop cumulative findings.

Pre-structured Case

Description

Assuming that the researcher has established an explicit conceptual framework, a rather precise set of research questions, and a clearly defined sampling plan, the pre-structured case begins with a case outline, developed *before* any data are collected. The outline will later include detailed data displays, as well as the narrative sections accompanying them. The outline is, in effect, a shell for the data to come. Over several rounds of field visits, the researcher fills in successive drafts of the case, revising steadily. The final version of the case is ready shortly after the last field visit (see Display 6.23).

Pre-structured Case Outline: Abbreviated Version

A. Beginning note: case methods and data

    I.   The context:

        a. The school: an overview

        b. The community context

        c. The school district

        d. The state context (SEA and legislature)

        e. The school: a more detailed picture

        f. Preconditions for change

    II. The improvement program as planned: an overview

    III. Why this program

    IV. The story of planning and implementation

        a. Chronology

        b. The process of planning and implementation

        c. The problems

        d. The assistance provided

            1. Sources, types, and adequacy

            2. Why this assistance?

        e. How problems were dealt with

            1. Managing and coping strategies

            2. Why these strategies?

    V. The program implementation effort

        a. Overall program extent and quality

        b. Prospects for the future

        c. Why implementation occurred as it did

    VI. The results

        a. Interim results

        b. Long-term results

    VII. Why these results?

    VIII. Lessions for improving the urban high school

Source: Miles, M. B., & Huberman, A. M. (1994). *Qualitative data analysis: An expanded sourcebook* (2nd ed.). Thousand Oaks, CA: Sage Publications.

Applications

We've alluded often to the problem of data overload in qualitative studies, which is exacerbated by the time required for processing field notes and for coding. In a study where time is limited and research questions are well specified, the pre-structured case is a way to focus and streamline data collection and analyses that are "quick and clean" and will more likely provide trustworthy results. These methods take on more importance in multiple-case studies, where comparability across cases is critical for warranted conclusions.

Example

In a study of reform processes in six urban high schools carried out by a staff of five researchers (Louis & Miles, 1990), the team developed a detailed conceptual framework and a set of 14 detailed research questions, such as the following:

- What barriers, problems, and dilemmas were encountered during planning/initiation and implementation of the school improvement project?

- What management and coping strategies were employed to deal with the barriers/problems/dilemmas?

With the research questions in hand, you can put together a clearly specified outline. Display 6.23 shows an abbreviated form of the one used in the study, with an eye toward a 40-page write-up of the case. A more detailed version was used by all the case researchers; the aim is to "drive the data collection by the anticipated product" (Miles, 1990). That is, the field-worker, knowing what the final write-up has to look like, collects the data needed to fill the shell. Specific data displays (matrices, organization charts, etc.) are also outlined in advance.

Because time normally is limited when this method is used, it helps to do advance planning for within-case sampling. For example, for the study's two research questions above, we wanted a good sample of the following:

- *Key actors*: people in coordinative positions

- *Key events*: meetings where problem solving and coordination occur

- *Core processes*: problems encountered during initiation, as well as early and later implementation, and coping strategies from a wide range of affected roles (teachers, building administrators, and central office personnel)

Given the limited time, it's also useful to plan a sequenced approach to data collection: Which research questions will be focused on during successive visits?

Analysis

With the outline clearly in mind, the researcher begins the first round of data collection. The raw field notes are coded without being transformed into write-ups. The researcher reviews the coded field notes and enters data directly into displays and the writing accompanying the analytic text—that is, the conclusions drawn from the displayed data. There will be instances of missing or unclear data and of unanswered research questions; these provide the targets for the next round of data collection. Early versions of the case outline can be limited to descriptive material, "reflective remarks," and a subsection on "puzzles and unanswered questions" in each chapter of the case.

This procedure is iterated until data collection and the completed case are done. Thus, the processes of data collection, analysis, and report writing are collapsed into one evolving procedure. With some experience, the researcher has a constant sense of being on top of the data and remains open to checking and extending the findings. Feedback from the study participants can be sought and incorporated along the way to verify and revise preliminary conclusions.

Display 6.24 shows how this analytic sequence differs from a more traditional one. Both are iterative, but the fieldwork in the pre-structured case is driven by the outline, as well as the emerging conclusions, and the report draft itself.

But Display 6.24 also points to a major weakness: Coding is done directly from field notes, not from a "public" write-up, and is much less subject to critique and refinement. So the method should *not* be used by inexperienced field-workers or by

Display 6.24

Traditional Analysis Sequence Compared With Pre-structured Case

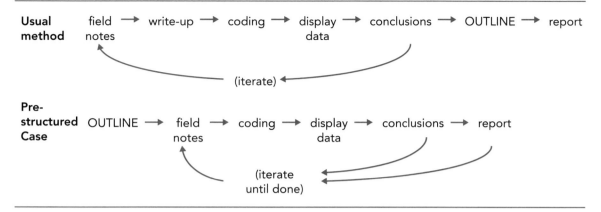

Source: Miles, M. B., & Huberman, A. M. (1994). *Qualitative data analysis: An expanded sourcebook* (2nd ed.). Thousand Oaks, CA: Sage Publications.

those unfamiliar with the type of setting being studied. Nor should it be used if the conceptual framework and research questions are not well spelled out. "In short, as with most things that matter, to do a pre-structured case *well*, you have to know what you are doing" (Miles, 1990, p. 48).

Notes

The pre-structured case method leans the researcher toward early—maybe too early—conclusion drawing. This tendency makes tunnel vision and undetected bias more likely. Even with experienced, knowledgeable researchers, we advise corrective tactics such as the following: (a) case development by a pair of researchers to ward off potential difficulties discussed above; (b) ensuring wide data sampling from a range of participants and settings; (c) **triangulating** (see Chapter 11) with different data collection methods, theories, or respondents; and—above all—(d) using colleagues to see whether different conclusions can be derived from your displays and write-ups.

Sequential Analyses
Description

A sequential analysis is not necessarily a specific set of methods or something that can be displayed but an intentional iteration of additional data collection and *reanalysis* to ensure a more robust set of findings and/or to build on the first cycle of interim findings for future research. Each wave of data collection leads to progressively more molar clustering and analysis.

Applications

A single interim analysis is rarely "enough." The first interim analysis should not only point to improved data collection but also lead to successively deeper, fuller waves of analysis by swinging back to coding, memoing, and assertion and proposition development as more detailed, better quality data become available and your cognitive map of the case gets richer and more powerful.

It's easy to fall into the trap of premature closure, a feeling of "rightness" that is grounded falsely—especially because early data collection is usually partial, flawed, and simplistic in some important respects. Basically, a good interim analysis is one that helps us reorient our view of the case. And any interim analysis should be the first of several. Their strength is their exploratory, summarizing, and sense-making character. Their potential weaknesses are superficiality, premature closure, and faulty data. These weaknesses may be avoided through intelligent critique from skeptical colleagues, feeding back into subsequent waves of data collection.

Example

McVea (2001) and a team of research colleagues conducted a series of separate qualitative studies from 1997 to 2001 that examined adolescent tobacco use. Each annual study not only informed but also provided additional research questions for the next year's project. Their first exploratory study investigated teenage smoking at one particular high school site. McVea reported that "despite the presence of written tobacco policies, the high school was not a 'safe haven' from smoking pressures. . . . The results from our first study raised an interesting question: Why didn't schools enforce their no smoking policies?" The research team's next annual project explored that question.

Analysis

McVea and colleagues' (2001) second study was driven by the most puzzling observation generated from the first study's fieldwork: Why didn't schools enforce their no smoking policies? The team interviewed adolescents and adults and reported,

> We discovered that administrators found rules difficult to enforce because of the large number of smokers, and the significant resources required to police their behavior. Teachers were concerned that driving students off campus to smoke caused them to miss class, and they feared punitive penalties caused more harm than tobacco use. Students interpreted the lack of enforcement as evidence that the faculty "didn't care" about smoking. Smoking students even commented about how the ability to smoke at school with friends contributed to their habit.

Armed with these findings, the third and next set of annual studies explored how smoking cessation programs could be implemented with teenagers. The research team discovered that peer relationships and influence play a strong role in whether an adolescent could or would stop smoking. Each year's study informed the next and enabled richer analyses and evaluation, plus constructive strategies for positive action and outcomes.

The example above was a broad brushstroke case of sequential analysis. As another and more specific example, a Belgian study of primary health care (Schillemans et al., n.d.) focused on the treatment of victims of incest. The researchers began with a group of 10 to 15 medical practitioners, meeting in a weekly "exploration group" for 2 years. Here are their successive analytic steps:

- Review the material from the first patient case (videotapes, documents, notes).
- Generate a first batch of codes from the case review, such as "fear of the dark," "speech difficulties," and "aversion to sexuality."

- Add more clinical codes from the specialized literature, such as "boundary between man and woman" and "violence."

- Examine further cases, and develop more codes through analytic induction.

- Develop a key hypothesis (e.g., that incest victims have weakly developed boundaries).

- Verify the hypothesis through interviews with several patients from the original set.

- Integrate these findings with the existing empirical and conceptual literature (e.g., on dissociated personalities).

- Extend the findings to a new sample (screening new cases for instances of incest) and a new analytic cycle.

Each step was a funnel for gathering more data on fewer, but progressively more vital, dimensions in the data set.

Overall, sequential analyses add value to the cumulative and final written product. The procedure lends more confidence to the researcher's findings in progress and provides dimensionality to the data corpus, thus better guaranteeing a richer analysis of details, nuances, and complexities.

Notes

See "Elaborative Coding" and "Longitudinal Coding" in Saldaña (2013) for additional methods of how sequential studies build on previous ones and inform the next series.

Closure and Transition

These exploratory methods are offered as initial ways of documenting and reassembling salient data into various display formats for the emergent enterprise that is qualitative inquiry. These methods alone, with a little bit of fine-tuning on your part, may even suffice for your particular research goals. They are offered as "first draft" heuristics for extracting what is important, for synthesizing and summarizing the most important details, for laying the groundwork for more in-depth analyses, and for reorganizing data to construct meaningful patterns from them.

The next chapter will present displays that more firmly rather than provisionally document the data. They are intended to provide, like this chapter, foundations for richer analysis, such as ordering, explaining, and predicting.

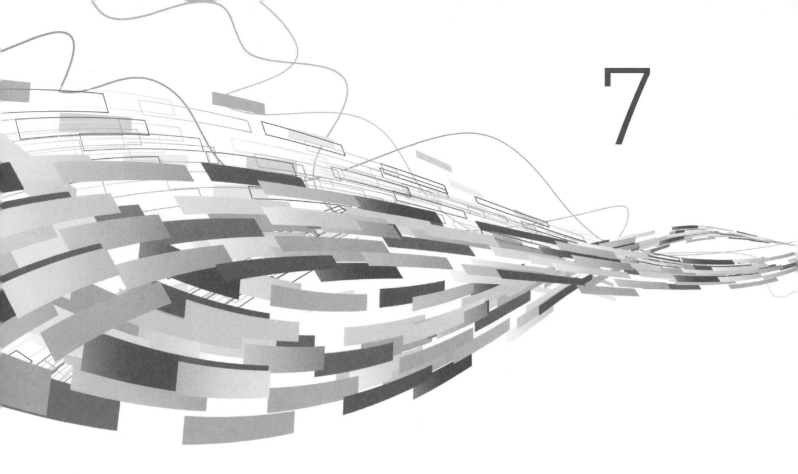

Methods of Describing

Chapter Summary

This chapter illustrates methods for organizing condensed qualitative data, from highly systematic to artistically rendered ways, for purposes of descriptive documentation. The descriptive profiles focus on describing participants, variability, and social action.

Contents

Introduction
Describing Participants
    Role-Ordered Matrix
    Context Chart
Describing Variability
    Construct Table
    Conceptually Clustered Matrix
    Folk Taxonomy
Describing Action
    Vignettes
    Poetic Display
    Cognitive Maps
Closure and Transition

Introduction

Wolcott (1994) advocates that *description* is qualitative representation that helps the reader see what you saw and hear what you heard. A solid, descriptive foundation of your data enables higher level analysis and interpretation. Usually, it is hard to explain the "hows" and "whys" of something satisfactorily until you understand just *what* that something is.

You begin with a text, trying out codes on it, then moving to identify patterns, categories, or themes, and then to testing hunches and findings, aiming first to delineate the "deep structure" and then to integrate the data into an explanatory framework. In this sense, we can speak of data transformation as information that is condensed, clustered, sorted, and linked over time. The researcher typically moves through a series of analysis episodes that condense more and more data into a more and more coherent understanding of *what*—building a solid foundation for later analyzing *how* and *why* (Wolcott, 1994).

Describing Participants looks at the relationship dynamics of the people you study. *Describing Variability* charts the spectrum and landscape of what we're finding in the field. And *Describing Action* documents the experiences and processes of our participants from systematic to artistically rendered ways.

Describing Participants

The *role-ordered matrix* charts the essential characteristics relevant to the study of the various participants. A *context chart* illustrates the hierarchies and interrelationships within, between, and among the participants.

Role-Ordered Matrix

Description

A role-ordered matrix sorts data in its rows and columns that have been gathered from or about a certain set of "role occupants"—data reflecting their views. The display systematically permits comparisons across roles on issues of interest to a study and tests whether people in the same role see issues in comparable ways (see Display 7.1).

Applications

People who live in groups and organizations, like most of us, and social scientists who study groups and organizations know that how you see life depends, in part, on your role. A *role* is a complex amalgam of expectations and actions that make up what you do, and should do, as a certain type of actor in a setting—a family, a classroom, a committee, a hospital, a police department, or a multinational corporation.

A role-ordered matrix groups, summarizes, and compares different people's role perceptions about selected topics or issues that enable the researcher to compare and contrast those perceptions. For example, mothers tend to see the world differently than fathers. Bosses tend not to see the frustrations faced by workers, partly because they are distant from them and partly because subordinates often censor the bad news when reporting upward. A teacher's high-speed interactions with several hundred children over the course of a day have a very different cast to them from the principal's diverse transactions with parents, vendors, secretaries, central office administrators, and other teachers. We each experience the world differently, and a role-ordered matrix is just one way of documenting those varied experiences.

Example

We (Miles and Huberman) draw on our school improvement study for an example. The innovation involved is an intensive remedial program, implemented in a high school, emphasizing reading in the subjects of English, science, and math. The question of interest is "How do people react to an innovation when they first encounter it?" This general question can be unbundled into several subquestions, such as the following:

- Which aspects of the innovation are salient and stand out in people's minds?

- How do people size up the innovation in relation to its eventual implementation?

- What changes—at the classroom or organizational level—do people think the innovation will require?

- How good a fit is the innovation to people's previous classroom styles or to previous organizational working arrangements?

Keeping in mind that we want to see answers to these questions broken out by different roles, we can consider which roles—for example, teachers, department chairs, principals, central office personnel—could be expected to attend to the innovation and could provide meaningful reactions to it. The matrix rows could be roles, but if we want to make within-role comparisons, the rows should probably be *persons* and clustered into *role domains*. It might be good, too, to order the roles according to how far they are from the actual locus of the innovation—from teachers to central office administrators. The columns can be devoted to the research subquestions. Display 7.1 shows how this approach looks.

The researcher searches through coded write-ups for relevant data, and the data entered in each cell are a brief summary of what the analyst found for each respondent. The main decision rule was as follows: If it's in the notes, and not internally contradicted, summarize it and enter a phrase reflecting the summary. There are also "DK" ("don't know") entries, where data are missing because the relevant question was never asked of that person, was asked but not answered, or was answered ambiguously.

Analysis

Now, we can begin looking down the columns of the matrix, both within and across roles, to see what is happening. Scanning the first two columns (Salient Characteristics and Size Up) shows us that many teachers—notably in English—see the new remedial program as *prescriptive*, with little latitude given for adaptation (tactics: **counting** and **making comparisons**). And the teachers who see the innovation as prescriptive are also those who have used it the longest, suggesting that prescriptiveness was highest when the program was first introduced (tactic: **noting relations between variables**). A number of teachers also mention *complexity* (but note that first-year users are more likely to see the program as simple and easy to use, suggesting program stabilization).

Display 7.1

Role-Ordered Matrix: First Reactions to the Innovation

TEACHERS	Salient Characteristics	Size Up	Anticipated Classroom or Organizational Changes @	Fit With Previous Style or Organizational Setting @@
+ REILLY 4th year	Highly structured	Little latitude	DK-1	DK-3
+ KENNEDY 4th year	Frightening format Overload of objectives Reams of handouts	Difficult, complicated No latitude	Teaming (loss of independence) No Scope Magazine use	Poor; user felt she would be locked into structure and others' schedules
+ FARR 1st year	Skill-oriented, organized Activities well planned Pre- & post testing good	Simple, clear Easy to use & understand	Less freedom to change direction	Fairly good; user views self as structured, organized
+ ROGERS 2nd year	Prescriptive Rigid	Confusing Simplistic content	Working with basic students for 1st time	Composition assignments fit well; grammar, etc. simple-minded
+ FLEMING 4th year	Prescriptive Use of media Teaming Heavy monitoring	Many materials Very complex, not quite clear	Working w/ other Ts Mastering all materials	DK-2
* BENNING 1st year	Objectives too broad Good content	Similar to prev. school's program, easy to use	Break down objectives Add games, activities Give objectives to kids	Close fit, when anticipated changes made
* THATCHER 2nd year	(wrote science curriculum) Skill-oriented Reading emphasis	Too detailed	DK-1	Fair; reading was new; fewer labs
# WOJICK 1st year	Variety of modes (workbooks, worksheets, computer terminals)	Easy to use; level & format right	DK-1	DK-2
# MUSKIE 2nd year	Computer terminals Short worksheets	1st 1/2 flawed; 2nd 1/2 on target Good variety	DK-1	DK-1

		Salient Characteristics	Size Up	Anticipated Classroom or Organizational Changes @	Fit With Previous Style or Organizational Setting @@
DEPT. CHAIRS	VAN RUNKEL Science Chrmn	Science content revision Reading reinforcement Flexibility in activities	Questioned content reorg'n would it fit together?	None—same teachers, using new curriculum	Good fit: Program replaced old curriculum
	MANNHOELLER English Chrmn	Orderly curriculum w/ horizontal, vertical org'n Reinforcement of 3 strands	Concept is right Depends on being used as it's set up	DK-1	Good fit: Program designed in part to fill basic English course slot
PRINCIPAL	MCCARTHY Tindale East	DK-2	DK-2	DK-2	Good fit: Order is maintained; no special requirements
CENTRAL OFFICE	CROWDEN Dir of Curriculum	3 strands of level I Sequential, comprehensive Reinforcement	Works if followed Any teacher can use successfully	None—program designed to fit structure	Close fit: same staff, teachers wrote curriculum, same auth. structure
	MANN Superintendent	DK-2	DK-2	DK-1	Good fit: Program is a successful curriculum revision effort in district

+ = English teacher
* = science teacher
# = math teacher
DK = Don't know
DK-1 = question not asked of informant
DK-2 = asked, but not answered (strayed from question, didn't know answer)
DK-3 = ambiguous answer
@ Classroom changes question asked of teachers; organizational one asked of others.
@@ Personal style fit question asked of teachers; organizational fit question asked of others.

Source: Miles, M. B., & Huberman, A. M. (1994). Qualitative data analysis: An expanded sourcebook (2nd ed.). Thousand Oaks, CA: Sage Publications.

When we drop down to department chairs and central office administrators, the picture is somewhat different. They are more likely to take the "big picture" view, emphasizing the "curriculum," "strands," and the like. Although they too emphasize prescriptiveness ("Depends on being used as it's set up" or "Works if followed"), they either do not give clear answers on the issue of complexity or (as in the case of the curriculum director, a major advocate of the program) say that "any teacher can use [it] successfully." But teachers, faced with an initially demanding, rigid program, are not so sure, it seems (tactic: **making comparisons**).

Moving to the third column (Anticipated Classroom or Organizational Changes) of Display 7.1, we can see role–perspective differences. Two teachers mention teaming as an anticipated change, one that curtailed their freedom and made them accountable to peers' schedules and working styles. Administrators, the field notes showed, considered the teaming necessary to implement the program's several strands and as a way of helping weaker teachers do better through learning from stronger ones. Even so, they do not consider it a salient change, saying either that no organizational changes are required ("The program is designed to fit the structure") or that they do not know whether organizational changes were anticipated.

Finally, if we continue the **making comparisons** tactic, the fourth column (Fit With Previous Style or Organizational Setting) shows a range of "personal fit" for different teachers, depending on their views of the content, their own styles, and the organizational issues involved. The administrators, however, uniformly emphasize good fit at the organizational level, stressing the appropriateness of the curriculum and its fit into the existing structure; the director also invokes the fact that teachers wrote it.

In short, a matrix of this sort lets us see how perspectives differ according *to the role*, as well as *within a role*. In this case, users from the English department who came in at the onset of the program had an initially tougher time than later users or math and science users. A within-role analysis, moving across rows, shows that the superintendent, as might be expected, knows very little about the innovation. More surprisingly, the principal does not either. In this case, a recheck with the field notes (tactic: **following up surprises**) told the field-worker that the formal role description for high school principals in this district actually forbids them from making curriculum decisions, which are the province of the curriculum director and department chairs.

We also can apply the tactic of **making if-then tests**. If the director and the chairs have a shared province of work (curriculum decisions), then their views of the innovation should resemble each other more closely than the teachers' views. Looking vertically once again, we can see that department chairs' views are much more like those of central office administrators than those of teachers.

The role-ordered matrix display emphasizes different roles as *sources* of data and perceptions. It is also possible to develop a role-ordered matrix that treats roles as *targets* of others' actions or perceptions. (For example, how are teachers treated *by* department chairs, principals, and central office personnel?)

Clarify the list of roles you consider to be most relevant to the issue at hand; avoid overloading the matrix with roles that are clearly peripheral. Differentiate the matrix by subroles (e.g., teachers of math or science) if relevant. If your case is an individual, role-ordered matrices may well be helpful in showing how role partners view or interact with the person at the center of your case.

Notes

Indicate clearly when data are missing, unclear, or not asked for in the first place. Return to field notes to test emerging conclusions, particularly if the decision rules for data entry involve, as in this case, a good deal of condensation. Role-ordered matrices, because of our prior experience with role differences, can lend themselves to too quick conclusion drawing. Ask for an audit of your analysis from a colleague (see Chapter 11).

Context Chart

Description

A context chart is a network, mapping in graphic form the interrelationships among the roles and groups (and, if appropriate, organizations) that make up the contexts of individual actions (see Display 7.2).

Applications

One problem a qualitative researcher faces is how to map the social contexts of individual actions economically and reasonably accurately—without getting overwhelmed with detail. A context chart is one way to accomplish these goals. Context charts work particularly well when your case is an individual—they show you the real richness of a person's life setting.

Most qualitative researchers believe that a person's actions have to be understood in their specific contexts and that contexts cannot be ignored or held constant. Contexts can be seen as immediately relevant aspects of the situation (where the person is physically, who else is involved, what the recent history of the contact is, etc.), as well as the relevant aspects of the social system in which the person appears (a classroom, a school, a department, a company, a family, a hospital ward, or a local community). Focusing solely on individual actions without attending to their contexts runs the risk of misunderstanding the meanings of events. Contexts drive the way we understand those meanings, or, as Mishler (1979) notes, meaning is always within context, and contexts incorporate meaning.

Most people do their daily work in organizations: They have superiors, peers, and subordinates; their work is defined in a role-specialized way; and they have different relationships with different people in other roles in their social vicinity. But you are not simply drawing a standard organizational chart; you are mapping salient properties of the context. Also, your chart will not be exhaustive or complete. It is a collection of organizational fragments or excerpts. (In Display 7.2, e.g., custodians, secretaries, and the immediate subordinates of most of the school district office personnel are excluded.) Context charts also can be drawn for people in families or in informal groups or communities.

Example

Networks ought to reflect the core characteristics of organizations: authority/hierarchy and division of labor. So it ought to show who has formal authority over whom and what the role names are. But those things don't tell us very much. We should also know about the *quality* of the working *relationships* between people in different roles.

Context Chart for Tindale East High School and District

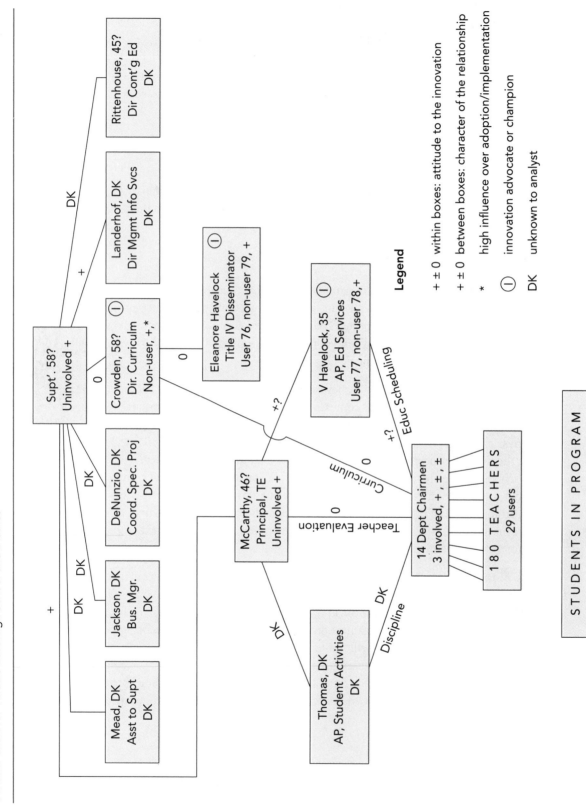

STUDENTS IN PROGRAM

Legend

+ ± 0   within boxes: attitude to the innovation

+ ± 0   between boxes: character of the relationship

*   high influence over adoption/implementation

Ⓘ   innovation advocate or champion

DK   unknown to analyst

Source: Miles, M. B., & Huberman, A. M. (1994). *Qualitative data analysis: An expanded sourcebook* (2nd ed.). Thousand Oaks, CA: Sage Publications.

Suppose you were interested, as we were, in organizations called schools and school districts—and with the general problem of how innovations enter and are implemented in those organizations. The display should show us who advocated the innovation, who is actually using the innovation, and people's attitudes toward it (whether or not they are using it). The display should show us how the specific school we are studying is embedded in the larger district organization. Above all, we need a display that will not overload us with information but will give us a clear, relevantly simplified version of the immediate social environment.

Display 7.2 shows how these requirements were met after a field-worker made a first visit to Tindale East, a high school involved in implementing a new reading program. The analyst selected out the roles and groups that are most critical for understanding the context. District office roles are above, school roles below. The network is thus partially ordered by roles and by authority level.

For each individual, we have a name, the age (a feature the analyst thought was important in understanding working relationships and career aspirations), a job title, whether the individual was a user of the innovation or not, and whether his or her attitude toward the innovation was represented through magnitude codes:

+ = positive

± = ambivalent

0 = neutral

Special symbols (such as *) are applied when the individual was an innovation advocate or influenced implementation strongly. The relationships between individuals are also characterized (positive, ambivalent, and neutral). Once past the upper echelons, the display simply counts individuals without giving detail (a secondary context chart at the level of individual teachers was also developed but is not shown here).

To get the data, the analyst consults field notes and available organization charts and documents. The decision rules look like this:

- For information such as job title, number of persons, and so on, assume accuracy for the moment, and enter it.

- A relationship rating (how X gets along with Y) should not be discounted by the other party to the relationship, though it need not be directly confirmed.

- The "innovation advocate" and "high influence" ratings should be given only if there is at least one confirmation and no disconfirmations.

- If there is ambiguous or unknown information, enter "DK."

Analysis

After a context chart has been constructed, the researcher reviews the hierarchies, flows, and magnitudes entered, in combination with the field notes, to develop an analytic memo or narrative that tells the relationship story thus far. An analytic excerpt about Display 7.2 reads as follows:

Looking at lines of authority, we can see that only one central office person (Crowden) has direct authority over department chairs as they work on the innovation. Crowden is not only an advocate but also has high influence over implementation, and seems to have a license from the superintendent to do this.

The department chairs, it appears, have three other "masters," depending on the immediate issue involved (discipline, teacher evaluation, scheduling). Because, in this case, the innovation does involve scheduling problems, it's of interest that V. Havelock is not only an advocate, but has actually used the innovation and is positive toward it. We might draw the inference that Crowden serves as a general pusher, using central office authority, and V. Havelock aids directly with implementation issues; the field notes support this.

Note, too, that Principal McCarthy (a) is not accountable to the superintendent for curriculum issues and (b) has a good relationship with V. Havelock. Perhaps McCarthy gets his main information about the innovation from Havelock and thus judges it positively.

So the chart shown in Display 7.2 helps us place the actions of individuals (e.g., Crowden, V. Havelock) in context to understand their meaning. For example, when Crowden, discussing the innovation, says, "It is not to be violated; its implementation is not based on the whim of a teacher at any moment in class, and its success is not dependent on charismatic teachers," the chart helps us understand that this prescriptive stance is backed up with direct authority over department chairs for curriculum issues—an authority that is accepted neutrally. In short, the analyst has been employing the tactic of **seeing patterns or themes**, as well as **subsuming particulars into the general** (see Chapter 11 for more on these tactics).

The symbols employed for Display 7.2 were Miles and Huberman's original magnitude codes, but you are not bound to using them. Context charts can employ other visual devices to enhance analysis. For example, dashed lines can be used to show informal influence, while thick lines suggest strong influence. Font size can be used to represent power relationships—for example, the names in a larger or bolded font have more authority than the names in a smaller font. Circles can be drawn enclosing informal groups and subcultures. Linkages to other affecting organizations in the environment can be added. Physical contexts (e.g., a classroom, the teacher's desk, resource files, student tables and chairs, and entrances) can be mapped to help understand the ebb and flow of events in a setting. And for an organizational context that seems to change a lot over a short time, revised context charts can be drawn for comparison across time.

Notes

Use context charts early during fieldwork to summarize your first understandings and to locate questions for next-step data collection. Keep the study's main research questions in mind, and design the context chart to display the information most relevant to them. If you're new to qualitative research, keep your first context charts simple. They can be embroidered as you continue the fieldwork.

Describing Variability

A *construct table* shows the variability or range of a central construct in a study. A *conceptually clustered matrix* charts participants' varying perspectives about selected concepts. And a *folk taxonomy* systematically charts the unique ways in which participants organize and categorize their worlds.

Construct Table

Description

A construct table includes data that highlight the variable properties and/or dimensions of one key construct (or concept, variable, category, etc.) of interest from a study (see Display 7.3).

Applications

Construct tables are particularly valuable for qualitative surveys, grounded theory, and phenomenological studies since they enable an analyst to focus on one core item of interest (a construct, concept, variable, core category, phenomenon, etc.). Traditional

Display 7.3

Lifelong Impact: Variability of Influence

Lifelong Impact	Supporting Respondent Quotes	Gender	Class of	Occupation
none	"It really has not changed my adult life at all."	male	1982	Quality Manager for a Manufacturing Company
little to none	"Although I don't feel like being involved in theatre has changed my life, it definitely changed my high school experience. It was something I worked hard at, enjoyed, and looked forward to."	female	2006	High School English Teacher
some, in combination	"Any career success I've experienced is largely due to the combination of process thinking developed in engineering school and, more significantly, my theatre, speech and debate experience in high school. I learned to communicate effectively, write well, speak clearly and distinctly, engage and hold an audience with pacing, inflection, movement, etc."	female	1984	Global Leader for Distribution and Sales Force Effectiveness [for a major corporation]
high	"My high school speech coach/drama teacher is one of the main influences in my life. She taught me much and helped me grow in ways that I am profoundly grateful for. Were it not for her guidance, I think my life would probably be much different today."	male	1999	Internet Strategy Consultant
very high	"Theatre and speech saved mine and my brother's lives."	male	1999	Hollywood Sound Effects and Dialogue Editor

grounded theory charges the researcher to examine the *dimensions* or variable ranges of a property, and a construct table assembles that variability for analytic reflection.

Although you may have a general idea in advance about the properties and dimensions of some major variable, such as "lifelong impact," such variables do not usually become clear until real case data have been explored in some depth. Cross-case construct tables are an excellent way to bring together and examine a core concept because the way the variable plays out in different contexts illuminates its nature.

Example

McCammon et al. (2012) surveyed 234 adults by e-mail to gather their perceptions of how their participation in high school theatre and speech programming may have influenced and affected their adult life course trajectories. There were certainly influences on careers, since approximately half of the respondents currently worked in the entertainment industries. The other half pursued careers in fields ranging from business to education to health care but still looked back fondly on their high school theatre and speech activities. The vast majority acknowledged a lifelong impact from arts participation during their high school years, yet not everyone testified that the impact was comparable. *Variability* in the amount and quality of lifelong impact was observed, and these needed to be documented and acknowledged for a more credible and trustworthy analysis.

Display 7.3 is a table that includes salient data about the construct *Lifelong Impact*. The variability of the construct is illustrated through five selected respondent quotes, including the participants' genders, graduation years from high school, and current occupations, since these were deemed potentially important variables for later analysis. The researcher-assigned assessments of Lifelong Impact range from "none" ("It really has not changed my adult life at all") to "very high" ("Theatre and speech saved mine and my brother's lives").

Analysis

The construct table is a case study of sorts. It contains representative data about one important element in your study that merits enhanced analysis. The variability of that element challenges the researcher to ponder questions such as the following:

- *Why* does variability exist in these data?
- What specific *conditions* might have influenced the variability?
- In what ways might this variability *influence and affect* other consequences and outcomes?

These questions are particularly important for grounded theory studies.

The following analytic narrative was developed to explain the variability of Lifelong Impact. The final two sentences of the excerpt further down preface the analytic findings to emphasize the *conditionality* of participation in high school speech and theatre programming. The researchers did not want to sweepingly suggest that arts education is a magic bullet for curing social ills and for human development but that meaningful lifelong impact is contingent on several factors, such as an outstanding teacher, challenging classroom content, high expectations of quality, and others:

These five participant responses highlight the *variability* of lifelong impact. The first and second quotes suggest that high school theatre is not necessarily an epiphanic or life-changing experience for everyone, but it can, as the second quote illustrates, function as an important program for adolescent enrichment and engagement. The third quote suggests theatre and/or speech experiences alone, in and of themselves, cannot be solely credited with generating a successful adult career for those who choose nontheatrical professions. The fourth quote suggests that a teacher in the field can have a significant influence on a student during his adolescent development, which may in turn significantly affect his adult life course. And the fifth quote suggests that the art form, guided by a nurturing teacher, can literally and powerfully influence and even save a human life.

We cannot assert that immersed participation in high school theatre or speech programming will benefit everyone to the same degree as they progress through the adult life course. But survey responses collectively suggest a set of *ideal* conditions to maximize the *potential* of lifelong impact. (Adapted from McCammon & Saldaña, 2011, p. 92)

Further analysis revealed that high school graduation year—that is, the respondents' generational cohorts—played a significant role in the way memories were recalled and perceived. Gender and current occupation played a less important role in survey patterns.

Scanning the construct table (and reviewing related portions of the database as needed) enables you to see the range and thus the parameters of your data. This keeps you from constructing too narrow an assertion about your observations and helps you modify your interpretive claims to be more inclusive of the breadth of findings from your data.

Notes

Keep a construct table short and sweet. Its primary goal is to focus on the variability of *one* item of interest in a study through a sample of representative data. See the Role-Ordered Matrix and Conceptually Clustered Matrix displays (in this chapter) for formats that contain much more data for interrelationship analysis.

Conceptually Clustered Matrix

Description

A conceptually clustered matrix has its rows and columns arranged to bring together major roles, research subtopics, variables, concepts, and/or themes together for at-a-glance summative documentation and analysis. Deciding what composes a row and column heading can happen in two ways: (1) *deductively*, the analyst may have some a priori ideas about key concepts, themes, or theories that will be explored in a study or, (2) *inductively*, during early analysis, you may find that participants are giving very similar or vastly different responses to questions or that unexpected variables, concepts, and themes are emerging. The basic principle is conceptual or thematic documentation of data in matrix cells, which may or may not be accompanied by researcher-assigned evaluative descriptors (see Displays 7.4 and 7.5).

Applications

Many studies are designed to answer a lengthy string of research questions. As a result, doing a separate analysis and case report section for each research question is

Display 7.4

Conceptually Clustered Matrix: Motives and Attitudes (Format)

Participants	Research Questions			
	Motives (types)	Career Relevance (none/some)	Centrality (low/mod /high)	Initial Attitudes (fav., neutr., unfav.)
Users U$_1$				
U$_2$, etc.				
Administrators A$_1$				
A$_2$, etc.				

Source: Miles, M. B., & Huberman, A. M. (1994). *Qualitative data analysis: An expanded sourcebook* (2nd ed.). Thousand Oaks, CA: Sage Publications.

likely to tire out and confuse both the analyst and the reader. One solution is to cluster several research questions so that meaning can be generated more easily. Having all of the data in one readily surveyable place helps you move quickly and legitimately to a boiled-down matrix by making sure that all the data fit into a reasonable scheme and that any evaluations or ratings you make are well-founded.

Conceptually clustered matrices are most helpful when some clear concepts or themes have emerged from the initial analysis. They also can be used with less complex cases, such as individuals or small groups.

Example

In our (Miles and Huberman) school improvement study, we had a general question about users' and administrators' **motives** for adopting a new educational practice, and a more specific question about whether these motives were *career centered* (e.g., whether participants thought they could get a promotion or a transfer out of the project). So here we had an a priori idea of a possible relationship between two concepts. Then, during data collection, we saw some inkling of a relationship between the motives questions and two others: (1) a *centrality* question (whether the innovation loomed larger than other tasks in the daily life of a user) and (2) an *attitude* question (whether the participant liked the new practice when first introduced to it). We wondered whether a relationship existed between people's motives and their initial attitudes toward the practice.

The best way to find out would be to *cluster* the responses to these questions. Not only is there a relationship to probe, but there is also a general theme (initial attitudes) and a possibility of handling three research questions and their concepts at the same time.

The conceptually clustered matrix is a format that

- displays all of the relevant responses of all key participants;
- allows an initial comparison between responses and between participants;

- lets us see how the data can be analyzed further (e.g., repartitioned or clustered);

- for multicase studies, lends itself easily to cross-case analysis and will not have to be redone; and

- for multicase studies, provides some preliminary standardization—a set of content-analytic themes that all case analysts will be using.

When you are handling several conceptually or thematically related research questions together, a likely start-up format is a simple participant-by-variable matrix, as shown in Display 7.4. Thus, we have on one page a format that includes all respondents and all responses to the four research questions (i.e., the concepts of interest in this study). Note that we have set up comparisons between different kinds of participants (users and administrators), so it is role ordered as well as conceptually ordered. The format also calls for some preliminary sorting or scaling of the responses: types of motive, career relevant or not, degree of centrality, and valence of initial attitudes.

Next, we go back to coded segments of data keyed to the research questions and their suggested concepts. The analyst notes down the *Motives* given by or attributed to a participant and then tries to put a label on the motive. One participant, for example, gave several motives: She heard how good the new practice was (social influence), her principal was "really sold on it" and "wanted it in" (pressure), most other teachers were using it or planned to—"It's what's coming" (conformity), and using the new practice was an occasion to "keep growing" (self-improvement). At this stage, it is best to leave the start-up labels as they are, without trying to regroup them into fewer headings that cover all participants; this practice gives you more degrees of freedom while still providing a preliminary shaping of the data.

Turning to *Career Relevance*, the second concept, the analyst summarizes in a phrase or sentence the relevance of adopting the practice for each participant. The next task is to look for evidence of the *Centrality* of this new practice for people and what their *Initial Attitudes* seemed to be. For these two columns, the analyst assigns a general rating, backing it with specific quotes. When these data are entered in the matrix, we get something like Display 7.5.

Display 7.5 contains about as many data as a qualitative analyst can handle and a reader can follow. The analyst has ordered participants according to their time of implementation (Early Users, Second Generation, and Recent Users) and their roles (Users and Administrators) and, within the group of users, has included a Nonuser to set up an illustrative contrast between motives for adopting and motives for refusing the new practice.

For cell entries, the analyst reduced the coded chunks to four kinds of entries: (1) labels (e.g., self-improvement), (2) quotations, (3) short summary phrases, and (4) ratings (none/some, low/high, and favorable/unfavorable). The labels and ratings set up comparisons between participants and, if needed, between cases. The quotations supply some grounded meaning for the material; they put some flesh on the rating or label and can be extracted easily for use in the analytic text.

The summary phrases explain or qualify a rating, usually where there are no quotations (as in the Career Relevance column). In general, it's a good idea to add a short

Display 7.5

Conceptually Clustered Matrix: Motives and Attitudes of Users, Nonusers, and Administrators at Masepa

		Motives	Career Relevance	Centrality	Initial Attitudes Toward Program
Early Users	R. Quint	Self-improvement: "To get better. I had to change"…. "Maybe I wasn't teaching the best ways." Pressure: "They wanted us to do it." Social influence: "Everybody was saying what Gail's doing is great."	None—improvement of practice	High: "Biggest thing I've ever done that somebody else told me to do."	Neutral: "There wasn't any appeal. They said it worked so I was going to try it."
	L. Bayeis	Observation: Saw G. Norrist do it and "was impressed." Fit to personal style: "I like structure." Practice improvement: "looking around for a different way to teach reading." Novelty: "you get tired of always doing the same old thing."	Vehicle to turnkey trainer role: also became Title I Coordinator	High: "most important thing I've been involved with."	Favorable
Second Generation	F. Morelly	Social influence: heard from several friends about program Opportunity, effort justification: "I took the training for recertification credit. After all that, I had to follow through." Pressure: "He (Weelling) is the reason we do it here. He's so enthusiastic about it."	None—possibly stabilizing her job at the school	High: "This is the only new thing I've done since I've been out of school…. I had to invest so much."	Neutral, apprehensive
	L. Brent	Social opinion, influence: "I heard how good it was." Pressure: "(Weelling) was really sold on it. They really want it in." Conformity: Most doing it or planning to in the school: "it's what's coming." Self-improvement: occasion to "keep growing."	None, possibly fear	High: "It's been a nightmare."	Unfavorable, once training began
Recent Users	V. Sharpen	Obligation: requirement to obtain teaching post: "I didn't have a choice." Practice-improvement: complementing pre-service training	Ticket to teaching job in the district	High: "My first job"	Neutral, apprehensive

	Motives	Career Relevance	Centrality	Initial Attitudes Toward Program
A. Olkin	Social influence: "heard it was good." . . . "a good friend liked it." Pressure: "strongly encouraged" by Weelling and Dahloff Observation, modeling; saw G. Norrist. "She really impressed me."	None: felt obligated by administration	High: "This was really the big one for me."	Neutral mixed feelings
S. Sorels	Observation: "It was so good for my own kids . . . tremendous change in reading, spelling, work habits."	Ticket to full-time teaching position	High: "This was really a big step for me—a big move...[nothing else] as high as this in my career."	Favorable: "I was excited about it."
Non-User				
C. Shinder	Relative disadvantage: "My program was better." Poor fit with personal style: "too scholastic. too programmed."	None	N/A	Unfavorable
K. Weelling Principal	Met need: "I was looking for a highly structured, skill-oriented reading program." Novelty, promise of practical improvement: intrigued by reading about mastery learning; wanted to see it in operation.	None at first: later, appreciates the visibility	High: "Largest investment I've ever made."	Neutral, then favorable
Administrators				
J. Dahloff Curriculum Coordinator	Relative advantage, face validity of program: "well organized"; could be used for other subject matters. Social influence: "impressed" that outstanding teachers favored the program. Practice improvement: beginning teachers ill-prepared in reading. "We didn't know what to do with them . . . They just had to learn on the job."	Another in a series of implementations	Moderate: "It was one thing among a lot of things I was working on."	Favorable
W. Paisly Asst. Sup't	Social influence: "talked into it" by J. Dahloff	None	Low: "It was no big deal."	Neutral

Source: Miles, M. B., & Huberman, A.M. (1994). Qualitative data analysis: An expanded sourcebook (2nd ed.). Thousand Oaks, CA: Sage Publications.

quote or explanatory phrase beside a label or scale; otherwise, the analyst is tempted to work with general categories that lump together responses that really mean different things (as seen in the "high" responses in the Centrality column). If lumping does happen and you are puzzled about something, the qualifying words are easily at hand for quick reference.

It's important to hold on to the common set of categories, scales, and ratings for each case—even if the empirical fit is poor in one or another of these columns—until the full set of cases can be analyzed.

Analysis

Reading across the rows gives the analyst a thumbnail profile of each participant and provides an initial test of the relationship between responses to the different questions (tactic: **noting relations between variables**). For example, L. Bayeis does have career-relevant motives, sees the practice as very important, and is initially favorable. But R. Quint's entries do not follow that pattern or a contrasting one. We have to look at more rows.

Reading down the columns uses the tactic of **making comparisons** between the Motives of different users and administrators, as well as comparisons between these groups. It also enables similar comparisons between responses to the Career Relevance, Centrality, and Initial Attitudes data.

A scan down the columns of Display 7.5 provides both information and leads for follow-up analyses. The tactic of **making contrasts/comparisons** leads to conclusions. For example, there is some career relevance in adoption for users but practically none for administrators. Centrality is high—almost overwhelming—for users but less so for administrators. Users are less favorable initially than administrators.

Looking across rows, we can use the tactic of **noting relations between variables** and see that for two of three career-motivated users a relationship exists among the variables: High centrality and favorable attitudes are also present. But the opposite pattern (low career relevance, low centrality, and neutral/unfavorable attitudes) does not apply. In fact, it looks as if some people who are neutral would have been favorable were they not so apprehensive about doing well (tactic: **finding intervening variables**).

In sum, a conceptually clustered matrix brings together key data from key participants into a single matrix. The goal is to summarize how things stand with regard to selected variables, concepts, or themes of interest. Avoid using more than five related research questions for a conceptually clustered matrix, otherwise the mind will boggle. There will be too many data to see inclusively at one time and too much time spent manipulating blocks of data to find clusters and interrelationships.

Notes

Conceptually clustered matrices need not be organized by persons or roles, as in Display 7.5. More general concepts and themes can be the ordering principle in the rows as well as in the columns. For example, rows can consist of cells broken into *Types of Problems*, with columns divided into various *Forms of Coping Strategies*. Less emphasis is placed on specific cases and people and more on the conceptual and thematic matters of the study.

Folk Taxonomy

Description

A folk taxonomy is best described by a series of its unique constituent terms explained in a particular order.

McCurdy, Spradley, and Shandy (2005) identify

> categories that categorize other categories *domains* and the words that name them *cover terms*. . . . Taxonomies are simply [hierarchical] lists of different things that are classified together under a domain word by members of a microculture on the basis of some shared certain attributes. (pp. 44–45)

Spradley (1979) further defines a *folk taxonomy* as "a set of categories organized on the basis of a single semantic relationship." The taxonomy "shows the relationships among *all* the folk terms in a domain" (p. 137). A verbatim data record to extract folk terms is necessary for constructing a taxonomy. But when no specific folk terms are generated by participants, the researcher develops his or her own—called *analytic terms*.

Semantic relationships are somewhat akin to "if-then" algorithms and include types such as the following (Spradley, 1979):

Form	Semantic Relationship
1. Strict inclusion	X is a kind of Y
2. Spatial	X is a place in Y, X is a part of Y
3. Cause–effect	X is a result of Y, X is a cause of Y
4. Rationale	X is a reason for doing Y
5. Location for action	X is a place for doing Y
6. Function	X is used for Y
7. Means–end	X is a way to do Y
8. Sequence	X is a step (stage) in Y
9. Attribution	X is an attribute (characteristic) of Y (p. 111)

As an example, "fruit" can be a domain/cover term, with "berries" as one kind of fruit—a semantic relationship of *strict inclusion*: X is a kind of Y. The category of berries continues with its own list, such as strawberries, raspberries, blueberries, blackberries, and so on, but without hierarchy at this level—in other words, a strawberry is not more important or more significant than a blackberry, so it doesn't matter in what order the types of berries are listed. "Apples" are then classified as another kind of fruit, with its list of granny smith, delicious, honey crisp, and so on.

In sum, a folk taxonomy is an organized network list of participant- and sometimes researcher-generated terms that are appropriately classified and categorized (see Display 7.6).

Applications

Concepts can't always be properly sorted into matrix rows and columns. Sometimes a network format is needed, such as a taxonomic diagram, to illustrate the interconnected complexity of social life.

A Folk Taxonomy of the Ways Children Oppress Each Other

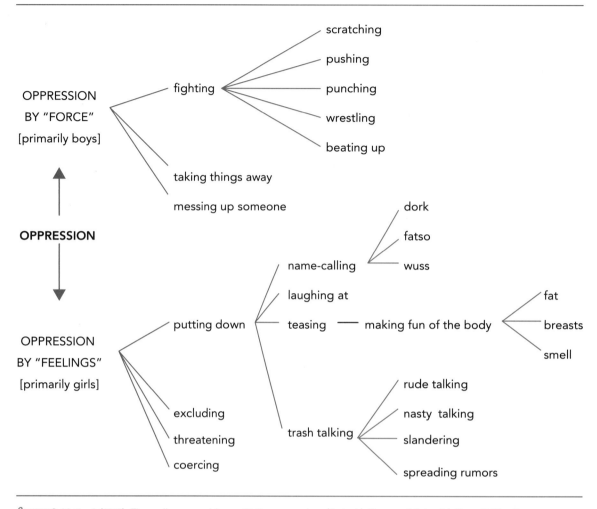

Source: Saldaña, J. (2013). *The coding manual for qualitative researchers* (2nd ed.). Thousand Oaks, CA: Sage Publications.

Taxonomies are useful when large or complex sets of unique terms appear in participant data, and researchers' sense of their organization seems necessary to better understand the subculture or microculture's ways of perceiving and living in its immediate social world. Taxonomies also help with classifying and categorizing various related pieces of data—a primary analytic step in synthesizing a massive set of field notes, interview transcripts, and documents. The goal is not to impose some artificial order onto the messiness of everyday living and working but to bring enhanced cognitive clarity for the analyst's interpretations of the people he or she is learning from and about.

Example

Saldaña (2005) and his research team explored how fourth- and fifth-grade children at one particular elementary school "oppress" each other. Participant observation, written surveys, and whole-class interviews were prepared for a short-term artists' residency to teach children, through dramatic simulation, how to proactively deal with bullying and peer pressure. The term *oppression* was key to the study, and it was defined to the children. After they grasped its meaning, they offered to the researchers examples of oppression they themselves experienced or witnessed at school and at home:

Fourth-Grade Boy [group interview]:	Sometimes when we're playing games and stuff, and this one boy comes over and he says, "Can I play with you guys?", and people say, "No, you're not our kind of people, so you better get out now."
Fifth-Grade Girl [written survey response]:	I was made fun of my fatness. I was called fat, huge fatso are you going to have a baby. I was sad all the time. I'm trying to luse wiaght but I just gain, gain and gain. Wiaght. I have not lose eney wight. I have not stoped being appresed.

These children's experiences were examples of the *means–end* semantic relationship: X is a way to do Y, or *excluding* is a way to oppress; *name calling* is a way to oppress. After all of these (often heart-wrenching) stories were collected, they were descriptively coded as to the types of oppressive acts they illustrated, for further analysis.

Analysis

The proper classification and categorization of individual items for taxonomy development can be conducted through a variety of systematic methods ranging from item-by-item queries with participants, to card and pile sorts, to follow-up interviews (Bernard, 2011; Spradley, 1979, 1980). Which method you choose depends on your own knowledge of the folk terms and their contextual meanings. Most often, intimate familiarity with your data corpus enables you to code and extract these folk terms directly from the database and onto a text-based software page or graphics program. A recommendation is first to cut and paste the array of terms into a traditional outline format and then to transfer that arrangement into network format with nodes and lines. Most often, nothing more complex than deep reflection and logical reasoning help you figure out how the terms align according to their semantic relationship (X is a kind of Y, X is a way to do Y, etc.).

Display 7.6 (from Saldaña, 2013, p. 162) shows an excerpt from the folk taxonomy constructed to illustrate the ways in which children oppress each other. Long story short, the children themselves told the researchers that oppression was either by "force" or by "feelings," usually enacted by boys and girls, respectively. From these two major categories, forms of physical and verbal oppression were arrayed. Some were folk terms told to us by children (e.g., *fighting*, *scratching*, and *pushing*), while others were researcher-constructed analytic terms that identified the types of oppression children described but had no vocabulary for (e.g., *excluding*, *coercing*, and *slandering*).

As with matrices, eyeballing and scanning the taxonomy may lead to analytic insights or questions for further investigation. For example, the folk term *putting down* has the most complex set of extended nodes and lines, suggesting not only that this type of oppression may be more frequent among older children but also that verbal belittling is potentially more violent than physical harm. For the action research project at the elementary school, these findings suggested that the adult team focus on how to get children to reduce their verbal put-downs and to offer students constructive strategies for coping with verbal abuse from peers.

Note that not everything in this (and possibly any other) taxonomy is perfectly bounded. For example, "taking things away" from someone may be a physical act of "force," but it can eventually lead to victim "feelings" of loss and hurt. There are many shades of grey, and exceptions to virtually every rule. The taxonomy is not a perfect model of the ways in which humans classify things in the social world. It is, at best, an analytic heuristic for mapping complexity to grasp at a glance the constituent elements of a culture.

Most CAQDAS programs include graphic capabilities to draw taxonomies. Some programs, such as ATLAS.ti, can "calculate" and display a visual model that illustrates your codes' organizational arrangement based on their frequency and researcher-initiated linkages. CAQDAS programs can also arrange and manage your codes into hierarchies and trees, based on your input.

Notes

Analysts may use the taxonomic method to sort out their own theoretical ideas exclusively—being careful, of course, to call it a researcher rather than a folk taxonomy. This is particularly advised for those employing grounded theory, who might construct a taxonomy composed of their codes: from theoretical, to axial/focused, to in vivo/process/ initial codes (see Saldaña, 2013).

Describing Action

Vignettes capture significant moments or the action of an extended portion of fieldwork into evocative prose renderings. A *poetic display* condenses data into poetic formats for capturing the essences and essentials of meanings. And *cognitive maps* diagram an individual's thinking processes as he or she goes through a series of actions.

Vignettes

Description

A vignette is a focused description of a series of events taken to be representative, typical, or emblematic in the case you are studying. It has a narrative, story-like structure that preserves chronological flow and that normally is limited to a brief time span, to one or a few key actors, to a bounded space, or to all three. The vignette can be written solely by the researcher or collaboratively with research team members and/or research participants. A vignette can range from being as short as a single paragraph to as long as a chapter (see the example under "Analysis" further down).

Applications

Like poetic displays (described next), vignettes are rich prosaic renderings of primarily fieldwork observations but can also include adaptations of stories embedded within interview transcripts. Examples are a day in the life of an intensive care unit nurse, the events in a typical college faculty meeting, the story of how a key management decision was reached over a period of several weeks, and the way in which a student solves a particular math problem.

Evocatively written vignettes can be a useful corrective when your data—coded, displayed, and pondered on—somehow lack meaning and contextual richness. Collaboratively written vignettes offer an opportunity to engage study participants actively in producing, reflecting on, and learning from the data.

During early data collection, as a researcher becomes more familiar with how things work in the case at hand, he or she often finds rich pockets of especially representative, meaningful data that can be pulled together in a focused way for interim understanding. Vignettes offer a way to mine such pockets fairly easily. They are also helpful in formulating core issues in a case—that is, your theory of what is happening—for yourself, for your study colleagues, and for external consumers of interim reports that may be required. They can be embedded usefully in a longer and more formal case report as well.

Example

Saldaña (1997) conducted an ethnography of an inner-city, largely Hispanic, arts magnet school in the southwest, whose theatre program was headed by a novice White female teacher. One of the key themes that emerged from the study was the theatre teacher's unconditional support for her students. Despite the ethnic differences between Nancy, the middle-class White teacher, and her lower income Hispanic students, a sense of mutual respect was evident in selected interactions.

One of the events observed during the fieldwork period was a school district–wide speech tournament for its junior high school students. Further down are excerpts from the raw field notes that were taken during this off-campus event. They are sketchy, hastily written jottings about a slice of action that happened over no more than 3 minutes of real time:

> Beatriz did a "don't drink and drive" speech. Elian shouted, "You go, Bea!" as she was coming up the stage. Beatriz spoke softly, little inflection. Needed prompting from another Martinez School girl about 4 times. When Beatriz comes back to the row Nancy rubs her shoulder. Beatriz looks hurt yet smiles, and as if she's about to cry.
> *OC: Even though there may not be much competence in comparison to the others, the Martinez School team seems to have a lot of support. Like in Damn Yankees, the baseball team may not be good, but they've got "heart."*

These notes do not give the total picture to an outside reader of what the researcher was observing, thinking, and feeling at the time. Thus, a narrative vignette that more fully describes the significance of the event is merited.

Analysis

There are no hard-and-fast guidelines for writing a vignette, though some may prescribe that the content should contain sufficient descriptive detail, analytic commentary, critical or evaluative perspectives, and so forth. But literary writing is a creative enterprise, and the vignette offers the researcher an opportunity to venture away from traditional scholarly discourse and into evocative prose that remains firmly rooted in the data but is not a slave to it.

Below is a vignette about the jottings presented in the example above, composed to illustrate why this seemingly small slice of social action held special significance for the researcher and the study's key findings:

The well-dressed eighth grade persuasive speaker from Canton Junior High spoke with clarity about her topic—adopting shelter animals. She obviously had been coached well to present a polished argument with confidence and volume. After finishing her flawless speech, the hundred or so student and teacher spectators in the auditorium applauded loudly as she stepped off the stage.

The facilitator of the event stood up from the judge's table and spoke to the assembly: "Thank you. Next: Beatriz Guzman from Martinez School."

Beatriz, in her quiet and unassuming way, rose from her chair and scooted across her seated classmates as Elian shouted, "You go, Bea!" Nancy, her coach, smiled as she passed and gave her a "rah-rah" pep-rally gesture. Beatriz, dressed in a pale yellow dress, walked hesitantly toward the stage, obviously nervous, walking up each stair step to the platform with measured care so as not to trip as someone had done earlier.

Beatriz walked to the center of the stage as her student prompter, Maria, took her place below, script in hand, ready to offer Beatriz a line in case she forgot her one-minute memorized persuasive speech (a safety measure permitted by speech tournament rules for young contestants).

Beatriz began and continued to speak softly with a monotonous voice. About four sentences into the speech, she said: "And when people get arrested for drunk driving . . ." There was a long and uncomfortable pause as Beatriz stared blankly into the darkened auditorium. Nancy looked helplessly at Beatriz and leaned forward in her seat. The student prompter cued, "their lives are. . . ." Beatriz shut her eyes, looked downward briefly, then raised her head and continued: "their lives are ruined forever."

Her speech continued for less than a minute. She needed prompting for forgotten lines three more times. On the final line of her speech, "And that is why people shouldn't drink and drive," Beatriz started leaning toward her right, as if she wanted to quickly finish and run off the stage. When she delivered her final line, the audience clapped politely as they had been instructed to do, with Beatriz's schoolmates cheering and calling out an occasional "Yay!" for her.

Beatriz returned quickly to her seat and sat next to Nancy, both of them silent for a few seconds as the next contestant from another school walked confidently toward the stage. Nancy stretched her arm across Beatriz's shoulder and pulled her student close. Beatriz leaned her head against her teacher's motherly body as Nancy started gently rubbing her student's back. Beatriz smiled through her hurt and looked as if she were about to cry. The two young women sat and said nothing to each other. They really didn't need to say anything at all.

Later that evening, as I reflected on the events of the day, I thought about Beatriz and her deer-in-the-headlights moment on stage—a moment that will probably never be forgotten for the rest of her life—and the reassuring comfort Nancy gave her afterward. It was such a peaceful yet riveting moment for me to observe: a young girl leaning against a young woman in a moment of unconditional support after failure. All I could think of was Nancy's love for her students and the realization that she's just so damn *human*.

Erickson (1986) advocates that writing a vignette after reading through field notes can be a powerful means for surfacing and clarifying your own perspective on what is happening. The method generates "an analytic caricature (of a friendly sort) . . . that highlights the author's interpretive perspective" (p. 150). A well-written vignette as a concrete, focused story will be vivid, compelling, and persuasive to a reader that the researcher has "been there." If it is not really representative, you and your readers run the risk of misunderstanding the case it refers to. Using multiple vignettes helps, but the question "Is this really typical?" must always be asked.

If you choose to make your vignettes collaborative constructions with your participants, it helps to meet with several of them to explain the vignette idea. Each person then chooses a situation to be described, makes some notes, and retells or writes an account in everyday language. The researcher reads the typed or transcribed account, makes marginal notes and queries on it, and sends it back to the writer for review. The notes and queries are discussed, and the researcher produces a revised and expanded version, later sent back for further review and discussion. A final version (with pseudonyms replacing real names) can then be circulated to others in the fieldwork setting—an extra benefit in terms of recognition and potential learning for participants.

Notes

The best discussion of this method we have found is in Erickson (1986). Seidman (2006) describes a more extended version called a "profile," a narrative summary using a participant's own words from interview transcripts to describe experience over an extended time period. Of course, the fields of narrative inquiry and oral history have developed unique and intriguing methods for extensions of vignette writing. See the Appendix for recommended resources in these subject areas.

Poetic Display

Description

Poetic displays arrange carefully selected portions of qualitative data into traditional and variant poetic structures for the evocative representation and presentation of a study, its findings, or a key participant's perspectives (see the display under "Analysis" further down).

Applications

At times, the researcher can feel overwhelmed by the massive amount of detail in a database and needs to grasp its most important or salient contents. One of poetry's unique features is its ability to represent and evoke human experiences in elegant language. Thus, the literary genre can be used as one way to extract core meanings from a large collection of texts.

Poetic displays are arts-based representations and presentations of qualitative data that capture the essence and essentials of the corpus from the researcher's perspective. Their constructions are primarily exploratory for the researcher's use, but a completed poem could be included in a published report if it is of sufficient artistic and scholarly caliber.

A poetic display brings the reader very close to a condensed set of data that forbids superficial attention by the analyst. You have to treat the data set—and the person it came from—seriously because a poem is something you engage with at a deep level. It is not just a figurative transposition but an emotional statement as well.

Example

A female principal of an arts magnet school was interviewed about the site's philosophy and mission. Here is just one verbatim excerpt from an hour-long interview about her perceptions of the school and its goals for students:

> It's, um, it's a very different kind of environment because what we're trying to do here is create whole people, give them the opportunity to become lifetime learners, um, to think that learning is joyful, to support them and to, um, be respectful of the backgrounds they bring to us. And that's very different from having a school in which there is a curriculum and these are, these things you have to learn. We haven't been able to find any single thing that people have to learn. You don't have to know the alphabet, you can always just put it down. You don't have to know the multiplication tables, you can carry them in your hip pocket. What you have to learn is attitudes. You know, we want them to have a taste for comprehensive elegance of expression. A love of problem solving. These, these are attitudes, and those are what we're teaching. And we try to teach them very respectfully and joyfully. And that's different—I know it's different.

A poem could (and should) be constructed from the entire interview transcript to holistically capture the principal's major perspectives or some facet that struck the analyst as intriguing. But for illustrative purposes only, a poem will be constructed solely from the transcript excerpt given above.

Analysis

Verbatim theatre playwright Anna Deavere Smith attests that people speak in "organic poetry" through their everyday speech. The listener needs to be sharply attuned to a speaker's rhythms, parsing, pausing, and, of course, significant words and passages of text that transcend everyday discourse to become insightful and meaningful communication.

The researcher becomes thoroughly familiar with the data corpus and extracts significant and meaningful in vivo words and phrases from the text. In the first sentence of the transcript above, for example, the phrases "whole people" and "lifetime learners" stood out as significant passages that were highlighted. This technique continued with the 170-word transcript.

Selected passages are then reassembled on a separate page to experiment with their arrangement and flow as poetry. Not everything extracted from a database will be needed, and some grammatical leeway may be necessary to change the structure of a word now and then as it gets reformatted into verse.

Eventually, the analyst took what were the selected words and phrases from the 170-word transcript and made artistic choices to compose a 23-word poem that, to him, represents the philosophy, mission, and goals of this particular site—an artistic rendering of an arts-centered school:

Teach attitudes:
    Create whole people
    Lifetime learners

Learn attitudes:
    A love of problem solving
    Elegance of expression

Teach and learn:
    Respectfully
    Supportively
    Joyfully

Two points that need to be remembered are that (1) the selection, organization, and presentation of data in a display are decisive analytic actions and (as in this case) need to be done in a thoughtful, lucid way and (2) displays owe as much to art and craft as they do to science. Attend to the poet within you to help find the organic poetry within your participants.

Classic literary poetry can stand on its own, but research as poetry almost always needs some type of introductory framing or supplemental narrative for the reader to contextualize or expand on the artwork. Also, acknowledge that poetry has a distinctive set of conventions and traditions, as does academic scholarship. Footnotes and citations of the academic literature have no place in the poem itself; save these, if necessary, for any accompanying prose narrative.

Notes

Do not fall into the paradigmatic trap of feeling the need to defend or justify your use of poetry as research if you choose to present and publish it. Many practitioners in the field of qualitative inquiry have transcended the outmoded perception of poetry as an "experimental" and "alternative" (read "marginalized") form of research, and now, they see it as a more *progressive* one. But realize that if you do choose to write poetry, it must be artistically sound to make a persuasive case as research representation.

For more on found poetry, poetic structures, and their applications as qualitative research representation and presentation, see Mears (2009) and Prendergast, Leggo, and Sameshima (2009).

Cognitive Maps
Description

A cognitive map displays a person's representation of concepts or processes about a particular domain, showing the relationships, flows, and dynamics among them. The visual map helps answer the question "What may be going through a person's mind as he or she experiences a particular series of actions and/or reflects on an experience?" Descriptive text accompanies the map for explanation (see Display 7.7).

Display 7.7

A Cognitive Map of One Person's Housecleaning Process

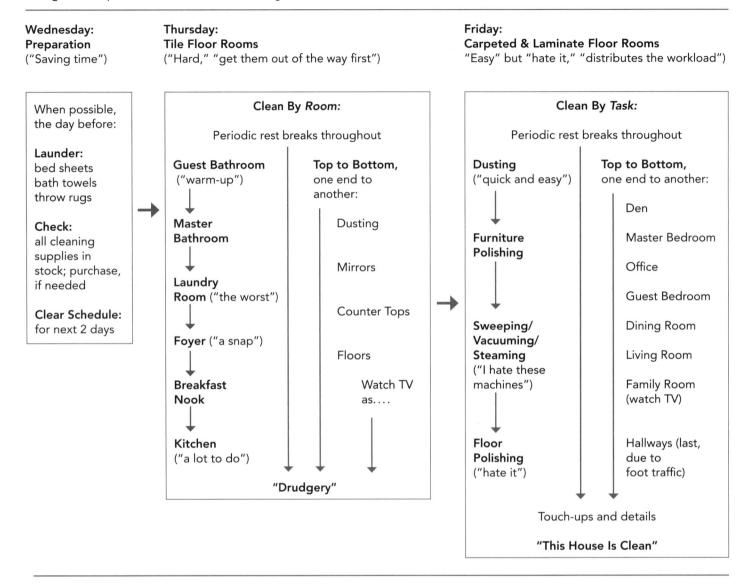

Wednesday:
Preparation
("Saving time")

Thursday:
Tile Floor Rooms
("Hard," "get them out of the way first")

Friday:
Carpeted & Laminate Floor Rooms
"Easy" but "hate it," "distributes the workload"

When possible, the day before:

Launder:
bed sheets
bath towels
throw rugs

Check:
all cleaning supplies in stock; purchase, if needed

Clear Schedule:
for next 2 days

Clean By *Room*:

Periodic rest breaks throughout

Guest Bathroom ("warm-up")

Master Bathroom

Laundry Room ("the worst")

Foyer ("a snap")

Breakfast Nook

Kitchen ("a lot to do")

Top to Bottom, one end to another:

Dusting

Mirrors

Counter Tops

Floors

Watch TV as....

"Drudgery"

Clean By *Task*:

Periodic rest breaks throughout

Dusting ("quick and easy")

Furniture Polishing

Sweeping/ Vacuuming/ Steaming ("I hate these machines")

Floor Polishing ("hate it")

Top to Bottom, one end to another:

Den

Master Bedroom

Office

Guest Bedroom

Dining Room

Living Room

Family Room (watch TV)

Hallways (last, due to foot traffic)

Touch-ups and details

"This House Is Clean"

Applications

There are times when the visual representation of concepts and processes is more effective than narrative alone. If we put stock in the classic folk saying "A picture is worth a thousand words," then cognitive maps are one way of efficiently and elegantly portraying what may be going through people's minds as they reflect on or enact an experience.

Many of our examples so far have been complex, multilevel cases. But cases are often focused at the individual level. We need displays that show us the complexity of the person. People's minds—and our theories about them—are not always organized hierarchically as in folk taxonomies. They can be represented fruitfully in nonhierarchical network form: a collection of nodes attached by links, and/or bins extended with arrows.

But qualitative researchers are not mind readers and most likely not brain surgeons, so we can never truly know what's going through someone else's mind. The cognitive map then is our best attempt to put into fixed form the dynamic and sometimes idiosyncratic thinking processes of a participant.

Example

Some research studies examine the mundane in humans' lives to understand concepts such as roles, relationships, rules, routines, and rituals—the habits of daily existence (Duhigg, 2012). The mundane example illustrated here is housecleaning, which we will soon learn is not as simple or as "mindless" as it may seem to be. Some people put a great deal of thought into it to develop time-efficient patterns of action across time.

An older and slightly arthritic married woman is interviewed at her home about her housecleaning routines. She shows the interviewer where all her cleaning supplies (broom, dust mop, glass cleaner, furniture polish, etc.) are kept; she then takes the interviewer through each room of her four-bedroom home, pointing out specific tasks and challenges during her every-other-week "cleaning days":

Woman: I clean my house over two days, not because it takes that long to do it, but at my age it's easier to space it out over two half-days. I do all the tiled rooms on the first day, then the carpeted and laminate floor rooms on the second day. . . .

Interviewer: Why do you clean tile rooms the first day?

Woman: Because they're the hardest and I want to get them out of the way first. And since they all use sort of the same cleaning supplies, I just move them from one room to another. . . . I usually start out with the bathrooms.

Interviewer: Which one gets done first?

Woman: Sometimes it doesn't matter. I might clean the smaller one first to "warm up" for housecleaning, then tackle the master bath[room], which takes about three times as long because I have to clean the shower stall and there's more mirrors and stuff in there. . . . Then I do the laundry room, and you can see I have to deal with cat litter in here. And it takes awhile to move everything around because there's so little space. It might look like a small room but it actually takes about 20, 25 minutes for me to clean. Then I go to the foyer, and that's a snap—5 to 10 minutes at most. Then I go to the breakfast nook and kitchen, and you know how long *that* takes.

Interviewer: Well, I have a much smaller kitchen. (*laughs*) How long does it take for you?

Woman: Top to bottom for the kitchen, about an hour? I always start at this end (*pointing to the coffeemaker on the counter*) then work my way around to the sink last. Well, the floor is last, cleaning that with the steamer. And when the floor's dry, I put the throw rugs back down on it.

The interview continues, covering in detail the woman's second-day cleaning routines.

Throughout, specific questions were asked by the interviewer to ascertain *what*, *where*, *how*, and *why* things are done in certain ways. Time was also discussed and demarcated into *when* and *for how long*, since the interviewee herself assigns ranges of minutes it takes to clean each room in her home. The basic goal of the interview is to collect sufficient information to construct a cognitive map of a person's process. In other words, we need to gather enough data to answer the question "*What may be going through a person's mind as he or she experiences a particular series of actions and/ or reflects on an experience?*" This includes not just facts but reasoning, memories, and emotions as well.

The initial interview is transcribed and reviewed. Follow-up questions, if needed, are composed for a second interview. The transcripts then become the verbal directions for designing the visual map.

Analysis

Drawing and constructing a cognitive map *is* the analysis, for you are trying to visually represent a real-time process. Tools available to you are paper and pencil, "sticky notes" and a wall board, or graphics/modeling software such as those found in most CAQDAS programs. Whatever method works best for you is fine, so long as you realize that you will be going through several mapping drafts before you feel you've captured the process on paper or on a monitor screen. You'll also discover that alternately drawing a map and writing the accompanying narrative help inform each other. After a draft of a cognitive map, the narrative gets written, which then stimulates a redrafting of the map and clarification of the narrative's details, and so on.

Display 7.7 shows the resulting cognitive map of this case study's housecleaning process, extracted from interview data and visually represented through captions, text, bins, nodes, lines, and arrows. The visual display also needs an accompanying narrative to explain the nuances of her thinking (excerpts):

Housecleaning is dreaded but nevertheless "prepared for" a day ahead of time. To the mildly arthritic Janice, the every-other-week task is a "necessary evil." When time permits, any laundering of towels, throw rugs, and bed sheets is done on a Wednesday so that Janice doesn't have to "hassle" with it as she's cleaning house on Thursday and Friday. This is just one way of making a burdensome task less strenuous.

Time and *energy* are two important concepts she thinks about when housecleaning. The routine is highly organized from over two decades of living in this home. On Day 1 of formal housecleaning, Janice's strategy is to tackle the "hard" rooms first to "get them out of the way." This strategy enables her to continue for approximately three hours (which includes numerous short breaks, due to her arthritis) to complete her scheduled tasks with sufficient energy: "If I save the hardest rooms for last, they'd probably never get done, or get done only part way. Bathrooms are the worst; I hate cleaning them, so that's why I do them first—get them out of the way."

Day 1's six tile floored rooms each have a preparation ritual: "Before I start each room, I bring into it everything I'm going to need for cleaning it: the Windex, paper towels, steamer, duster, trash bag. . . . That way, I don't have to waste time going back and forth to get this and that—it's all in the room, ready to go." Each room cleaning routine also follows two spatial patterns: "Clean from top to bottom—wall stuff first, then to counters, then the floor," concurrent with analog clock-like movement: "Start at one end of the room and work my way around it."

The process described above is the researcher's interpretation of what's going through a person's mind. But cognitive maps can also be collaboratively constructed between the researcher and participant. The procedure engages the respondent and the researcher in joint work, simultaneously building the display and entering data.

After an initial interview about the experience or process, the researcher transcribes the exchange and extracts key terms, concepts, in vivo codes, and so on. Each one gets written on its own "sticky note," and a follow-up mapping interview is scheduled with the participant.

At the audio-recorded mapping interview, the participant is given the sticky notes and is asked to arrange them on a large poster-size sheet of paper on a wall "in a way that shows how you think about the words." When this task is complete, the researcher asks, "Why are they arranged this way?" The researcher draws lines around concepts that the person says belong together, and evokes a name for the group, which also is written on the display. The question "What relationship is there between _____ and _____?" leads to the person's naming of links between concepts and/or concept groups, and those too are written on the display.

During preliminary analysis, the researcher listens to the recording of the mapping discussion, clarifies any errors, and writes a descriptive text that walks through the complete map. The revised map and narrative are fed back to the respondent to ensure that it is an accurate representation of the concept or process.

This version of cognitive mapping makes for maximum idiosyncrasy—and complexity—in the results. A simpler version (Morine-Dershimer, 1991) asks the respondent to generate a list of *concepts* related to a major topic. The major topic is placed in the center, and then other concepts are placed around it, with unnamed links radiating out to them, and from them, to other concepts in turn.

Cognitive maps have a way of looking more organized, socially desirable, and systematic than they probably are in the person's mind. Allow for those biases when making analyses and interpretations. Also acknowledge that one person's cognitive map does not necessarily represent others' ways of thinking and acting in comparable situations. (For example, when the husband of this case study cleans the house, he chooses to accomplish the task in 1 day instead of 2. He begins at one end of the house and works his way from one room to the adjacent room, regardless of flooring surface, until he reaches the other end of the house.)

Notes

Cognitive maps also can be drawn from preestablished narratives such as interview transcripts, fiction, or other longer documents. Here, the analyst is interrogating the text rather than the person. You can even use cognitive mapping techniques to clarify your own ideas or analytic processes about the meaning of a particular set of data.

For a quirky and humorous fictional media representation of participant observation and cognitive mapping, see the outstanding Norwegian/Swedish film *Kitchen Stories*.

Closure and Transition

These methods for describing social settings and action are documentary processes. They condense a vast array of data into more coherent forms for answering one of the inquiry's most basic questions: "What is happening here?" Sometimes a research study's goals are focused solely on description, but other goals may include deeper explorations into the "whys" of what humans do.

Exploring and describing are two foundation methods for analyzing qualitative data. In Chapter 8, we will arrange data into more systematic and ordered formats for constructing even more patterns across time, processes, and cases.

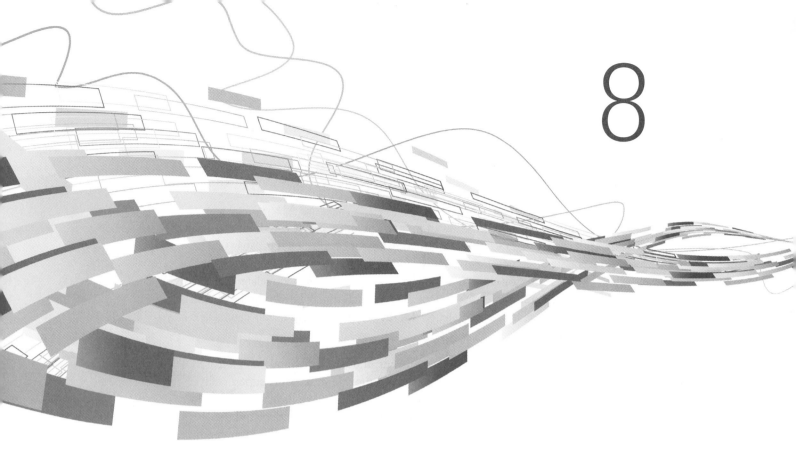

Methods of Ordering

Chapter Summary
....

This chapter outlines methods for ordering condensed data according to time, processes, and cases. The ordering provides foundations for determining sequences and hierarchies for further analytic work.

Contents
....

Introduction
Ordering by Time
    Event-Listing Matrix
    Growth Gradient
    Time-Ordered Matrix
Ordering Processes
    Decision Modeling
    Event–State Network
    Composite Sequence Analysis
Ordering by Cases
    Case-Ordered Descriptive Meta-Matrix
Closure and Transition

Introduction

A third major family of displays *orders* data by time, processes, and cases, preserving the chronological flow and permitting a good look at what led to what, and when. Once past initial description, some form of ordering is typically very helpful. Ordering matrices by time enables the analysis of phases, stages, cycles, and possibly influences and affects (the preferred terms over the outmoded "cause and effect"), suggesting causation.

Life is chronology; we live in a flow of events. But although we can think of ourselves as being in the midst of a river of events, that metaphor breaks down because the river's flow is not one-dimensional. Some events occur in one domain of life, others elsewhere. Some events are close to us, some distant. Some events are related coherently to other events, and others are adventitious. And though it may be stating the obvious, events long ago in time have consequences for the present. Distant events can have consequences for close events.

As for cases, looking across them deepens our understanding and can increase generalizability. But cross-case analysis is tricky. Simply summarizing superficially across some themes or main variables by itself tells us little. We have to look carefully at the complex configuration of processes within each case and understand the local dynamics before we can begin to see a patterning of variables that transcends particular cases. Thus, combining "process" and "variable" approaches is needed for methods of ordering.

Ordering by Time uses chronology as an organizing framework for examining data as they change across time. *Ordering Processes* examines how "big picture" composite journeys can be diagrammed. *Ordering by Cases* hierarchically arranges individuals, groups, and sites according to designated variables of interest.

Ordering by Time

An *event-listing matrix* documents selected actions during selected periods of time. A *growth gradient* illustrates the development of a variable throughout a range of time. And a *time-ordered matrix* shows the concurrent pathways of multiple variables and researcher evaluation notes during selected periods of time.

Event-Listing Matrix

Description

An event listing is a matrix that arranges a series of concrete events by chronological time periods, sorting them into several categories (see Display 8.1).

Applications

Qualitative researchers are always interested in events—what they are, when they happened, and what their connections to other events are (or were)—to preserve chronology and illuminate the processes occurring. A process, after all, is essentially a string of coherently related events. Typically, these interests lead to the production of an extended narrative arranged in a proper time sequence (usually without flashbacks or flash forwards).

Display 8.1

Event Listing, Banestown Case

"Score-On" Time Periods

Level	Contextual Press 1976–1978	Emergence of the Problem Oct. 1978	Awareness and Proposal of Solution Nov. 1978	Approval and Preparations Jan.–Feb. 1979	Training and Beginning Operations March–April 1979	Expansion, New Openings Sept. 1979	Budget Reduction, Disruption May 1980
State/ Macro	minimal competency levels, testing introduced in state schools			proposal discussed, approval at state level	Smithson middle school teachers, 2 admins, trained at D/D site (4 days, early March)		Reduction in Title I allocations
District	supplemental skills program introduced in reading and math	– alarm at failure rate – internal solutions proposed, found unacceptable	* officials see SCORE-ON at 'awareness fair' – IV-C proposal rapidly drawn up, submitted	* Smithson pupil folders screened – appointments made of Smithson lab teacher and aide	– 30 4th grade pupils selected for Smithson lab – materials, technical assistance intensified for Smithson lab	– staff active in extending Smithson, launching new labs * funding for all lab staff at Smithson taken over by Title I	* reduction in county, Title I budgets – proposed staff cuts, transfers in elementary schools
Local Schools	pressures begin to raise minimal levels			* continuation for following year planned for 5th grade in 2 middle schools; teachers named	– rooms, staffing completed for middle schools – 2 other elementary schools authorized to implement in the fall	lab opens at Carrington, Banestown Middle modified version opens at Smith Camp, South End	– middle schools unaffected by cuts – threat of discontinuation at Banestown Middle (conflicts)
Smithson School	large numbers of low achievers placed in FACILE classes	* 4th grade teachers report 40 pupils 1–3 grade levels behind – teachers unfavorable to central office proposals	– teachers approve pull-out lab formula	– lab teacher and aide replaced; some disgruntlement – lab room created, minimally equipped	– Smithson lab opens (late March) – preparations inadequate, materials not arrived, scheduling difficulties	Smithson expands to 45 pupils in 3rd, 4th grades – new teacher added for morning sessions	* major shifts in lab staffing announced to teachers – program to be cut back, focused on grades 1–3, limited to 1.5 posts

* barometric event

Source: Miles, M. B., & Huberman, A. M. (1994). *Qualitative data analysis: An expanded sourcebook* (2nd ed.). Thousand Oaks, CA: Sage Publications.

Narratives are indispensable if we are to understand a complex chronology in its full richness. The problem is that going straight to an extended narrative from written-up field notes runs an acute risk: You can tell a story that is partial, biased, or dead wrong—even though it may look vivid, coherent, and plausible to a reader. The event listing is a good way of guarding against false chronologies. It creates a matrix-based outline for your narrative.

Example

In the school improvement study, we (Miles and Huberman) wanted to display events during the adoption and implementation of an innovation at the school level, showing them by different phases or time periods of the process.

Keeping the classic left-to-right convention for the passage of time, we might make columns of the matrix list successive time periods. These could be defined arbitrarily (e.g., Year 1, Year 2), or more organically by empirically derived phases or stages of the adoption-implementation process. Perhaps some events are more critical than others, serving to cause new events or to move the process forward into a new phase. Rows of the matrix, in this case, deal with the locale of events: state, district, and local levels.

Display 8.1 shows how this technique worked out for a 1970s innovation called SCORE-ON, a laboratory for teaching remedial math and reading skills to children "pulled out" of their regular classes. The time periods (Contextual Press 1976–1978, Emergence of the Problem Oct. 1978, etc.) were initially defined conceptually from a general adoption-implementation model, but labels for each period came from the actual core activities during that period. A new time period was defined when a significant shift in activities occurred. The analyst marked "barometric events" (those that moved the process on into the next time period or phase) with an asterisk.

The analyst focused mainly on Smithson School (bottom row) and wanted to have that as the most local of the locales. However, the innovation was also implemented in other schools (next row up). And events could be sorted into district and state/macro levels, which, in turn, influenced the lower levels.

An exploratory interview question asked people to describe the history of the innovation ("Can you tell me how SCORE-ON got started in this school?"). Follow-up probes fleshed out the sequence from innovation awareness to adoption, how and by whom key decisions were made and the reasons involved. Other questions dealt with outside agencies and events and "anything else going on at the time that was important." Similar questions were asked about events during the implementation process.

The analyst looked at coded field notes (here, the codes are any that include the subcode CHRONOLOGY) and extracted accounts of specific events, such as "4th grade teachers report 40 pupils 1-3 grade levels behind" or "officials see SCORE-ON at 'awareness fair'." The analyst defined an event as a specific action or occurrence mentioned by any respondent and not denied by anyone else. If at least two people said the event was important, crucial, or "made a big difference" to what happened subsequently, an asterisk was assigned to designate it as a "barometric event."

Analysis

A quick scan across the display shows us that the process of change is strikingly rapid. A problem seen in one elementary school in the fall of 1978 by the fourth-grade teachers apparently leads to the discovery and introduction of an innovation (SCORE-ON) that was in place in five district schools by the fall of 1979.

A look at the asterisks helps explain some of the speed: the active involvement of central office officials after they saw the innovation at an awareness fair, leading to justificatory events such as the pupil folder screening and to specific school-level planning and the appointment of specific teachers to manage the remedial laboratory. State-level competency requirements were the backdrop, and the teachers' report of problems was probably an alarm or trigger that set off actions already fueled by concern at the district level about meeting state requirements.

When we note the repercussions of an externally driven budget crisis during the latter school year (September 1979–May 1980), we can infer that the original availability of Title I funds might have played a strong part in the original changes.

These are plausible hunches about the meaning of the data in Display 8.1. To check them out, the analyst can piece together a focused narrative that ties together the different streams into a meaningful account, a narrative that could only with difficulty have been assembled—or understood—from the diverse accounts spread through the field notes. Here are some excerpts from the focused narrative the analyst produced. They should be read in conjunction with Display 8.1:

> A special impetus was given in the fall of 1978, when the six fourth-grade teachers at Smithson noticed that they had an unusually large cohort (40) of incoming pupils who were one or more grade levels behind in reading achievement. . . . Thirty-eight of these forty had come out of the [existing] FACILE program in the first to third grades. It is not clear how so many of these pupils got to the fourth grade, but no one was surprised. . . .
>
> The teachers were worried that either promoting or retaining so many pupils would cause problems; they were leaning toward retention, but feared a massive protest by parents. Essentially, they were covering themselves by announcing early in the year that they had inherited, not created, the problem. . . .
>
> During this phase, a circular announcing Federal funding . . . came to the central office from the State superintendent. An awareness conference, presenting a series of projects, many of them keyed to remedial skill development, was to take place nearby. At Mrs. Bauers' initiative—and with an eye to a solution for the problem at Smithson School—a contingent from the central office (Mrs. Bauers, Mrs. Robeson, Mr. Rivers) attended the presentations and was attracted to SCORE-ON. It seemed a relatively flexible program, easy to integrate into the school in pull-out form. It was directed specifically to the bottom quartile in reading and math.

Note several things here: (a) the narrative, which is both straightforwardly descriptive and analytic, helps knit together and flesh out events at different levels of the chart, (b) the analyst can add explanatory conditions or states that show how one event led to another, (c) the return to the field notes often turns up other critical events or supporting information not originally in the display, and (d) the narrative is more understandable when read in conjunction with the display, and vice versa. When the first version of the display is filled in, start a draft of a focused narrative. That step will require you to return to the field notes as you go. Stay open to the idea of adding new events to the listing or subtracting events that seem trivial or irrelevant.

For a careful reconstruction, the events in a listing can be dated within cells. Time periods can be specified much more narrowly or cover a very brief time span (e.g., 1 hour in a classroom). Events from a listing also can be shown as a network-like flow that includes more general states or conditions, such as "lack of enthusiasm" (see "Event–State Network" later in this chapter). Barometric or significant events in cells can be color coded in red to highlight their importance during the at-a-glance review.

The problems we face in understanding event flows are those of sorting out the different domains of events, preserving the sequence, showing the salience or significance of preceding events for following events—and doing all of this in an easily visible display that lets us construct a valid chronology. The event listing helps ground the analyst's understanding of a complex flow of events, especially for longitudinal qualitative studies, and increases confidence in the associated chronological account. It also lays the basis for the beginnings of a causal analysis: what events led to what further events and what mechanisms underlay those associations (see Chapter 9).

Notes

Event listings can be limited much more sharply to "critical incidents," defined as important or crucial, and/or limited to an immediate setting or compressed time frame. These matrices can be done at many different levels of detail, but keep the rows to a maximum of four or five levels, and be sure they represent a meaningfully differentiated set of categories. Do not go finer than the study questions dictate.

Even more selectively, events can be shown as a flow limited to an individual's major events, each demarcated and connected with the causal pushes that may have moved the process from one event to another. Display 8.2 shows a diagram adapted from display work models by Pillet (personal communication, 1983).

The case here is one of Saldaña's (1998, 2003, 2008a) longitudinal qualitative studies of a young man from kindergarten through his late 20s. The successive Educational and Occupational experiences are indicated in the left column; at the right, we see the researcher's summary of the Personal major crises and forces moving concurrently throughout the education and work history of the case studied. The researcher uses this not just as an event-listing chronology but as a visual *chronicle* of significant periods and epiphanies from a young life.

Growth Gradient

Description

A growth gradient is a graphic display that illustrates the amounts, levels, or qualities of changes across time through the use of points and links accompanied with text (see Display 8.3).

Applications

Events can sometimes be conceptualized as associated with some underlying variable that changes through time. That variable can serve as the purpose for or central theme

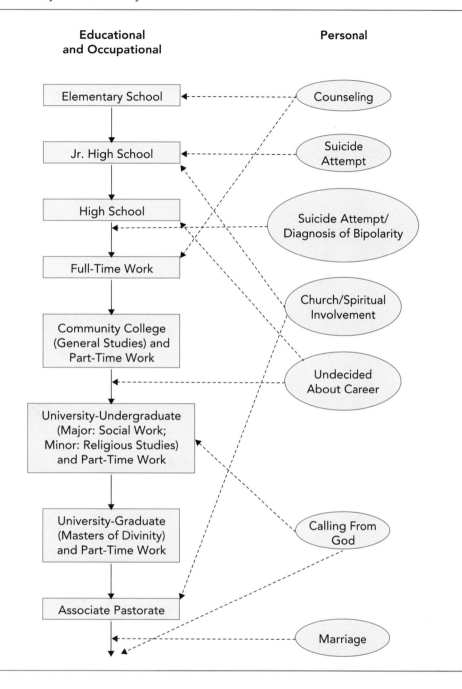

of a growth gradient. The illustration provides a long-term picture of a process or a cumulative, "connect the dots" map of related events.

A growth gradient tells the story of a variable's journey across time. So it is particularly appropriate for qualitative longitudinal or evaluation studies, for ethnographies, and especially for those research projects with a mixed-methods component.

Display 8.3

Growth Gradient for ECRI Innovation, Masepa Case

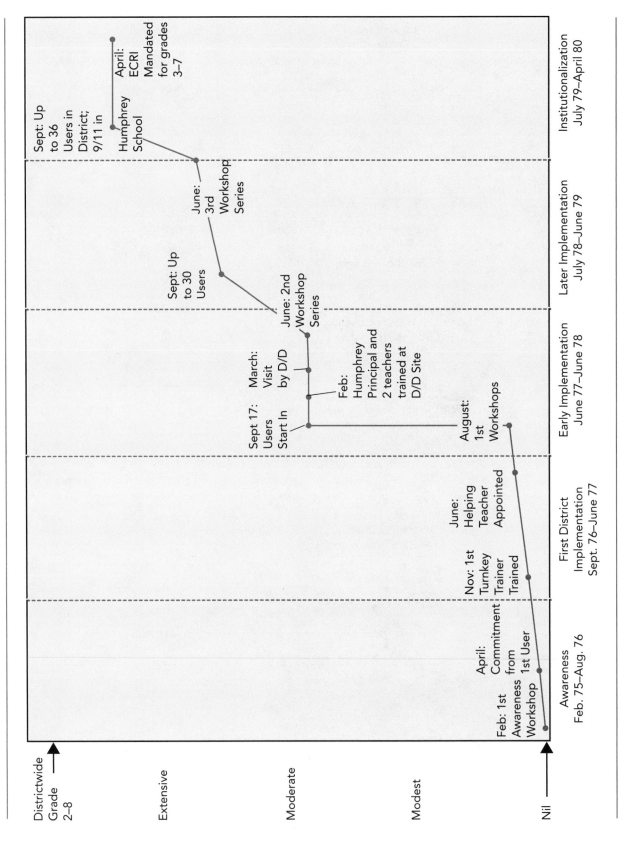

Source: Miles, M. B., & Huberman, A. M. (1994). *Qualitative data analysis: An expanded sourcebook* (2nd ed.). Thousand Oaks, CA: Sage Publications.

Example

In Display 8.3, we see a simple network display designed to show the growth gradient of an innovation's use in one case for our (Miles and Huberman) school improvement study. The network is ordered chronologically, with five distinct and separated periods. The vertical dimension shows the numbers of users, and the horizontal dimension represents time. The points or *nodes* are noteworthy events, and the lines or *links* have the implicit meaning "is followed by." Each point is labeled with a more specific month and sometimes a date to mark an event that seemed to the analyst significant to the innovation's implementation and history.

Analysis

Here the analyst is interested in the main variable, *internal diffusion (spread) of an innovation*, defined as growth in the number of teachers using it. That variable is represented in network form as a single line between points. But the analyst has attached various critical events to the line—appointments of key personnel, training, and the like—that help expand our understanding of the movements of the main variable. You can get a clear idea of the tempo of expansion and can see which events were especially critical (e.g., the August 1 workshops in 1977). More generally, you can see that workshops appear to be the main mechanism for expanding use of the innovation.

The growth gradient also reveals that it took between 4 and 5 years in the 1970s to achieve "extensive" use of the innovation across various school sites. Some administrators may perceive this as a typical time frame for substantive change to occur and declare the innovation project a success. Other administrators, especially in the fast-paced 21st century, may interpret this as a too slow-moving process that, next time, might be integrated more rapidly into the curriculum through earlier workshop presentations, strategically scheduled right before the school year begins.

Growth gradients can map out not just increases but also decreases, stability, surges, turning points, the erratic, and the idiosyncratic through time (Saldaña, 2003). These patterns are particularly revealing when they seem to emerge gradually or accumulate considerably. You can also map out two or three variables at the same time on a growth gradient, which may reveal some interesting interrelationships and possibly causation factors at work (see Chapter 9).

At least one axis of a growth gradient is time, and the other axis is a range, continuum, or dynamic of some type, be it numbers (1, 2, 3), general amounts (few, some, many), evaluative measures (poor, satisfactory, excellent), frequency (rarely, sometimes, often), direction (negative, neutral, positive), intensity (weak, moderate, strong), position (conservative, moderate, liberal), quality (fractured, ambivalent, unified), and so on. The items you place on nodes in a growth gradient should be related in some way to the primary variable you're examining. The brief event phrases you place on the nodes should be "just enough" to help you properly interpret changes and turning points in the historic timeline.

Notes

Don't be reluctant to use what may seem like a quantitative method with qualitative data. The growth gradient is an effective application for simultaneously assessing long-term quantitative *and* qualitative change. See Belli, Stafford, and Alwin (2009) for calendar and time diary methods for long-term data collection, management, and analysis of qualitative data.

Time-Ordered Matrix

Description

A time-ordered matrix has its columns arranged chronologically by time period to determine when particular phenomena occurred. Row contents depend on what else you're studying. This matrix is somewhat comparable with the event-listing matrix profiled above, but the time-ordered matrix emphasizes *sequence*, *timing*, and *stability* of processes and experiences (see Display 8.4).

Display 8.4

Time-Ordered Matrix: Changes in the CARED Innovation (a Work Experience Program)

		Planning Period Jan.–June 1977	First Year 1977–1978	Second Year 1978–1979	Third Year 1979–1980
Developer Components	**Individualization**			Some tendency to "batch" students, encourage standard projects, etc.	
	Student responsibility and time use	Added logs/time sheets	Added "accountability" scheme for discipline	Added system of passes for students to leave room	Refusal to accept late work; students were failed
	Direct exposure to work experience				Some tendency to reduce individualization/ exploration aspects; more long-term placements; convenience location of jobs
	Program requirements/ curriculum		Added direct instruction on basic skills, separate from job	More competencies required	More competencies and project required
	Learning strategies	Did not include employer seminars; intensified "competencies" experience	Wrote new "competencies" Discarded learning style instrument New basic skills materials	Student learning plan only 1 semester; more basic skills emphasis	Journal more routine communication; less counseling emphasis
	Parental involvement		Parent advisory committee added	Advisory committee mtgs dwindled and stopped	Reduced level of detail in reporting to parents
Other Aspects	**Time and credits**	Reduced to 4-hr time block; students must take 1 other course			
	Student selection			Moved away from full-random selection to self-selection plus a few random	Lower SES
	Program size		32 students	64 students	70 students, cut to 50 in 2nd semester; 25 for next year (juniors only)

Source: Miles, M. B., & Huberman, A. M. (1994). *Qualitative data analysis: An expanded sourcebook* (2nd ed.). Thousand Oaks, CA: Sage Publications.

Applications

With qualitative data, you can track sequences, processes, and flows, and are not restricted to "snapshots." The time-ordered matrix displays time-*linked* data referring to phenomena that are bigger than specific "events," so as to understand (and perhaps later explain) what was happening.

Use a descriptive time-ordered matrix like this when your data are fairly complete, to begin developing possible explanations that can be tested by moving back to the coded field notes.

Example

In our (Miles and Huberman) school improvement study, we were concerned with how an innovation changed and transformed across time during several years of implementation. We predicted that most innovations would show such changes as they were adapted to the needs of users and the pressures of the local situation.

We broke down the innovation into specific Developer Components or Other Aspects, using these as rows of the matrix. The columns of the matrix are time periods from early through later use. If a change in a component occurred during the time period, we could enter a short description of the change. A blank cell would mean no change—a nice feature that permits seeing *stability*, as well as change.

Display 8.4 shows how this matrix looked. The innovation, CARED, is a work experience program for high school students. The official components were those specified by the original program developer. These Developer Components do not necessarily exhaust important aspects of the innovation, so there are rows for Other Aspects, such as time and credits or student selection. Such aspects usually appear after initial fieldwork and direct experience with the use and meaning of the innovation.

The columns are time periods, starting with the initial planning period (because we expected changes while this relatively demanding and complex innovation was readied for use). The three succeeding school years follow.

In this case, the analyst was looking for changes in the innovation, component by component. Those changes could be found in the coded field notes, where innovation users were asked whether they had made any changes in the innovation's standard format. Follow-up probes asked for parts that had been added, dropped, revised, combined, or selected out for use. We used the decision rule that if a reported change was confirmed by at least one other staff member and not disconfirmed by anyone else, it should be entered in the matrix.

Analysis

Only a few analytic observations culled from the matrix are described below.

Looking across the rows of Display 8.4, you can begin to see drifts or gradual shifts expressing an accumulated tendency underlying specific changes. For example, the row "Program requirements/curriculum" shows an increasing tendency to make *stiffer achievement demands* on students (the tactic here is **noting patterns, themes**—see Chapter 11). The component "Student responsibility and time use" suggests that a process of exerting more and more *control* over student behavior is occurring (e.g., the accountability scheme, the system of passes, etc.).

At this point, the analyst can deepen understanding by referring back to other aspects of the field notes, notably what else people said about the changes or the reasons for them. In this example, a staff member said, "Your neck is on the block . . . the success and failures of the students rebound directly on you." So the increased emphasis on control might come from the staff's feelings of vulnerability and mistrust of students (tactic: **noting relations between variables**).

What else is happening? We can note an important structural shift in the second year: moving away from random student selection to self-selection. The field notes showed that this decision was precipitated by principals and counselors who opposed entry by college-bound students and wanted the program to be a sort of safety valve for poorly performing, alienated students. Thus, the program became a sort of "dumping ground" or "oasis" (tactic: **making metaphors**) for such students. But look at the "Program size" row. Though the program doubles in the second year, it cuts back substantially in the third year. In this case, severe funding problems were beginning to develop (tactic: **finding intervening variables**).

The report could either contain the analytic text, pulling together the strands we just wove, or present the table along with it. But Display 8.4 may be too busy and unfocused for the reader—it is more an interim analysis exhibit than a report of the findings. One way of resolving these problems is to boil down the matrix to (a) verify the tendencies observed in the initial analysis and (b) summarize the core information for the researcher and the reader.

Display 8.4 could be condensed in myriad ways. One approach is to standardize the several drifts by naming them—that is, finding a gerund such as *controlling* or *tightening up* that indicated what was going on when a change was made in the innovation (tactic: **clustering**) and then tying that drift to its local context, inferring what the changes mean for the case. The result appears in Display 8.5 as a summary table.

Reading the Tendency column and using the tactic of counting the number of mentions for each theme confirms the accuracy of the initial analysis. The core themes are, indeed, stiffer achievement demands ("Going academic"), more control, increased routinization ("Simplifying"), and reduced individualization ("Standardizing"). You might even try for an overarching label to typify the set—something like "Self-protective erosion," thus subsuming particulars into the general—and this labeling can kick off the final analytic text, usable in the report of findings.

A scan of the Significance/Meaning for Site column helps in summarizing the underlying issues, which we identified as exhaustion, lack of local endorsement, and the discrepancy between the demands of the innovation and the organizational procedures and norms in the immediate environment.

Overall, for time-ordered matrices, consider whether the rows are organized in a sensible way. You may need to regroup them into streams or domains. Consider whether a boiled-down, summary matrix is needed to advance your understanding or that of the reader. Also be sure the time periods chosen are a good fit for the phenomena under study. They should be fine enough to separate events that you want to keep in sequence, rather than blending them into one big pot. Use Content-Analytic Summary Tables (see Chapter 6, Display 6.20) to pull together and look at data from the display if it is too complicated.

Display 8.5

Summary Table for Verifying and Interpreting Time-Ordered Matrix: Changes in the CARED Innovation

Component	Tendency	Significance/Meaning for Site
Individualization	Standardizing	Undergoes individualization, shows streamlining as response to demandingness
Student responsibility	Controlling, tightening up	Reflects staff feelings of vulnerability, mistrust toward students
Exposure to work	Simplifying, standardizing	Response to demandingness: cutting back on innovativeness of the project
Program requirements	Going academic	Shows vulnerability, marginality of project in the two high schools—again cutting back on innovativeness of CARED
Learning strategies	Going academic, de-individualizing, simplifying, standardizing	More "routinization" overall
Parental involvement	Cutting back, simplifying	Response to demandingness
Time and credits	Cutting back, going academic	Done early: reflects principals' opposition to project, etc.
Student selection	Self-selecting	Project becomes "dumping ground" but also gets stronger endorsement from counselors, principals
Program size	Growing, then dwindling	Reflection of funding problems and possibly of under-endorsement

Source: Miles, M. B., & Huberman, A. M. (1994). *Qualitative data analysis: An expanded sourcebook* (2nd ed.). Thousand Oaks, CA: Sage Publications.

Notes

In this profile's example, the time periods were relatively long (a full school year), but depending on the phenomena under study, they could be shorter (semesters, months, weeks, days, hours). The cell entries here were specific *changes*. But you can also enter specific *events*, such as decisions, actions, key meetings, or crises.

The rows of this matrix were components or aspects of an innovation. Many other types of rows can be used in a time-ordered matrix: *roles* (principal, teacher, student, parent), *event types* (planned/unplanned, critical actions), *settings* (Classroom 1, Classroom 2, playground, principal's office, central office), or *activity types* (teaching, counseling, formal meetings).

By relabeling the matrix rows, you can examine time-related events or states *across* cases. Data from several cases can be displayed in a way that respects chronology for assessing change (if any) in longitudinal, action, and evaluation studies. For looking at the general flow of events *within* a case, see the methods of event-listing matrix and event–state networks in this chapter.

Ordering Processes

Decision modeling maps out specific choices and actions we take for a particular process. An *event–state network* illustrates how events and their transitional states can be plotted as a flow diagram. And a *composite sequence analysis* integrates multiple participants' journeys into a single diagram.

Decision Modeling

Description

A decision model is a visual graphic that outlines the thoughts, plans, and choices/decisions made during a flow of actions embedded in a range of conditions (see Display 8.6).

Display 8.6

One Person's Decision Model for Saving Money

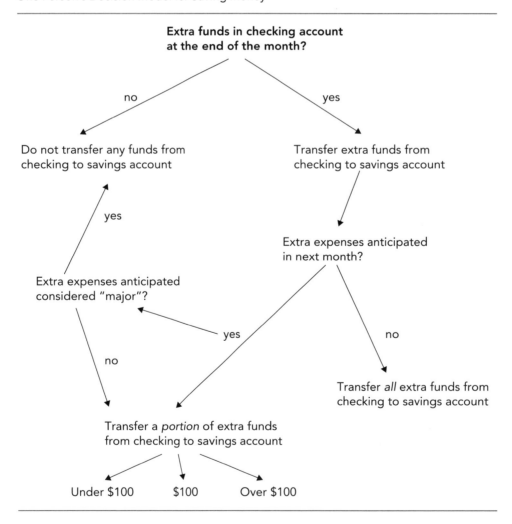

Applications

Sometimes you want to know how a basic process plays out across an individual or a number of cases and to build a general model of just how it works. One such process is decision making and its related actions by individuals. Decision modeling is either an individual or a collective display of the options available for a particular process and the possible pathways that can be taken—usually but not exclusively—based on "yes" or "no" alternatives.

The method is very useful for making the inexplicit visible and clear and can also be used for recurring decisions involving many people and complex situations (e.g., patient care in an intensive care unit, serving a meal to a party in a restaurant, dealing with customer complaints). This sort of display lends itself well to improving practice or recasting policy. The model is also effective for diagramming more open-ended participant decision-making processes that will help answer the following example research questions: How do high school students decide to attend a particular university? What is involved in moving from recreational to addictive drug use? Why do some women's support groups disband?

Example

During the recession from 2008 onward, a researcher was interested in whether lower-middle-class citizens were able to save money during an uncertain economic period for the country. The researcher pilot interviewed several participants and learned (perhaps not surprisingly) that the decision to save money depended on variables such as the participant's employment status, annual income, financial obligations, outstanding debts, age, and so on. But other affective factors also came into play, such as fear of an uncertain future, dedication to one's family security, habits of frugality, and so on.

Display 8.6 illustrates a single adult working male's decision-making process for "saving money." The primary window for this process is toward the end of the month, when he assesses how much remains in his checking account. The action items (i.e., the transfer of funds from a checking to a savings account) for the model in the display were extracted from an interview with the individual:

Participant: If there's some money at the end of the month, that's leftover in checking, I'll either transfer that extra into my savings account, or keep it in, in case there's some kind of expense coming up next month.

Interviewer: On average, how much do you transfer into savings at the end of the month?

Participant: It depends, really. Ballpark is about a hundred dollars, but sometimes it's less, maybe more, depending on what kind of bills I've had for the month. If I know there's gonna be a big major expense coming up, like dental work next month, I won't transfer anything into savings, I'll just keep it in checking 'cause I'm just gonna have to spend it anyway.

The interview continues with questions to clarify the participant's decision-making processes; hypothetical alternatives that may influence and affect his decisions are also posed to him (e.g., "What do you do if you're short on cash at the end of the month?" "How do credit cards, if you have any, affect your savings plans?")

Analysis

After the interview, the researcher reviews the transcript and maps out with pencil and paper the participant's decision-making processes for saving money. The two primary things to remember about a first-draft decision model is to (1) stick with a very focused task—"saving money" is a lot simpler to plot than "long-term planning for retirement"—and (2) start with listings of simple decision-making questions and actions that can be furthered through "yes" and "no" alternatives. You may feel as though this is abhorrently reductive of the richness of what you're trying to model. But this is just a starting point to get you thinking about the *actions* necessary to further *other actions*. And things will get more complex with each additional person you interview about his or her process of saving money. New alternatives will literally enter the picture, and your model will extend beyond "yes" and "no" to reveal Pathway Option 1, Pathway Option 2, Pathway Option 3, and so on.

The procedure for composite decision modeling can be done iteratively: The criteria mentioned by the first person are used in the interview with the next person, and so on. Repeated interviewing of multiple participants is usually needed, along with attempts to disconfirm the model through feedback and verification, and checking with a new, uninterviewed sample of people. Gradually a composite decision model for saving money is built. Or a full set of individual decision models like Display 8.6 can be done and then generalized into a composite. The next step is to test the composite model through interviews with a *new* population, using all of the decision criteria.

Our actions in life are not always a series of strictly "yes" or "no" decisions. As the participant above wisely noted, "It depends." The decision model approach is stronger on *logical* order rather than narrative order as such. It strips away nuanced but nonessential information yet retains the key conditions and specifies contingently the decisions to be made. It's essential to preserve the validity of each separate decision model; each person's path must be represented accurately, even though some more idiosyncratic features may need to be generalized to a more abstract version.

Decision making can be a complex cognitive process, depending on the task at hand, for there is a flurry of thoughts that can race quickly through a person's mind as alternatives beyond "yes" or "no" are considered, benefits to self and others are weighed, moral and ethical soliloquies are pondered, and best- and worst-case outcomes are hypothesized. The decision model attempts to generalize across individuals, but it does not limit itself to generalities. Some models can plot the emotional complexities of and inner motivations for our decision-making dilemmas.

This profile is a gloss of the full procedures and methods, for composite decision modeling is a prescribed process with modest statistical tasks. For more detailed instructions and examples, see Bernard (2011) and Bernard and Ryan (2010).

Notes

The decision model is somewhat comparable to the cognitive map (see Chapter 7, Display 7.7). But the decision model focuses on and examines one particular process and its actions, while the cognitive map attempts to chart more extended and open-ended experiences.

Event–State Network

Description

An event–state network is a visual and processual adaptation and representation of an event-listing matrix (see Display 8.1). Events are represented as boxes; the sharp edges imply specificity and a narrow time span. States (or conditions) are represented as bubbles; round edges imply more diffuseness, less concreteness, and existence over a longer time. You connect the boxes and bubbles by lines and arrows to show what led to what. States or conditions are not as time limited as events and often serve as the mediators or links between specific events (see Display 8.7).

Applications

A matrix is a cell-based, linear construct that organizes events chronologically. But the tight borders of a matrix do not enable processual illustration of the sometimes multiple and overlapping events happening simultaneously within and driven by specific states and conditions. If life is complex and interconnected, then sometimes our analytic representations and displays need to reflect that complexity and interconnectedness, rather than condense it to more manageable understandings.

An event–state network portrays both the *actions* of participants (as events in boxes) and the *conflicts or rationales* (as states in bubbles) that initiate their actions. The network is thus a heuristic for deducing from data not just *what* happened but the possible motivations for *how* and *why*.

Example

By the time an event-listing matrix is generated, you usually have a set of implicit generalizations about why things happened as they did. Event–state networks are a way of making those ideas explicit and verifiable. Display 8.7 shows an excerpt from an event–state network drawn from the data in the event-listing matrix in Display 8.1.

Analysis

Once an event-listing matrix is done, a network can be generated somewhat quickly. If you wish to work by hand first, write one event per "sticky note," generate state or condition sticky notes as you go, and arrange the emerging network on a large sheet of poster paper, drawing arrows as you go. This method is an especially helpful step toward assessing causal dynamics in a particular case. To create state or condition sticky notes (a) recheck the field notes for evidence of the antecedents and/or consequences of specific events and (b) surface your generalized understandings of what was moving events along in the process you are studying.

For those who wish to create this illustration with computing software, selected CAQDAS programs such as NVivo permit you to create such networks easily, shifting and changing them as your understanding grows. Word text boxes are a more accessible option.

A cell-by-cell matrix is not necessarily required preparation for drawing a network, but it very helpful. In large-scale qualitative studies with a massive database, it is essential to have a firm grasp on the categorical/thematic and processual understandings before tackling a network. In small-scale qualitative studies with a more manageable

Display 8.7

Event-State Network, Banestown Case (Excerpt)

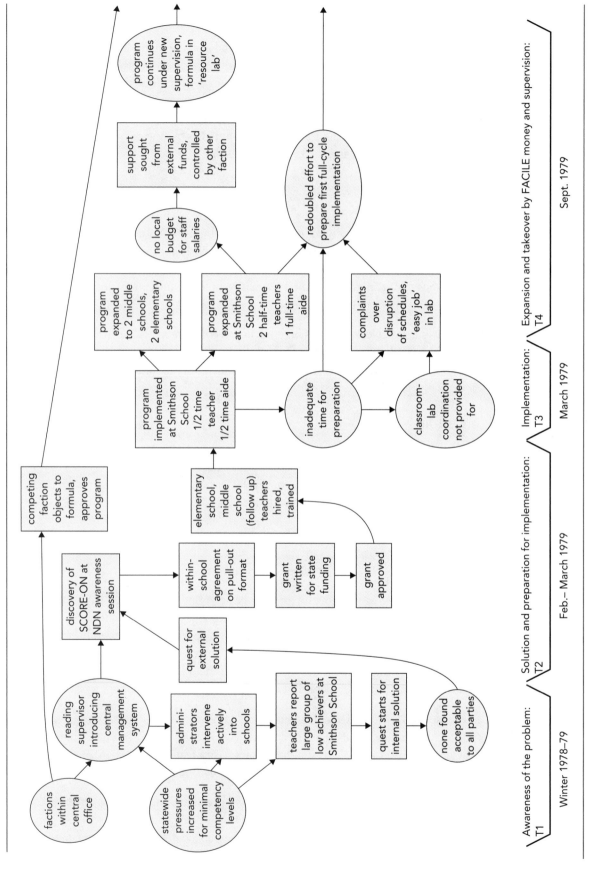

Source: Miles, M. B., & Huberman, A. M. (1994). *Qualitative data analysis: An expanded sourcebook* (2nd ed.). Thousand Oaks, CA: Sage Publications.

database, you can experiment with drawing networks *as a way of getting to* categorical/thematic and processual understandings.

Have a colleague examine your network without explanation to see if he or she can follow the processual trail. The audit may also generate valuable discussion for redesigning the drawing. For example, another analyst examined one of Saldaña's diagrams and took issue with how one state led to another. Saldaña agreed and even felt that his colleague's suggestion was correct. But the data suggested otherwise; how the researchers felt the process *should* happen was not the way the *participants* said it did. Thus, the participants' version was accepted as the final say for the network.

Notes

Event–state networks are a visual and processual way to make sense of a text-based event-listing matrix. It does not usually help to accompany the network with a long narrative text; the display itself is more economical and illuminating. But a summary set of analytic comments may be useful.

Composite Sequence Analysis

Description

A composite sequence analysis extracts typical stories or scenarios from multiple individual cases to develop a collective network that represents their common and unique features in meaningful sequences and paths (see Display 8.8).

Applications

There are analytic occasions when you need to describe multiple participant journeys through time. These stories can be told through individual narratives and then through a thematically connected one. But the length and number of these individual stories may be too much to grasp in one sitting. A composite sequence display graphically illustrates the participants' collective journey across time (and/or space), while maintaining the tangential and idiosyncratic veer-offs necessary for texture and detail.

Longitudinal research is also interested in demarcated periods of time, such as phases, stages, and cycles (Saldaña, 2003). These patterned periodicities provide us with a short- and long-term understanding of how the rhythms of life or work may proceed. We are better prepared for the journey if we know what may lie ahead. Thus, there is predictive utility in composite sequence analysis and display design.

Example

This example comes from Huberman's (1989, 1993) life cycle study of 160 teachers. Huberman was interested in what he called career trajectories of teachers. He was working from 5-hour interviews with secondary-level teachers, all of whom had divided their careers into phases or stages. They themselves provided the names or themes for each phase, rather than responding to a stimulus list.

First, the material for each case was condensed into a 25-page protocol, with an identical format for each participant. For each person's career trajectory, the sequence of themes was mapped, with the features of each theme added in. An initial theme labeled "Drowning," for example, was often characterized by features such as difficulties with keeping discipline, exhaustion, unpredictability, feelings of professional inadequacy, overload, and the like.

Compostite Sequence Analysis: Career Trajectory Data for 11 Cases (Huberman, 1989)

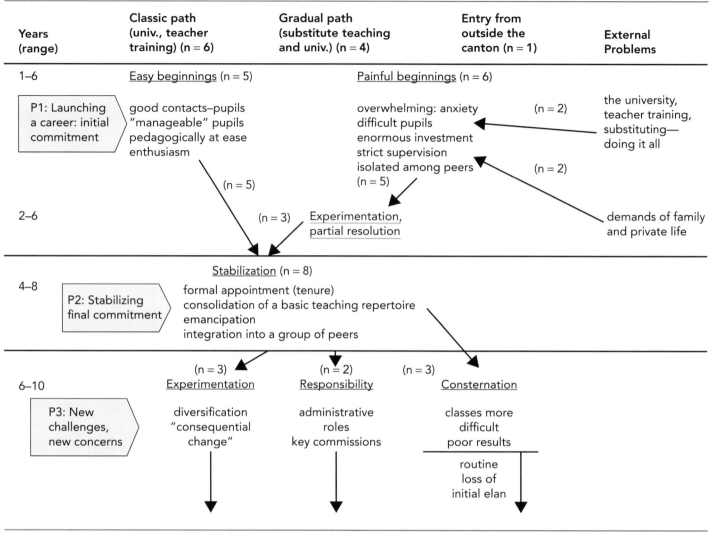

Source: Huberman, A. M. (1989). The professional life cycle of teachers. *Teachers College Record, 91*(1), 31–57.

How could you begin to group the cases, phase by phase, to see any "families" of trajectories? The first step was to group cases *within* phases. The decision rules for grouping cases within a given phase were that (a) the theme itself had to be denotatively or connotatively identical and (b) at least two features had to be the same. For example, one participant might name a "stabilizing" phase and another a "settling down" phase, while both teachers were at the same point in their sequence and each used two of the same features to describe that phase (e.g., gaining tenure, having a basic instructional repertoire).

Graphically, this procedure amounts to an "overlay" of individual trajectories, although it is clear that seen up close, each career is qualitatively distinct. But we do get, as Wittgenstein put it so well, "family resemblances," with some intersections, along with the distinctive properties.

Analysis

Let's illustrate these intersections by a look at Display 8.8. It depicts 11 teachers, 1 of 16 subgroups; here we have women with 5 to 10 years of teaching experience at the lower secondary level.

At the left is the range of years of teaching experience within phases and a series of general phases defined by the researchers in light of the phase names given by the participants:

P1: Launching a career: initial commitment

P2: Stabilizing: final commitment

P3: New challenges, new concerns

Within each general phase are subgroups. For example, of the 11 women, 5 describe their initial phase in terms of "Easy beginnings" (tactic: **clustering**). The common features are noted under the theme. Six women evoke "Painful beginnings," again with a list of features, and 4 mention external problems (parallel work at "the university" and "teacher training"; "demands of family and private life"). Through experimentation and trials and errors, these problems are attenuated for 3 women.

The second phase, *Stabilization*, is common to nearly all. It is, in effect, one of those archetypical stages in the teaching career. Note, however, that $n = 8$, meaning that 3 of the original cohort of 11 have not followed the sequence but rather have taken another path (not shown on the display). In that sense, the sequential analysis gets progressively more stringent. It groups only participants who have attached identical or analogous themes to the same sequence of phases.

Display 8.8 shows a third phase for this cohort, "New challenges," in which the paths diverge still more into three tracks: (1) *Experimentation* (3 teachers), (2) *Responsibility* (2 teachers), and (3) *Consternation* (3 teachers). Once again, these thematic names are provided by the participants.

In this study, the researchers were taking a variable-oriented approach while still trying for a narrative ordering of the data. They were hunting for correspondences across the full set of 160 participants. By reviewing 16 charts like the one just shown, they came out with four modal sequences. The first scenario—the prime sequence in Display 8.8—accounts for 17% of the population and was called "Recovered harmony":

Painful beginnings → Stabilization → Experimentation

Another sequence represents 25% of the sample—by no means the majority, but a strong cluster—a clutch of people describing their career progression in terms of "Reassessment":

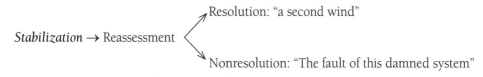

Taken together, the four scenarios located account for 65% of the sample. Much has been lost in the condensation of 25 pages of interview data to a bare-bones sequence in Display 8.8. But we argue that, in conceptual terms, it is this last scenario-building exercise that tells us most graphically how the case narratives cluster—in this instance, how the teaching career plays out for different subgroups of its members. And we have successfully linked a case-oriented with a variable-oriented approach, protecting case sequences and gaining the conceptual power that cut-across variables can bring.

The most important preparatory work for constructing a composite sequence display is having a solid grasp on how the phases are narratively told and what researcher- or participant-generated words/phrases best describe and label the phases. This is one of those analytic tasks that asks you to consider what all of the differences—or at least most of them—have in common. You may also discover that working concurrently and back and forth on both the narrative and the display will help inform the other's development.

Notes

This method reinforces that network displays can handle narrative complexity more easily than matrices can.

For an excellent longitudinal qualitative study that describes five different early-career decisions in teaching, see Cochran-Smith et al. (2012).

Ordering by Cases

A *case-ordered descriptive meta-matrix* hierarchically organizes cases according to selected criteria to compare common variables or outcomes of interest.

Case-Ordered Descriptive Meta-Matrix

Description

A case-ordered descriptive meta-matrix contains first-level descriptive data from all cases, but the cases are *ordered* (e.g., high, medium, low) according to the main variable being examined. Thus, it coherently arrays the basic data for a major variable across all cases (see Displays 8.9 and 8.10).

Display 8.9

Ordered Meta-Matrix: Format for Student Impact Data

		Direct effects		Meta-level & side effects	
CASES	Program objectives	Positive	Negative	Positive	Negative
CASE 1 *(highest impact)*					
CASE 2 *(next)*					
etc.					

Source: Miles, M. B., & Huberman, A. M. (1994). *Qualitative data analysis: An expanded sourcebook* (2nd ed.). Thousand Oaks, CA: Sage Publications.

Applications

Case-ordered displays array data case by case, but the cases are ordered according to some variable of interest, so that you can easily see the differences among high, medium, and low cases. It's a powerful way of understanding differences across cases to help answer questions such as the following: What are the real patterns of more and less X in the cases? Why do we see more X at one site or case and less of it in another? This makes the method particularly suitable for evaluation and action research studies.

Example

In our (Miles and Huberman) school improvement study, we were interested in a variable we called "student impact." We had interviewed not only students themselves but also teachers, parents, administrators, and counselors—and had looked at formal evaluation data as well. We wanted to assemble this information in one place and understand the differences among cases that showed high, medium, or low student impact.

Our interviewing and data retrieval focused not only on "direct" student outcomes (e.g., improved reading test scores) but also on what we called "meta-level" or more general outcomes (e.g., increased interest in school activities) and "side effects" (e.g., "zest in experimental program leads to alienation from regular classes"). We also wanted to track both positive and negative effects of the innovation on students.

How can the cases be ordered? You can look at the relevant sections of each case report and note the general level of student impact the writer of the case report had claimed. You place the cases in rough order, and then you reskim the text in each case report to see whether the first impression is justified or whether the ordering should be changed. Some programs aimed high, shooting for everything from student achievement to self-concept, while others were more focused, hoping only, say, for the improvement of reading skills. The reading also showed us that the data were of variable robustness—ranging from detailed and thorough achievement data, interviews, and questionnaire responses to nearly unsupported opinion.

That range suggests the usefulness of a format like Display 8.9. The idea here is to show the objectives and to enter data in the form of phrases or sentences in the appropriate cells. This way, we keep more of the raw data, and we can see how outcomes are related to objectives. Our own matrix legend/shorthand to show the data source (i.e., Attribute Codes) was as follows: U for user, A for administrator, E for evaluator, S for student, P for parent, and so on. If the impact was seen as strong, the letter would be underlined; if uncertain, a question mark would be added; if the evidence was conflicting, an X would be added (i.e., Magnitude Codes).

From relevant sections of each case report, we look for coded material on direct and meta-level outcomes and summarize the material in a set of brief sentences or phrases, one for each distinct outcome. We can arrange the data in the Program Objectives and the Direct Outcome columns in parallel fashion to make comparisons easier. Skills and achievement goals might be placed first, followed by affective/attitudinal and other outcomes.

After the data are all assembled into the matrix, review again: Are the cases correctly ordered from high to low student impact? In this case, some criteria for a "high" rating are as follows:

Case-Ordered Descriptive Meta-Matrix (Excerpt): Program Objectives and Student Impact (Direct, Meta-Level, and Side Effects)

CASES		Direct Outcome		Meta-Level Outcomes and Side Effects	
High Impact	**Program Objectives**	**Positive**	**Negative**	**Positive**	**Negative**
Perry-Parkdale (E)	Basic skills (reading, math, communication, etc.) Life skills (critical thinking, citizenship) Life competencies (credit, health, etc.) Job-finding skills Entry-level work skills, career training Decision-making skills Self-responsibility and initiative Matching interests/abilities to job information Understanding of others Know socioeconomic trends: career knowledge Sex role awareness Better parent-child communication	Same or better on basic skills scores U, better math (12th grade girls) E P Specific job skills S E P U Career planning and choice: aids goalless Job exploration attitudes positive E How interests fit jobs, what to look for in job E: identity, explore career options C A Experience with world of work: head start C U S Career, occupational knowledge E Preparation for real world of work Experience in working with adults: P communicating with them better U	Less exposure to academic courses C	Personal development, identity, U E P Better communication with adults U S Self-confidence U E P S Increased attendance U Responsibility, motivation U C E P Staying in school (lower-level students) C A U Help goalless students A Improved peer relations U Getting permanent job S Parent-child communication P	Some students "get lost" again after a while U Some bide time, don't "deliver" U Program more effective with girls U Alienation from regular school activities C A S Irresponsibility, "can't handle freedom" P U
Masepa (E)	Improvement in full range of language arts skills (see at right) More on-task behavior Improved discipline	Increased skills: vocabulary U A P, spelling U A, phonetics Ux, punctuation U, reading comprehension Ux E, reading decoding U, grammar U, written expression U Low achievers more productive Ux	Retention levels not good U Too little diversity Student fatigue U	Concentration, study skills Fewer discipline problems U A More attentive to errors U Better academic self-concept U More enjoyment, enthusiasm U A Work with less supervision, more responsible A U Less time lost, more time on task U A E Rapid students progress faster E	Some lagging, failing mastery tests U Boredom U
Moderate Impact					
Canon (L)	Increased achievement Clearer career interests Friendliness Improved self-concept as a learner More internal locus of control	Career knowledge U A C Work on new interests U		Achievement composite (use of resources) E Better classroom attitude U Attitude to school E U Self-concept as learner (HS) F Friendliness E Social studies (elem) Self-understanding E	Little effect on achievement U

(Continued)

CASES	Program Objectives	Direct Outcome		Meta-Level Outcomes and Side Effects	
		Positive	Negative	Positive	Negative
Moderate Impact					
Calston (E)	Basic reading skills, plus use of reading as tool for learning: literature appreciation: reading for enjoyment	Increased criterion referenced test scores A U More reading skills Ux		Learning to work independently self-managing U A Self-motivation A: children like independent work U Children proud to come to school A Children not competing A Reduced discipline problems A	
Moderate to Low Impact					
Dun Hollow (L)	Eliminate stereotyping of Eskimos Knowledge of Eskimo history, customs, current life Create positive image of Eskimo culture	Some learning of culture, reduction of stereotypes U A More reading skills Ux	Information too detailed U		Some students behind in language arts U
Low Impact					
Burton (E)	Knowledge & practical skills re political/government/legal processes (voter education, state government, individual rights)	Concept learning, by being in different roles U Experience in active learning approach A	No effects discernible U		

Legend for sources of data:

U = user
A = administrator
C = counselor
P = parent
E = evaluator
S = student

Underlined letters refer to mention by at least two persons
x = presence of dissenting or conflicting opinion

(E) = externally-developed innovation
(L) = locally-developed innovation

Source: Miles, M. B., & Huberman, A. M. (1994). *Qualitative data analysis: An expanded sourcebook* (2nd ed.). Thousand Oaks, CA: Sage Publications.

1. The program is achieving most of its aims.

2. The program is also achieving other positive meta-level and side effects.

3. These judgments are corroborated, either through repeated responses from one role through cross-role agreement, or through evaluation data.

Display 8.10 shows how this kind of data display worked out. The rows show two cases (Perry-Parkdale, Masepa) where student impact was high, two where it was moderate (Carson, Calston), one where it was moderate to low (Dun Hollow), and one where it was low (Burton). (For simplicity, we show an excerpted table, with only 6 of our 12 cases.)

Analysis

At first glance, Display 8.10 looks daunting and overloading. But first try a "squint analysis" by asking where in the table the data look dense or sparse.

Looking across rows, we can see that positive effects are more frequent than negative ones (tactic: **making contrasts, comparisons**). Another squint shows us that cases where many negative effects are noted (e.g., Perry-Parkdale, Masepa) are cases where much is being attempted (in terms of the Program Objectives column). Apparently, large efforts are more likely to spin off negative effects along with the positive ones (tactic: **noting relations between variables**).

Looking at the two right-hand columns shows significant meta-level and side effects in nearly all cases (tactic: **noting patterns, themes**); in only the lowest impact case (Burton) do we see none at all. Perhaps this pattern means that the claims for meta-level changes in moderate-impact cases are suspect. Maybe so—they are less likely to have repeated mention (underlines) and have fewer instances of multiple-role confirmation (tactic: **using extreme cases**).

To clarify the last two columns, we defined meta-level outcomes as congruent with the program's purposes but affecting the more general aspects of students' functioning. Note the reading program at Calston: It led to the direct outcome of improved reading skills; but by providing interesting materials and opportunities for independent student work, it may have induced the meta-level outcome of increased student self-direction. Side effects are more unintended: Note the alienation of Perry-Parkdale students, who liked their program's concreteness and relevance but thereby came to dislike their regular high school's courses and activities.

During analysis of a case-ordered descriptive meta-matrix, first do a general squint. What does the matrix look like—where is it dense, where empty? Draw conclusions, and write them out. Then, look down particular columns, **comparing/contrasting** what things look like for high, medium, and low cases. It may be useful to look at more than one column at a time to **note relations between variables**.

A first-cut case-ordered descriptive meta-matrix can be big. We sometimes have used up to 20 columns in trying to sort out a wide range of variables that might bear on the main "ordering" variable. Excel database software comes in very handy for these types and sizes of matrices. Expect to make several cuts at the format of the matrix before you settle on the one best for your purposes. Recheck the ordering of cases at several points as you proceed; ask a colleague to confirm or argue with your ordering. For less complex databases, it often helps to enter actual direct quotes from case reports, rather than constructed sentences or phrases. They give an even more direct grounding in the data for the analyst and the reader.

Notes

Miles and Huberman's classic Display 8.10 employed a legend of single letters and symbols to differentiate between sources and corroboration of data. Today, software such as Word and Excel can color code or use rich text features and varying font sizes to separate different types of data from one another in a matrix and make them much more visually discernable at a glance.

A case-ordered descriptive meta-matrix is usually a fundamental next step in understanding what's going on across cases. Assuming that you have a good basis for ordering the cases, it's far more powerful than a partially ordered matrix: Patterns can be seen for high, medium, and low cases; and the beginnings of explanations can emerge. "Aha" experiences are likely. Generally speaking, time spent on this is well worth the investment because so much later analysis rests on it.

Also remember that rows and columns can be transposed for your analytic goals. It's usually easier to show effects by rows rather than columns, simply because there is more space to write headings there. You can create a *case-ordered effects matrix* that sorts cases by degrees of the major cause being studied and shows the diverse effects for each case. The focus is on *outcomes* across multiple cases when multiple variables also need to be examined simultaneously (see Display 8.11).

Display 8.11

Case-Ordered Effects Matrix Template

CASES, by assistance provided

Effects on the innovation	Substantial						Moderate			Low		
1.												
2.												
3. . . .												
Effects on individuals												
1.												
2.												
3. . . .												
Effects on the organization												
1.												
2.												
3.												
4. . . .												

Source: Miles, M. B., & Huberman, A. M. (1994). *Qualitative data analysis: An expanded sourcebook* (2nd ed.). Thousand Oaks, CA: Sage Publications.

Case-ordered effects matrices are especially useful when you anticipate a wide diversity of effects from a general cause—itself varying across cases. They fall just about at the fuzzy boundary between cross-case description and explanation, providing leads for theory building and testing. The matrix also helps you avoid aggregation, keeping case data distinct, and lets you look at deviant cases. In sum, a case-ordered effects matrix enables you to bring together and order several cases, variables, and time simultaneously to see their multiple outcome configurations.

Closure and Transition

Most ordering displays are complex because we are attempting to multidimensionally and simultaneously document cases, ranks, variables, actions, time periods, outcomes, and/or assessments. Basic software literacy and access for most of us are limited to two-dimensional renderings, when we wish we could draw in three dimensions or animate some of our graphics. But two-dimensional matrices and figures bring us one step closer toward understanding complex participant processes.

Exploring, describing, and ordering data are necessary prerequisites for the next chapter's methods: *explaining*. Rich and insightful answers are generated from posing "how" and "why" questions.

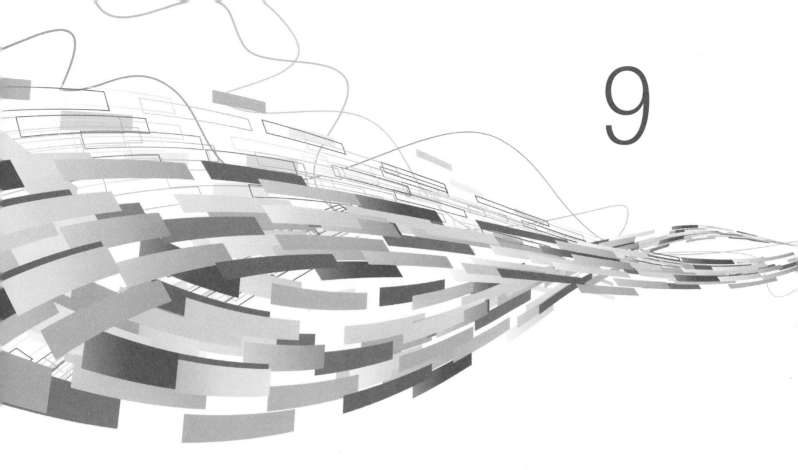

Methods of Explaining

Chapter Summary

This chapter explores how displays can be used to construct explanations for interrelationships, change, and causation. Matrices and networks are carefully designed and plotted to map research stories of antecedents, sequences, and outcomes.

Contents

Introduction
Explaining Interrelationship
    Variable-by-Variable Matrix
Explaining Change
    Effects Matrix
    Case Dynamics Matrix
Explaining Causation
    Causal Chains
    Causal Network: Within-Case Analysis
    Causal Network: Cross-Case Analysis
Closure and Transition

Introduction

We've been profiling methods for developing coherent descriptions of *what* and *how* things happen across a number of cases. In this chapter, we turn to questions of *why*.

Why things happen is at the forefront of the research experience, once you're past the basic problem of understanding just *what* is happening. That question is also a salient one for people in their day-to-day lives; questions of "why" and "how come" and answers beginning with "because" appear constantly in day-to-day interactions.

The conventional view is that qualitative studies are only good for exploratory or descriptive forays and that strong explanations, including causal attributions, can be derived only through quantitative studies, particularly the classical experimental–control design. We consider this view mistaken. Even the most elegant quantitative procedures deal primarily with associations, not really causes. They can only develop plausible possibilities smoothed across many persons and situations. We consider qualitative analysis to be a very powerful method for assessing causation. But we have to go far beyond assertion, showing an empirical basis for the claim that *Y* is explained or caused/influenced by *X*.

Good explanations need to link the explanations given by the people we are studying with explanations we develop as researchers. But this link presents problems. Explanations offered in daily life have many flaws—and so do researchers' explanations. People may not always offer rational reasons for why something happens. Some may reduce the complexity of an event to a single root cause. Munton, Silvester, Stratton, and Hanks (1999) offer that "beliefs about causality can, and often do, involve multiple causes and multiple outcomes. . . . In sequences of attributions, an outcome in one attribution can become a cause in the next" (p. 9). Causes are not only multiple but also "conjunctural"—they combine and affect each other as well as the "effects." Furthermore, effects of multiple causes are not the same in all contexts, and different combinations of causes can turn out to have similar effects. Thus, to Saldaña (2003), *influences and affects* may be the more accurate way to reconceptualize the positivist construct of "cause and effect." But in this volume, *effects* as a term will be used more often to harmonize with the methodological display principles of causation established by Miles and Huberman.

Morrison (2009) advises that we should carefully consider the nuanced differences between a cause, a reason, and a motive and to keep our focus primarily on people's intentions, choices, objectives, values, perspectives, expectations, needs, desires, and agency within their particular contexts and circumstances: "It is individuals, not variables [like social class, sex, ethnicity, etc.], which do the acting and the causing" (p. 116). People are not like billiard balls, each progressing in its own direction after they've been struck. People have complex intentions operating in a complex web of others' intentions and actions. Another line of reasoning emphasizes the "disorderly" nature of social facts; they are more chaotic and less coherent than our minds make them. There ought to be ways for us to understand how human events and meanings, actions and intentions, are chained over time, as slippery and disorderly as they may be.

Just as there's no clean boundary between description and explanation, there's no precise demarcation between general "explanation" and "causation." It's not fair to say that determining causation is necessarily a stronger form of explanation than others. At the minimum, we can note that causation decisively brings in the question of *time*: We are concerned with finding out what led to what. Prior events are assumed to have some connection with following events, even though that connection may not be neat and clear.

So assessing causation is essentially a retrospective matter. Even if we do a classic experiment, we cannot tell what the effects were until afterward. It can proceed by the creation and parsing of stories, the flow of connected events in context. In the *process* mode, we'll be likely to assemble chronologies, pay attention to time, and look for connections within the big picture. In the *variable* mode, we'll be likely to code small chunks of data, retrieve them, and look for similarities and conceptual patterns, with less regard to setting, sequence, and the passage of time. Clearly, *both* stances will be needed at different points in a study. The issue is being aware of your analytic assumptions and acting on them appropriately, moving back and forth between story and concept modes to deepen each.

Qualitative analysis, with its close-up look, can identify *mechanisms*, going beyond sheer association. It is unrelentingly *local* and deals well with the *complex* network of events and processes in a situation. It can sort out the *temporal* dimension, showing clearly what preceded what, either through direct observation or through *retrospection*. It is well equipped to cycle back and forth between *variables* and *processes*—showing that stories are not capricious but include underlying variables and that variables are not disembodied but have connections over time.

Explanatory matrices usually require more careful attention to various forms of ordering. And multiple cases are extraordinarily helpful in both generating explanations and testing them systematically. In a real sense, they are our best resource for advancing our assertions and theories about the way social life works. But we should not delude ourselves that scientific explanation is somehow lofty, wholly determinate, and precise. Research never "proves" anything; at best, it *suggests*.

In this chapter, *Explaining Interrelationship* examines how variables interact and interplay. *Explaining Change* looks at the multiple pathways leading toward outcome variables. And *Explaining Causation* provides methods for displaying and narrating the "how" and "why" of a study's outcomes. Also, refer back to *Explanatory Effects Matrix* and the accompanying Display 6.15 on page 141 in Chapter 6 for a preliminary charting of causes for further analysis.

Explaining Interrelationship

Interrelationship is one of the foundation principles for methods of explaining change and explaining causation. *Variable-by-Variable Matrix* first explores the interaction and interplay between multiple pairs of variables to see whether they apply to selected cases.

Variable-by-Variable Matrix

Description

A variable-by-variable matrix has two main variables in its rows and columns. Specific properties or components of each variable are individually listed and ordered by intensity. The cell entries, rather than being data bits, are case names, so that we can see which cases (themselves also ordered on a variable) include a specific type of interaction or interrelationship between the two main variables (see Display 9.1).

Display 9.1

Variable-by-Variable Matrix: Coping Strategies and Problems, by Case

STYLE	Coping Strategies	Program Process	Program Content	Target Pop.	Skill Lacks	Attitudes	Crises	Competing Demands	Low Control	Physical Setting	Resources
	Can't determine	BURR	ALAMEDA						CARUSO		
DO NOTHING	None	CHESTER			CARUSO	CHESTER			CHESTER		
TEMPORIZE	Delaying/avoiding		CARUSO			CHESTER					
DO IT THE USUAL WAY	Short-run coping	CARUSO CHESTER	CARUSO							CARUSO	CARUSO
	Using existing meetings/roles	ALAMEDA BURR CARUSO CHESTER	CHESTER								ALAMEDA CARUSO
	Action-taking	CARUSO									
	People-shuffling		CARUSO?			AGASSIZ	CARUSO CHESTER				CARUSO
EASE OFF	Program modification		BURR	AGASSIZ BURR CARUSO	BURR?	BURR		BURR			
DO IT HARDER	Symbolic support					AGASSIZ CARUSO CHESTER		AGASSIZ			
	Rewards/incentives					AGASSIZ ALAMEDA BURR CHESTER					
	Negotiating										CHESTER
	Pressuring/requiring					BURR CHESTER					
BUILD PERSONAL CAPACITY	Person-changing	ALAMEDA		AGASSIZ ALAMEDA BURR?	AGASSIZ						

STYLE	Coping Strategies	Program Process	Program Content	Target Pop.	Skill Lacks	Attitudes	Crises	Competing Demands	Low Control	Physical Setting	Resources
BUILD SYSTEM CAPACITY	New orchestration structure	ALAMEDA CARUSO	CARUSO		ALAMEDA						ALAMEDA CARUSO
	New interaction arenas			BURR							
	Vision-building/ sharing		AGASSIZ			AGASSIZ ALAMEDA BURR					
	Monitoring		CARUSO								
	Rolling planning					ALAMEDA					
	Ongoing assistance		AGASSIZ								AGASSIZ
ADD NEW PEOPLE	Re-staffing					ALAMEDA BURR					
	Increasing control							AGASSIZ	BURR?		AGASSIZ?
REDESIGN THE SYSTEM	Empowering	AGASSIZ ALAMEDA BURR?				AGASSIZ ALAMEDA					
	Role redesign										AGASSIZ
	Organization redesign										AGASSIZ ALAMEDA

Legend

AGASSIZ High School [more successful]

ALAMEDA High School [more successful]

BURROUGHS [BURR] High School [moderately successful]

CARUSO High School [less successful]

CHESTER High School [less successful]

? = Cases with less researcher certainty

Source: Miles, M. B., & Huberman, A. M. (1994). *Qualitative data analysis: An expanded sourcebook* (2nd ed.). Thousand Oaks, CA: Sage Publications.

Applications

Sometimes, after cases have been analyzed carefully, you begin to notice that a few major variables are in play, underlying many specific phenomena. Normally, you would like to know how these variables are connected or interrelated. The problem is how to keep the richness of specific indicators of the main variables, so as to see in more depth what the core relationships are.

A variable-by-variable matrix arranges individual properties or components of variables into distinct row and column headings to detect what types of associations or intersections may be occurring within cases and their data. It is both descriptive and ordered, exploratory and explanatory, for it matches cases with two variables to encourage you to explain why the interrelationship is suggested in the matrix.

Example

In a study of urban high school reform (Louis & Miles, 1990; Miles, 1986), one of the questions of interest was how schools coped with the inevitable problems encountered during the change process. The researcher had clustered and categorized the types of *problems* reported and ordered them from most to least "tractable" or solvable (see the column headings of Display 9.1). Problems such as program process and program content were relatively easy to deal with; problems stemming from the school's physical setting or available financial resources were judged as more difficult to resolve, on the basis of prior studies of educational reform. The first ordering was adjudicated with other members of the research team.

The researcher also developed, from the five high school cases at hand, a list of 23 coping strategies (the second column from the left): What do you do when faced with a problem? The strategies listed under coping strategies, such as delaying/avoiding, people shuffling, vision building/sharing, and role redesign, were sorted into nine stylistic clusters, such as DO NOTHING, DO IT THE USUAL WAY, DO IT HARDER, and REDESIGN THE SYSTEM. These clusters were then ordered according to a major shallow–deep dimension, one end of which was "shallow, soft, informal, less penetrating" and the other "deeper, more structurally oriented, deliberate, and person-changing." Here, too, the first cut required colleague feedback and revision.

Once the conceptual work was done, the matrix design was plotted: Rows were coping strategies, and columns were problem types. The cell entries were the five high school case names: Agassiz and Alameda had the most successful implementation; one case, Burroughs, was moderately successful; and Caruso and Chester were the least successful. Instances of problems and the associated coping strategies used were drawn from case report displays, field notes, and researcher judgments. The problem was sorted into the appropriate column, and the strategy used was identified by the researchers most knowledgeable through their fieldwork and case analysis. If more than one strategy had been used for the same problem, more than one cell entry was made. When the researcher was less certain about the problem-coping connection, the symbol "?" was added to the cell entry after a school's name. Altogether, 76 problem-coping pairs were entered for the five sites.

Analysis

Variable-by-variable matrix analysis relies primarily on eyeballing the results and making inferences about the connections. The analyst, looking at the top part of the table, wrote,

Most of the instances of "shallow" coping (DO NOTHING, TEMPORIZE, DO IT THE USUAL WAY) appear in the two less-successful sites: Caruso and Chester (tactic: **noting patterns, themes**).

Second, moving to the lower region of the table, it is quite striking to note that the deeper managing and coping strategies (BUILD PERSONAL & SYSTEM CAPACITY, ADD NEW PEOPLE, REDESIGN THE SYSTEM) are used mostly by more-successful sites. Except for the New orchestration structure and the Monitoring strategies at Caruso, such strategies are mostly absent in the less successful sites. The Burroughs moderately successful site employs a few "deep" strategies, but fewer than Agassiz and Alameda.

Then the analyst saw another **pattern**, a bit more complex. He focused on the Agassiz and Alameda sites and wrote the following:

> These sites actually use a very wide range of strategies, *except* for None and Delaying/avoiding. The feeling is one of actively doing whatever the problem seems to require, but having a repertoire that includes vigorous managing and capacity-building interventions where they are needed. . . . [They] show "deeper" coping for the more difficult problems.

To check the meaning of these findings further, the researcher returned to the case reports, to a section where the analyst had described the typical *results* of problem-coping efforts, and made a summary table shown in Display 9.2 (tactic: **replicating a finding**). This summary table not only synthesizes the findings, it helps pull together and support the variable-by-variable matrix associations.

Display 9.2

Summary Table: Typical Consequences of Coping, by Case

Agassiz	Most problems have been acknowledged, addressed, and solved.
	Main consequences is an increase in individual and collective self-confidence (both teachers and students).
	More downtown (central office) respect for school.
Alameda	Reduced anxiety, built more constructive norms.
	Better mesh with staff development, met teacher needs.
	New roles and empowerment meant that principal could be reassigned [without disruption of program].
Burroughs	Increased respect for principal's authority.
	Staff schism: people either big fans or opponents.
	Little investment by new staff in program.
	As trained staff moved to other schools, new staff did not know or have skill in program.
Caruso	Problems slightly ameliorated, but will recur.
Chester	Moderate coordination of the curriculum alignment part of the program, but of the remainder not.
	Problems will continue.

Source: Miles, M. B., & Huberman, A. M. (1994). *Qualitative data analysis: An expanded sourcebook* (2nd ed.). Thousand Oaks, CA: Sage Publications.

The more the properties and components of variables listed in the matrix rows and/ or columns, the more is the preparatory work required to review the data corpus and fill in the cells. But this is a worthwhile investment of time and energy to learn whether any interaction and interplay exist. This can transcend basic descriptive association to potentially explanatory reasoning.

The time dimension can be added to a variable-by-variable matrix by identifying cell entries as occurring earlier or later during some time period. Each cell entry could also include a magnitude code indicating how "successful" a strategy turned out to be. (In this particular display, did the problem recur, lead to new problems, or was it effectively solved?)

Notes

The cut-and-paste functions of Word tables and Excel databases permit easy rearrangement of rows and columns for exploratory analyses. Most CAQDAS programs have the ability to quickly assemble and display variable-by-variable (or code-by-code or category-by-category) matrices, thus enabling convenient examination of what possible interrelationships may be present within specific cases. Most of these programs can also provide statistical information as to the strength of an association.

Explaining Change

Both of these profiles illustrate a research story's trajectory and outcome with a focus on change, but they also serve as foundation methods for explaining causation. An *effects matrix* generally explains *what* eventually happened, while a *case dynamics matrix* charts *how* the outcomes came to be.

Effects Matrix

Description

An effects matrix displays data on one or more outcomes as the study requires. Effects are always outcomes of *something*—for example, a global program, an independent variable, an intervening variable. There is always at least an implicit predecessor, and the basic principle in an effects matrix is a focus on *dependent* variables (see Display 9.3).

Applications

In many studies, the researcher is interested in outcomes. An evaluator may want to know what changes a particular program or treatment brought about in its target population. A more descriptive researcher may simply want to know where things stood at the end of some process. A researcher aiming at explanations will usually want to have a good look at some main dependent variables of interest (e.g., reading scores, dropout rates, school social climate) before turning to predictor variables. These are examples of "ultimate" outcomes. This label may sound pretentious, but it only means that the variable is the last one being looked at in a temporal or causal chain. A researcher will be interested, too, in preceding outcomes, which usually are labeled "intervening" or "intermediate."

The problem for the qualitative researcher is how to select and display data that will faithfully represent the changed state of persons, relationships, groups, or organizations,

Display 9.3

Effects Matrix: Organizational Changes After Implementation of the ECRI Program

Effect Type	Early Use 1st and 2nd Years		Later Use 3rd Year	
	Primary Changes	Spin-Offs	Primary Changes	Spin-Offs
Structural	Scheduling: ECRI all morning, rescheduling music, phys. ed. Helping teacher named: has dual status (teach/admin)	Cutting back on math, optional activities Two separate regimens in school Ambiguity of status and role	Integrated scheduling, cross-age grouping in grades 2-6	Less individual latitude: classroom problems become organizational problems
Procedural	No letter grades, no norms Institutionalizing assistance via helping teacher	Parents uneasy 2 regimens in class Teachers insecure Loosens age-grading system In-house assistance mechanism implanted	ECRI evaluation sheets, tightening supervision More uniformity in work in all classes	Teachers more visible, inspectable Problems, solutions more common, public
Relational/ Climate	Users are minority, band together	Cliques, friction between users, non-users	Tighter academic press Perception by teachers of collective venture	Reduction in "fun activities," projects (e.g., Xmas) More lateral help More 'public' distress

Source: Miles, M. B., & Huberman, A. M. (1994). *Qualitative data analysis: An expanded sourcebook* (2nd ed.). Thousand Oaks, CA: Sage Publications.

seen as one or more outcomes of interest. Words are much harder to manage in this respect than numbers. For qualitative data, clarifying just which outcomes have occurred is not always an easy process. Conceptual clarity is at a premium.

Example

When an organization, such as a school, implements an innovation, the possibility exists that the organization may change in some way as a consequence. Although some innovations can be "dropped into" an existing structure, serving as a replaceable part, most innovations turn out to make demands on the system and have ripple effects. The organizational response often shows up in the form of something new—new attitudes, new rules, new procedures, and new structures. In the school improvement study, we (Miles and Huberman) wanted to study the changes in local schools that were traceable to their having implemented an innovation. The Exemplary Center for

Reading Instruction (ECRI) innovation in this example is a relatively demanding, rather structured, language arts program being implemented in an elementary school. It takes a behaviorist approach to word recognition, phonetics, composition, and vocabulary.

First, we need to make clear what makes up the bundle called an "outcome" (in this case, organizational change). What parts or aspects does it have? Display 9.3 shows how this worked out. The analyst decided that the outcome "organizational change" has three basic parts: (1) structural changes, (2) procedural or operating changes, and, more general, (3) relational or social climate changes.

Second, the analyst, reflecting on the particular case at hand, believes that such aspects of organizational change should be displayed separately for the early-use period (first and second years) and for later use, when 9 of the school's 11 teachers were users of the innovation.

Third, the analyst wants to distinguish between primary changes—those directly following from the requirements of the innovation's implementation—and those termed *spin-offs*—secondary effects, some of which may not have been fully anticipated. Because the usual convention (at least in a culture where the printed word is read from left to right) is that later events should be displayed to the right of earlier events, the analyst puts the time dimension in columns and the outcome types in rows.

The cell entries in Display 9.3 are brief phrases describing specific organizational changes found in the coded write-ups of field notes. The original question to teachers, their principal, and several central office personnel was "Did any changes occur in the organization of the school or the district during this period?" Follow-up probes asked about specific structural or "setup" changes, procedural changes, and climate or feeling shifts. The decision rule was that any change reported and verified by a document or at least one other respondent would be condensed to a summary phrase for entry into the matrix.

Analysis

A look at the left side of the table shows us that the major structural change was rescheduling previously separate language arts activities into one integrated morning period; this change required rescheduling of the subjects taught by circulating teachers (music, physical education). This change, in turn (see the Spin-Offs column), created two separate daily regimens, because the scheduling was done for two ECRI users in the first year and five in the second year. Other teachers were on the old schedule.

Other early changes included use of mastery levels, rather than letter grades, and the creation of a new helping teacher role to assist new users of ECRI. We can see by moving vertically down the columns that (as has been found in much social psychological research) structural changes tend to lead to procedural changes and, in turn, to climate/ attitudinal changes (tactic: **making conceptual/theoretical coherence**). In this case, the pressure, insecurity, and special attention led to a "we unhappy few" climate change, where users banded together. Moving across the climate row, we can see the spin-off effect: cliques and friction.

Moving to the right half of the matrix (Later Use, 3rd Year), we can note that because 9 of 11 teachers were now involved, scheduling became more integrated and close supervision and uniformity were more typical. And it is suggested that the fuller scale, more regulated implementation now is seen by teachers as a collective venture. Looking across from primary changes to spin-offs, we observe that teachers are both more likely and better able to express the need for help and to give and receive it (tactic: **building a logical chain of evidence**).

This display lets us see how structural changes induce procedural and attitude changes. We can see how first-level changes lead to later consequences (spin-offs), and we can see how organizational changes flowed and developed over the 3-year period. Naturally, these conclusions all need to be confirmed, tested, and verified—for example, by **looking for negative evidence** or **checking out rival explanations**. But we have a good running start on what the effects added up to. If we simply had bundled all of the reported organizational changes into one content-analytic summary, all of this information would have been lost.

Effects matrices also can be organized by specific *persons*. You can show, for example, the changes in concepts, attitudes, and behavior experienced by several teachers as a result of their use of an innovation through quoted interview excerpts. Effects matrices might also employ magnitude codes such as + or - or numeric ratings of some kind to display users' perceptions of the outcomes.

Effects data can be retrieved from observation or available documents, as well as from interviews. And the typical "program"—a treatment aimed at achieving outcomes—has some type of evaluation component attached to it, with some already collected data, which can be incorporated as well.

Finally, outcomes can be sorted according to their directness. Some outcomes are "direct" effects, like the primary changes just noted. Others are more general; they might be termed "meta-effects," outcomes that go considerably beyond the immediate direct effects the innovation is supposed to have. And we can think of "side effects," outcomes quite far away from the original intention.

Notes

It is most unlikely that any innovation is perfectly implemented and happily accepted by everyone involved. If your effects matrix does not include negative (undesired) outcomes, be prepared to give a good justification for the reader.

Case Dynamics Matrix

Description

A case dynamics matrix displays a set of forces for change and traces the consequential processes and outcomes. The basic principle is one of preliminary explanation (see Display 9.4).

Applications

The analyst, during and after data collection, is constantly trying to link data with explanations and trying to understand why specific things happen as they do and how people in the cases explain why things happen as they do. A case dynamics matrix illustrates, in a preliminary way, the explanations that seem relevant to a particular question.

Display 9.4

Case Dynamics Matrix: The IPA Innovation as a Force for Organizational Change in the District and Its Schools

Strains, Difficulties Created	Underlying Issues (as Seen by Researcher)	How Coped With	How Resolved: Type of Resulting Change
Conflicting expectations: should parents or teachers do activities?	Work load. Parent-teacher role conflict.	"Explaining" that teachers could not take primary responsibility for out-of-school activities.	Increased use of "batched" activities, many set up by coordinator (P).
View that forms and procedures were "extra," overloading.	Work load. Autonomy, resistance to control.	In-service assistance.	Repeated revision and simplification of forms and procedures; production of an operating manual. Reduction of expectations (no home visits, fewer conferences) (P).
User uncertainty and resistance to use.	Autonomy.	In-service assistance. Management Team interviews of all staff.	See above. Also creation of in-service committee (S), with coordination through Management Team (P).
Extra time requirements.	Work load.	Initially, via volunteerism, high commitment.	Use of substitutes (P). Dismissal of school during conference days (P). Reduction of expectations (above).
Program is complex, demanding, externally funded.	Authority, coordination, accountability.	Early creation of Management Team, addition of elementary teachers.	Institutionalization of Management Team (S). Heightened expectations for teacher upward influence (C). Lowered morale when expectations violated (C).
Enthusiasm of "advocate" teachers led to peer criticism.	Autonomy.	Quieting conflicts through informal discussion. Informal coordination and referral.	Norms supporting flexibility and colleague influence within schools, and cross-school interaction (C). Increased linkage and closer interaction between schools (C). Hobby Day (P).

(S) Structural change
(P) Procedural change
(C) Climate change

Source: Miles, M. B., & Huberman, A. M. (1994). *Qualitative data analysis: An expanded sourcebook* (2nd ed.). Thousand Oaks, CA: Sage Publications.

Example

Suppose you were interested, as we (Miles and Huberman) were, in the school improvement study, in the question of how and why an innovation induces change in the organization implementing it. That is an important "why" question because the history of many educational innovations is that they are either shrugged off or absorbed into routine operating procedure, disappearing without a trace. Under what conditions does this *not* happen?

If we are looking for causes, we might start with "dynamic" issues—things with a pushing or demanding quality. In this instance, they might be "demands," "requirements," or "strains" that the innovation carries with it. These can be in rows of the matrix. For columns, we could include underlying issues or assumptions about the meaning of these demands, the organizational coping responses, and how things finally settled down in terms of the resulting organizational changes.

Display 9.4 shows how this works out. The innovation is a program for doing individualized educational planning for all students in a school district, not just those involved in special education. As such, it had been deliberately designed locally to be an organizational, districtwide change, with its procedures to be used routinely by all staff.

Looking through coded field notes, the analyst can pick out chunks of material marked by relevant codes. In this case, the coded data were as follows:

- Implementation problems
- Effects on organizational practice
- Effects on organizational climate
- Explanations for effects on the organization

The analyst has also decided to sort organizational effects into three exhaustive general classes: (1) structural, (2) procedural, and (3) climate.

The decision rules for data entry in Display 9.4 were as follows: (a) locate distinctly different "demands," and summarize in a phrase or two the essence of the demand, the coping method, and the resolution; (b) use only data that are not contradicted by other informants; (c) for "underlying issues," move up a level of abstraction, drawing on ideas about organizational theory and the explanations site people offer, and enter concepts that seem most relevant.

Analysis

As always, *any* display forecloses some issues. Here, the analyst is looking at only those demand-caused effects that actually constituted an organizational change and is tacitly excluding demands that cause no organizational effects or are absorbed without a trace.

In this sort of matrix, much analysis occurs during the actual data entry, which is done by moving across each row. By the time the row is filled in, the analyst has a first sense of what the dynamics have been (tactic: **noting patterns, themes**). Analytic, summarizing text can be written by cycling back as needed to the written-up field notes for amplification and clarification. Here is an example of such text for the first row of Display 9.4:

> The enthusiasm of the "early settlers" in IPA was strong; teachers would often spend a weekend with one of their five children, doing special activities. But as the program expanded, there was tension and role conflict: Parents somehow expected teachers to carry out all the activities. Official explanations that parents and students would have to "take responsibility" were only partially effective; the most favorable estimate was that only 25-30 percent of parents actually helped out, and a few were actually resistant to "nonschool" activities. The gap had to be filled by the coordinator, who was increasingly expected to set things up and carry them out.

Similar analyses can proceed row by row.

We can also look at the types of resulting change in the last column (How Resolved), noting that genuine structural changes are fewer than procedural or climate changes (tactic: **counting**). And we can look down the Underlying Issues column to see that issues of workload and autonomy are occurring repeatedly (tactic: **clustering**). Cycling back to the How Resolved column, we can see that workload issues were generally resolved through routinization and reduction of effort.

Using the tactic of **making contrasts, comparisons**, we can see that autonomy issues were resolved in an interesting, unexpected way: increased interdependence and colleague influence. When the analyst runs into such a conclusion, it poses a puzzle: how to shed light on an unpredicted finding. This calls for the tactic of **following up surprises**. Reviewing field notes further, the analyst comments,

> It also appeared that the program induced more elementary-secondary contact and collaboration—partly because many teachers were themselves parents, and experienced the IPA program in that role (and could notice poor or partial implementation as well as benefits).

With this type of display, we aren't wholly stuck in row-by-row analyses and can see how rows influence each other—even though this is not as rich as a network display would be.

The data in this sort of explanatory matrix are at several removes from the actual field notes, so the display will work best as a summarizing, clarifying, puzzle-posing (but not always puzzle-solving) device. Cycling back to the field notes is often a helpful move.

Case dynamics matrices, rather than starting with "strains," as this example did, can start with "dilemmas." Columns could be labeled as follows with appropriate cell entries:

- Dilemmas (the problems)
- Issues (why they were perceived as problems)
- Who did what (the actions taken by individuals to resolve the dilemmas)
- Final resolution (the outcomes of the actions)

Some cell entries may also include cases of nonchange. A column could be added easily that emphasizes stability and nonchange data—particularly on outcomes that might have been expected a priori to change as a result of the initial push or strain. That addition, in turn, suggests the need for an "explanations" column.

Notes

Review (or have a colleague review) the first versions of your matrix to see what you are excluding and what analyses you will and will not be able to make. Ask someone else to look at the completed matrix and tell you what your analytic assumptions seem to be.

Explaining Causation

The three methods in this section build on each other and incorporate selected principles from *Explaining Interrelationship* and *Explaining Change*. *Causal Chains* illustrates the trajectory or path of an individual story line in the data. *Causal Network: Within-Case Analysis* integrates several causal chains into an interrelated system, while *Causal Network: Cross-Case Analysis* builds on and combines several within-case networks. These are perhaps the lengthiest and most complexly described of the analytic methods thus far, but there are just three profiles we offer for guidance toward explanatory development.

Causal Chains

Description

A causal chain is a researcher-constructed linear display of events, actions, and/or states that suggests a plausible sequence of causes and effects (see Displays 9.5 and 9.6).

Applications

During the early stages of causal modeling, it helps to make simplifying assumptions about what leads to what, placing causes and effects in a linear chain. Such a chain helps the analyst lay out explicitly what may be causing certain phenomena. Although the chain does represent a simplification, that very simplification carries with it the seeds of a fuller explanation.

Causal chains are useful just because they require little elaboration or textual explanation. They are a rapid, simple way to communicate with colleagues (and final readers) about the meaning of—the mechanisms underlying—a process. They can be elaborated and linked with other chains to form causal models or to build within-case causal networks.

Example

Display 9.5 shows an analyst's effort to understand how teachers using an innovation that stressed Individualization and Pupil-Centeredness came to experience a change in themselves they called "Letting Go." The labels for each bin in between the arrows were developed by the researcher after a review of coded field notes and analytic reflection on a key teacher outcome from the study.

Analysis

A causal chain is similar to a story outline for a narrative—a condensed treatment of sorts before the full explanation is given for what led to what and why. The analyst expands on the processes suggested by Display 9.5:

Display 9.5

Causal Chain: Illustration

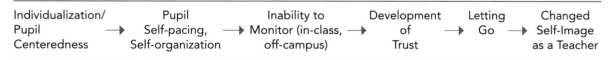

| Individualization/ Pupil Centeredness | → | Pupil Self-pacing, Self-organization | → | Inability to Monitor (in-class, off-campus) | → | Development of Trust | → | Letting Go | → | Changed Self-Image as a Teacher |

Source: Miles, M. B., & Huberman, A. M. (1994). *Qualitative data analysis: An expanded sourcebook* (2nd ed.). Thousand Oaks, CA: Sage Publications.

There is something like an implicit contract between parties that pupils going off campus will not "betray" their teachers in return for pastoral care . . . [or that] in classroom-bound projects, pupils will complete their work and do the requisite exercises or mastery tests in return for individual help with difficult concepts or operations.

We have left out some steps [in this display]. For example, Pupil-Centeredness also leads to Relational Closeness (not shown) and to a better grasp of Individual Ability Levels and Emotional States. Trust then develops as a result of the Bond Between Staff and Pupils (Trust Violation was a common motif at many sites).

Causal chains can be used to study less constructive processes—sequences with negative outcomes. Display 9.6 presents one chain explaining why an initially ambitious innovation eventually was discontinued, with energy expenditures dwindling steadily. The labels of each action, event, and/or state should be concise yet descriptive enough to give a reader with no background knowledge of the study a general idea of what happened through time.

Keep a causal chain limited to a maximum of five to seven descriptive blocks or bins. Remember that this is a thumbnail sketch of a much larger portrait and is only one thread of sequences in a complex tapestry of interwoven fieldwork stories. You can explore a sequence by tracing significant events forward in time (from A to B to C), or start with an outcome and work backward to determine its antecedent causes (from C to B to A).

Notes

The causal chain deliberately uses the positivist construct of "cause and effect" because the display design is linear. Networked, interwoven, and multidirectional causal chains illustrate qualitative "influences and affects" (see Saldaña, 2003).

Causal Network: Within-Case Analysis
Description

It is assumed that some variables exert an influence on others: Variable X brings variable Y into being, or variable X increases variable Y and decreases variable Z. A causal network is a display of the most important variables (represented in boxes) in a field study and the relationships among them (represented by arrows). The plot of these relationships is unidirectional rather than bidirectional or correlational, to suggest that one or more variables lead to another variable(s). In a causal network, the analyst traces the emergence and consequences of a particular theme and orchestrates it with others. To be useful, the display should have accompanying analytic text describing the meaning of the connections among variables (see Displays 9.7 [network fragment], 9.8 [network excerpt], and 9.11 [complete network]).

Display 9.6

Causal Chain: Illustration

Source: Miles, M. B., & Huberman, A. M. (1994). *Qualitative data analysis: An expanded sourcebook* (2nd ed.). Thousand Oaks, CA: Sage Publications.

Display 9.7

Casual Fragment: Mastery of a New Educational Practice

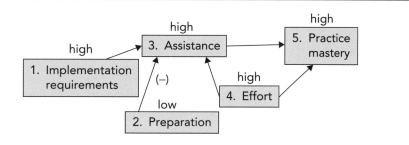

Source: Miles, M. B., & Huberman, A. M. (1994). *Qualitative data analysis: An expanded sourcebook* (2nd ed.). Thousand Oaks, CA: Sage Publications.

Applications

Participants walk around with a cognitive map in their heads that provides a frame for action and perception and explains what causes what in their world. Much of field research has to do with schema absorption and re-elaboration; you go around recording individuals' mental cause maps, putting them together, and making connections with your own evolving map of the setting. But causation is not unilateral. Thus, how do you get a reasonable handle on the overall "plot" of the research story—the flow of events in a particular case—and not get lost in a blur of everything affecting everything else?

Basically, a causal network illustrates through a study's variables how one thing led to another in linear yet interwoven patterns. A causal network builds a progressively integrated map of case phenomena and, for multiple cases, aligns their maps to make a cross-case map that contains more generalizable causal explanations. It neatly assembles and "anthologizes" into one thematic display all the stories of your individual cases.

A causal network is an abstracted, inferential picture organizing field study data in a coherent way. In this profile, we review how to do this for a single case; afterward, we outline a multiple- or cross-case approach. Developing good causal maps that respect complexity and are plausibly connected with those of respondents is the challenge. Meeting this challenge helps the analyst avoid intellectual overload and produces results that are systematic and verifiable.

Example

Causal network construction necessitates a step-by-step outline of "how to." Thus, foundation principles will be discussed first, followed by their integration.

Inductive and Deductive Approaches to Building Causal Networks.

Basically, you have to plan from the beginning of data collection to produce a causal network display, so that successive rounds of data collection, interim analysis of all the data, and iterations of the network itself all build toward that end. But there are two different ways of approaching the task: (1) inductively and (2) deductively.

In the *inductive* approach, the researcher discovers recurrent phenomena in the stream of field experiences and finds recurrent relations among them. These working hypotheses are modified and refined progressively as fieldwork progresses. The causal network emerges piecemeal and inductively. It has regularity and pattern; some things happen only when others do or don't. These things and the links between them acquire their own names or labels, and cluster into the probable influences and affects they appear to engender—and the analyst has a causal network.

In *deductive* strategy, the researcher has some a priori orienting constructs and propositions to test or observe in the field. These analytic units are operationalized and then matched with a body of field data.

Induction and deduction are actually dialectical rather than mutually exclusive research procedures. Nevertheless, the deductive researcher *starts* with a preliminary causal network, and the inductive researcher *ends up* with one. Wolcott (1992) calls the approaches "theory-first" and "theory-later." In either approach, the initial version is amended and refined as it is tested against empirical events and characteristics. By the end of data gathering, both types of researchers are about at the same place. Both are substantiating a cause-and-effect/influences-and-affects network, but the deductive conceptualist has a top-down model, and the inductive constructivist has a built-up one.

In principle, you could draw a full causal network for the case during the early stages of a study, then go back to the field for cumulative testing and refining. We do not advise this. The risk is that a network vision sets in too early. A final "coherent" picture emerges before the individual parts of the picture have been carefully studied individually and in combination. The analyst constructs a premature causal network and begins to use it to (mis)interpret all the phenomena of interest. The better alternative is to save full causal network drawing and analysis for later in the project, making it perhaps the last analytic exercise.

Causal Fragments.

Earlier in this chapter, causal chains were profiled and illustrated as a linear construct. Many of those same principles will apply to the discussion of causal fragments below, but the linearity of the chain now "bends" here and there to accommodate the complexity of network models.

Display 9.7 shows a causal fragment. This one puts together variables concerning the mastery of a new educational practice. The story can be told quickly, point by point or box by box:

Box 1. A demanding project with high Implementation requirements . . .

Box 2. began with low or inadequate Preparation, and was . . .

Box 3. bailed out by high levels of Assistance, which then . . .

Box 4. increased local Efforts, and ultimately. . .

Box 5. facilitated Practice mastery.

The minus sign (-) indicates inverse causal influence; low Preparation led to high Assistance in this particular case.

Try to assemble a few such fragments from your study without necessarily connecting one to another. Play around; do some causal noodling, fiddle with other fragments. Don't try to connect variables that don't go together empirically, even if on logical grounds they "should." Some variables, like some blood types, don't commingle well.

In the style of causal mapping we're describing, we (Miles and Huberman) do not advise bidirectional arrows/flows from one box to another. They rapidly bewilder the mind ("after all, everything affects everything else"). For graphic and intellectual clarity, we have found it better to stick with one-way arrows, which provide a temporal order to the diagrammed research story. For anything that justifiably "loops," accumulates, or cycles back (e.g., a bad economy leads to high prices, which leads to a worse economy, which leads to higher prices, which leads to . . .), show the recurring action through new boxes, not through bidirectional arrows. Saldaña advises that if bidirectional arrows *are* used, the narrative should explain and justify their use (see Display 5.2).

A useful next step is to take these fragments out to the field to see how and whether they work. This step can include showing the rough diagram to a case participant (tactic: **getting feedback from participants**) to get confirmation or revision recommendations.

If you're new to qualitative research, start with causal fragments. They can be profitably done early and repeatedly as a basis for discussion with your critical friends. Causal fragments are useful if your case is defined as an individual—and *very* useful if you are studying several individuals.

Event–State Networks as Precursors to Causal Networks.

Displays we have discussed up to now can inform and feed causal network analysis. Analyzing conceptually clustered matrices (Chapter 7), for example, lets you tease out the relationships within one of the variable families. Effects matrices (Chapters 6 and 8) are exercises in identifying cause–effect relations. Both clustering and cause–effect inferencing are at work in case dynamics matrices (this chapter). In other words, causal analysis goes incrementally; you are testing individual paths more rigorously and, at the same time, building a cognitively meaningful, integrated causal map. But the event–state network (Chapter 8) in particular gets us almost there.

Display 9.8 shows an excerpt from the final causal network, with the variable numbers keyed to the corresponding variables in the event–state network. Display 9.9 shows an excerpt from the original event–state network for the case in our illustration (Perry-Parkdale).

Usually, there will be markedly fewer causal network variables than event–state boxes and bubbles. (This would be the case here had we shown a fuller excerpt from the event–state network and had we taken the three case-specific variables out of the causal network.)

In most instances, case-specific events and states such as those in Display 9.9 can be turned into more generic network variables. They give you more powerful explanations, usable in other cases. Plus, there's much analytic power in working from a specifically temporal, process-oriented display (an event–state network) toward a variable-oriented display that still retains temporality (a causal network).

The lesson here is this: Use your previous analytic display work about your data for threads to weave your causal network tapestry.

Display 9.8

Excerpt From a Causal Network: Perry-Parkdale School

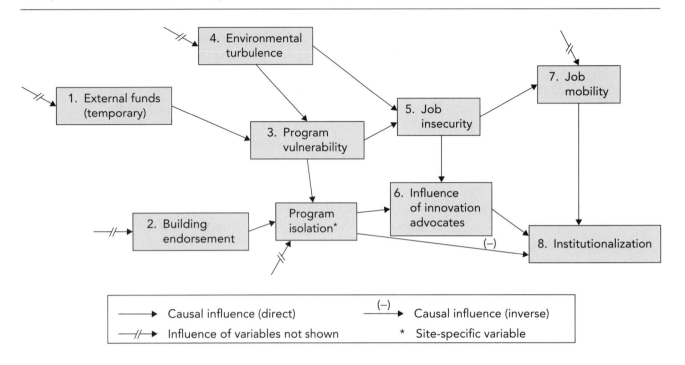

→	Causal influence (direct)	
—//→	Influence of variables not shown	
—(−)→	Causal influence (inverse)	
*	Site-specific variable	

Display 9.9

Excerpt From an Event-State Network: Perry-Parkdale School

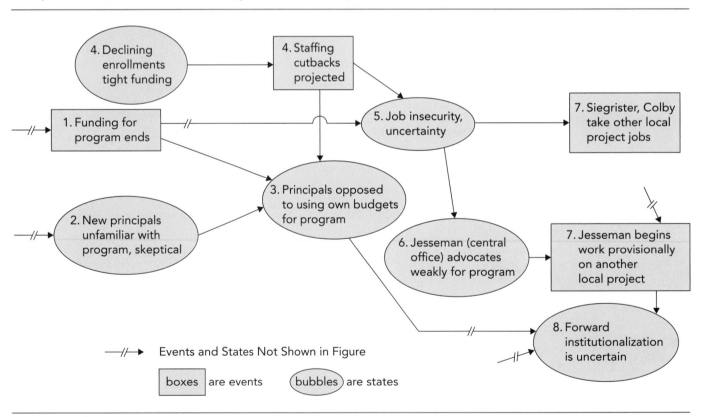

—//→ Events and States Not Shown in Figure

[boxes] are events ⬭bubbles are states

Source: Miles, M. B., & Huberman, A. M. (1994). *Qualitative data analysis: An expanded sourcebook* (2nd ed.). Thousand Oaks, CA: Sage Publications.

Generating a Causal Network Variable List.

Late during data collection, you may be ready to assemble the remaining fragments of the full causal network. But a useful first step is to generate the full set of network variables as a written list. This, too, is an exercise in playful brainstorming. The idea is to list all the events, states, factors, processes, outcomes, and so on that seem to be important and then to turn them into variables. For instance, the several fights between employees will become "organizational conflict." The first pass should be exhaustive, the next one more selective. The first list should be combed for redundancies and overdifferentiation (e.g., three types of fighting between employees).

As an illustration, Display 9.10 presents a list of core variables generated in our school improvement study. (This was a complex, multicase study; the list for single, simpler cases would be much shorter.)

Display 9.10

List of Antecedent, Mediating, and Outcome Variables: School Improvement Study

Antecedent or Start Variables	Mediating Variables	Outcomes
Internal funds	External funds	Stabilization of use
Career advancement motivation	Program adoption (E)	Percentage of use
Assessed adequacy of local performance	Program concept initiative (L)	Student impact
	District endorsement	User capacity change
Environmental turbulence	Building endorsement	
	Influence of innovation advocate	Institutionalization
	Implementation requirements	Job mobility
	Adequacy of initial user preparation	
	Program-district fit	
	Program-building fit	
	Program-user fit	
	Assistance	
	User commitment	
	User skill	
	Program transformation	
	Teacher-administrator harmony	
	Validation effort (L)	
	Stability of program leadership	
	Stability of program staff	
	Organizational transformation	

Legend:
   (E) externally developed innovation
   (L) locally developed innovation

Source: Miles, M. B., & Huberman, A. M. (1994). *Qualitative data analysis: An expanded sourcebook* (2nd ed.). Thousand Oaks, CA: Sage Publications.

Note the three general temporal categories:

1. *Antecedent or start variables:* the baseline conditions within the field site that will later change

2. *Mediating variables:* those events, states, processes, and/or factors that initiate changes or action of some kind

3. *Outcomes:* the consequent results of antecedent and mediating variables

Just as drawing causal fragments is effective preliminary work for a network display, composing a variable list is also important foundation work. It lets you know what specifically gets entered into the boxes and encourages you to hypothesize about what led to what. Causation coding (Saldaña, 2013) is an effective way of generating lists of antecedent and mediating variables and their outcomes for display work.

Assembling Data Fragments: Codes, Analytic Memos, and Summaries.

As profiled earlier, Second Cycle Pattern Codes (Chapter 4) symbolically represent bigger chunks of data and often become candidates for inclusion in a causal network. In essence, they signal a *theme* or *pattern* that can be integrated into the network. For example, in our study of Perry-Parkdale, we noticed that teachers using innovations described their experiences in terms such as "Finally I felt really on top of it," "It got easier when I knew how," "It's a snap now," and "Basically, I learned how to do it right." We labeled this pattern of responses, and thus the underlying variable, "User skill" and made a box for it.

Analytic memos and other analytic processes on interrelationship, coupled with exploratory and descriptive summaries, synthesize discrete pieces of data into an evidential chain that suggests causation. You think, roughly, "These variables are present or absent together (they covary), while others look random or unconnected." The tactic is **building a logical chain of evidence**. But with more knowledge, you begin to think more elaborately: "Some of these variables are coming into play *before* others, varying *with* others, or having an *effect* on others, and that effect seems to change when *other* variables are taken into account." You have the rudiments of a causal network that contains well-founded assertions about *directions* of influence among *sets* of variables.

Ideas ultimately need to get drawn on paper or on a monitor, and fragments of your thinking and analyses start coming together into one place by doing the following:

- Translate your preliminary analytic work into *variables,* that is, something that can be scaled (high to low, big to little, more to less).

- *Rate* the variable (e.g., high, moderate, low). How much of it is in the case?

- Draw a *line* between pairs of variables that *covary,* that is, that appear together consistently in the case, that have some kind of relationship—for example, more of one variable goes with less of another.

- Draw a *unidirectional arrow* between each variable that comes first (temporally) and those later ones it appears to influence. *Influence* here means that more or less of one variable determines to some extent the rating of another. The rating of the second variable might have been different had the first one not been there—a reasonable "mechanism" is involved.

- If two variables covary but seem to have only a tepid or oblique influence on each other, probably another latent variable needs to be found to join the two (tactic: **finding intervening variables**). Review the full list of codes to see whether one fits here.

It is important to note that not all variables may need accompanying ratings or scales (high, medium, low) to be eligible for inclusion as causal network boxes. The example used in this profile includes them since the original study had evaluation objectives.

Analysis

Display 9.11 shows the resulting causal network for one case. At first, it may look complex and forbidding. But look at one section of it (say, starting at the upper left) in conjunction with some text, like this:

> The first three antecedent variables (1, 2, and 4) worked out this way: The state mandate (2) for well-planned career education programs, together with assessment of local performance as less than adequate (1), led to a search for new programs (3), which proved to be a good fit (7) with district characteristics, and hence to district endorsement (8), and to adoption of the program (9).
>
> But these were not sufficient causes of adoption. Inadequate local funds (4) to cover existing programs led to a ceaseless search for add-on funds (6) as almost a "way of life" for the district. That search led to getting temporary external funds (14) for a three-year period; they were the other basic cause of adoption (9).
>
> The program, when adopted, proved to have substantial implementation requirements (10), which dictated the need for assistance (18), and also exerted a good deal of pressure for careful selection of high-quality staff (21), and for careful preparation (19) of them to carry out the program. The heavy implementation requirements (10), and to some degree the assistance provided (18), induced a good deal of user commitment (20), and in turn user skill (26), which was also high because of staff quality (21). High user skill, in conjunction with the fact that the program was quite well stabilized (27) by late 1980, brought about a reasonable degree of student impact (30).

Text and network together communicate more than either could alone. We are moving toward an *explanation*—not just a description—of what happened at Perry-Parkdale. This network has taken more than 300 pages of field notes down to a few dozen boxed words and arrows on one page; the network and the text tell economically how and why things turned out as they did.

Streams.

Drawing the network is done in the same way you analyze it: stream by stream. Some streams—unbroken chains of variables—are long. Look at the one that runs through these numbered boxes: 1 > 3 > 7 > 8 > 9 > 10 > 20 > 26 > 30 > 31 > 32. Others are conveniently shorter, like the bottom stream: 5 > 33 > 32. Within an unbroken stream, multiple channels usually lead in different directions or end up at the same place via a different route. Those also should be drawn in.

Streams can be drawn most easily—especially if the event–state network is used as the preceding try—from antecedents forward in time. It is also possible to take a

Display 9.11

Causal Network for Perry-Parkdale CARED Program

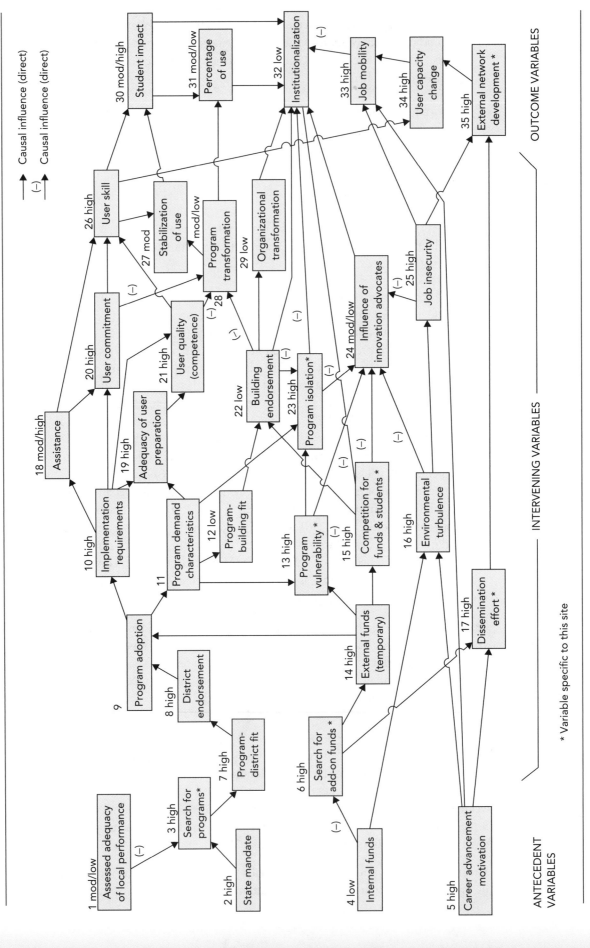

Source: Miles, M. B., & Huberman, A. M. (1994). *Qualitative data analysis: An expanded sourcebook* (2nd ed.). Thousand Oaks, CA: Sage Publications.

dependent variable and work backward, but then, it is important to run it forward again to be sure the links are coherent and empirically justified. You'll inevitably find cross-stream connections, and they can be drawn in as the network evolves.

Often, these streams can be given a name—a scenario or theme—and this labeling makes them easier both to analyze and to report. For example, along the bottom stream, variables 5 > 17 > 35 > 34 have a "cosmopolitanizing" theme: People go outside their environments in connection with a new project, and the experience both stretches them and sets up career shifts. Or again, staying along the bottom of the network, boxes 4 > 16 > 25 > 33 add up to a "casualty" (*casualty*, not causality) stream: low money, high turbulence (usually in the form of budget cuts), staff instability, and ultimate staff reassignments.

Streams also can be labeled according to the level of dependent variables, such as *high student impact scenarios*, *low institutionalization scenarios*, or *high job mobility scenarios*. These similarly named scenarios can be very different, even within the same case. For instance, one high job mobility scenario involves a promotion or desirable transfer, whereas another involves an unwanted reassignment or even a layoff.

Finally, causal networks can have a predictive function. In drawing a variable stream with two or three substreams leading out to the dependent variables, you are in a position to say something like "Effect D is likely to occur when predictors A, B, and C occur in sequence," or "To get high levels of J, you need high antecedent levels of G, H, and I but not necessarily of E and F." These statements have modest weight in a single-case analysis, but they perk up noticeably when several within-case sets show the same or a similar pattern.

The Causal Network Narrative.

Drawing conclusions from the network goes along with its production. Like all time-related representations, this one tells a story—really, several stories. You can write out a chronological narrative including each of the major streams, starting at the beginning. Display 9.12 presents the complete narrative for the causal network shown in Display 9.11.

Writing the narrative usually does several things. First, it forces you to be less mechanistic and more coherent; turning a network into clear text requires you to be honest and explicit about what you think is causing what. (Corrections and revisions are very typical.) Second, it provides an opportunity for expansion: You can explain why variables are related, why they are rated differently, why some precede others, which ones matter more, and so on. Third, both products—the network display and the narrative text—are the basic material to be handed to a colleague for reaction and revision. It's nearly impossible to map a causal network "right" the first time. Someone else who knows the database can review it and suggest improvements. When a causal network and its narrative are revised to coherent form, they can be used to generate more general explanations on a multicase level.

Final Recommendations.

Be cautious about giving tacit weights to individual network variables. Presumably the ones with more arrows leading to them are more significant, but a stream-level analysis cancels this out. In fact, a variable with too many arrows leading to it becomes a nuisance, because it multiplies the possible number of streams.

Narrative for Causal Network: Perry-Parkdale CARED Program

The first three antecedent variables (1, 2 and 4) worked out this way. The state mandate (2) for well-planned career education programs, together with assessment of local performance as less than adequate (1), led to a search for new programs (3), which proved to be a good fit (7) with district characteristics, and hence to district endorsement (8), and to adoption of the program (9).

But these were not sufficient causes of adoption. Inadequate local funds (4) to cover existing programs led to a ceaseless search for add-on funds (6) as almost a "way of life" for the district. That search led to getting temporary external funds (14) for a three-year period; they were the other basic cause of adoption (9).

The program, when adopted, proved to have substantial implementation requirements (10), which dictated the need for assistance (18), and also exerted a good deal of pressure for careful selection of high-quality staff (21), and for careful preparation (19) of them to carry out the program. The heavy implementation requirements (10), and to some degree the assistance provided (18), induced a good deal of user commitment (20), and in turn user skill (26), which was also high because of staff quality (21). High user skill, in conjunction with the fact that the program was quite well stabilized (27) by late 1980, brought about a reasonable degree of student impact (30).

The stream of causality refers essentially to internal program dynamics. What was happening at the *district and building* level?

Moving back to program demand characteristics (11), we note that certain aspects of the program (such as its removing students from high school control, and from high school courses and activities) caused poor fit between the program and the sending buildings (12). That poor fit led to lack of endorsement (22) from building principals, counselors, and teachers. Poor endorsement was further weakened by the presence of competition for funds and for students (15), induced by the fact that external funds (14) were temporary in nature.

Temporary funding, together with the program's demand characteristics (11) (for example, student were visible to employers, had to be responsible, and could easily behave like "assholes") also made for a good deal of program vulnerability (13). As a consequence, the staff tended to operate the program in a rather isolated fashion (23), to buffer it against the consequences of vulnerability when the immediate environmental endorsement (22) was weak. Certain programs demand characteristics (11), such as the intensive time block, reinforced isolation (23) as well.

An added set of causal variables was also in play. The career advancement motivation (5) of key central office staff and principals operated to induce a good deal of turbulence (16) in the district. This turbulence effectively reduced the influence of those who were advocating the innovation (24); for some advocates, influence was weakened by job insecurity (25).

So although the program was transformed and altered (28) to some degree to meet the objections stemming from low building endorsement (22), achieved a modest increase in percentage of use (31) for a while, and was, as we have seen, proving reasonably effective with students (30), these factors were not enough to ensure the program's institutionalization (being built into the system) (32).

Rather, the weak building endorsement (22), the program's isolation (23), the competition for funds and students (15), and the weak exercise of influence by innovation advocates (24) resulted in weak institutionalization (32). So, it seems likely, did the departure of program staff, whose mobility (33) was driven by both career advancement motivation (5) and job insecurity (25). It also seems likely that the very user capacity development (34) induced by experience with skillful use of the program (26), enhanced by the external network of contacts (35) generated through the dissemination effort (17), also contributed to the decision of staff members (and it seems, possibly the director) to move on.

Taken as a whole, these explanations seem baroque and complex. But there is fairly clear evidence that each causal link worked as described. The chart will look less complicated if one notes that the chart contains four basic streams: the *program development* stream across the top, the *building/district* stream in the middle, the *career stream* near the bottom, and the external *dissemination/networking* stream last. In many respects the final outcomes can be seen as stemming from conflicting pressures across the streams.

Source: Miles, M. B., & Huberman, A. M. (1994). *Qualitative data analysis: An expanded sourcebook* (2nd ed.). Thousand Oaks, CA: Sage Publications.

We advise (a) always writing accompanying text to clarify and summarize the streams and (b) increasing the credibility of any given network and narrative by subjecting them to colleague and even participant critique. Keep in mind that you may be building too much order and purpose into loose-ended, inconclusive events. Get others to entertain a more chaotic view.

Doing a causal network forces a more inferential level of analysis that pulls together the data into a single summarizing form. You have to look at all the data and the preceding conclusions and map them in a coherent way. If you've done it right, you will have respected the complexity of local causality as it has played out over time and successfully combined "process" and "variable" analyses.

Notes

Remember that a causal network is only as good as the analyses whose shoulders it stands on: the original codes, conceptual clusters, and displays. That caveat sends us back to the quality and coverage of the data and the trustworthiness of data collection methods. Good models are only as good as the measures and simpler analyses they derive from.

Selected CAQDAS programs are equipped to help draw causal streams for you, based on your input during analytic entry. You, however, must specify and verify the connections of what leads to what.

Causal Network: Cross-Case Analysis
Description

A cross-case causal network analysis is a *thematic narrative* derived from systematic comparison of within-case causal network displays. All cases in a sample are analyzed using variables estimated to be the most influential in accounting for the outcome or a core variable. You look at each outcome measure and examine, for each case, the stream of variables leading to or "determining" that outcome. Streams that are similar or identical across cases, and that differ in some consistent way from other streams, are extracted and thematically interpreted. The basic principle is that of developing one or more meta-networks that respect the individual case networks from which they have been derived (Huberman & Miles, 1989; see Display 9.13 for a subnetwork example).

Applications

Causal network *within-case* displays show how to make an inclusive, explanatory analysis of single-case data. A *cross-case* causal network, with its core list of variables found to have significance across several cases, is a powerful way to move from case-specific explanations to more generalizable constructs and theory. We are going from local causation to clusters or "families" of cases sharing important attributes.

Example

Because cross-case causal networking involves manipulating several sets of boxes and arrows at the same time, it can be confusing to explain. So let's break down the process into successive analytic steps. We'll work from a familiar example and take an outcome variable that lends itself easily to cross-case analysis.

Display 9.13

Subnetwork: Variable Streams Leading to High Job Mobility, Perry-Parkdale Case

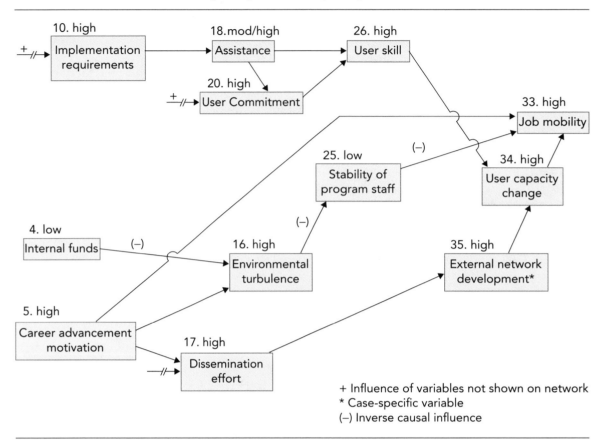

+ Influence of variables not shown on network
* Case-specific variable
(−) Inverse causal influence

Source: Miles, M. B., & Huberman, A. M. (1994). *Qualitative data analysis: An expanded sourcebook* (2nd ed.). Thousand Oaks, CA: Sage Publications.

Assembling the Causal Networks. We will assume that you have the basic building blocks of within-case causal networks (discussed above) for each of your cases:

- The list of core variables (see Display 9.10 for an example)

- The causal network (see Display 9.11)

- The accompanying narrative (see Display 9.12)

In our (Miles and Huberman) school improvement study, for example, we had 12 such networks and narratives, incorporating a core list of some 35 variables, together with 6 case-specific variables. It helps to have each within-case causal network display printed out and posted on a wall or another display surface.

Isolating the Causal Streams for Each Case That
Lead to the Dependent Variable Being Analyzed.

This is the major task. Let's assume, for purposes of illustration, that you want to see how an outcome called "job mobility" is determined in a study of people's role and career shifts. We begin by looking at the predictors of that outcome for one case. We start with an exhibit we have seen already, the causal network for the Perry-Parkdale case (Display 9.9). But to make the cross-case causal network analysis easier to follow, let's extract the streams from the causal network that led to job mobility, as shown in Display 9.13.

We've pulled out the *subnetwork* of variables leading to the outcome of job mobility. The job mobility box (Number 33) has three arrows leading to it, from Boxes 5, 25, and 34. Two of those boxes, in turn, have others leading to them along what we call a stream. The streams leading to "job mobility" are easy to see if you scan backward from Box 33 to the preceding boxes. It helps to go only two steps back from the outcome measure. The boxes reached in that way can be thought of as "immediate" causes of the outcome; earlier boxes on the causal stream are "remote" causes (generally).

To understand the five streams within the subnetwork, we have two tools. First, we can read across each stream to see what is happening—what the theme or logical succession is. To do that, we have the variable labels and their ratings. For instance, take the substream 5 > 17 > 35. The message here is that key participants at Perry-Parkdale were interested in getting promoted (5), which led to a more energetic effort to disseminate (17) the innovation they had developed to others outside their home district (35), where, presumably, some interesting jobs might be found.

Working from the bottom of the display, let's look at the five streams that led to job mobility (Box 33):

- 5 > 17 > 35 > 34 > 33
- 5 > 33
- 5 > 16 > 25 > 33
- 4 > 16 > 25 > 33
- 10 > 18 > 20 > 26 > 34 > 33

To be sure that such an interpretation is plausible, we have the second tool: the causal network narrative (see Display 9.12, the narrative for the case discussed here). The narrative nails down the context, shows the temporal and causal relationships mapped on the network, and explains why the variables are chained as they are.

But here is where analysis takes a real qualitative turn. Each job mobility stream in Display 9.13 is not just a causal chain but a *story* with an accompanying *theme*:

- 4 > 16 > 25 > 33: This stream looks ominous—low funds, high turbulence, high job insecurity, low stability of program staff, high job mobility. Reading the narrative confirms our impression that this is a *casualty* scenario: Low funding led to local uncertainties about continuing the project, which caused project staff to be shifted to other jobs.

- 5 > 16 > 25 > 33: This stream adds the "career advancement motivation" variable and thereby strengthens the *casualty* theme; people did not get promoted or reassigned to desired job slots, even though they had hoped to.

- 5 > 33: Some people got to where they wanted via the project. For now, let's call this one an *opportunism* stream.

- 5 > 17 > 35 > 34 > 33: Some made desirable job shifts, but in what looks like a socially redeeming way. The dissemination effort may be fed by career advancement motives, but the process of spreading the project to other districts develops training and consulting skills (capacity changes) that then are used on the next job. Reading the narrative to get a clearer sense of what is happening here yields a *career crystallization* theme: People doing the disseminating realize that they want to go on doing this kind of work rather than return to their former jobs.

- 10 > 18 > 20 > 26 > 34 > 33: The stream itself is upbeat: Local staff take on a stiff project (high implementation requirements), receive decent assistance, develop strong commitment, master the project (high user skill), develop new capacities, and move to desirable new jobs. Let's call this stream *success-driven advancement*.

Don't try for a theme or scenario name until you have looked at several cases. A stream usually has a stray predictor or two, and you need to wait until these strays can be separated out from those variables appearing consistently, which will give the name to the stream. To provide a proverb for the rest of this analysis, "Where there's a stream, there's a theme."

Analysis

Pattern matching is discovering whether a pattern found in one case is replicated in others as well, suggesting a common scenario. Are the same patterns of core variables involved? Are the ratings (high, moderate, low) the same? Let's take another high job mobility case, extracting the streams leading to that outcome. Display 9.14 presents the result for the Calston case.

Only two streams lead to the "job mobility" variable, and both highlight the same scenario. If you look back at the *casualty* stream/theme for the Perry-Parkdale case (Display 9.13), three of the same variables (internal funds, environmental turbulence, stability of program staff) are here. Better still, they are in the same sequence and have identical ratings.

Let's try another case. Display 9.15 shows the extracted portion for Banestown.

Display 9.14

Subnetwork for Job Mobility, Calston Case

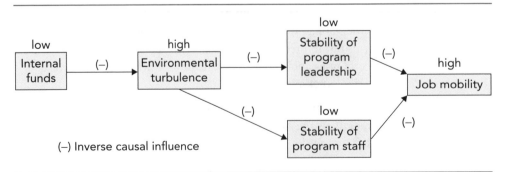

Source: Miles, M. B., & Huberman, A. M. (1994). *Qualitative data analysis: An expanded sourcebook* (2nd ed.). Thousand Oaks, CA: Sage Publications.

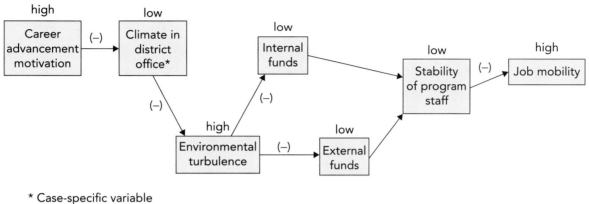

* Case-specific variable
(−) Inverse causal influence

Source: Miles, M. B., & Huberman, A. M. (1994). *Qualitative data analysis: An expanded sourcebook* (2nd ed.). Thousand Oaks, CA: Sage Publications.

This is clearly another *casualty*-themed case. If we take out the case-specific variable ("climate in district office") and the "external funds" variable, we have the same variables, identically rated, as in Perry-Parkdale, although not in the same order. Here, the "internal funds" variable comes after, not before, the "environmental turbulence" variable. But reading the case narrative produces the same, sad scenario of dashed career hopes; the shift in sequence means little.

Let's look at one more example in Display 9.16.

By now, you probably can dissect the network more rapidly. Three arrows lead to high "job mobility," but so do five possible streams. The first one—variables 20 > 18 > 26 > 36 > 37—should be familiar; it is the *success-driven advancement* stream/theme we saw at Perry-Parkdale, at least in the immediate causal variables, those closest to the criterion measure: skill, capacity change. The sequence is the same, and the ratings are identical.

Let's try another stream: 27 > 31 > 37; this looks like the *opportunism* scenario at Perry-Parkdale. Finally, let's take a third stream: 39 > 38 > 37. This is the same sequence as the final three predictors in the Calston *casualty* scenario, which itself is virtually identical to the Perry-Parkdale *casualty* scenario. (To confirm this, the analyst rereads the causal network narratives for the three cases.)

At the end of this analysis, the 40+ streams for the 12 cases fell into the four *thematic families* we identified along the way:

1. *Casualty* scenarios

2. *Opportunism* scenarios

3. *Success-driven advancement* scenarios

4. *Career crystallization* scenarios

Moreover, the analyst can move up an analytical notch and cluster *cases* rather than individual streams. For example, both Perry-Parkdale and Plummet have successful and

Display 9.16

Subnetwork for Job Mobility, Plummet Case

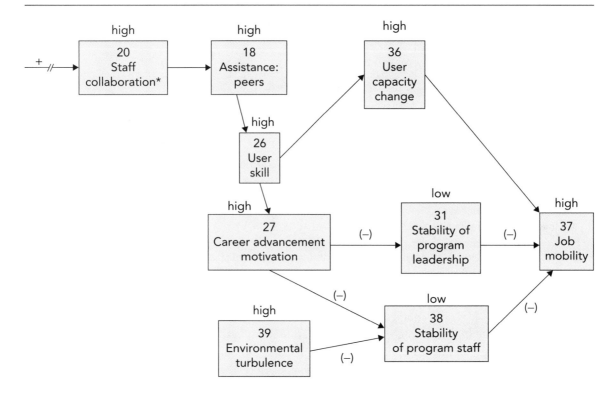

* Case-specific variable
+ Influence of variables not shown on network
(−) Inverse causal influence

Source: Miles, M. B., & Huberman, A. M. (1994). *Qualitative data analysis: An expanded sourcebook* (2nd ed.). Thousand Oaks, CA: Sage Publications.

unsuccessful job mobility scenarios; some people get what they are after, and others do not. This was also obtained for other cases; we could group them at the case level as a *win–lose* scenario/theme.

In a sample of cases, we have not only comparability but also *variability*. There are moderate and low job mobility cases, and we have to be sure their causal flows are either different or contrary to the ones in the high job mobility cases. Ideally, the low cases would have some of the same *variables* in the same or similar *sequences* as for the high cases, but the *ratings* would be different. For example, high internal funds, combined with low environmental turbulence and high staff stability, would lead to low job mobility—the opposite of the casualty scenario but with the same variables in the same order. That would strengthen the analysis and increase its explanatory power. We now can claim with more confidence that job mobility is caused by a *particular combination* of funding, turbulence, and staff stability, because both high and low mobility result from the same interaction of these variables.

Confirmation of the emerging scenarios/themes can range from research team discussion and consensus to a series of logic-based decision rules, such as the following:

- The most immediate predictor variables—the two or three closest to the outcome measure—are the same and are in the same sequence.

- The common predictors have the same ratings (high, moderate, low).

- The outcome themes are different (or absent) in cases with a differently rated outcome variable (e.g., high, moderate, low).

In a single-case study, making and revising a variable list is fairly straightforward. In a multiple-case study, we are at a decisive moment. For cross-case comparisons, the same variables will be used to analyze 5, 10, or 20 cases. For this to happen, ideally each of the variables should be empirically meaningful in all cases. Of course, you should leave slack for two likely situations: (1) there will be some case-unique variables and (2) some variables will be influential in most but not all cases. In the former instance, the final causal network will contain some case-specific variables, labeled as such. In the latter instance, some network variables will be dropped (with an explanation) from the cases where they contribute little or nothing to the analysis.

Finally, back out of certain dead ends. Dead ends are streams that make no sense and need to be broken up, even though they seem common across cases. And if a cross-case scenario doesn't square with the network narrative, the scenario needs to be revised.

Notes

We've found that the basic operations for cross-case causal network analysis are very similar to those used for within-case causal networks. The lesson again here is *use your previous analytic display work about your data for threads to weave your causal network tapestry*.

Displaying a cross-case causal network is possible, but we forego an example here. This is one case in which words, in the form of themes and an accompanying explanatory narrative, are the stronger and more elegant display strategies for your analytic efforts. Selected CAQDAS programs can provide the software necessary for such complex modeling, but you must still, as the data analyst, initiate and justify the boxes' labels and pathways.

Closure and Transition

Remember that research never proves anything; at best, it suggests. Explaining through these methods "why" something happened the way it did is an evidence-based but nonetheless good-faith effort to map causation. It is a complex and slippery enterprise that requires the analyst to find the story lines in data, constructed through systematic investigation of "What happened next?"

With explaining comes the groundwork for predicting, the method outlined in the next chapter.

10

Methods of Predicting

Chapter Summary

This chapter presents methods of displaying efforts that attempt to predict outcomes based on careful and nuanced analysis of antecedents. These methods rely on earlier displays that serve as foundations for documenting and hypothesizing about possible trajectories of action.

Contents

Introduction
Methods of Predicting
- Making and Testing Predictions
- Predictor-Outcome-Consequences Matrix
- Causal-Prediction Models

Closure and Transition

Introduction

Futurists and inventors ask themselves three questions when they think about visions for the world:

1. What is possible? (i.e., What *might* happen?)

2. What is plausible? (i.e., What *could* happen?)

3. What is preferable? (i.e., What *should* happen?)

These same questions may also apply to qualitative researchers attempting to predict and theorize about their studies for future, comparable contexts.

But no one can predict the future with 100% accuracy. Even statisticians with their sophisticated mathematical models give themselves margins of error. Research-based predictions and theories are well-informed but, nevertheless, provisional visions about what might, could, and should happen.

Methods of Predicting

Making and Testing Predictions outlines a series of heuristics for proposing hypotheses and building theory. *Predictor-Outcome-Consequences Matrix* illustrates how to document, order, and chart antecedent variables that lead to primary outcomes and consequences. *Causal-Prediction Models* completes the series by showing how primarily matrix data transform into network displays for explanatory analysis and theory or predictive construction.

Making and Testing Predictions

Description

Predictions are inferences that a researcher makes about the probable evolution of case events or outcomes over the following months or years. The predictions are drafted at the time of analysis, held, and then submitted to case participants later (e.g., 6–12 months, but timing obviously depends on the nature of the cases and predictions involved). Participants respond to (a) the accuracy of the predictions and (b) the accuracy of the reasons given to justify them. Although predictions can originate from virtually any researcher process, they are more solidly grounded when they derive from causal/explanatory displays (see Display 10.1).

Applications

History, Napoleon is supposed to have said, is the version of past events that people have decided to agree on. And field researchers, who depend heavily on local participants' perceptions in building a descriptive and explanatory write-up of the site, are likely to get sucked into collective perceptions that lend coherence to such a write-up. There are many ways to avoid obvious biases in the data being collected, but there are fewer ways of getting around collective, consensual ones. Also, participants may not agree—either with parts of your write-up or with one another. People witnessing the same events may make sense of them in quite different ways and give discrepant accounts.

Display 10.1

Prediction Feedback Form

School District	Dun Hollow	Name _____

Our Predictions (Made with June 1980 data)   Date _____

1. <u>Institutionalization</u>: that is, the degree to which the Eskimo units have become a durable, built-in or routine part of the ongoing operation in the district.

Our Prediction

> The curriculum will not be incorporated into the district after the field test at Carr and Tortoise Area Schools.

<u>Your Description of the Actual Situation Since Then</u>

Actual Situation

There are probably many factors leading to the actual situation. The most important ones are:

A. _____
_____

B. _____
_____

C. _____
_____

D. _____
_____

E. _____
_____

F. _____
_____

Please rank these factors you have listed in their order of importance by putting next to the letter A – F nos. 1 for the most important, 2 for the next most important, etc.

Source: Miles, M. B., & Huberman, A. M. (1994). *Qualitative data analysis: An expanded sourcebook* (2nd ed.). Thousand Oaks, CA: Sage Publications.

In three studies where we fed back causal networks, we found only modest discrepancies among participants, or between them and us. But there was some disagreement, and we were left sitting on it, trying to think of a way to get resolution. We did invent one approach: testing the validity of your findings by predicting what will happen in your case after 6 months or a year. Presumably, if the analysis is expressed clearly, it has some implications or consequences (using the **if-then** tactic). These can be spelled out and operationalized. The real-world results can be checked out later in a new field contact through the tactic of **getting feedback from participants**. The result is the qualitative researcher's rich, full-fledged prediction of a slice of social life, which in turn helps with current ways of working and living and forewarns us of potential obstacles as we strive toward our goals.

Generating predictions is a good experience: You have to take a hard look at the data and analyses and address their portent explicitly. It's a way of clarifying a general theory about your case by generating multiple predictions about different aspects of the case. It's also a validation device, even when participants' responses are equivocal. Predictions also bring in additional, well-targeted data that can be appended to a case report. Finally, participants feel rewarded; many enjoy the status that comes from their solicited opinion.

Is prediction making worth the time? Yes, if you want to know how good your analysis really is or if much is riding on it. No, if your main thrust in a study is descriptive rather than explanatory or predictive.

Example

Making a Prediction.

A prediction exercise must be built into your study's budget and timeline. In our (Miles and Huberman) school improvement study, we had been looking retrospectively at 3 or 4 years of change efforts in schools. It made sense to plan for a follow-up, a year after fieldwork ended, to see whether our analyses had not just explanatory but predictive power.

To see how this process works, take a look back at Display 9.11 on page 244 in Chapter 9, and find variable/Box 32 on the network: *Institutionalization*. It has a "low" rating, indicating that the innovation at this site has not become a durable, built-in, routine part of ongoing operations. The rating on this variable is a function of the several paths leading to it, both from other outcome variables (e.g., 30 *Student impact*, and 31 *Percentage of use*) and from variables farther back on the causal streams. Schematically, the causal network says that *Institutionalization* is as low as the combined function of the variables leading up to it; they are the likely causes of the *Institutionalization* "effect."

In testing the plausibility of the causal analysis, we asked two predictive questions: (1) What is likely to happen to the innovation between now and next year at this time? (2) On which factors are we basing that estimate?

Looking over the causal network and accompanying text, and reviewing our collective displays for the study, the analyst decided that the program was in trouble. The data suggested that the innovation was a peripheral one, that its benefits were less than its demands on staff, that its support was soft, that competing practices had not been eliminated, and that its funding was uncertain.

But there were some promising signs—the program was operating on a regular, daily basis, and it was getting positive results with turned-off students—but they were buried in a pile of pessimistic indicators. *The analyst predicted that the project would be phased out gradually in the course of the following year*.

Justifying the Prediction.

Now that a prediction has been made, it needs to be justified through the data. Here is where your display work provides evidentiary support.

Back to our example: On page 244, Display 9.11's causal streams leading to Box 32, *Institutionalization*, look foreboding. The stories that the interrelated variables tell are as follows:

- The project makes for a poor program fit (Box 12) and is not supported by teachers or administrators (Box 22). It has not worked through to a better fit by changing the organization (Box 29).

- The project is vulnerable because of its demands, its isolation, and its dependence on soft money (Boxes 11, 13, 14, and 23).

- It competes for funds and students (Box 15).

- Its support in the central administrative office is uncertain for a variety of reasons (Box 24).

- Key project staff are about to leave (Box 33).

- The number of students projected for the following year is lower than for the previous year (Box 31).

These are the reasons for the dire prediction. You weight all of these indicators by their degree of influence; this is also a way of getting the number down to four or five, which is all that a participant can be asked to respond to. Display 10.2 shows the five that were settled on.

Looking for Contrary Data.

If you look only for the factors supporting a prediction, you'll probably make a poor one. Making a good guess is a function of weighting the odds for one outcome against another. It's important to consider the factors that could work *against* the prediction (tactic: **looking for negative evidence**).

In the same example (Display 9.11) were indications that the project was well entrenched in routine operations, that it appeared to pay off for a normally hard-to-reach pupil public (Boxes 30 > 31 > 32), and that it had some central office support (24).

Display 10.2

Factors Supporting "Institutionalization" Prediction

A. Poor district record of institutionalizing soft-money programs.

B. Unlikelihood of strong support from new principals: some counselors indifferent: some elective-subjects teachers are hostile.

C. Lukewarm support from central office.

D. Financial squeeze in district: declining enrollments, staff cutbacks, lowered external funds. Program vulnerable because of high unit costs.

E. "Tightening up" mandate to principal: Program may be seen as a "frill," with lax control over students.

Source: Miles, M. B., & Huberman, A. M. (1994). *Qualitative data analysis: An expanded sourcebook* (2nd ed.). Thousand Oaks, CA: Sage Publications.

Factors Working Against "Institutionalization" Prediction

A.   Possibility of dissemination funding, which would call for continued implementation.

B.   Program meets needs (oasis, dumping ground, safety valve) for alienated, undecided students who are not college bound.

C.   Program well installed (recruitment, job sites, monitoring and instrution), well stabilized.

D.   Program might be folded in to new vocational education center and be funded through it.

Source: Miles, M. B., & Huberman, A. M. (1994). *Qualitative data analysis: An expanded sourcebook* (2nd ed.). Thousand Oaks, CA: Sage Publications.

Pooling these indicators with a contextual and trend analysis of the case as a whole, the analyst came up with four factors, shown in Display 10.3, that could "spoil" the pessimistic prediction.

Analysis

Selecting Participants to Confirm/Disconfirm the Prediction.

Before the predictions are sent out, an ethical review is important: Can this information be damaging to these individuals or to their colleagues in any way? General predictions usually have little harmful potential, in contrast with person-specific information. But the question needs careful attention.

The prediction and its justification are given to key participants at the site 1 year later, with a request for data on the current, actual situation about which the prediction was made. Normally, you choose participants who (a) have proven reliable, (b) are in a position to know the current situation, and (c) occupy differing roles and have somewhat differing perspectives.

Display 10.4 shows a response form from one of the three case participants. Factors A through E on the top part of the chart are the "supporting factors" we listed earlier; Factors A through D on the bottom part are the "spoilers." This respondent agrees that most of the supporting factors were pertinent in determining the way things turned out 1 year later. The other participants made similar, but not identical, judgments on all of the predictors (e.g., two thought central office support was stronger and the "tightening up" was a more pertinent predictor).

As for the factors working against the prediction, the two high "pertinence" estimates suggest that the analyst had underrated the possibility of more external funding and the importance of the "dumping ground" function of the project. (The two other participants agreed, but they also felt that C and D were influential factors that bettered the chances of institutionalization. So we are still caught in the dilemma of differing perceptions among respondents—a dilemma that sometimes can be resolved by follow-up phone interviewing.)

Display 10.4

Filled-Out Response Form From Case Informant for "Institutionalization" Prediction

Pertinence Ratings:
1 = not pertinent
2 = pertinent, but not important in causing current situation
3 = important factor in causing current situation

Our Predition

| The program will undergo a transitional year in 1980–81, during which time it will be phased out. |

	Factors we thought would support our prediction	Pertinence (write in appropriate number below)	Brief explanation (why you say this)
A.	Poor district record of institutionalizing soft-money programs.	2	It could have been different with a more aggressive leader sold on the idea.
B.	Unlikelihood of strong support from new prinicipals; some counselors indifferent; some elective-subjects teachers hostile.	2	One new prinicipal was supportive; the other not. Counselors reflected the principals' attitudes.
C.	Lukewarm support from central office.	3	This true. In four years neither the Supt. nor the Deputy have ever visited the room. The new Assistant spent 30 min. there last year.
D.	Financial squeeze in district; declining enrollments, staff cutbacks, lowered external funds. Program vulnerable because of high unit costs.	3	
E.	"Tightening up" mandate to principals: Program may be seen as a "frill," with lax control over student.	1	I wasn't aware of the "tightening up" toward the program. Student behavior-yes.

	Factors we thought could work against our prediction	Pertinence (as things turned out)	Brief explanation
A.	Possibility of dissemination funding, which would call for continued implementation.	3	As long as state funds are available, a demonstration program will be available.
B.	Program meets needs (oasis, dumping ground, safety valve) for alienated, undecided students who are not college bound.	3	This year more students were less motivated then ever before.
C.	Program well installed (recruitment, job sites, monitoring and instruction), well stabilized.	1	I don't think this matters at all to the decision-makers.
D.	Program might be folded in to new vocational education center, and funded through it.	1	I have not heard this said regarding the voc. ed center, through I've thought it has possibilities under state guidelines which allow for student community placement under contracts with employers.

Source: Miles, M. B., & Huberman, A. M. (1994). Qualitative data analysis: An expanded sourcebook (2nd ed.). Thousand Oaks, CA: Sage Publications.

Limit the number of variables or outcomes for which you make predictions (say, to four or five), and keep the explanatory factors for each to the same number or less. Define each of the outcome variables specifically, or else participants may give confusing responses. You should not ethically expect site personnel to carry out what amounts to professional work without some form of compensation. We offered a modest reader's fee for participants' time and feedback to our prediction response forms.

Assessing the Prediction.

How about the researcher's prediction itself—that the program would be phased out? The prediction is probably in trouble because participants felt that some of the "spoiler" factors were pertinent and important. As it turned out, our prediction was too pessimistic. The project was reduced in scale, and its status was transitional—but it was still around, though barely.

Central office support apparently was stronger than estimated, owing to the successful and still necessary dumping ground function and the possibility of receiving new external funds to disseminate the project to other districts. The district office had decided to fund the project for one more year but had cut project staff and students by half. We counted our accuracy as only moderate.

We did better at predicting *Institutionalization* at other field sites; one other was moderately accurate, and the rest were high/moderate to highly accurate. Furthermore, the explanations given by us and the site people overlapped reasonably well (58% of the assigned causes were in full agreement).

As the causal network in Display 9.11 shows, this was a difficult prediction to make, in light of the number of streams and the fact that not all led to the same conclusion. The predictions for the other outcome variables shown at the outcome end of the network (e.g., student impact and job mobility) were easier to make and were on the nose.

Notes

This exercise has some limits. Unless you go back to the field, you are relying solely on self-report data. And predictions can be wrong for reasons that have little to do with their internal validity. A few unanticipated events, such as the sudden death of a key participant or a budget crisis, can wreak havoc on the best-laid projections of an analyst. Though you may try to imagine the intrusion of unanticipated events as part of the predictive work, surprises and the idiosyncratic can never be fully anticipated.

Predictor-Outcome-Consequences Matrix

Description

A predictor-outcome-consequences matrix arrays cases and data on three components: (1) main *antecedent* variables that you think may be the most important contributors to (2) main *outcome* or criterion variables, then (3) the predicted *consequences* of the outcomes. The basic principle behind the three-component matrix is explanatory rather than purely descriptive; we want to see whether particular antecedents and outcomes predict or account for consequences.

This analytic model does not necessarily "predict the future," per se, for the specific cases you're investigating. Rather, you're strategically documenting what has already actually happened to the cases in order to discover whether, in retrospect, certain antecedent variables or factors, and in what combination, foreshadowed—that is, predicted—particular outcomes and consequences (see Display 10.5).

Applications

Cross-case matrices can be used to explore and test relationships between two, then among several, variables. It's also possible to do more directly explanatory work with cross-case matrices, moving beyond probabilistic predictions to more causal (deterministic) analyses. We can hook a chain of predictors to some intermediate outcome and then show the later consequences of that outcome—the outcome of the outcome. Such a display is especially good when you are looking at an intermediate or intervening variable that is not construed as a "final" outcome.

Use a predictor-outcome-consequences matrix when you want to see how several contributing factors function *together* in relation to different levels of a criterion measure. It's variable oriented but keeps the configuration of variables for each case. This matrix and its accompanying analysis also provide opportunities to develop conditional hypotheses, though they may only be site specific to the contexts of the cases.

Example

In the school improvement study, we (Miles and Huberman) found that some cases had an easy, smooth time during early use and others had a rougher time. What accounted for this difference? In other words, which prime factors, coming before or during early use, were associated with more or less smoothness? We had already done some preliminary analysis on "preparedness factors" (e.g., available resources and materials, skills and training of school personnel, etc.), which we will not go into here due to the excessive detail, which will confound rather than clarify the method profile. The important thing to note from that analysis is that we assigned *dynamic descriptors* to each case's variable under examination. For example, we assessed for each site whether

- the *Required practice changes* were major, moderate, or minor;
- the *Actual size and scope of the innovation* was large, moderate, or small;
- the *Actual classroom/organizational fit* of the innovation was good, moderate, or poor;
- the *Central office's commitment to change* was high, moderate, or low;
- the *Smoothness or roughness of early implementation* was very rough, rough, smooth, mostly smooth, or mixed; and
- other variables.

The use of these magnitude descriptors is not intended to reduce or seemingly quantify our observations. Rather, it is intended to make *comparative and evaluative* analyses across cases and between variables more possible and manageable.

In Display 10.5, the first goal is to predict the degree of *Assistance* provided at the 12 field sites (which are ordered in the left-hand column). To do this, the analyst assembled the most likely predictors emerging from the individual cases and from preceding cross-case analyses.

The first three *Antecedent Conditions* columns (*Actual size/scope of innovation*, *Required practice change*, and *Actual classroom/organizational fit*) deal with variables

Display 10.5

Predictor-Outcome-Consequences Matrix: Antecedents and Consequences of Assistance

SITES	Antecedent Conditions						Assistance		Consequences	
	Actual size/scope of innovation →	Required practice change →	Actual classroom/organizational fit →	Strength of implementation requirements #	Scale of funding →	Central office commitment to change →	Admin. latitude →	Outcome: Overall presence	Smoothness/Roughness of early implementation	Practice-stabilization (later implementation)
Scale of Assistance										
Substantial assistance										
Masepa (E)	large	major	mod/good	12 of 15	$30–50K	high	low	**high**	very rough	mod
Plummet (L)	large	mod/major	good/poor*	12 of 15	$300K	high	high	**high**	very rough	mod
Carson (L)	large	major	mod/good	12 of 15	$96K	high	mod	**mod/high**	rough	mod
Tindale (L)	large/mod	major	mod	12 of 15	$87K	high	low	**mod/high**	rough	high
Perry-Parkdale (E)	mod	mod/major	mod	10 of 15	$300K@	mod	high	**mod/high**	mixed	mod/high
Banestown (E)	small/mod	major	mod	10 of 15	$5.6K	high	high	**mod**	very rough	mod
Initial assistance, then minimal										
Lido (E)	small	mod	mod	7 of 15	$6.1K	low	high	**low/mod**	mostly smooth	mod/high
Astoria (E)	small	minor	good	3 of 15	none	high	high	**low/mod**	smooth	high
Calston (E)	small	mod	poor	9 of 15	none	mod/high	mod/high	**low/mod**	mixed	mod/high
Nearly none										
Dun Hollow (L)	small	minor	poor	7 of 15	none	low	mod	**low**	rough	low
Proville (L)	mod	minor	mod	7 of 15	$180K	high/low	high	**low**	very rough	low
Burton (E)	small	minor	good	3 of 15	$3.1K	mod/high	high	**low**	smooth	mod

(E) = externally developed innovation

(L) = locally developed innovation

* = good at district level, poor for students

= weighted sum of three variables at left, scaled 1–5

@ = local innovation funds, to adopt

+ = disseminate externally developed innovation

Source: Miles, M. B., & Huberman, A. M. (1994). *Qualitative data analysis: An expanded sourcebook* (2nd ed.). Thousand Oaks, CA: Sage Publications.

that are bundled together and given a numerical weight in the fourth column, signifying *Strength of implementation requirements*. A high "score" of 15 was possible.

Then we have three more *Antecedent Conditions* columns (*Scale of funding*, *Central office commitment to change*, and *Administrative latitude*). The *Overall presence* as a level of *Assistance* is listed in the next column. A mod/high or low/mod rating meant that our assessment fell in between the two words (i.e., "moderately high" and "low to moderate," respectively). We made these predictive ratings based on the antecedent variables that came before them on the matrix, coupled with earlier analyses on preparedness factors, plus our insider research knowledge of the 12 cases' subtleties.

If we wanted to, we could have stopped the analysis here and ended up with a two-component predictor-outcome matrix. But the display can be helped with another objective: looking beyond *Assistance* to its *Consequences* during *early* implementation (next to last column) and during *later* implementation (last column). In other words, although the degree of *Assistance* was a dependent variable for an earlier analysis, it is, in turn, the chief predictor of the two later *Consequences*.

Analysis

The next step is to get into a *multivariate* prediction mode, taking those antecedent or predictor variables that we have good reason to believe are contributing to outcomes and assessing their separate and combined effects for consequences.

The analyst is looking to see whether the predictors that best accounted for the degree of assistance make sense and lead to different levels of later outcome. So we have the rudiments of a *causal chain* appearing in the matrix. But we are going beyond a simple configuration in each case to understanding, if we can, the actual *causal mechanisms* involved.

The analyst begins to piece together this mosaic by looking for possible explanatory configurations and by cycling back to the case-level reports to see whether the emerging picture makes sense. Here, the analyst saw one cluster of cases and variables (small practice change, high latitude, and small-sized innovation) with its countervailing cluster (large practice change, lower latitude, and large innovation size). He then could look back at the case reports to see whether such animals actually existed and whether the hypothesis about the size of attempted changes affecting early smoothness was plausible in each case or not (tactic: **replicating a finding**).

Of course, eyeballing the matrix and looking for patterns is the best way to compose predictions. One analyst developed three assertions using basic if-then logic:

1. When there is virtually no on-site preparation assistance for an innovation, later program stabilization will tend to be low.

2. Even when there is substantial on-site preparation assistance for an innovation, early program implementation will be rough, but later program stabilization will most likely be moderate.

3. The amount of on-site funding for an innovation does not appear to effect the program's eventual early implementation or later stabilization; but no funding at all generally equates to minimal on-site preparation assistance (which, in *some* cases, could lead to lower program stabilization later).

These assertions or statements about what *did* happen at 12 particular sites are written in the present tense, comparable to *hypotheses*—projections or predictions of what *could* happen or *most likely would happen* if another comparable program innovation were to be initiated in the future at these sites. Also, notice that they are conditional, meaning that phrases such as "tend to," "does not appear to," "most likely," "in *some* cases," and so on, are woven into the statements. No one can predict the future with any exact certainty, not even statisticians. Therefore, couch your qualitatively derived predictions with a touch of humility.

Begin work with a manageable number of candidate antecedent variable predictors chosen on the basis of good sense, conceptual plausibility, and empirical groundedness. More than 12 at a time is a formula for overload; don't let predictors balloon. A pure fishing expedition is never helpful; the conceptual framework or the data from the cases should be providing promising clues from the outset. Expect that one matrix will lead to another and that the next one will be smaller and better informed as a result of the first one.

Work with the matrix descriptively before you work with the relationships between the variables; that is, go down each column first (tactic: **noting patterns, themes**) and then start **comparing, contrasting** columns. If there is too little variation in the matrix, be content with what you can extract descriptively, or focus solely on the variables that *do* have some range.

Notes

Although this method is not designed to "predict the future" for the specific study you're working on, there's nothing that says you can't plausibly predict midway through your fieldwork what might happen, and then later see if your predictions of outcomes and consequences were correct (or not). Depending on the scope of your study and the persuasiveness of your argument, there may be transferability of your predictions to other comparable settings, contexts, and conditions.

This profile illustrated a three-component model: predictor, outcome, and consequence. For small-scale or short-term studies, you may wish to explore a simpler two-part prediction and outcome model (discussed below in Display 10.7).

Causal-Prediction Models

Description

A causal-prediction model is a network of variables with causal connections among them, drawn from multiple-case analyses. Although empirically grounded, it is essentially a higher order effort to derive a testable set of propositions about the complete network of variables and interrelationships. The principle is one of theory building and thus prediction (see Display 10.6).

Applications

Carefully ordered meta-matrices, time-ordered matrices, or effects matrices can begin to tell us a lot about what goes with what. Variable by variable, we can understand that *X* comes before *Y*, and more of *X* goes with more of *Y*; that less of *Z* goes with more of *Y*; and perhaps that *W* looks unrelated to *X*—unless you take varying levels of *V* into account. This is all rather atomistic, though. Two problems remain.

The first is beginning to transcend mere association and to arrive at *interrelationship*—something like a judgment that variable *X* not only precedes *Y* in time

Display 10.6

Causal-Prediction Model Tracing User Practice Changes

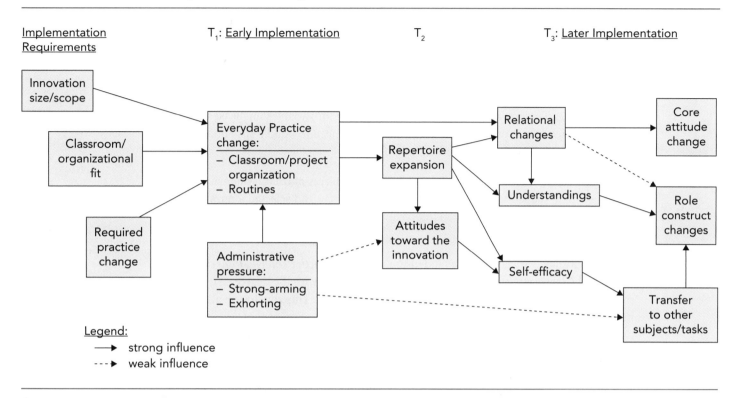

Implementation Requirements

T₁: Early Implementation

T₂

T₃: Later Implementation

Legend:
⟶ strong influence
--→ weak influence

Source: Miles, M. B., & Huberman, A. M. (1994). *Qualitative data analysis: An expanded sourcebook* (2nd ed.). Thousand Oaks, CA: Sage Publications.

but also looks coherently connected to it: If *X* goes up for some reason, we would expect *Y* to go up or down, as well.

The second problem is how to go beyond mere list making to something like an integrated set of relationships among the variables: in short, a *model*. In practice, these problems usually need to be solved together, and they require a network rather than a matrix display.

We have discussed in Chapter 9 the practical problems of assessing causality and of forming a sensible, data-grounded causal network. The question at hand is this: Given multiple-case data in ordered matrix form and a set of variable-oriented conclusions, how can you integrate those findings into a general visual model of the variables involved that specifies causal and thus theoretical/predictive connections clearly? A causal-prediction model is proposed as one heuristic.

Example

Preliminary Displays: Variables and Outcomes.

In the school improvement study, we (Miles and Huberman) asked the question "In what way do users of an innovation change their 'practice' after using the innovation—and what determines greater or lesser amounts of practice change?" Because causal-prediction modeling is usually a second-order activity drawing on other displays, we need to discuss the preliminary displays first.

Throughout this book, there have been many displays related to the school improvement study, some of which have focused on exploring, describing, ordering, explaining, and predicting the variables, actions, processes, phenomena, states, events, outcomes, consequences, and so on, of the participants. We draw on those displays plus field notes and additional analytic insights made along the way to contribute ideas for the causal-prediction model. These will be discussed later.

Preliminary Display: Predictors and Outcomes.

We first need to look at the question of which predictor variables might be associated with the particular outcomes in this study. For that we need to build a *case-ordered predictor-outcome meta-matrix* (see Display 10.7).

The analyst in this case chose to order the cases in terms of overall intensity of the outcome (high, moderate, moderate-low, small/no change) and selected a number of predictors that seemed to have been important on a case-by-case basis in inducing user practice change.

In this instance, the analyst concluded that *Required practice change*, *Project size/ scope*, and *Classroom/organizational fit* were all associated with the degree of user practice change (tactic: **making contrasts, comparisons**). This conclusion also involved another tactic: **checking the meaning of outliers**. For example, the analyst noted that the moderate-sized program at Proville was simply sabotaged by dissatisfied users, so there was no opportunity for user practice change to occur. The analyst also noted that *General attitude during implementation* was a poor predictor because it was largely positive, except in cases where discontinuations took place (Dun Hollow, Proville).

Finally the analyst saw that *Administrative pressure* of a *Direct* sort was, by itself, not a very good predictor. But if it was combined with *Indirect* pressure (exhorting, reinforcing), the consequences were clear: A carrot-and-stick approach was associated with greater user practice change (tactic: **finding intervening variables**).

Analysis

Building the Causal-Prediction Model.

Now you begin reflecting: How can the associations noted in matrix displays be transformed and integrated into a meaningful explanatory network model? So far, the analysis has been mostly variable oriented. Let's apply four process-oriented rules of thumb:

1. Order the model *temporally*: Learn which relevant variables occur first in time, which occur along the way during implementation, and which might be seen as early and later outcomes.

2. Consider which variables might reasonably be expected to have a direct *impact* on other variables, both preceding them in time and having a plausible direct connection.

3. *Check case participants' explanations*: What causal linkages do they claim are present? Consult the field notes.

4. Consider what available *research and theory* have to say about causal connections and their predicted outcomes. (In this case, past studies of implementation and individual learning theory might suggest relationships among variables.)

Display 10.7

Predictor-Outcome Matrix: Predictors of Magnitude of User Practice Change

Early Implementation Requirements

Magnitude of change, by sites	Required practice change *	Project size/ scope	Classroom/ organizational fit	Index of early implementation requirements @	General attitude during implementation	Administrative pressure: Direct: Strong-arming	Administrative pressure: Indirect: exhorting, reinforcing
High Change							
Masepa (E)	major	large	mod/good	14	+	high	high
Plummet (L)	mod-major	large	good/poor #	12	+	low	high
Moderate Change							
Banestown (E)	major	small/mod	moderate	10	+	mod	high
Tindale (L)	major	large/mod	moderate	12	+	high	high
Carson (L)	major	large	moderate	13	+	low	high
Perry-Parkdale (E)	mod-major	mod	moderate	10	+	low	low/mod
Moderate-Low Change							
Calston (E)	moderate	small	poor	9	+	mod	mod
Lido (E)	moderate	small	moderate	7	+	low	mod
Small-No Change							
Burton (E)	minor	small	good	3	+	low	mod
Dun Hollow (L)	minor	small	poor	7	-	mod	low
Proville (L)	minor	moderate	moderate	7	-	mod	mod
Astoria (E)	minor	small	good	3	+	low	low

(E) = externally developed innovation

(L) = locally developed innovation

* = Discrepancy between users' customary instructional practices and those required to implement the innovation at the time of initial use

= Good in the district, poor for needs of incoming students

@ = sum of 5-point scales for first 3 columns.

Source: Miles, M. B., & Huberman, A. M. (1994). *Qualitative data analysis: An expanded sourcebook* (2nd ed.). Thousand Oaks, CA: Sage Publications.

Using these rules, you have to noodle for a while. As with other network displays, it helps to put variables on index cards or "sticky notes," move them around into various configurations, and look at the connections that seem plausible and sensible. If you have some user-friendly CAQDAS graphic software, use that. Display 10.6 shows the model that finally emerged from our own process. Let's look at some of its aspects.

First, the analyst concludes that the innovation's three *Implementation requirements* are logically prior to what happens when it is implemented. So he places *Innovation size/scope*, *Classroom/organizational fit*, and *Required practice change* as antecedents of some aspects of user practice change.

From the Display 10.7 matrix, we can suggest that the easiest (hence possibly earliest) things to change are classroom routines. The analyst, reflecting a moment and reviewing case data, also realizes that such routines are being changed, not by magic, but by the form of organization of the project and the way it is carried out in classrooms. So those are drawn in as the immediate *Everyday Practice* changes during early implementation. The model is growing.

Where should *Administrative pressure* fit in the model? It occurs mainly during early implementation, the field notes show, and the analyst reasons that it probably has a direct effect on *Everyday Practice* changes: The strong-arming and exhorting serve to keep the immediate short-run practice changes in place. (Prior educational implementation research tends to support this linkage, contributing to the strength of the model's prediction component.)

The analyst also postulates that the *Administrative pressure* has weaker, later effects as well (suggested through dashed lines): It encourages positive *Attitudes toward the innovation* itself (through the strong-arming and exhorting) and makes it more likely that users will *Transfer* their learnings to *other subjects and tasks*.

From Early (T1) Through Later (T3) Implementation.

Once the initial user changes in practice have taken place, what is a reasonable model that would get us to the other, "deeper" outcomes noted in Display 10.6? It almost surely is not a linear chain but a network. We have to consider how succeeding types of changes in teachers might influence and affect each other. Here again, the four rules of thumb apply. The analyst also has the variables and outcomes from earlier relevant displays as an empirical start.

The analyst culled from previous displays and field notes that the project's *Routines*, given some teacher experience with them, lead to *Repertoire expansion* (i.e., teachers have new things they know how to do). From this expansion came positive *Attitudes toward the innovation*.

These two practice changes have further consequences. An expanded repertoire leads to *Relational changes* (e.g., more willingness to share one's new knowledge with other teachers); and it deepens teachers' *Understandings*—of classroom dynamics, of their own and pupils' roles, and, in some cases, of school and district dynamics.

Finally, both repertoire expansion and positive attitudes to the innovation lead to increased *Self-efficacy* (i.e., I am more skilled in doing this good new thing, therefore I feel good about myself professionally).

After a good deal of implementation, *Core attitude* changes (e.g., "I was learning to be flexible") come essentially from the teacher's working relations with peers, as well as with students themselves. The analyst also proposes that *Role construct* changes (e.g., reconceptualizing "structured" teaching as productive rather than authoritarian) come essentially from basic understandings and from the successful experience of transfer to other subjects and tasks. *Transfer*, itself, comes mainly from *Self-efficacy*, in this model: The better I feel about my competence, the more likely I am to try my new ideas and practices in other aspects of my work.

All of these variables were mapped into Display 10.6, the causal-prediction model. Think of the final result as a carefully interwoven series of causal chains from the school improvement study, with transferable possibilities to comparable sites and contexts. Each stream is a story about the project and its participants across time, and their points (or variables) of convergence are moments of interrelationship. The structure of the causal-prediction model with its "What happens next?" scenarios outlines the accompanying narrative we compose for readers to tell them, "This is what happened, and this is *why* it happened *in this particular sequence*." This implies that we are proposing a theory; and *theories are about prediction*.

Recommendations for Causal-Prediction Model Development.

It sometimes helps to make submodels that are wholly linear ($W \to X \to Y \to Z$), as a simplifying strategy (see the methods profile for *causal chains* in Chapter 9). It's also useful to consider a backward-mapping approach: You begin with final outcomes and reason back along the causal byways (Which variable, in principle, would have to be changed in order to induce this change?).

It often happens that you feel blocked, unable to understand how variable A could lead to variable C in any plausible way. There must be one or more other variables in the picture that affect the outcome. Use the tactic of **finding intervening variables** to generate a variable B that comes between A and C.

Another analyst could well have come out with a somewhat different causal-prediction model. The rules of thumb may be weighted differently, or they may turn up alternative, equally compelling accounts. You should subject the "final" causal model to verification, most easily through colleagues and participants, who can help you clarify the assumptions you are making and suggest alternative views (tactic: **checking out rival explanations**). Given a causal-prediction model with which you are reasonably satisfied intellectually, return once again to the written-up field notes for evidence of disconfirmation or needed revision. Of course, the true test of a causal-prediction model is if the same sequences occur in different settings in the future.

Notes

Expect to do several versions of the causal-prediction model. Use a simple technology that permits flexibility in rearrangement—index cards and "sticky notes" do indeed work well for the initial stages of display design. Once those are relatively set, transform the bins to digital representations with modeling software. Get advice from colleagues; don't close up too fast. Return repeatedly to field notes to check, test, and extend the model. It usually helps to refer back to preceding matrices, with a good look at **outliers** and **extreme cases**. When a specific, well-understood case does not fit the model, *change the model* to accommodate that information, instead of trying to explain away the "inconvenient" information.

Closure and Transition

Prediction is a slippery concept in qualitative inquiry, but there may be some occasions in which projection of what might, could, and should happen is a necessary outcome of our research endeavors. We advise that you predict, propose, hypothesize, and theorize only after rigorous analysis and careful reflection on the consequences of your statements.

We have completed five chapters on methods of qualitative data analysis through display: exploring, describing, ordering, explaining, and predicting. The next chapter offers several methods for further analytic work—ways of better ensuring the credibility and trustworthiness of your findings.

Chapter 11 - Drawing and Verifying Conclusions

Chapter 12 - Writing About Qualitative Research

Chapter 13 - Closure

Part

3

Making
Good Sense

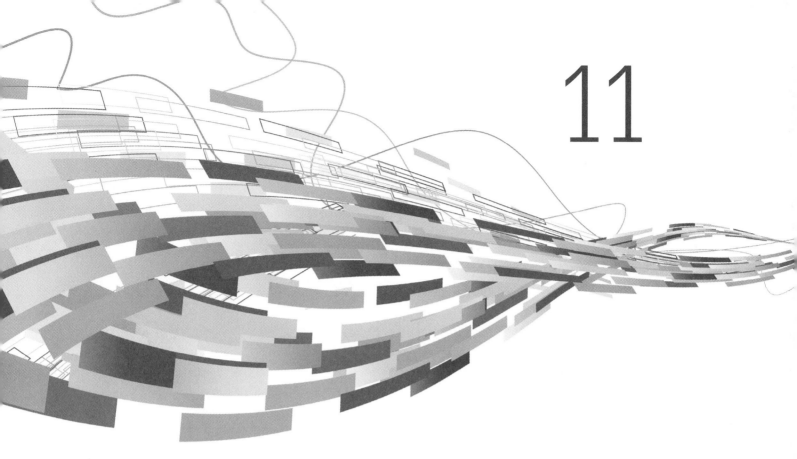

Drawing and Verifying Conclusions

Chapter Summary

This chapter offers additional analytic tactics for generating meaning from data and for testing or confirming findings. Standards for assessing the quality of conclusions are proposed, along with methods for documenting a researcher's analytic processes.

Contents

Introduction

Tactics for Generating Meaning

    1. Noting Patterns, Themes

    2. Seeing Plausibility

    3. Clustering

    4. Making Metaphors

    5. Counting

    6. Making Contrasts/Comparisons

    7. Partitioning Variables

8. Subsuming Particulars Into the General

9. Factoring

10. Noting the Relations Between Variables

11. Finding Intervening Variables

12. Building a Logical Chain of Evidence

13. Making Conceptual/Theoretical Coherence

Tactics for Testing or Confirming Findings

1. Checking for Representativeness

2. Checking for Researcher Effects

3. Triangulating

4. Weighting the Evidence

5. Checking the Meaning of Outliers

6. Using Extreme Cases

7. Following Up Surprises

8. Looking for Negative Evidence

9. Making If-Then Tests

10. Ruling Out Spurious Relations

11. Replicating a Finding

12. Checking Out Rival Explanations

13. Getting Feedback From Participants

Standards for the Quality of Conclusions

Objectivity/Confirmability

Reliability/Dependability/Auditability

Internal Validity/Credibility/Authenticity

External Validity/Transferability/Fittingness

Utilization/Application/Action Orientation

Analytic Documentation

The Problem

Illustration

Closure and Transition

Introduction

This is a substantial chapter, at the core of the book. The displays we've described are tools for analysis. But how do you use them? As you work with any display, there's always a flow of specific analysis *tactics*—that is, ways of drawing and verifying conclusions that you use during the process. These tactics have been named in **boldface** in the preceding chapters. Now, we discuss each in detail. Following that, we turn to the question of the goodness—the *quality*—of the conclusions you reach. The chapter concludes with a look at the documentation of qualitative analyses.

The creativity scholar Sir Ken Robinson is attributed with offering this cautionary advice about making a convincing argument: "Without data, you're just another person with an opinion." We add to that the following: "Without verification, you're just another researcher with a hunch."

Tactics for Generating Meaning

In this section, we discuss 13 specific tactics for drawing meaning from a particular configuration of data in a display. Usually, we describe the general analysis situation being faced, explain the tactic, and then give one or more examples, sometimes referring back to previous sections (where the tactic was noted in **boldface**). If we can muster advice, we present that too. But the real test of these tactics comes in the using.

People are meaning finders and meaning makers; they can usually make sense of the most chaotic events. Our equilibrium depends on such skills: We keep the world consistent and predictable by organizing and interpreting it. The critical question is whether the meanings you find in qualitative data are trustworthy and "right." The following section discusses tactics for testing or confirming meanings, minimizing bias, and ensuring to your best ability the quality of the conclusions.

First, here is a quick overview of tactics for generating meaning, numbered from 1 to 13. They are arranged roughly from the descriptive to the explanatory and from the concrete to the more conceptual and abstract.

Noting patterns, **themes** (1), **seeing plausibility** (2), and **clustering** (3) help the analyst see "what goes with what." **Making metaphors** (4), like the preceding three tactics, is a way to achieve more integration among diverse pieces of data. **Counting** (5) is also a familiar way to see "what's there."

Making contrasts/comparisons (6) is a pervasive tactic that sharpens understanding. Differentiation sometimes is needed too, as in **partitioning variables** (7).

We also need tactics for seeing things and their relationships more abstractly. These include **subsuming particulars into the general** (8); **factoring** (9), an analog of a familiar quantitative technique; **noting the relations between variables** (10); and **finding intervening variables** (11).

Finally, how can we systematically assemble a coherent understanding of data? The tactics discussed are **building a logical chain of evidence** (12) and **making conceptual/theoretical coherence** (13).

1. Noting Patterns, Themes

When you're working with text or initial displays, you often note recurring patterns, themes, or "gestalts" that pull together many separate pieces of data. Something jumps out at you and suddenly makes sense.

Some examples of patterns from the school improvement study were

- the frequent citing of a "miracle case" (a failing student who was rejuvenated by the innovation) as either an explanation or a justification for the project,

- "deep coping" as a problem-solving style in a high school staff group, and

- the use of "administrative latitude"—the freedom to alter an innovation in return for trying it at all.

What kinds of patterns can there be? As usual, we can expect patterns of *variables* involving similarities and differences among categories, and patterns of *processes* involving connections in time and space within a bounded context.

Pattern finding can be very productive when the number of cases and/or the data overload is severe. McCammon et al. (2012), for example, analyzed responses from 234 returned open-ended surveys. The patterns constructed from the mixed-methods data resulted in 30 major categories, which were then synthesized into three major themes, then into one key assertion.

The human mind finds patterns almost intuitively; it needs no how-to advice. But patterns don't just happen; we construct them from our observations of reoccurring phenomena. The important thing is to be able to (a) see added evidence of the same pattern and (b) remain open to disconfirming evidence when it appears. Patterns need to be subjected to *skepticism*—your own or that of others—and to conceptual and empirical testing (Does it really make conceptual sense? Do we find it elsewhere in the data where it was expected? Are there any counterexamples?) before they can represent useful knowledge.

2. Seeing Plausibility

It often happens during analysis that a conclusion is plausible, makes good sense, and "fits." If a colleague asks you how you came to the conclusion or what you based it on, the initial answer is something like "I don't really know. It just feels right." Many scientific discoveries initially appeared to their authors in this guise; the history of science is full of global, intuitive understandings that, after laborious verification, proved to be true. So plausibility, with intuition as the underlying basis, is not to be sneered at.

But people are meaning finders, even in the most genuinely chaotic data sets. Patterns can be found even in random data, as the activities of numerologically obsessed people show (see the films π, *A Beautiful Mind*, and *The Number 23*). So plausibility can easily become the refuge of analysts who are too ready to jump to conclusions.

During the documentation of our own analysis efforts, we often found ourselves giving the "plausibility" basis for the conclusions we drew, particularly in the early stages of analysis. Nearly always, it turned out, plausibility was an initial impression that needed further checking through other tactics. Plausibility in this sense was a sort of *pointer*, drawing the analyst's attention to a conclusion that looked reasonable and sensible on the face of it—but what was the real basis involved?

Here's a brief illustration: McCammon et al. (2012) analyzed their survey data by *gender* to observe whether men and women responded differently to their high school arts experiences. Saldaña hypothesized and "felt sure" that major differences would appear, based on his earlier research with audience response trends. But after data analysis, no *major* gender differences were found. There were nuances of experience that women remembered and men did not, but the projected differences were just not present in the data. Saldaña even thought, "This can't be right," and he subjected the qualitative data to reanalysis tactics—**counting** and finding new ways of **making contrasts/comparisons** with the data—but nothing new was discovered. (The most revealing differences actually occurred between other stratifications, such as age cohort.)

So the moral is "Trust your 'plausibility' intuitions, but don't fall in love with them. Subject the preliminary conclusions to other tactics of conclusion drawing and verification."

Incidentally, a somewhat more trustworthy tactic involves noticing a *lack* of plausibility. When a conclusion someone is advancing just doesn't make sense, it's a bit safer to rule it out. But not completely safe. Counterintuitive or puzzling findings sometimes can be extraordinarily stimulating and rich, so they should be allowed their day in the sun, too. (We will discuss the tactic of **following up surprises** later.)

Most of the conclusions drawn during analysis are substantive, based on the content. But the analyst is constantly drawing *procedural* conclusions along the way as well: to transpose two rows in a matrix, to add or discard a column, to collapse the data into a summary table, and to change a decision rule for data entry. It's important to log and report the procedural decisions made (the final matrix, the operative decision rules, etc.).

3. Clustering

In daily life, we're constantly clumping things into classes, categories, and bins: Things that do not move around but grow are called "plants," things that move around and have babies are called "animals," and things that move around, have four wheels, have an engine run by fossil fuels or electricity, and carry people are called "automobiles." Most categories require other categories to define them: "wheel," "engine," "babies."

The next step often is to figure out what to call clusters. For example, the process of transforming hundreds of pages of interview transcripts and field notes into a one-page matrix or network display might be called "condensing" the data. But to others, it might be called "distilling," "synthesizing," "abstracting," "transforming," and even the abhorrent "reducing" the data. Even though these are different words and processes, they *kind of* mean the same thing. We have clustered them and now need to assign a word or phrase that represents all of them. Shall one of the six words be chosen as their representative? Or shall we compose a completely new umbrella label for the six of them? (This is where a thesaurus comes in handy. But, ultimately, it's your call as the analyst.)

Just as we are pattern-finding people, we are also cluster-making people. We categorize and organize the vast array of things in our lives to feel a sense of comfort and security in their ordering. Roles, rules, relationships, routines, and rituals are clusters of patterned actions—what some generically label as our habits (Duhigg, 2012). Clustering is a tactic that can be applied at many levels to qualitative data: at the level of events or acts, of individual participants, of processes, of settings/locales, of sites or cases as wholes, of time periods, and so on. In all instances, we're trying to understand a phenomenon better by *grouping* and then *conceptualizing* objects that have similar patterns or characteristics.

But, occasionally, clusters are not always mutually exclusive and may overlap. For example, a student most often is in *either* an undergraduate *or* a graduate program. That's easy enough. But what's the undergraduate student's major? Well, it's complicated. He's a double major in social work and religious studies, *and* he's concurrently enrolled in the university's Honors College. Yes, he's male. And gay. And Hispanic. And a first-generation college student. And so on. Life is not neatly bounded and discrete as it once might have seemed. As the analyst works at clustering, the operations become more and more complex and extended—just as sorting things into "animals" and "plants" is a (perhaps deceptively) simpler task than sorting various kinds of wheeled machines (automobiles, trucks, golf carts, airplanes, ski-lift gondolas, and floor polishers) into sensible clusters. Clustering is our best attempt to categorize what seems to belong together.

Here are some additional examples.

Focusing on *participants*, we asked high school students to name the cliques they observed at their school. They identified clusters such as "preppies," "jocks," "goths," "skaters," "band kids," "stoners," "math geeks," "cheerleaders," and so on.

At the level of *processes*, we clustered the activities involved in coping with the problems of later implementation of an innovation: "reaching up," "improving," "debugging," "refining," "integrating," "adapting," and "extending." Processes are best identified in the form of gerunds ("-ing" words) to connote action.

At the level of both *processes* and *phases*, another example comes from our look at teachers' and administrators' job mobility, which clumped rather easily into these categories: "moving in," "moving out," "moving up," "moving in and up," "moving out and up," and "moving over."

It's also possible to cluster *settings* where site-specific *actions* occur. For example, in schools, we might sort places where people interact into the following clusters:

- Formal instructional (classroom, gym)
- Informal instructional (library, media center)
- Formal adult work (meeting room, office)
- Informal adult association (faculty lounge, corridor)
- Mixed (cafeteria, playground)

Clustering also can be seen as a process of moving to higher levels of abstraction (see **subsuming particulars into the general** later in this chapter).

We can see from these examples that clustering is a general name given to the process of inductively forming *categories* and the iterative sorting of things—events, participants, processes, settings, and so on—into those categories. When less complex things are being sorted (events, participants, etc.), the clustering tactic typically relies on aggregation and comparison (What things are like each other/unlike each other?) and is closely interwoven with the creation and use of attribute codes.

Clustering techniques do not have to be completely self-invented. There is a long tradition of content-analytic, coding, and categorizing techniques dealing directly with issues of unitizing and clustering qualitative data that can be very helpful (see Richards, 2009; Saldaña, 2013; Schreier, 2012).

4. Making Metaphors

The notion that research should focus only on matter-of-fact, literal description, with cautious, later ventures into interpretation and meaning, is responsible for much intellectual poverty and misery.

That sentence itself is stuffed (a metaphor) with metaphors (cautious ventures, poverty, misery). Metaphors, seen as one major type of trope or literary device, involve comparing two things via their similarities and ignoring their differences. As Morgan (1980) notes, calling a boxer "a tiger in the ring" evokes fierceness, grace, and power—and ignores striped fur, fangs, and four-leggedness. Metaphors are thus a partial abstraction.

The people we study use metaphors constantly as a way of making sense of their experience. We do the same thing as we examine our data. The issue, perhaps, is not *whether* to use metaphor as an analysis tactic but to be *aware* of *how* we—and the people we study—use it.

For instance, suppose you found yourself referring to "the empty nest" when you looked at an interview with someone who has grown children. You are, in effect, making allusions to an important environmental setting ("nest"), the idea of nurturance aching for a newly absent but grown-up object, and the acknowledgment that nurturance to the point of nest leaving has taken a good deal of time. But you may also be assuming that the nest itself is of little value and will be abandoned—and not considering the idea that the nest may be refilled with a new brood.

So the *richness and complexity* of metaphors are useful. The empty-nest metaphor leads us farther than a single variable, such as "a parent's separation anxiety," would. Our metaphor lets us see new theoretical possibilities (e.g., maybe if socialization for independence is weak, the child will regress).

What else is true of metaphors? They are *data-condensing devices*, taking several particulars and making a single generality of them. For instance, the "scapegoat" metaphor pulls together into one package facts about group norms, the treatment of those perceived as "deviants," social rituals, and social rationalizations. This ability is not to be sneezed at. Qualitative researchers looking at mountains of field note write-ups are grateful for any device that will reduce the bulk without locking out multiple avenues for analysis.

Metaphors are also *pattern-making devices*—for ourselves and for the people we study. For example, in the school improvement study, we found at one site that the remedial learning room was something like an oasis for the pupils sent there for part of each day. (A teacher used the word spontaneously, and we began to see the pattern.) The metaphor "oasis" pulls together separate bits of information: The larger school is harsh (like a desert); not only can students rest in the remedial room, but they also can get sustenance (learning); some resources are very abundant there (like water in an oasis); and so on. Such metaphors also help place the pattern noted in the larger context (in this case, the harsh, resource-thin school).

Metaphors are also excellent *decentering devices*. You step back from the welter of observations and conversations at the field site and ask, "What's going on here?" Because metaphors will not let you simply describe or denote a phenomenon, you have to move up a notch to a more inferential or analytical level. The remedial learning room does not look like an oasis, and most people are not actually describing it that way, nor is anyone behaving literally like an exhausted Bedouin under a date palm.

Finally, metaphors or analogies are ways of *connecting findings to theory*. The "oasis" metaphor makes you think of how institutions develop compensating mechanisms to reduce the stress they put on role occupants or of how they nurture as well as isolate deviants. Or you start considering social control mechanisms more generally. Metaphoric thinking effectively unites reason and imagination. Lakoff and Johnson's (1980) *Metaphors We Live By* is essential reading on this topic.

The metaphor is halfway from the empirical facts to the conceptual *significance* of those facts; it gets you up and over the particulars en route to the basic social processes that give meaning to those particulars. So a few words of advice for metaphor makers:

- Stay aware of the metaphors you and people in your study are using, often with only partial awareness. Dig into them for implicit meanings, for more explicit exploration and testing.

- Don't look for overarching metaphors too early in the study. It distracts you from fieldwork, and it leads to hasty judgments that clamp down on the meaning of what you are studying. You start to look around less, and you project the metaphor on things that are, at best, remotely related to it.

- Being cognitively playful helps generate metaphors. Ask yourself, "If I only had two words to describe an important feature at this site, what would they be?" or "What does it feel like?" The trick is to move from the denotative to the connotative. Instead of the social or the personal, go to biological, mechanical, or spatial domains to find useful metaphors.

- Interaction helps. Groups stimulate their members' thinking by increasing the inputs, bringing in ideas from a new angle, and creating a contagiously playful thinking environment.

- Know when to stop pressing the metaphor for its juice. When the "oasis" starts to have camels, camel drivers, a bazaar, and a howling sandstorm, you know you're forcing things. Use it as long as it's fruitful, and don't overmetaphorize. Remember that the two things compared in a metaphor always have differences.

There are other literary devices available to qualitative inquirers, such as irony (the view from the opposite, sometimes incongruous or paradoxical side), along with synecdoche (linking instances to a larger concept) and metonymy (representing a whole in terms of one or more of its parts). Gibbs (2007) describes how romance, tragedy, and other literary genres can be used effectively for narrative inquiry.

5. Counting

In qualitative research, numbers tend to get ignored. After all, the hallmark of qualitative research is that it goes beyond *how much* there is of something to tell us about its essential *qualities*.

However, a lot of counting goes on in the background when judgments of qualities are being made. When we identify a theme or a pattern, we're isolating something that (a) happens a number of times and (b) consistently happens in a specific way. The "number of times" and "consistency" judgments are based on counting. When we make a generalization, we amass a swarm of particulars and decide, almost unconsciously, which particulars are there *more often*, which *matter more* than others, which *go together*, and so on. When we say that something is "important," "significant," or "recurrent," we have come to that estimate, in part, by making counts, comparisons, and weights.

So it's important in qualitative research to know (a) that we are sometimes counting and (b) when it is a good idea to work self-consciously with frequencies, *and when it's not*.

There are three good reasons to resort to numbers: (1) to see rapidly what you have in a large batch of data, (2) to verify a hunch or hypothesis, and (3) to keep yourself analytically honest, protecting against bias.

Seeing What You Have

Numbers, we noted earlier, are more economical and manipulable than words; you "see" the general drift of the data more easily and rapidly by looking at distributions. For instance, in the school improvement study, we asked participants why they were using the new school practices we were studying. We got a mass of answers from several participants at each of the 12 field sites. It seemed that many people were saying that they had been pushed, more or less gently, into these projects, rather than diving in voluntarily. To see more clearly, we did a content analysis of the responses, totaled them, and derived Display 11.1.

It turns out that 62% (35 of the 56 respondents) mentioned administrative pressure and constraint. And, counterintuitively, very few of the practices were adopted to solve problems. There also seemed to be a general "professional development/capacity enhancement" theme (challenge, shaping projects, professional growth). Seeing that theme, gauging the importance of the "constraint" motive, and noting the infrequent problem-solving incentive were all helpful. We saw the overall trends, got some new leads, and saw some unexpected differences. All these findings helped in the subsequent nonquantitative analysis.

Verifying a Hypothesis

McCammon et al.'s (2012) mixed-methods survey examined, in part, whether any gender differences occurred between adult men's and women's responses about their high school arts experiences. Saldaña hypothesized that there would be. On a 4.00 "strongly

Display 11.1

Reasons Given for Adoption by Users

Reasons/Motives	Number of Respondents Mentioning Item (N = 56)
Administrative pressure, constraint	35
Improves classroom practice (new resources, relative advantage over current practice)	16
Novelty value, challenge	10
Social (usually peer influence)	9*
Opportunity to shape projects	5
Professional growth	5
Gives better working conditions	3
Solves problems	2
Provides extra money	1
Total	86

*Seven mentions from one site

Source: Miles, M. B., & Huberman, A. M. (1994). *Qualitative data analysis: An expanded sourcebook* (2nd ed.). Thousand Oaks, CA: Sage Publications.

agree" scale, the female respondents' mean was 3.85 and the male respondents' mean was 3.93 to the prompt "I have good memories from my [high school] speech and/or drama participation." But when we "crunched the numbers" through a *t* test, there was no statistically significant difference on a *p* < .05 standard between these two mean ratings. And the *qualitative* content analysis of their narrative responses to this prompt also confirmed no major differences between men's and women's experiences. So counting in the form of a statistical operation disconfirmed the hypothesis and made for a more trustworthy analysis.

Keeping Yourself Analytically Honest

We had expected from the start that careers would be important in the school improvement projects we studied. The more data we got, the more it seemed that "innovating" was a vehicle for moving up, in, over, or out (seldom down). The finding seemed important, was potentially controversial, and might have been a result of our expectation. So we actually counted the number of job moves (63 for 12 sites) and estimated how many could be attributed to the innovation (83% were). Afterward, we felt far more comfortable about the claims we were making. For example, it seemed that only 35% of the job-related shifts were upward ones, contrary to our earlier impression.

As qualitative researchers, we work to some extent by insight and intuition. We have moments of illumination—things "come together." The problem is that we could be wrong. Doing qualitative analysis with the occasional aid of numbers is a good way of testing for possible bias and seeing how robust our insights are.

6. Making Contrasts/Comparisons

Although comparisons are supposedly odious, they are what we do naturally and quickly when faced with any life experience, including looking at a qualitative data display. How does *X* differ from *Y*? Comparison is a time-honored, classic way to test a conclusion; we draw a contrast or make a comparison between two sets of things—persons, roles, activities, variables, cases as a whole—that are known to differ in some other important respect. This is the classic "method of differences" heuristic. A few examples from our work described in earlier chapters are as follows:

- *Contrast tables* show how exemplary cases vary in extreme ranges of their change, from "high" to "low" to "negative" degrees of user change (see Display 6.21).

- *Growth gradients* display time on one axis and degree on another axis, enabling a comparison of changes across time (see Display 8.3).

- *Predictor-outcome-consequence matrices* array cases by high and low outcomes and use that leverage to examine the impact of possible predictors. In our example, the comparison was between the *magnitude* of change, showing which predictors were present in "high-change" sites but not in "small-/no-change" sites (see Display 10.6).

We advise you to make sure that the comparisons made are the right ones and that they make sense. Take a moment before you display a comparison, and think, "How big must a difference be before it makes a difference?" You do not always need a statistical significance test to fall back on. The *practical* significance is what you need to assess.

7. Partitioning Variables

There are times when *differentiation* is more important than integration. It may occur to you at some point in your analysis: "Whoa—that variable is not really one variable but two, or maybe even three."

Partitioning or subdividing variables can occur at many points during analysis. At the stage of initial conceptualization, it pays to "unbundle" variables rather than assume a monolithic simplicity. For example, the general variable of "preparedness" to carry out an innovation can be partitioned into subvariables or components, ranging from the state of the user ("commitment," "understanding," "skills") to the availability of materials and the actions taken by administrators ("time allocation," "in-service workshops").

When you are designing matrix formats, variable partitioning is also useful; more differentiation lets you see differences that might otherwise be blurred or buried. Rather than a single column of *Outcomes*, it may help to partition that into two columns: (1) *Short-Term Effects* and (2) *Long-Term Consequences*.

When is variable partitioning a good tactic? The first answer: Divide variables in the early stages (conceptualizing, coding) to avoid monolithism and data blurring. The second answer: Partition a variable when it is not relating as well to another variable as your conceptual framework (or other available data) has led you to expect.

Finally, we should say that variable partitioning is not a virtue in itself. Extreme differentiation can lead to complexity and atomization, and poor mapping of events and processes. When you divide a variable, it should be in the service of finding coherent, integrated descriptions and explanations.

8. Subsuming Particulars Into the General

Clustering involves clumping together things that "go together" by using single or multiple dimensions. A related tactic is to ask, "What is this specific thing an instance of? Does it belong to a more general class?" This tactic is similar to the analytic processes for pattern coding and focused coding (see Chapter 4). Classic grounded theory calls this the "constant comparative method." You are trying to categorize a particular action, event, participant, state, and so on, into a more abstractly defined class. That class may have been predefined, or it may have emerged as a result of coding or analytic memoing.

For example, in the school improvement study, we noted specific statements made by teachers and administrators, such as the following:

- "If you want to depart from the guide, ask me and also tell me why you want to do it and how it will fulfill the guide's objectives."

- "The basic philosophy is there, but the use of [the innovation] is flexible, and doesn't require use of all units."

- "In this program you're like a robot . . . but I learned that if I wanted to change something I would just go ahead and do it. . . . I learned to cut corners and do it just as well."

These statements can be subsumed into a more general class: the presence of high or low *administrative latitude* given to teachers to adapt or alter an innovation, a variable that turned out to be very important in explaining the amount of adaptation that occurred.

Subsuming particulars into more general classes is a conceptual and theoretical activity in which you shuttle back and forth between first-level data and more general categories that evolve and develop through successive iterations until the category is "saturated" (new data do not add to the meaning of the general category).

Arbitrary abstraction, however, gets you nowhere. Suppose you observed a teacher writing her name on the dry-erase board on the first day of school. That specific action can be subsumed into a larger class of "written communication," then into a larger class of "information transmission," and finally into a still larger class of "human action." That is a sort of taxonomic classification without useful meaning, however. You cannot decide in a vacuum which of these classes is "right" or "best." There must be a clear linkage to the study's conceptual framework and research questions.

9. Factoring

"Factoring" comes from factor analysis, a statistical technique for representing a large number of measured variables in terms of a smaller number of hypothetical variables. These second-order variables (factors) may have some "communality." So what is the qualitative researcher's version of factoring? Making patterns of patterns, or categories of categories.

Most of the tactics we've discussed are designed to do two things: (1) condense the bulk of the data and (2) find patterns in them. Noting patterns/themes, clustering, and making metaphors are all pattern-forcing exercises. The task essentially is saying to yourself, "I have a mountain of information here. Which bits go together?" When you create a Pattern Code (see Chapter 4), you are proposing that several disparate but related pieces of data have something in common. What they do or are is the factor, and the process by which you generate it is factoring. In other words, we're tightening up the data even further by making a smaller number of patterns from a larger number of patterns, or a smaller number of categories from a larger number of categories. Time for an illustration.

Hager, Maier, O'Hara, Ott, and Saldaña (2000; see also Saldaña, 2013) examined a state department of education's new arts standards document and how it was received by high school theatre teachers. (Long story short, the majority of teachers rejected it because it was poorly written and developed with virtually none of their input.) The focus group interview transcript data generated 52 different Versus Codes, which were then clustered into comparable groups to form eight descriptive categories:

1. Arts Standards Development
2. Curricula
3. Teacher Resistance
4. People
5. Political Ideologies
6. Testing and Graduation Requirements
7. Exclusion and Marginalization
8. Institutions

The next analytic step was to *factor* these categories—in other words, to categorize these eight categories into an even tighter and smaller number of categories. Given below is how the analyst factored the eight into the resulting three categories, which were labeled with war imagery because tensions were high among the participants and the metaphor seemed apt for this study:

Category 1: Human and Institutional Conflicts—The "Fighters"

Subcategories:

    People

    Institutions

    Political Ideologies

Category 2: Standards and Curriculum Conflicts—The "Stakes"

Subcategories:

    Curricula

    Arts Standards Development

    Testing and Graduation Requirements

Category 3: Results of Conflicts—The "Collateral Damage"

Subcategories:

    Exclusion and Marginalization

    Teacher Resistance

These three new categories were eventually transformed into "versus" phrases (e.g., Your Way vs. Our Way) that served to thematically represent the data.

The consequential question for this analytic tactic is "Do these factors make any meaningful difference, or are they essentially decorative?" The factors have to contribute to our understanding of the case or of its underlying dynamics. Otherwise, they are no more useful than the big, gift-wrapped boxes that unpack into a succession of smaller but equally empty gift-wrapped boxes, leaving us at the end with a shapeless heap of ribbon, paper, and cardboard.

10. Noting the Relations Between Variables

The idea of the interrelationship between variables has been discussed throughout the book thus far, but let's examine it as an analytic tactic.

Networks are most easily depicted as sets of boxes and arrows; the boxes are the variables, and the arrows show relationships between them. Once you are reasonably clear about what variables may be in play in a situation, the natural next query is "How do they relate to each other?"

What sort of relationship can we envision between variables *A* and *B*? A variable is something that varies. Thus, we might have the following:

1. *A+, B+* (both are high, or both are low at the same time)

2. *A+, B–* (*A* is high, while *B* is low, or vice versa)

3. $A\uparrow$, $B\uparrow$ (*A* has increased, and *B* has increased)

4. $A\uparrow$, $B\downarrow$ (*A* has increased, and *B* has decreased)

5. $A\uparrow$, then $B\uparrow$ (*A* increased first, then *B* increased)

6. $A\uparrow$, then $B\uparrow$, then $A\uparrow$ (*A* increased, then *B* increased, then *A* increased some more)

These don't cover all of the possible permutations, of course.

Relationship 1 is a direct association: Both variables are high (or low) at the same time. For variables that are "all or nothing," this relationship can be read as follows: When *A* is present, *B* is also present, or both may be absent.

Relationship 2 is the inverse. With Relationship 3, we are noting that changes have occurred recently in *A* and in *B* in the same direction; Relationship 4 is the inverse. No claims are necessarily being made that the changes are linked; they are just present.

In Relationship 5, we verge toward causation: *A* changed, then *B* changed (and—not shown—there is a reasonable belief that *A* could have caused *B*). If *A* is an evening of heavy drinking and *B* is a headache the next morning, there is a presumptive connection. But little connection is likely—in most cases—if *B* is a morning headache and *A* is the announcement of the new city budget. (Still, if the headache belongs to the mayor, maybe. . . .)

Finally, in Relationship 6, we see a mutual relation: A change in *A* leads to a subsequent change in *B*, then to a subsequent change in *A*. The strength of these associations can vary: We can have decisive, strong, clear relationships—or feeble, weak, ambiguous ones. And, as Morrison (2009) reminds us, causation can be direct or indirect, mediated through other variables.

The basic analysis tactic here involves trying to discover what sort of relationship—if any—exists between two (or more) variables. The important thing to keep in mind is that we are talking about *variables or concepts*, not necessarily specific actions.

Even when we focus on specific events, usually underlying or more general variables are involved. The event of an evening of heavy drinking and the event of the morning headache do not quite affect each other directly. All sorts of variables are at work: the presence of certain chemicals in the beverage involved and the body's ability to metabolize alcohol, the amount consumed, the time intervening, and so on.

How are relationships detected? We propose in this book that displays are an especially strategic way to see them: Data bearing on two or more variables can be arrayed for systematic inspection, and conclusions drawn. Network displays help us look at more complex configurations and show the temporal dimension more clearly.

People tend to think in causal terms. The risk in trying to understand relationships between two variables is jumping too rapidly to the conclusion that *A* "causes" *B*, rather than that *A* happens to be high and *B* happens to be high. Here, it helps to shift to verification tactics (discussed later), such as proposing and **checking out rival explanations**, **ruling out spurious relations**, or **using extreme cases**.

Drawing in skeptical colleagues to use one or more of these tactics can be very useful. One friend of ours says that any causal statement made about a social situation should be reversed immediately to see whether it looks truer that way:

- "The students are late to class because they hate the teacher." (Resistance driven by dislike)
- "The students hate the teacher because they are late to class." (Lateness, caused by other reasons, leads to dislike—perhaps mediated by the teacher's reactions to tardiness)

That example may sound a little fanciful, but the reversal exercise is useful. In our school improvement study, we considered this conventional statement: "Teacher involvement and commitment lead to more effort in using the innovation." Then, we considered the reverse: "High teacher effort leads to teacher involvement and commitment." That made good theoretical sense in terms of cognitive dissonance theory. And we had seen several examples of cases where early strong teacher effort led to later increases in commitment.

11. Finding Intervening Variables

It often happens during analysis that two variables that "ought" to go together according to your conceptual expectations, or your early understanding of events in the case, have an inconclusive interrelationship. Another puzzle is the case of two variables that do go together, but without making much sense. The analyst cannot quite figure out *why* they go together.

In both of these conditions, looking for other variables that may be in the picture is a useful tactic. Your initial analysis may be showing that $A \rightarrow C$, but you may be thinking, "Yeah, but something's missing. Where's '*B*'? And what *is* '*B*' anyway?"

To start the example, look at Display 11.2.

In the school improvement study, we observed that schools adopting innovations accompanied with large funding changed more than those adopting less well-funded innovations. That finding leaves a great deal unexplained. Why should it be that a well-funded innovation "induces" more organizational change?

In this case, the analyst created a case-ordered matrix of other possible correlates of organizational change, such as "environmental pressure," "problem-solving orientation," "implementation requirements," and "administrative support." A careful scan showed that the original relation (Display 11.2) could be understood much more realistically when several other variables entered the picture (see Display 11.3). Here, we see that "Size of funding" is part of a web of other variables.

Display 11.2

Two-Variable Relationship

Source: Miles, M. B., & Huberman, A. M. (1994). *Qualitative data analysis: An expanded sourcebook* (2nd ed.). Thousand Oaks, CA: Sage Publications.

Two-Variable Relationship With Intervening Variables

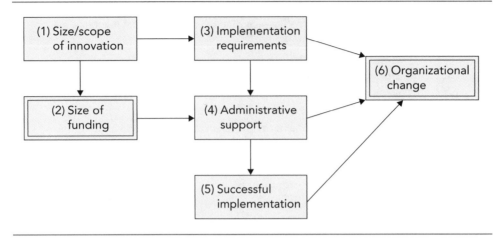

Source: Miles, M. B., & Huberman, A. M. (1994). *Qualitative data analysis: An expanded sourcebook* (2nd ed.). Thousand Oaks, CA: Sage Publications.

Larger innovations (Box 1) carry more funds with them (Box 2). The funds increase the support administrators give (Box 4), but so do the heavier implementation requirements (Box 3) of larger innovations. Organizational change (Box 6) comes from at least three sources: (1) the direct requirements of the implementation itself (Box 3), (2) administrative support (Box 4), and (3) the degree to which implementation is successful (Box 5). As the network revealed, *Administrative support* is a very central intervening variable.

In this example, the effort to clarify a plausible but puzzling relationship led to a much clearer—if more complex—formulation. Simpler cases of finding intervening variables also exist. Finding intervening variables is easiest with multiple examples of the two-variable relationship to look at, contrast, and compare.

12. Building a Logical Chain of Evidence

We've discussed **noting patterns**, **making metaphors**, **clustering**, **subsuming particulars into the general**, and **factoring**. With these tactics, discrete bits of information come together to make a more economical whole that, analytically speaking, is more than the sum of its parts. How do you actually accomplish this? Is there some kind of heuristic you can use? Let's start with an example.

In the study of interorganizational arrangements between schools and universities, we happened on one especially successful case. It was a "teacher center" connected to a rural state college and undertaking a variety of in-service training activities for schools within a radius of some 60 miles.

We developed a logical chain of factors that could be leading to success, as seen from the state college side and from the school side (see Display 11.4). The logical chain of evidence goes like this.

The state college might regard service and outreach activities as very central (1). Because of that, we would expect college staff to see the benefits (2) of a teacher

Display 11.4

Example of a Chain of Evidence Supporting an Observed Outcome

STATE COLLEGE

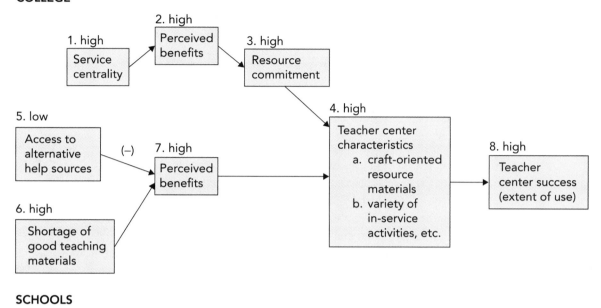

SCHOOLS

Note: (–) = inverse influence

Source: Miles, M. B., & Huberman, A. M. (1994). *Qualitative data analysis: An expanded sourcebook* (2nd ed.). Thousand Oaks, CA: Sage Publications.

center as high (which they did). That should, in turn, lead to higher resource commitment (3) to the center; such commitment was found in the form of money and staff.

Looking at the school side, we found few other opportunities for in-service help (5), and a shortage of good teaching materials (6); both of these should lead to high perceived benefits (7) from using the center—if the center did, in fact, give good in-service help and provide new materials. As it turned out, the high resource commitment did permit that; teacher center assets (4) and extent of use (8) were high.

This example illustrates how to build an evidential chain. Some minimal conditions have to be met. *Several* participants with *different* roles have to emphasize the factors independently and *indicate the causal links*, directly or indirectly (e.g., "We didn't have any other facility to go to in order to find out about new materials, so the center looked good" = the link between 5 and 7). You have to *verify* the logical predictions and the claims (e.g., the actual funds committed, the lack of alternative resource sources, the activities actually undertaken). *Countervailing evidence* has to be accounted for.

How does building a chain of evidence differ from causal network methods? This approach is more tactically and specifically oriented. Building a chain of evidence requires painstaking verification *at each step*: Does this really happen, and what would we logically predict as a consequence—and does that consequence appear in the data? We are stringing together a series of **if-then** tactics: "If that were true, we should find X. We do find X. Therefore, . . . "

Furthermore, the *relationships have to make sense*: There must be a logical basis for the claim that "perceived college benefits" lead to "resource commitment." The *chain must be complete*: The stream from antecedents to outcomes should have no gaps. For instance, in Display 11.4, the link between 3 and 4 is not so obvious. The college might have committed resources and might come up with another model or a center with different characteristics. Committing resources does not translate automatically into, say, craft-oriented resource materials. Something is missing in the logical chain and needs to be filled in.

You construct this evidential trail gradually, getting an initial sense of the main factors, plotting the logical relationships tentatively, testing them against the yield from the next wave of data collection, and modifying and refining them into a new explanatory map, which then gets tested against new cases and instances. This is the classic procedure of analytic induction.

At its most powerful, the method uses two interlocking cycles. One is called "enumerative induction," in which you collect a number and variety of instances all going in the same direction. The second is called "eliminative induction," in which you test your hypothesis against alternatives and look carefully for qualifications that bound the generality of the conclusion. When qualitative researchers invoke "progressive focusing," they are talking about enumerative induction; when they get into "constant comparisons" and "structural corroborations," they are switching into a more eliminative inductive mode of work. The "modus operandi" logic used in several professions as a troubleshooting device—for forensic pathologists, garage mechanics, clinicians, detectives, classroom teachers—is a good example of a back-and-forth cycling between enumerative and eliminative induction.

13. Making Conceptual/Theoretical Coherence

When you're trying to determine what someone's actions "mean," the mental exercise involves connecting a discrete fact with other discrete facts, then grouping these into comprehensible and more abstract patterns. With the preceding tactics, we're moving up progressively from the empirical trenches to a more conceptual overview of the landscape. We're no longer dealing with just observables but also with unobservables and are connecting the two with successive layers of inferential glue.

The next step is to move from metaphors and interrelationships to *constructs*, and from there to *theories*. We need to tie the findings of our study to overarching, across-more-than-one-study propositions that can account for the "how" and "why" of the phenomena under study.

In the school improvement study, we came to notice that people at some of the field sites were literally exhausting themselves in the course of using new instructional practices. These very people were also making strong claims that the practice had substantially improved reading scores or children's attitudes toward school. The interesting part was that data to substantiate the outcome claims were either nonexistent or gave little support for them.

These are the "facts" from which we made a pattern. Field site participants could—and did—agree with the facts, but they didn't put them together as we did. To some extent, we were only able to see the pattern because things were happening otherwise at *other* sites—less investment, fewer claims, or more accurate claims. Multicase field research is very useful in providing contrast and variance.

Let's call the pattern we saw "consensual delusion"—everyone agrees that more is happening with outcomes than there really is. The metaphors, in gerund form, might be "group thinking," "self-deluding," or "wish fulfilling." We also could sketch out a logical flowchart like the one shown in Display 11.4 to get a fix on how this happens at the several sites. But we are still within the confines of our study. The analyst now has to ask, "Do any broader constructs put these facts together the way I am putting them together?" In principle, gerunds should help. The first one (group thinking) points toward group behavior, the next one (self-deluding) toward individual cognitive process, and the third one (wish fulfilling) toward motivational dynamics.

We picked up an appropriate and powerful construct from classic cognitive social psychology: *effort justification* (Festinger, 1957). To justify the effort expended, you "see" more results than are objectively there. This action led us into the domain of *cognitive dissonance* and how people learn to love that for which they have suffered.

Where does this process get us? For starters, it tells us that our finding has a conceptual analog, which lends more plausibility to the finding and to the concept, which is now empirically grounded in a new context. It also helps explain why such a pattern occurs. And it throws light on larger issues (e.g., how people, at our sites and more generally, cope with uncertainty). Finally, the construct can be trained back on our cases to explain related but puzzling phenomena. For example, we can now see why objective criteria (the test scores) are being systematically ignored, when they are easily available.

We have progressed here from the bottom up—from the field to the concepts. The steps are (a) establishing the discrete findings, (b) relating the findings to each other, (c) naming the pattern, and (d) identifying a corresponding construct. We are making conceptual "additions" to the observed data to make them applicable more broadly.

It is perfectly legitimate, and sometimes necessary, to work from the top down—from a conceptual framework or theory to the collection of information testing its validity. Of course, you have to stay open to the idea that the concept is inapplicable or has to be bent or discarded when you see the data. Concepts without corresponding facts are hollow.

Tactics for Testing or Confirming Findings

We've spent some time on particular tactics for generating meaning—making and interpreting findings at different levels of inference. Now, we need to confront the issue of *validity* or *trustworthiness*. Qualitative analyses can be evocative, illuminating, masterful—and wrong. The story, well told as it is, does not fit the data. Reasonable colleagues double-checking the case come up with quite different findings. The interpretations of case participants do not match those of the researchers. The phenomenologist chuckles, reinforced in the idea that there is no single reality to get "right"—but cannot escape a sneaky feeling that, in fact, reasonable conclusions are out there somewhere. In this section, we review some general guidelines for judging the "goodness" of qualitative research—that is, what researchers can do at the tactical, operating level to test and confirm the findings.

First, let's take a general view of the problem: Many, if not most, qualitative researchers work alone in the field. Each is a one-person research machine: defining the problem, doing the sampling, designing the instruments, collecting the information, condensing the information, analyzing it, interpreting it, and writing it up. A vertical monopoly.

And when we read the reports, they are most often heavy on the "what" (the findings, the descriptions) and rather thin on the "how" (how you got to the "what"). In most cases, we don't see a procedural account of the analysis, explaining just how the researcher got from 500 pages of field notes to the main conclusions drawn. So we don't know how much confidence we can place in them. Researchers are not being cryptic or obtuse. It's just that there are few guidelines for explaining to their colleagues what they did, and how. (And, in all fairness, the page limit for journal articles also forces researchers to briefly sketch their methodology paragraphs.)

We need to be mindful in qualitative research about the multiple sources of analytic bias that can weaken or even invalidate our findings. Some of these biases have been identified in mainstream research methods textbooks; the archetypical ones include the following:

- *The holistic fallacy:* Interpreting events as more patterned and congruent than they really are, lopping off the many loose ends of which social life is made— that is, sloppy research

- *Elite bias:* Overweighting data from articulate, well-informed, usually high-status participants and underrepresenting data from less articulate, lower status ones

- *Personal bias:* The researcher's personal agenda, personal demons, or personal "axes to grind," which skew the ability to represent and present fieldwork and data analysis in a trustworthy manner

- *Going native:* Losing your perspective or your "bracketing" ability, being co-opted into the perceptions and explanations of local participants

We draw on some of the research methods literature as we discuss tactics for testing and confirming findings. The language of confirming and verifying is bolder than what we can usually achieve. But the intent is still there: How can we increase our—and our readers'—confidence in what we've found?

We describe 13 tactics, beginning with ones aimed at ensuring the basic quality of the data, then moving to those that check findings by examining exceptions to early patterns, and concluding with tactics that take a skeptical, demanding approach to emerging explanations.

Data quality can be assessed through **checking for representativeness** (1); **checking for researcher effects** (2) on the case, and vice versa; and **triangulating** (3) across data sources and methods. These checks also may involve **weighting the evidence** (4), deciding which kinds of data are most trustable.

Looking at "unpatterns" can tell us a lot. **Checking the meaning of outliers** (5), **using extreme cases** (6), **following up surprises** (7), and **looking for negative evidence** (8) are all tactics that test a conclusion about a pattern by saying what it is *not* like.

How can we really test our explanations? **Making if-then tests** (9), **ruling out spurious relations** (10), **replicating a finding** (11), and **checking out rival**

explanations (12) are all ways of submitting our beautiful theories to the assault of brute facts or to a race with someone else's beautiful theory.

Finally, a good explanation deserves attention from the very people whose actions it is about—the participants who supplied the original data. The tactic of **getting feedback from participants** (13) concludes our list.

1. Checking for Representativeness

When we develop a finding in a field study, we quickly assume it to be typical, an instance of a more general phenomenon. But is it? And if it is, *how* representative is it?

People typically make a generalization and then illustrate it ("For example, my friend . . . "), but they would be hard put to come up with several more instances of a supposedly widespread occurrence. To compound the problem, people as information seekers—and as processors—are far more likely to see *confirming* instances of original beliefs or perceptions than to see disconfirming instances, even when disconfirmations are more frequent.

Operating alone, without any standardized or validated instruments, the field researcher runs several risks of generalizing wrongly from specific instances. Here are some of the most common pitfalls, and their associated sources of error:

The first pitfall, **sampling nonrepresentative participants**, highlights the fact that you can talk only with people who can be contacted; some people are harder to contact than others. This problem in itself signals something particularistic; their accessibility may be connected with workload, lack of cooperativeness, or both. Anthropologists have often warned of field-workers' tendency to rely too much on articulate, insightful, attractive, and intellectually responsive participants; such people often turn out to be in the local elite.

The second pitfall, **generalizing from nonrepresentative events or activities**, results from the researcher's noncontinuous presence; you have to infer what is happening when you are not there. When you observe a dramatic event (a crisis, an argument), the tendency is to assume that it has "built up" when you were absent or that it symbolizes a more general pattern. These are plausible but certainly not well-grounded inferences.

The third pitfall, **drawing inferences from nonrepresentative processes**, is looking for underlying processes explaining what you've seen and heard. But if the samples of events and activities are faulty, the explanation cannot be generalized beyond them. If an emerging account makes good logical sense (to you) and fits well with other, independently derived analyses, you lock onto it and begin to make a stronger case for it. The problem is that you might have *plausibility* but not *confirmability*.

The real problem with selective sampling and hasty generalizing is that you can slide incrementally into these biases, with the first layer preparing the ground for the next. Gradually, you become a prisoner of your emerging system of comprehending the case. There is no longer any possibility, cognitively speaking, of standing back or reviewing critically what you have observed up to then. What you now understand has been accumulated very gradually from within, not drawn validly from without.

So if you want to stand back and review critically, you need someone else to do it—or you must build in safeguards against self-delusion. We've already reinforced the former approach (critical friends, colleagues, other field-workers, research team members, auditors) throughout the methods profiles, so let's offer some additional safeguards.

Automatically assume that you are selectively sampling and drawing inferences from a nonrepresentative sample of cases, be they people, events, or processes, in the first place. You are guilty until you prove yourself innocent by extending the "universe" of your study. How?

1. Increase the number of cases.

2. Look purposively for contrasting cases (negative, extreme, countervailing).

3. Order the cases in various ways in a matrix to see who or what may be missing.

4. Randomly sample people and phenomena within the site(s) you're studying.

The last two procedures correspond to the "stratification" and "randomization" conventions used by experimental researchers to enhance internal validity. But while the experimental researcher uses the conventions *early*, as anticipatory controls against sampling and measurement error, the qualitative researcher typically uses them *later*, as verification devices. That use allows you to let in all the candidate people and data, so the most influential ones will have a chance of emerging. But you still have to carry the burden of proof that the patterns you ultimately pinpoint are, in fact, representative.

2. Checking for Researcher Effects

Outsiders to a group influence insiders, and vice versa. So it is with the researcher who disembarks in a field setting to study the "researchees." You are likely, especially at the outset, to create social behavior in others that would not have occurred ordinarily. That behavior, in turn, can lead you into biased observations and inferences, thus confounding (an appropriate term in this instance) the natural characteristics of the setting with the artificial effects of the researcher–researchee relationship. Unconfounding them is like moving through a hall of mirrors.

So we have two possible sources of bias here:

1. The effects of the researcher on the case

2. The effects of the case on the researcher

Field study researchers are often less worried about Bias 1 because they typically spend enough time on-site to become part of the local landscape. But that, of course, increases the hazard of Bias 2: being co-opted, going native, swallowing the agreed-on or taken-for-granted version of local events.

Although we discuss these biases as they occur during site visits, they influence the analysis deeply, both during and after data collection. The researcher who has gone native remains native during analysis. The researcher who has influenced the site in un-understood ways suffers unawares from that influence during analysis.

Bias 1 occurs when the researcher threatens or disrupts ongoing social and institutional relationships by doing nothing more than simply being there. People now have to figure out who this person is, why he or she is there, and what might be done with the information being collected. While they are figuring that out, participants typically will switch into an on-stage role or special persona, a presentation of self to the outsider. (They have other personae, of course, for fellow insiders, as Goffman [1959] shows so well.)

Even after this preliminary dance, participants will often craft their responses to appear amenable to the researcher and to protect their self-interests. For some analysts, local participants' interests are fundamentally in conflict with those of the researcher, who might penetrate to the core of the rivalries, compromises, weaknesses, or contradictions that make up much of the basic history of the site. Insiders do not want outsiders—and sometimes other insiders—to know about such things. So the researcher, who is usually interested in uncovering precisely this kind of information, must assume that people will try to mislead and must shift into a more investigative mode.

Field research can, at bottom, be considered as an act of betrayal, no matter how well-intentioned or well integrated the researcher is. You make the private public and leave the locals to take the consequences.

But that is not the only way Bias 1 can occur. In some instances, Biases 1 and 2 can team up to create "artifactual" effects as a result of the complicity between the researcher and local actors. This is Rosenthal's (1976) famous "experimenter" effect.

We've been caught napping several times on this one. For instance, one field site in the school improvement project was about to phase out the project we had come to see. For some mysterious reason, the phase-out decision was cancelled during our time on-site. The reasoning, which we unraveled only after several more days, was that the practice *had* to be better than it appeared because university researchers had come from so far away to see it. There was also the desire to avoid a public indictment; the researcher and/or the public reading her research might convey the impression that the school had botched things.

Bias 1 can take still other forms. For example, local participants can implicitly or explicitly boycott the researcher, who is seen variously as a spy, a voyeur, or a pest. Or the researcher can inhibit the local actors. After several days on-site and multiple interviews, people are not sure anymore how much the researcher has found out and assume—wrongly in most cases—that the researcher knows too much. This opinion then triggers Bias 2: The researcher accordingly becomes more reassuring or, alternatively, moves into the investigative-adversarial mode. Both strategies are likely to affect the data being collected.

Assuming, then, that you have only a few months, weeks, or even days on-site, how can these two interlocking forms of bias be countered? Below is a short shopping list of suggestions, many of which are treated in far more detail in fieldwork-related literature.

A. Avoiding Biases Stemming From Researcher Effects on the Site

- Stay on-site as long as possible; spend some time simply hanging around, fitting into the landscape, taking a lower profile.
- Use unobtrusive measures where you can, such as reading the site's publically accessible documents.

- Make sure your intentions are clear for participants: why you are there, what you are studying, how you will collect information, and what you will do with it.

- Consider co-opting a participant—asking that person to be attentive to your influence on the site and its inhabitants.

- Do some of your interviewing off-site in a congenial social environment (cafe, restaurant, participant's home), by way of reducing both your threat quotient and your exoticism.

- Don't inflate the potential problem; you are not really such an important presence in the lives of these people.

B. Avoiding Biases Stemming From the Effects of the Site on the Researcher

- Avoid the "elite" bias by spreading out your participants; include lower status participants and people outside the focus of your study (peripheral or former actors).

- Avoid co-optation or going native by spending time away from the site; spread out your site visits.

- Be sure to include dissidents, cranks, deviants, marginals, isolates—people with different points of view from the mainstream, people less committed to tranquility and equilibrium in the setting.

- Keep thinking conceptually; translate sentimental or interpersonal thoughts into more theoretical ones.

- Consider finding a participant who agrees to provide background and historical information for you and to collect information when you are off-site (such co-optation may be more useful, in bias-reduction terms, than the information provided).

- Triangulate with several data collection methods; don't overly depend just on talk, just on observation, or just on documents to make sense of the setting.

- If you sense you are being misled, try to understand and focus on why a participant would find it necessary to mislead you. Follow that trace as far upstream as you can.

- Do not casually show off how much you do know; this is a covert plea for confirmation that deludes only the person making it.

- Show your field notes to a colleague. Another researcher is often much quicker to see where and how you are being misled or co-opted.

- Keep your research questions firmly in mind; don't wander too far from them to follow alluring leads or drop them in the face of a more dramatic or momentous event.

As with all such lists, following some items gets you in trouble on others. For instance, if you have only a few days on-site, off-site interviewing may be too costly. Or you may be co-opted by the participant you are trying to co-opt.

Bias detection and removal take time. The more time you have, the more layers you can peel off the setting to get to the core explanatory factors and the less subject you are to Biases 1 and 2. However, we take that with a grain of salt. Long exposure can just push up Bias 2 and make Bias 1 harder to see.

We say again that people who are discreet, savvy in the environment under study, and conceptually ecumenical are often able to get to the core of a case in a matter of days, sidestepping both types of researcher bias and coming away with good-quality data. It's possible that the methodologists demanding months or years on-site before valid data can be obtained are confusing time with competence.

3. Triangulating

Much has been written about triangulation as a near-obligatory method of confirming findings. Stripped to its basics, triangulation is supposed to support a finding by showing that at least three independent measures of it agree with it or, at least, do not contradict it. But it's not as simple as that. For one thing, if two measures agree and one does not, you are stuck with a deeper question: Which do you believe? (See the film *Minority Report*.)

Triangulation is similar to the modus operandi approach used by detectives, mechanics, and primary care physicians. When the detective amasses fingerprints, hair samples, alibis, and eyewitness accounts, a case is being made that presumably fits one suspect far better than others; the strategy is pattern matching, using several data sources. Diagnosing engine failure or chest pain follows a similar approach. The signs presumably point to the same conclusion and/or rule out other conclusions. Note the importance of having different kinds of measurements, which provides repeated verification.

What kinds of triangulation can there be? Following Denzin's (2001) classic distinctions, we can think of triangulation by *data source* (which can include persons, times, places, etc.), by *method* (observation, interview document), by *researcher* (Investigator A, B, etc.), and by *theory*. To this, we add *data type* (e.g., qualitative texts, audio/video recordings, quantitative data). How to choose which? The aim is to pick triangulation sources that have different foci and different strengths, so that they can complement each other. In some senses, we are *always* faced with triangulating data, whether we attend to it or not.

As an example, Saldaña's studies on child audience responses to theatre employed multiple measures: (a) live audience observations and field notes of the events, (b) audio and video recordings of audience responses to the performance, (c) audio-recorded focus group interviews with children after the performance, (d) drawings or written assessments by children of the productions they viewed, (e) play script dramaturgical analyses, (f) interviews with selected teachers and adult production company members, and (g) relevant theories from the professional research literature in areas such as child development, psychology, education, media, and performance studies.

What can we expect from triangulation? We may get *corroboration* from three different sources, which enhances the trustworthiness of our analysis. But sometimes we may get *inconsistent* or even directly *conflicting* findings. At best, this can push us to more closely examine the integrity of the data collection methods and even the data themselves. Inconsistent and conflicting findings force us to explain why they exist. It may be due to an undetected variability of something that we need to consider or unanticipated anomalies and outliers in the phenomena we're studying that merit closer examination. Sometimes the inconsistent and conflicting findings suggest that the researcher made a mistake somewhere along the way and needs to figure out what may have gone wrong. But sometimes the conflicting findings are a blessing because the different data collection methods used gather different facets of data, and their combined effects *build* on each other to compose a more three-dimensional perspective of the phenomenon.

Perhaps our basic point is that triangulation is not so much a tactic as a way of life. If you self-consciously set out to collect and double-check findings, using multiple sources and modes of evidence, the verification process will largely be built into data collection as you go along. In effect, triangulation is a way to get to the finding in the first place— by seeing or hearing multiple *instances* of it from different *sources* by using different *methods* and by squaring the finding with others it needs to be squared with.

4. Weighting the Evidence

Any given preliminary conclusion is always based on certain data. Maybe we should use the word some historians have employed: *capta*. There are events in the real world, from which we "capture" only a partial record in the form of raw field notes, from which we further extract only certain information in the form of write-ups, which we then call data. There is, in turn, further condensation, selection, and transformation as these data are entered into various displays and reports.

Some of these data are better than others. Fortunately, you can exploit that fact beautifully in verifying conclusions. If the data on which a conclusion is based are known to be stronger, more valid than average, then the conclusion is strengthened. Stronger data can be given more weight in the conclusion. Conversely, a conclusion based on weak or suspect data can be, at the least, held lightly and, optimally, discarded if an alternative conclusion has stronger data to back it up.

Basically, there is a very large range of reasons why certain data are stronger (valid) or weaker (less valid) than others. First, data from some participants are "better." The participant may be articulate and reflective and may enjoy talking about events and processes. Or the participant may be knowledgeable and close to the event, action, process, or setting with which you're concerned. In our study, for example, we gave more weight to school superintendents' judgments about district budget matters than we did to those of teachers about that topic.

Second, the circumstances of the data collection may have strengthened (or weakened) the quality of the data. Seeing with your own eyes what happened in a classroom is more reliable than overhearing faculty lounge gossip about the incident. Interviewing a participant during later rather than earlier stages of fieldwork may get you richer responses since you've had time to build rapport and trust.

Third, data quality may be stronger because of a field-worker's validation efforts. These may consist of several varieties (the bolded ones are discussed elsewhere in this chapter):

- **Checking for researcher effects** and biases
- **Checking for representativeness**
- **Getting feedback from participants**

- **Triangulating**
- Looking for ulterior motives
- Looking for deception

The last two have not been attended to in other sections. Douglas (1976) emphasizes that regardless of the degree of trust a field-worker may believe has developed, people in field sites nearly always have some reasons for omitting, selecting, or distorting data and also may have reasons for deceiving the field-worker (not to mention deceiving themselves). If you have entertained such a view of certain respondents, and of the data from them, and have done something to validate the data, more confidence is justified. Douglas offers a few strategies, which we have adapted:

- Check against "hard facts."
- Check against alternative accounts.
- Look for "the trapdoor"—what is going on beyond the obvious.
- Share your own personal story to open up the respondent.
- Share what you genuinely think is going on, and see how the respondent reacts.

Field-workers who rely mainly on trust may quail at such interventions or dismiss them as too intrusive. We have found that it pays to be skeptical, to expect to be lied to sometimes, to look for respondent self-deception, and to *gently* and *tactfully* question respondents from time to time on such matters.

Two added suggestions. First, we've found it useful to keep a running log of data quality issues (often in the form of analytic memos or OCs—observer's comments—in field notes), together with recurrent efforts to improve data quality in subsequent site visits. Second, when approaching the final write-up of a case analysis, it's useful to summarize your views of data quality—both for yourself and for your eventual readers. Here is an example from a case report in our school improvement study, which appeared after the researcher listed the number of interviews (46), informal talks (24), and observations (17) held during three site visits:

> The data base is probably biased toward administrators and central program personnel (3-6 interviews apiece), and may underrepresent those of normal program users, and certainly those of peripheral (and more disenchanted) people. So the information may be fuller about the ins and outs of operation as seen by key operators, and thinner on what day-to-day life in the Carson schools is like.

5. Checking the Meaning of Outliers

Any given finding usually has exceptions. The temptation is to smooth them over, ignore them, or explain them away. But *the outlier is your friend*. A good look at the exceptions, or the ends of a distribution, can test and strengthen the basic finding. It not only tests the generality of the finding but also protects you against self-selecting biases and may help you build a better explanation.

For example, in the school improvement study, we happened on one case where the new practice was seen by many teachers as a near-miraculous cure for local ills.

Although teachers found it hard to get on top of it, the project eventually led to dramatic increases in reading and composition scores. Enthusiasm was high.

Was it a "miracle cure"? To test the finding, we asked about people who either had not adopted the practice or had used it and found it wanting. After some thought, our key participants came up with one each.

Our interviews with these two people were instructive. First, we found that their reasons for not adopting were opposite to—and thereby coherent with—the reasons given by the other participants for adopting. Then, we found that the dissident user had not really mastered the innovation in the way the contented users had. We already had good evidence linking technical mastery to positive results. So our findings were strengthened, and we understood far better why deviant cases were deviant.

So it became clearer that the innovation was like a "miracle cure"only if it was technically well carried out. Furthermore, these outliers told us that there were more people like them around than the advocates had admitted. We realized then that we had oversampled the contented users and, in a sense, had been "sucked in" to the taken-for-granted version of events among the local teachers. In widening the sampling of discontented users thereafter, we got a somewhat different and more intricate picture of the case.

There are often more exceptions or deviant cases than you realize at first; you have to go looking for them. They do not come calling; nor do you usually think spontaneously of sampling for them. After all, they are inconvenient—not only hard to reach or observe but also spoilers of your artfully built, coherent version of case dynamics.

Remember, too, that outliers are not only people; they can consist of discrepant *cases*, atypical *settings*, unique *treatments*, or unusual *events*. You need to find the outliers and then verify whether what is present in them is absent or different in other, more mainstream examples (see **using extreme cases** next). Finding outliers is easier when you have well-ordered displays. Cases, roles, settings, events, and individuals can be shown in coherent relation to others. If you are still collecting data, display what you have, and go for the outliers. If things are closely clumped (no apparent outliers), consider where you might go to find some outlying persons, events, or settings. And, on following up, stay open to the eventuality that the exceptional cases can turn out to be prototypical ones.

In many cases, outlier analysis strengthens an original conclusion ("the exception proves the rule"). But be careful; don't force it. Stay open to the idea that the outlier is telling you something useful and important about how your conclusion needs modification.

6. Using Extreme Cases

We've just described the use of outliers in deepening preliminary conclusions. Outliers of a certain type, which we call extreme cases, can be very useful in verifying and confirming conclusions.

In Saldaña's (1995) exit interviews with sixth graders about their 7 years of theatre-viewing experiences since kindergarten, one interview question we posed to the young participants was "Is theatre necessary?" All except one child said "Yes"; it was the young boy who said "No" that was the extreme case in this instance. His explanation that "we don't have to have" theatre was not unexpected, as he was one of the lowest rated participants in the study over the past 7 years. But his "no" became part of the data record, and we now had to explain why, after so many years of free and mostly high-quality theatre experiences, he alone out of 30 children felt that theatre was unnecessary. Long story short, his "no" forced us to closely examine the varying *value* children attribute to the arts, and thus the landscapes of meanings and payoffs they offered to their young participants. That single "no" helped crystallize the conclusions of the study.

This is a tactic of "holding everything else constant"—looking for the most extreme case, where there should have been consensus but there wasn't. Note that you need conceptual and/or empirical knowledge of the variables involved; it cannot be done in a vacuum. You are not just looking for empirical outliers but are conceptually defining extreme cases and looking at whether they exist.

The second sort of extreme case is persons known to have a strong bias. For example, suppose you are talking with a very conservative administrator who you know from past contact is rather defensive. You ask him why the teachers he works with are reluctant to try innovations. He answers that it's due to his own lack of cooperation and support. That answer is very persuasive because you wouldn't expect this particular administrator to make such a statement at all.

To put this another way, look for the person in a site who would have the most to gain (or lose) by affirming or denying something, and pop the question. If you get a surprising answer (e.g., the person who has much to gain by denying the statement/question, in fact, affirms it), then you can be more confident. This maneuver requires you to have a good prior understanding of the person's typical stance and biases.

In a way, this is another style of differentially **weighting evidence** (discussed earlier). For example, if you are interviewing enthusiastic proponents of an innovation, their comments on the innovation's warts and trouble spots should be taken quite seriously. Once again, you are conceptualizing what "extreme" means and capitalizing on the data you find there.

7. Following Up Surprises

Surprises have more juice than outliers. When you are surprised, it usually means that something has occurred well outside the range of your expectations. You had an implicit theory of what was happening, such as "I am coming home after a hard day at the office." And—surprise! You walk into a roomful of friends who are giving you a half-birthday party 6 months in advance. So you laugh, bask in the attention, and maybe reflect on their kindness, and perhaps on the sneakiness of your significant other, who colluded with the plot to delude you—for a good cause, of course. And how did all of the shopping get done without your noticing?

In qualitative analysis, the party is less important than the follow-up reflection and sleuthing. What does this event tell me about my expectations, implicit theories, and taken-for-granted assumptions? And where can I go in my data to help me rebuild my theory?

Something that surprised Saldaña on his first day of fieldwork in an inner-city school in the mid-1990s Southwest was the combed back and "slicked" hairstyles of most of the Hispanic boys—a grooming nuance he realized had been within the culture since his own childhood 40 years ago. Also surprising was the realization that many young girls did not wear shorts or pants but wore dresses to school—unlike the clothing observed at middle-class, predominantly White elementary schools. These small fashion details made him rethink the larger cultural dynamics he was now surrounded by and how selected traditions and values still played a role in these Hispanic children's lives.

Following up surprises has three aspects. You (1) reflect on the surprise to surface your violated theory, (2) consider how to revise it, and (3) look for evidence to support your revision. You may also work from (2) to (3), hunting in a sniffing mode, to find new aspects of the case that possibly could lead to a new theory.

8. Looking for Negative Evidence

The tactic **looking for negative evidence** is easy to describe but, given people's pattern-making proclivities, not naturally instinctive. When a preliminary conclusion is at hand, the tactic is to ask, "Do any data oppose this conclusion, or are any inconsistent with this conclusion?" This is a more extreme version of looking for **outliers** (discussed earlier) and for **rival explanations** (discussed later). You are actively seeking *dis*confirmation of what you think is true.

Einstein is supposed to have said, "No amount of evidence can prove me right, and any amount of evidence can prove me wrong." That is so, in the abstract, but most of us act as if the converse were true. Our beautiful theories need few data to convince us of their solidity, and we are not eager to encounter the many brutal facts that could doom our frameworks. A good case study of such an effort is Cressey's (1953) classic study of embezzlers. Cressey revised his working hypotheses five times, looking for negative cases for each version in turn, using prior data, newly collected data, and the studies of others, until there was no disconfirmation.

Miller (n.d.) advises that "disconfirming instances should be handled with care." Discarding your original hypothesis too quickly and modifying it hastily to accommodate the negative evidence are both undesirable. Miller suggests that although one instance of negative evidence may be enough to require reconsideration, the *proportion* of negative to positive evidence should probably play a part.

Commission a friendly but curmudgeonly skeptic to take a good look at your conclusion at hand, avoiding your data display and seeking data back in the written-up field notes that would effectively disconfirm your conclusion. If such evidence is found, proceed to the formulation of an alternative conclusion that deals with the evidence.

Finally, note what might be called the "delusional error." The absence of negative evidence can never be decisive as a confirmatory tactic, as in the following exchange:

Question: Why do you have that blue ribbon on your little finger every day?

Answer: It's to keep elephants from following me.

Question: But there are no elephants here.

Answer: See? It's working.

9. Making If-Then Tests

If-then tests are the workhorse of qualitative data analysis. They are more focused than a generalized working hypothesis, which supports a general analytic direction.

A formal statement is "If X, then Y." It is a statement of expected relationship. Assuming X to be true (an important condition), we look to see whether Y is true. If Y is true, then we have a building block for understanding. We are a long way from a "law" about the relation of X and Y, which requires universality, linkage to a larger theory, and nontriviality, among other conditions. But we know more than we did and can take some next analytic steps—notably, making more if-then tests and connecting them into a general theory of what is happening.

Saldaña's (1999) study of adolescent social class and social consciousness was an opportunistic study that investigated why two different groups of teenagers, each from two very different social and economic backgrounds, responded quite differently to the same social issues–oriented workshop content. The lower socioeconomic group embraced the seriousness of the social issues addressed at a forum workshop and participated with respectful enthusiasm. But the upper socioeconomic group transformed the same content at their forum workshop into a parody and satire of the social issues we tried to address.

After reflection on these experiences, Saldaña put forth the following general proposition: *If* adolescents are from an upper social class background, *then* their social consciousness may not be as heightened as those from a lower social class. Of course, a reflective practitioner might also develop the following proposition: *If* workshop content is not relevant or meaningful for its participants, *then* they will reject the provided experiences. One can always think of exceptions or **negative evidence** that will force a revision of these propositions, but for this particular event, this is what was observed.

The use of the conditional future tense in the "then" statements helps remind us that we have to look to see whether the "then" has happened. Therefore, if-then statements are a way to formalize *propositions* for testing. The method of generating *predictions* involves linking together a large number of "ifs" to a single major "then." If-then statements are just a step away from constructing theories.

10. Ruling Out Spurious Relations

"Spurious" means something that's falsely attributed; a spurious relation means that you're connecting things together incorrectly. Suppose you've been able, through assorted tactics, to establish that variable *A* is indeed related to *B*. Whenever we see *A*, we see *B*, and vice versa. Before breathing a sigh of relief and proceeding to the next conclusion, it pays to consider the picture you are drawing:

$A \rightarrow B$

may in fact be more accurately portrayed as

where some third factor is in play, causing both *A* and *B* to occur.

This is an old logic problem, and we can draw a nice example from a classic Wallis and Roberts (1956) study from the *Journal of the American Medical Association*. Researchers noted that polio patients who traveled longer distances (average, 85 miles) to a hospital were more likely to die than patients who traveled less (average, 7 miles) and were more likely to die sooner (50% died within 24 hours, vs. 20%). They concluded, "The greater mortality in the transported group, occurring shortly after admission to the hospital, is a manifestation of the effect of long transportation during the acute stage of illness" (p. 285).

Wallis and Roberts (1956) suggest that a third variable may be influencing both *A* (transportation) and *B* (mortality)—the *seriousness of the initial attack*. All of the patients were seen in a certain hospital: Willard Parker, a noted center for the treatment of contagious diseases. Polio patients who lived farther away were probably brought to Willard Parker only if their condition was serious; milder cases would be treated nearer their own homes. Thus, the picture develops as shown in Display 11.5.

This interpretation can be checked out through the sort of display found in Display 11.6, with *N*s and mortality rates entered in the cells.

As Wallis and Roberts (1956) faithfully point out, even if the reanalysis could be done and it supported "seriousness of initial attack" as the real issue, you would have to do additional ruling out. Perhaps those coming from a distance had poorer basic health to begin with. Perhaps they came from an area where a particularly virulent strain of polio was widespread. And so on.

Finding a candidate third variable is not always easy, especially if the original explanation "makes sense," as the transportation–mortality link seemed to at first glance. The Willard Parker researchers did think of one third variable—length of prior illness—which showed no real difference. Then, they stopped, not realizing that the "Willard Parkerness" of Willard

Display 11.5

Possible Explanation of Spurious Relationship

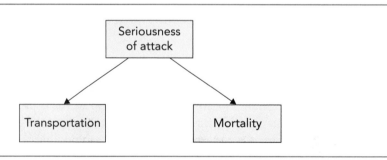

Source: Miles, M. B., & Huberman, A. M. (1994). *Qualitative data analysis: An expanded sourcebook* (2nd ed.). Thousand Oaks, CA: Sage Publications.

Display 11.6

Display for Testing Explanations in Display 11.5

	Local patients	Distant patients
Mild attack		
Severe attack		

Source: Miles, M. B., & Huberman, A. M. (1994). *Qualitative data analysis: An expanded sourcebook* (2nd ed.). Thousand Oaks, CA: Sage Publications.

Parker was probably in the picture. Had they been able to recruit Wallis and Roberts as friendly strangers partway through their analysis, the story might have been different.

The moral for qualitative researchers is the same. When two variables look correlated, especially when you think that they are causally associated, wait a bit and consider whether some third variable might be underlying/influencing/causing them both. Use a knowledgeable but detached colleague to help in the search. Then, consider new displays that will give you a clean look at third variables and their effects.

Doing this procedure in a more than cursory way takes time, so it is worth it mainly when you have a major (but perhaps surprising) conclusion or one on which a lot is riding, in practical terms.

Earlier, we discussed the tactic of **finding intervening variables**, but there we were concerned with understanding a tepid relationship better. Here, the issue is *undoing* a relationship you think looks plausible and strong.

11. Replicating a Finding

As we showed earlier in the section on **triangulating**, findings are more dependable when they can be buttressed from several independent sources. Their validity is enhanced when they are confirmed by more than one data collection instrument measuring the same thing.

Still, the fact that usually one person is doing all of this measuring with homemade instruments is a ground for precaution. Once you've latched onto a hypothesis that makes powerful sense of the case, it's the dickens to get rid of it. Confirmation seems, almost magically, to come from all quarters. New interviews, observations, and documents all appear to bring verification and to fit together coherently. Disconfirming evidence is absent or feeble. This is a heady and very slippery time, and it usually means you are knee-deep in the "holistic fallacy": putting more logic, coherence, and meaning into events than the inherent sloppiness of social life warrants. How do you protect against this?

One line of attack is to think in terms of study replication. If I can observe and reproduce the finding in a new context or in another part of my database, it is most likely a dependable one. If someone else can reproduce it, better still.

This tactic can be used in several ways. At the most basic level, you are replicating as you collect new information from new participants, from new settings and events. New data bolster or qualify old data by testing their validity and generality.

At a notch higher in the confidence scale, you can test an emerging hypothesis in another part of the case or data set. Such a test is more rigorous; it's harder to bootleg researcher bias into it. Even stiffer tests can be made by looking at multiple cases: finding a pattern in a cross-case display and then tracking carefully through all of the cases to see whether the pattern is repeated.

Even better, replicate in a brand new case, though we acknowledge that may be an extreme and ephemeral goal. Some brief words of advice:

- In cross-case studies, replication is an important part of the basic data collection effort. Emerging patterns from one case need to be tested in others. Be prepared in the course of fieldwork to do the kind of corroborative testing described here and in the section on **triangulation**.

- If provisions are not made in advance for replications, they will not happen; there is inevitably too little time and too much information still to compile.

- Doing replication at the very end of fieldwork, during the final analysis and write-ups, is very difficult and less credible. To test a hypothesis in another part of the data set assumes that all of the requisite data are there for the test to be made. They usually are not, unless the researcher has made sure to collect them beforehand in anticipation of just such an exercise.

Reasonably early in your study, think forward a bit. Imagine that your findings will turn out to be truly amazing, with profound implications for your field. Then, ask a friendly colleague to perform a rapid "replicability check." Based on a few hours' review of the project database and methods, how easy or difficult would it be *for your colleague* to repeat your study?

12. Checking Out Rival Explanations

Thinking that rival explanations may account for the phenomena you have carefully studied and masterfully unraveled is a healthy exercise in self-discipline and hubris avoidance. But that thought often gets lost in the shuffle. During data collection, you are often too busy making sense of the welter of stimuli. Later on, you tend to get married to your emerging account and usually opt for investing the scant time left to buttress, rather than to unhorse, your explanation. Then, during data analysis, it is often too late to test any other explanation than the one arrived at; the data necessary for doing that in any but a cosmetic way just aren't there.

But we think that the search for rival explanations is often more thorough in qualitative research than in most laboratory studies and that it's relatively easy to do. The competent field researcher looks for the most plausible, empirically grounded explanation of events from among the several competing for attention in the course of fieldwork. You are not looking for one account, forsaking all others, but for the best of several alternative accounts.

The trick is to hold onto several possible (rival) explanations until one of them gets increasingly more compelling as the result of more, stronger, and varied sources of evidence. Looking at it from the other end, you give each rival explanation a good chance. Is it maybe better than your main love? Do you have some biases you weren't aware of? Do you need to collect any new data?

One of the most intriguing yet puzzling findings in McCammon et al.'s (2012) survey of adults from various generations reflecting on their high school experiences was an outcome from data analysis of the most recent age cohort. When participants were asked about the challenges they faced as an adolescent, those who graduated during 2000–2010 described a general sense of disconnect and "fear" more than older age-groups. Saldaña hypothesized this as the result of living in an uncertain post-9/11 world and affirmation of the then current emotional angst in America's youth projected by Goleman (1995, 2007). But Saldaña was a researcher in his 50s who was trying to understand the responses of a generation that was in their 20s, so he turned to younger colleagues—his research assistants Matt Omasta and Angie Hines—for their perspectives. And they did indeed offer other factors to consider for hypothesis development, such as the generational search for "safe spaces" that school arts programs provided and the socio-psychological effects on the most recent generation by the rapidly developing social media and entertainment technology.

Foreclosing too early on alternative explanations is a harbinger of bias. You lock into a particular way of construing the case and selectively scan the environment for supporting evidence. Discounting evidence is ignored, underregistered, or handled as exceptional—thus further increasing your confidence in your erroneous thesis.

We should also note that closing too *late* on alternative explanations builds too weak a case for the best one. It also adds great bulk to the corpus of data. So rival explanations should be looked at fairly promptly in fieldwork and sustained until they prove genuinely unviable—or prove to be better. This step should happen, if possible, before most of the fieldwork is done. The same principle applies to analysis done after fieldwork. Check out alternative explanations early, but don't iterate forever.

It also helps to fasten onto discrepant information—things that do not fit or are still puzzling (tactics: **looking for negative evidence, following up surprises**). The trick is not to explain them away in light of your favorite explanation—that's a piece of cake—but rather to run with them, ask yourself what kind of alternative case these bits of information could build, and then check them out further.

A useful subtactic is as follows: During the final analysis, first check out the merits of the next best explanation you or others can think of as an alternative to the one you preferred at the end of the fieldwork. "Next bests" have more pulling power than fanciful alternatives.

13. Getting Feedback From Participants

One of the most logical sources of corroboration is the people you have talked with and watched. After all, an alert and observant actor in the setting is bound to know more than the researcher ever will about the realities under investigation. In that sense, local participants can act as judges, evaluating the major findings of a study through what has been colloquially labeled "member checking." Some of the display methods profiles encouraged feedback from case participants: commenting on a short summary of findings, evaluating the accuracy of a causal network, verifying researcher predictions.

Feedback may happen during data collection, too. When a finding begins to take shape, the researcher may check it out with new participants and/or with key participants. The delicate issue here, of course, is that of introducing bias (see **researcher effects**). Feeding things back in the course of a study may change participants' actions or perspectives. (In some genres, such as action research, critical ethnography, or community-based collaborative research, however, changing participants' actions and perspectives for the better *is* the goal.)

Still, we've seen some useful examples of thorough early feedback. In a phenomenological study, Melnick and Beaudry (1990) interviewed teachers and, then, in a second interview, fed back the transcript, which had been annotated with marginal remarks on themes, and follow-up questions; the transcript became the basis for shared reflection. Warner (1991) not only had children run camcorders of adult-child interaction and added their comments, but he also played back the video tapes for yet more comment by the children. The more emic the study, the more useful early feedback is likely to be.

There are also good reasons for conducting feedback after the final analysis. For one thing, you know more. You also know *better* what you do know—you are less tentative, have more supporting evidence, and can illustrate it. In addition, you can get feedback at a higher level of inference: on main factors, on causal relationships, and on interpretive conclusions. Finally, the feedback process can be done less haphazardly. You can lay out the findings clearly and systematically and present them to the reader for careful scrutiny and comment.

It is crucial that the reader be able to connect to the feedback—understand it, relate it to local experience and perceptions, *do* something with it (draw on it, cross out parts and add others, etc.). So *formatting* the feedback is crucial. Sending back an abstract, an executive summary, or the concluding chapter without transforming it into the language of the site—which the researcher has come to learn in the course of field research—is of little value if you are seriously after verification.

Some advice:

- If you don't plan deliberately for this exercise—setting aside the time, transforming write-ups into site-comprehensible language and formats, leaving time to incorporate the results of the exercise into your final write-up—it probably won't happen. There will be too many competing claims on your time.

- Think carefully about displays. As with analysis, matrices and networks work much better than text alone to help participants access the information. They will find it easier to get an overview, to see how the pieces fit together.

- Providing information at more macro-analytical levels of inference (e.g., main factors and relationships, causal determinants) has to be done very carefully by working up from particulars. If this is not done, participants may discount the whole exercise because the overarching findings look abstract or incomprehensible. Or they may swallow these macro findings whole because these read so "scientifically." Format your data, and feed them back in a participant-friendly way. Beyond this is the possibility of mutual enlightenment.

- Think very carefully before feeding back any specific incident. Will anyone's self-esteem, job chances, or standing in the organization be damaged by the report? (One of us once fed back first-draft case reports to people in five cases and was threatened with lawsuits in four of the five because of specific incidents in the reports—even though the incidents were reported accurately.)

- Don't expect that participants will always agree with you or with one another. If they always did, life at the site would be more conflict-free than you probably found it to be. People often have widely varying perceptions of the same phenomenon. Interpretivists consider this natural.

Data feedback is an occasion to learn more about the *case*, not only about the feedback.

Standards for the Quality of Conclusions

We've reviewed 26 tactics for drawing and verifying conclusions. How will you, or anyone else, know whether the finally emerging findings are *good*? That term has many possible definitions: possibly or probably true, reliable, valid, dependable, reasonable, confirmable, credible, trustworthy, useful, compelling, significant, empowering (add others of your choice). It's not enough to say that well carried out tactics will make for good conclusions.

In this section, we explore some practical standards that could help us judge the quality of conclusions. The battles in this domain have been extensive, and they continue. Many interpretivist researchers suggest that it is not really possible to establish standards or to specify criteria for good qualitative work—and that the effort to do so is somehow expert centered and exclusionary, not responsive to the contingent, contextual, and personally interpretive nature of any qualitative study.

But the problem of quality, of trustworthiness, of authenticity of the findings will not go away. The fact is that some accounts read better than others. Although we may acknowledge that "getting it all right" may be an unrealistic goal, we should, as Wolcott (1990) suggests, try to "not get it all wrong." (Would you be bothered if a journalist did not tell the truth about you or if a court dismissed a case against someone who had assaulted you, saying that everyone has different interpretations?)

Our view is that qualitative studies take place in a real social world and can have real consequences in people's lives; that there is a reasonable view of what happened in any particular situation (including what was believed, interpreted, etc.); and that we who render accounts of it can do so well or poorly and should not consider our work unjudgable. These are matters of merit, rigor, integrity, ethics, and accountability.

We cannot enter here into a discussion of how goodness criteria flow from epistemological positions. Rather, we remain broadly in the critical realist tradition and discuss five main, somewhat overlapping, issues: (1) the **objectivity/confirmability** of qualitative work, (2) **reliability/dependability/auditability**, (3) **internal validity/credibility/authenticity**, (4) **external validity/transferability/fittingness**, and (5) **utilization/application/action orientation**. Here, we are pairing traditional terms with those proposed as more viable alternatives for assessing the trustworthiness and authenticity of naturalistic research (Lincoln & Guba, 1985).

In each section, we describe the issues generally, without trying to straighten out all of the thorny problems involved. (Better people than us are still trying.) Then, we propose some practical guidelines that can be applied to qualitative work—your own or that of others. These are not rules to be stiffly applied but guidelines to consider when you reflect on the question "How good is this research report?"

Objectivity/Confirmability

The basic issue here can be framed as one of relative neutrality and reasonable freedom from unacknowledged researcher biases—at the minimum, explicitness about the inevitable biases that exist. This domain is sometimes labeled "external reliability," borrowed from classic quantitative terminology.

Some useful points to consider about this issue for a qualitative study are as follows:

1. The study's general methods and procedures are described explicitly and in detail. We feel that we have a complete picture, including "backstage" information.

2. We can follow the actual sequence of how data were collected, processed, condensed/transformed, and displayed for specific conclusion drawing.

3. The conclusions are explicitly linked with exhibits of condensed/displayed data.

4. There is a record of the study's methods and procedures, detailed enough to be audited by an outsider (Lincoln & Guba, 1985).

5. The researcher has been explicit and as self-aware as possible about personal assumptions, values and biases, and affective states—and how they may have come into play during the study.

6. Competing hypotheses or rival conclusions have been considered. The plausibility of rival conclusions has been examined.

7. The study's data are retained and available for reanalysis by others (as allowed by institutional review board regulations and any researcher–participant agreements).

Reliability/Dependability/Auditability

The underlying issue here is whether the process of the study is consistent, reasonably stable over time and across researchers and methods. We are addressing issues of quality and integrity: Have things been done with reasonable care?

Some useful points to consider about this issue for a qualitative study are as follows:

1. The research questions are clear, and the features of the study design are congruent with them.

2. The researcher's role and status within the site have been explicitly described.

3. The findings show meaningful parallelism across data sources (participants, contexts, times).

4. Basic paradigms and analytic constructs are clearly specified. (Reliability depends, in part, on its connectedness to theory.)

5. Data were collected across the full range of appropriate settings, times, respondents, and so on, as suggested by the research questions.

6. If multiple field-workers are involved, they have comparable data collection protocols.

7. When appropriate, intercoder agreement checks were made with adequate results.

8. Data quality checks have been made (e.g., for bias, deceit).

9. Multiple observers' accounts converge—in instances, settings, or times—when they might be expected to.

10. Forms of peer or colleague review are in place.

Internal Validity/Credibility/Authenticity

Here, we arrive at the crunch question: truth value. Do the findings of the study make sense? Are they credible to the people we study and to our readers? Do we have an authentic portrait of what we were looking at?

Validity is a contested term among selected qualitative researchers. Some feel that this traditional quantitative construct (with its components of face, content, predictive, etc., validity) has no place in qualitative inquiry. Alternative terms such as *verisimilitude* and *a persuasively written account* are preferred. But other qualitative methodologists continue to use the term purposefully because it suggests a more rigorous stance toward our work.

Wolcott (1990) went so far as to reject validity in our field and proposed that we should come to a deep *understanding* instead. Maxwell's (1992) thoughtful review distinguishes among the types of understanding that may emerge from a qualitative study: *descriptive* (what happened in specific situations), *interpretive* (what it meant to the people involved), *theoretical* (the concepts, and their relationships, used to explain actions and meanings), and *evaluative* (judgments of the worth or value of actions and meanings).

Saldaña calls this domain the "That's right!" factor. When an oral presentation is made of one's research and people in the audience are nodding their heads affirmatively, saying "M-hm" in agreement and (even better) exclaiming out loud, "That's right!" to the speaker after an assertion has been made, you can feel confident that some sense of resonance has been achieved between the research and the audience. Call this domain what you will; it's the write-up itself that matters in the end.

Some useful points to consider about this issue for a qualitative study are as follows:

1. Descriptions are context-rich, meaningful, and "thick" (Geertz, 1973).

2. The account rings true, makes sense, seems convincing or plausible, and enables a vicarious presence for the reader.

3. Triangulation among complementary methods and data sources produced generally converging conclusions. If not, the procedures for reconciling the differences and their results are explained.

4. The data presented are well linked to the categories of prior or emerging theory. The measures reflect the constructs at work.

5. Findings are clear, coherent, and systematically related—that is, unified (Charmaz, 2006; Eisner, 1991).

6. Confirmation procedures for assertions, propositions, hypotheses, conclusions, and so on, are described.

7. Any areas of uncertainty have been identified.

8. Negative evidence was sought (and, if applicable, found and accounted for in the analysis and write-up).

9. Rival explanations have been actively considered.

10. When possible, findings have been replicated in other parts of the database than the one they arose from.

11. The conclusions were considered to be accurate by the original participants. If not, a coherent explanation is offered.

12. If predictions were made in the study, their accuracy is reported.

External Validity/Transferability/Fittingness

We need to know whether the conclusions of a study—a case study, in particular—have any larger import. Are they transferable to other contexts? Do they fit? How far can they be generalized?

Grounded theorists attest that the methodology develops concepts and abstractions at a level that supports their transferability to other populations and contexts (Glaser, 2005). Some methodologists purport that any transfer of a study's findings to other contexts is the responsibility of the reader, not the researcher (Erickson, 1986). The generalizability of the case study has been a contentious issue, ranging from the researcher's analytic ability to find levels of universality in the case (Spradley, 1979, 1980) to frank admission that complex and site-specific contexts problematize the ability to construct theory and, thus, generalization (Clarke, 2005).

The generalizing process is far from mechanical, as Noblit and Hare (1988) note in their discussion of meta-ethnography: It is more like synthesizing two or more studies of similar phenomena. It is careful interpretation, not just "adding up." In this case, we again conclude that it's the write-up itself that matters in the end. How *persuasive* a case can the researcher make that the findings of $N = 1$ have meaning and resonance to other individuals, sites, and times?

Some useful points to consider about this issue for a qualitative study are as follows:

1. The characteristics of the original sample of persons, settings, processes, and so on, are sufficiently fully described to permit adequate comparisons with other samples.

2. The report specifies any limits on sample selection and critically examines its ability to generalize to other settings and contexts.

3. The sampling is theoretically diverse enough to encourage broader applicability when relevant.

4. The findings include enough "thick description" for readers to assess the potential transferability and appropriateness for their own settings.

5. A range of readers report that the findings are consistent with their own experiences.

6. The findings are congruent with, connected to, or confirmatory of prior theory.

7. The processes and outcomes described in the conclusions are applicable in comparable settings.

8. Any theories and their transferability are explicitly stated.

9. The report suggests settings where the findings could fruitfully be tested further.

10. When possible, the findings have been replicated in other studies to assess their robustness.

Utilization/Application/Action Orientation

Even if a study's findings are valid and transferable, we still need to know what the study does for its participants—both researchers and researched—and for its consumers.

Evaluation and policy studies in particular are supposed to lead to more positive and constructive actions; whether or not they do, real people's lives are being affected, and large amounts of money are being spent (or misspent). Action research, critical ethnography, and other community-based research projects are designed to clarify and rectify particular local problems through participatory engagement. At the very least, they heighten awareness among participants of selected social issues that affect them directly.

These research genres also raise questions of ethics—Who benefits from a qualitative study, and who may be harmed?—and of "evaluative validity" (Maxwell, 1992): judgments made about the worth, legitimacy, or goodness of actions or meanings.

Some useful points to consider about this issue for a qualitative study are as follows:

1. Value-based or ethical concerns and dilemmas are raised explicitly in the report.

2. The findings are intellectually and physically accessible to potential users.

3. The findings stimulate and provide intellectual "payoff" for a reader, and possibly ideas for his or her own related research project.

4. The level of usable knowledge offered is worthwhile, ranging from consciousness raising and the development of insight or self-understanding to broader considerations—a theory to guide action, or policy advice. Or it may be local and specific—corrective recommendations or specific action images.

5. The actions taken actually help solve a local problem.

6. Users of the findings have experienced a sense of empowerment or increased control over their lives (Lincoln & Guba, 1985).

7. Users of the findings have learned or developed new capacities.

Analytic Documentation

The Problem

Good qualitative research, like any other research, requires careful record keeping as a way of connecting with important audiences. The first audience is the *self*: well-organized electronic and hard copy files that help keep track of what was done along the way, suggesting ways of improving next steps and documenting all logistical matters related to the study.

The second audience is the *readers* of the research reports, who need to know what was done and how, as a way of assessing the credibility of the findings. Other researchers and journal peer reviewers make such judgments carefully, even obsessively. And other readers such as local participants, policymakers, managers, and the general public often raise questions such as "Whom did you talk to, anyway?" "How do you know?" "Why are you being so negative?" and "Where did you get that recommendation?"

The third audience is a subset of the second: *other researchers* who are interested in secondary analysis of the data, who want to carry out a metasynthesis of several studies, or who want to replicate the findings to strengthen or modify them.

For the latter two audiences, most journals require authors of empirical studies to report on their procedures as an integral part of the article. The formats are often so familiar that the author can almost fill in the blanks when writing sections on sampling, methods, and data analysis. For mixed-methods studies, it's also expected that you report relevant statistical data in standardized display formats.

There is, in other words, a traditional set of conventions for documenting empirical research and for reporting it, and a corresponding set of methods for verifying the report. But qualitative researchers don't have very clear alternatives to fall back on. We've borrowed a few conventions from the culture of quantitative-oriented journals. But the hybridity of the field has created multiple, open-ended reporting structures for progressive genres such as poetic inquiry, ethnodrama, narrative inquiry, and others. And selected schools of thought reject the very notion of "conclusions," considering them abhorrent abuses of researcher power to force fixed meanings on an uncertain social world. (The irony, of course, is that these same schools of thought seem to authoritatively assert their stances as fixed meanings.)

On the face of it, this is a curious state of affairs. Although qualitative studies are rich in descriptions of settings, people, events, and processes, they often say little about how the researcher got the information, and very little about how the conclusions were drawn. When procedures are left so opaque, we have only vague criteria for judging the goodness of conclusions: the "plausibility," the "coherence," or the "compellingness" of the study—all evocative but ultimately hollow terms. The researcher can always provide a plausible final account and, with careful editing, may ensure its coherence. If the writing is good, we will be won over by the undeniability and vividness of the report. But seemingly plausible and coherent accounts can be terribly biased, and vividness lands us in the "availability" heuristic, where we overweight concrete or dramatic data.

So we have an unappealing double bind. Qualitative studies cannot always be verified because researchers don't always report clearly on their methodology, and they don't report clearly on their methodology because there are not always required conventions for doing so. (Epistemological reasons may be claimed as well—for instance, the idea that a qualitative study is such a person-specific, artistic, private/interpretive act that no one else can viably verify or replicate it—but that takes us far from shore just now.) What do we do?

Methods sections are much more typical in dissertations, theses, and journal reports of traditional qualitative studies. They tend to follow a traditional outline and sequence:

- Central and related research questions
- Cursory literature review
- Conceptual or theoretical framework
- Methodology
  - Participants
  - Data collection methods
  - Data analysis procedures

We need to know a few additional things, if possible:

- Which kinds of qualitative designs do researchers actually use?
- How are sampling decisions actually made?

- What does the instrumentation look like, and how does the researcher know whether it is measuring accurately what it was meant to measure?

- How does fieldwork actually proceed?

- How are the data aggregated, condensed, partitioned, displayed, analyzed, and interpreted?

- Most fundamentally, how do researchers get from hundreds if not thousands of pages of field notes, interview transcripts, and documents to a final report?

Until we can share clear descriptions of qualitative research procedures, we cannot talk about them intelligibly with one another—let alone set up conventions for verification.

We have to begin, then, by logging and then describing our procedures clearly enough so that others can understand them, reconstruct them, and subject them to scrutiny.

Lincoln and Guba (1985) used the metaphor of the fiscal auditor who examines the books of a company to determine whether accounts have been kept satisfactorily and whether the "bottom line" is correct. Making such an audit depends on the auditee's having documented income, outlays, and transfers. Without such an audit trail, you cannot determine the dependability or the confirmability of the bookkeeping.

The first and basic audience for good documentation is the *self*. Even if no audit is ever intended, devices such as the researcher's journal, diary, and analytic memos strengthen the study *as it goes*. Second, they enable easy production of the methods section. Thorough auditing, as such, is relatively rare as far as we know. The audit metaphor is forbidding: It connotes an external, stern, obsessive expert and misses the idea that you, with close colleagues, can frequently look at documentation very fruitfully. There are also confidentiality issues to consider, with outsiders looking at personal data; institutional review board regulations may prohibit this unless approval has been made in advance to the regulatory body.

Illustration

We (Miles and Huberman) developed a documentation form focusing on analytic operations. (*Note:* It does not deal with issues of sampling, instrumentation, fieldwork, and so on.) The challenge was to come up with a documentation form that met several criteria: facility and rapidity of use, easy transfer into a methodological report, easy access and comprehension by a second reader, and believability/validity. There are some clear trade-offs—for example, comprehension and believability usually mean that the form requires some time and care.

We show in Display 11.7 a streamlined version of more elaborate efforts. We include it here for essentially heuristic, illustrative reasons, and we encourage others to develop their own documentation methods. The nature of good documentation of analysis operations is something we have to discover inductively.

As we used it, the form is focused on a single research question or issue (Item 1). Item 2 asks the researcher to explain, generally, what the analysis was designed to do and to situate it in the context of other analyses. Item 3 calls for a fairly complete description

Display 11.7

Qualitative Analysis Documentation Form

1. Research Issue being explored: _____
   FORM NO. _____

2. *In this analysis task, what, specifically, were you aiming to do?* (Give context and a short rationale; say whether focus is exploratory or confirmatory; make the connection with earlier analyses.)

3. *Description of procedures. Work sequentially,* keeping a log or diary of steps as you go through the analysis. Use a second sheet if needed. If the analysis task changes substantially, *use a new form, redoing items 1 and 2 above.*

_____ Analyst _____ Date _____

SPECIFIC DATA SETS IN USE (a)	PROCEDURAL STEPS (number each one, explain what was done, and exactly how it was done) (b)	DECISION RULES followed during analysis operations (c)	ANALYSIS OPERATIONS (enter codes)			CONCLUSIONS DRAWN from these specific analysis operations; give substance	RESEARCH COMMENTS, reflections, remarks on any of the preceding in brief
			Readying data for analysis	Drawing conclusions	Confirming conclusions		

(a) Indicate whether single or multi-site. May include: field notes; write-ups; summaries; documents; figures; matrices; tables; tape recordings; photos; film/video; others (specify).

(b) PROVIDE ALL RELEVANT DISPLAYS; give each a letter, describe briefly, and also give numbers of procedural steps where used.

   Work notes/work sheets: _____

   Interim data displays: _____

   Final data displays: _____

   Final text written (excerpts): _____

(c) Explicit list of actual rules used for "readying" data (clustering, sorting, scaling, etc.); may also apply to drawing/confirming conclusions.

Source: Miles, M. B., & Huberman, A. M. (1994). *Qualitative data analysis: An expanded sourcebook* (2nd ed.). Thousand Oaks, CA: Sage Publications.

(actually written as a log or diary during analysis), including the *data sets* in which the analysis was conducted, the *procedural steps*, the *decision rules* used to manage the data, the *analysis operations* involved, the preliminary *conclusions* to which the analysis led, and any concluding *comments*. All of this information goes on a single sheet, so that the analyst can log in the successive analytical steps and a reviewer (if any) can grasp quickly what was done.

The researcher indicates all relevant *displays* (materials used or developed in the course of analysis), so that they can be referred to easily. For a reviewer, they should be appended.

Make running notes for the *Procedural Steps* section as you go along; much gets lost in recollection. Then, it's easy to fill in the section with a few summary phrases, such as the following:

- Reviewed preliminary matrix format; entered data from two sites.

- Reviewed meta-matrix; decided to lump Lido case with Astoria and Carson.

- Went through causal network, reviewing links, adding and subtracting links to make final version.

Noting the exact *decision rules* used is important, especially for any operations involved in readying data for entry into displays. Making them explicit as you go along is very useful; it reduces error and can aid self-correction. Here are some examples:

- Theme was coded as present for a participant if mentioned repeatedly or with strong affect during the interview.

- Item was entered in display if mentioned by more than one participant at sites with more than three participants; at sites with fewer users, item was entered if mentioned by one participant, with no contradiction from others.

- Cutting point between "high" and "moderate" cases was made when half or fewer of the indicators were absent.

Making decision rules explicit is not only critical for data-readying operations but also important for conclusion drawing and confirmation. A reader will usually want to know how and why you concluded that variable *A* was a stronger predictor of the outcome than variable *B*, *and* how you verified or confirmed that conclusion. Your rules may be (alas) arbitrary, but they are your rules.

For tracking *analysis operations*, we (Miles and Huberman) developed an "in-house" code list (see Display 11.8). Scanning the list serves as a kind of prompt for the analyst, both helping label the operations followed and suggesting other avenues that might be followed. Note that although we have clustered the codes for convenience into three general categories, many of them may fall into any of the three categories. For example, COH (conceptual and theoretical coherence), though it appears under *Drawing conclusions*, can also be used to confirm or test conclusions. Or SUB (subsuming data under a higher level variable) can be seen as *Readying data for analysis* or as a way of *Drawing conclusions*.

Note that many of the items, along with the logic underlying their use, are tactics defined more fully in earlier sections. Because there is no standardized language about analysis operations and there are a variety of partial dialects from different disciplines,

Display 11.8

Code List for Analysis Operations

Readying data for analysis

TAB	tabulating coded segments
MAT	filling in matrices
CLAS	classifying, categorizing
RANK	ranking/weighting data
SMM	summarizing phrases, generating key words
SUB	subsuming data under higher level variable
SCAL	scaling, summing indices
COMP	computing, tabulating
SPLT	splitting one variable into two
PAR	partitioning
AGG	aggregating

Drawing conclusions

PLAUS	seeing "plausibility" only
GES	seeing a Gestalt, pattern, theme
MET	generating metaphors
CLUS	clustering
COUNT	counting/frequencies
CEN	establishing central tendencies
CONT	systematic contrasts/comparisons
FAC	establishing factors
REL	establishing relationships between variables/sets of variables
LOG	logical chain of evidence
INTV	establishing intervening/linking conditions
COH	conceptual/theoretical coherence
CAUSE	determining directional influence

TEMP	determining temporal order/ temporal relationships
INF	making inferences
INF-COMP	by computations
INF-DED	by deduction
INF-IND	by induction (e.g., determining antecedents, covariates, consequences)

Confirming conclusions

REPR	checking for representativeness
RES-EFF	checking for researcher effects
BIAS-CONTR	control for bias (specify)
TRI	triangulation
TRI-DATA	from different data sources
TRI-METH	from different methods
TRI-CONC	conceptually (different theories)
TRI-RES	from different researchers
WT	weighting of evidence
OUT	user of outliers, exceptions
EXTR-SIT	extreme situation verification
EXTR-BIAS	extreme bias verification
SURP	following up surprises
EMP	empirical evidence from elsewhere
NONEG	absence of negative evidence
IF-THEN	testing if-then relationships
FALSE-REL	checking false relation due to third variable
REPL	replication
RIV	test of rival explanation
FB	corroboration from informant feedback

Source: Miles, M. B., & Huberman, A. M. (1994). *Qualitative data analysis: An expanded sourcebook* (2nd ed.). Thousand Oaks, CA: Sage Publications.

we tried to find items that would have meaning to most researchers. We've aimed to keep our own terms clearly defined. We include no items for noting "insights," "bracketing," "structural corroboration," and "disciplined subjectivity" because it isn't clear to us, operationally, what these terms mean and how they actually work. Other researchers may have more success in this.

The next to last column of the Display 11.7 form asks for the researcher's substantive *Conclusions* in capsule form; they do not need to be detailed, and reference can be made to the analytic text in which they appear. The last column is open for the researcher to comment on confidence in the conclusions, reflect, make remarks, or vent any relevant feelings. This material helps clarify the meaning of the analysis episodes being reported.

We repeatedly found that indicating or appending all available *Displays* was crucial for other readers. It is simply impossible to understand the analysis procedures followed without direct recourse to such exhibits. The final analytic text is equally important. It's the end of the audit trail.

Documentation is not a separate, onerous task carried out for someone else. It's a method of improving the immediate analysis task being carried out, advancing the sophistication of later analyses, and deepening the confidence you have in the final conclusions. The value of feedback from a friend, colleague, reader, replicator, meta-evaluator, or auditor comes later as an add-on. A number of CAQDAS software programs automatically develop a dated log of analysis operations of certain sorts, such as code development, searches and queries, and analytic memo records.

Less complex documentation methods are not hard to find. Sometimes a detailed researcher journal or analytic memos may be all that are needed for your purposes. We offer these final recommendations:

1. Be clear in your own mind why you are doing documentation for this study. Is it for study steering and revision, for your own personal learning, for getting feedback from a colleague or other critical friend, for "methods section" reportage, or for a methodological article as such, for actual audit?

2. Any study has more or less riding on it. A high-stakes study (e.g., of an expensive but controversial program) demands more care.

3. Documentation detail also depends on your study's focus. With our interest in close depiction of analytical moves, we found that any given research question usually involved a flow of seven or eight analysis episodes, each using one of these documentation sheets. Less micro purposes, or fewer of them, would mean less detail.

4. Work with a form of the sort we have shown usually goes faster with a stepwise procedure. First, while actually conducting the analysis, make rough running notes; then order them, logging in the procedural steps, decision rules, and conclusions, giving enough detail to be clear; and then assemble the exhibits (tables, worksheets, text, etc.). After the analysis is complete, review the entries, cleaning them up where needed and adding analysis codes; then fill out the more reflective part.

5. It's not a good idea to do a thorough reflection on your analysis while doing the analysis. You need all the energy you can spare for the analysis itself. Avoid "laundering" or retrospective enlightenment. Do not let incomplete documentation forms pile up—that defeats your purposes. Do them as you go along.

6. Code lists can be used as cues for tactics or procedures you aren't using but could use. This flag will turn up automatically as you notice yourself using the same codes frequently; it probably means that you are relying too heavily on too few devices.

Closure and Transition

Tremendous amounts of tactics, guidance, advice, and recommendations were covered in this chapter. We do not mean to overwhelm you with this vast array of factors to consider in your data analyses. But we do feel they are important guidelines that can strengthen the quality and integrity of your qualitative work. Use these methods on an "as needed" or "as relevant" basis.

In the next chapter, we will explore the write-ups researchers must make for sharing their data-analytic efforts and findings with audiences.

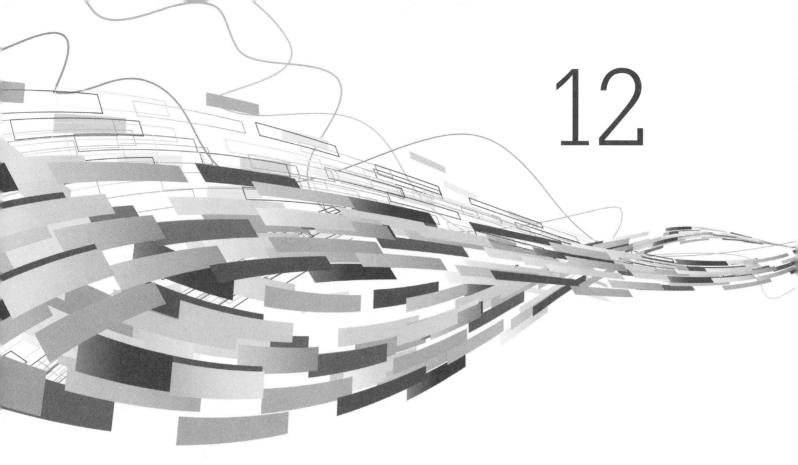

Writing About Qualitative Research

Chapter Summary

This chapter reviews the various choices available to researchers writing up the qualitative report. Extended examples from traditional and progressive forms are provided to illustrate selected "tales" or styles of writing. Advice for thesis and dissertation students is also provided.

Contents

Introduction
Audiences and Effects
    The Reader and the Writer
    Types of Effects
Voices, Genres, and Stances
    Writing Example
Formats and Structures
    Traditional Presentation Modes
    Progressive Presentation Modes
Closure and Transition

Introduction

Some form of reporting the results to others is a necessary component of virtually all qualitative research projects. But in what form? It's clear that the conventional formats long familiar to quantitative researchers, something like the following, are too schematic and constraining:

- Statement of the problem
- Research questions
- Methods
- Results
- Discussion
- Conclusions

A qualitative write-up could follow that format (and several do), but it's not the only one available to us. Normally, we'd have other expectations for a qualitative report.

For example, we might expect a close description of the setting and the major participants. We might look for a more circular linkage between research questions, methods, data collection, and interim analyses, as each analysis opened up new leads. And many qualitative analysts would not start with a conceptual framework but rather strive to end up with one. Qualitative data have special strengths: local groundedness, holism, temporality, access to causation, emphasis on meanings, and so on. Reporting formats can capitalize on them.

Zeller (1991) suggests that qualitative studies don't report data; they report "scenes"—that is, accounts of researchers' engagements over time with participants in their surroundings. Often, these reports may not be compiled into factually accurate accounts but rather serve as a corpus from which the researcher actively selects, transforms, and interprets the material at hand—sometimes without leaving traces of the successive steps taken along the way.

Zeller (1991) asks further whether qualitative field studies are different from the nonfiction novels or from slice-of-life case studies from the New Journalism movement. Do qualitative studies have a distinctive reporting format? As we've shown, even for data segments within a study, a set of field observations can be rendered differently—in poetic form, as a series of vignettes, as stories, or compiled in a meta-matrix. A blurring of the frontiers seems to occur between social scientific reporting and figurative or rhetorical renditions of aesthetic material.

The reporting of qualitative data may be one of the most fertile fields going; there are no standardized formats, and the ways data are being analyzed and interpreted are getting more and more varied. As qualitative data analysts, we have few shared canons of how our studies *should* be reported. Should we have normative agreement on this? Probably not now—or, some would say, ever.

Yet it's important to consider the choices you face in designing and writing reports. The challenge is to combine theoretical elegance and credibility appropriately with the many ways social events can be described and to find intersections between the propositional thinking of most conventional studies and more creative thinking. Just as a good analysis nearly always involves a blend of variable-oriented, categorizing, paradigmatic moves, and case-oriented, contextualizing, narrative ones, so does good reporting.

We do not offer a fixed set of ideas about reports and reporting but rather identify a series of *choices* you have in writing your accounts. They include choices about the report's audiences and the hoped-for effects on them, the voice or genre of the report, its style, its structure and format, and what will be done to ensure better use of the report.

Our stance is that these choices should be made clearly and deliberately in preliminary form—for interim reports, quite early, and for final reports, somewhat before the midpoint of a study. Otherwise, much effort can be wasted. Wolcott (2009) has an even stronger position: "You cannot begin writing early enough. . . . Would that mean someone might write a first draft before venturing into the field to begin observations or interviews? Absolutely" (p. 18). The point here is not advocacy of data-free writing but of early and continuous writing as a way to make your ideas—more and more informed by data—explicit.

Other researchers may be more leisurely and more indeterminate. But the issue is that *not* facing choices about writing is a choice—a de facto action that may lead you into unhappy, unforeseen circumstances when the crunch of producing a final report begins to make itself felt.

As we emphasize throughout the book, data analysis includes selecting, condensing, and transforming data; displaying these data in an organized way; and drawing and verifying conclusions from the condensed, displayed data. Any interim or final report will deal, more or less explicitly, with this flow of analytical processes and their resulting products.

Reporting is not separate from thinking or from analysis. Rather, it *is* analysis. And from our perspective, *a report is a display*. Reports display your organized accounts of what happened in the field, and they display your carefully considered analytic explanations of those events. Your report triggers within your readers the memories of their own personal experiences, plus their comparative and critical faculties. At its best, writing as a form of display presents new, intriguing ideas and stimulates the reader to perceive social life in different and insightful ways. Here, then, is a set of writing-related issues you face from the start, whether or not you decide to confront them directly.

Audiences and Effects

The Reader and the Writer

Reports are supposed to be written for specific audiences to achieve specific effects. But the familiar label "audience" obscures an important issue: You cannot exactly manage a fully rational specification of audiences or of the effects you want to achieve with them. Rather, in Erickson's (1986) terms, the reader is a co-analyst, experiencing the original setting vicariously, looking at the evidence, weighing the writer's interpretations and perspective, and noting how they have changed along the way.

Generally speaking, you need to make choices of reader types from a list like this:

- *Local participants and respondents:* the people who provided data
- *Program administrators and operators:* in evaluation studies, people running and/ or deciding about the program being looked at

- *Practitioners:* people engaged in the same sort of work as those studied, but in different settings
- Other researchers:
  - Colleagues in your own setting
  - Members of dissertation committees
  - Colleagues in your academic field
- *Policymakers:* governing boards, legislators, and agency officials
- *General readers:* purchasers of trade and e-books
- *Mass readers:* purchasers of magazines and newspapers, readers of Internet news sources

Types of Effects

What are you hoping will occur when a particular type of reader engages with your report? Although that cannot be really predicted or controlled, getting your *intentions* clear can make a profound difference in what the report will look like and how you produce it. Any qualitative research report may be written from certain general stances:

Scientific

- To heighten insight, illuminate, and deepen understanding
- To expand or revise existing concepts, theory, and explanations
- To convince the reader of the report's worth, truth, and value
- To advance the methodological craft of research
- To add to existing information on a topic

Aesthetic

- To entertain, amuse, and arouse feeling
- To enable vicarious experiencing

Moral

- To clarify and sharpen moral, ethical, and legal issues
- To emancipate, raise consciousness in, and free the reader from unrealized oppression

Activist

- To show connections between findings and local problems
- To enable improved decisions and to provide guidance for action
- To empower the reader and to increase a sense of control
- To mobilize specific action
- To support the reader in future use of the findings

One of the critical considerations is *which* effects you are intending for *which* types of reader. If your report is a dissertation and your audience is your committee (and only secondarily other researchers), then the effects of theoretical and methodological advancement—or perhaps, mostly, convincing the readers of the report's credibility—are likely to be central. On the other hand, if your audiences are policymakers and trade book readers, your intended effects may be different—for example, the illumination, moral clarification, and mobilization that Jonathan Kozol (1991) doubtless intended in his riveting depiction of urban schools in *Savage Inequalities: Children in America's Schools* and the insightful investigative journalism and social critique of America's minimum-wage injustices in Barbara Ehrenreich's (2001) *Nickel and Dimed: On (Not) Getting By in America.*

Voices, Genres, and Stances

How do we speak to the reader? Many choices are to be made, and no standard lexicon describes the overall tone, mode, and orientation of the report. Yet when we read a research report, we can almost immediately detect a pervasive stance, a flavor, a tone that defines the relationship between the writer and the reader.

Matters of style are connected with the choice of voice. Using a Latinate instead of Anglo-Saxon language, passive instead of active verbs, "objective" stances rather than honestly personal ones, and indirect locutions instead of straightforward talk has a long and dishonorable history in traditional research reporting. It serves only to wrap the writer in the mantle of "science," while mystifying and alienating the reader.

One common misconception some scholars have is that you need to "write smart" to be taken seriously or to prove that you know a lot, because it's a traditional discourse expected in scholarly/academic publications and presentations. Others "write smart" because they're arrogant elitists in love with their own intelligence, and they feel that lofty prose, big words, and abstract concepts are the only ways they can communicate their brilliance to others. We're not advocating that you "dumb down" your qualitative writing; but things can still be complex without being complicated. Write simply, write clearly, and write believably. Keep it real.

van Maanen's (2011) eloquent and classic *Tales of the Field* distinguishes among several possible voices or research tale types, with many examples from his own and others' work. Several of these can be compatibly mixed and matched within a single report:

Realist: a direct, highly detailed, matter-of-fact portrait, with methods left mostly undescribed, in which the field-worker is invisible and "interpretively omnipotent"

Confessional: written from the field-worker's viewpoint; includes methodological dilemmas, admission of errors, ethical issues, and behind-the-scenes glitches

Impressionist: personalized, atheoretical accounts, often story-like, aiming to link reality and the field-worker and to enable the reader's vivid reliving of the experience

Critical: focuses on the sociopolitical implications of fieldwork; critically examines, usually through a Marxist lens, the sociological and cultural underpinnings of human dynamics

Formal: traditional and conventional scholarly writing; details the methods, data collection, and data analysis procedures employed, with a systematic overview of results and theories

Literary: evocative narratives; utilizes the power of literary tones, styles, and devices to develop characters in active storylines as in "creative nonfiction"

Jointly told: collaborative, coauthored accounts, where the researcher and participants join together to create a polyvocal narrative of their collective experiences

Structural: a combination of theoretical reflection with first-person accounts; links the local to the general

Poststructural: "purposeful incompleteness and uncertainty"; inconclusive results to reinforce the flux of human nature

Advocacy: takes a deliberate moral perspective; examines inequities and power struggles to achieve social justice and to empower the oppressed

These voices have profound consequences for what is included in a report and what can be learned from it. For example, van Maanen notes that a realist voice tends to rule out alternative interpretations and/or to pretend that the interpretations come straight from the respondents. Confessional tales may overfocus on the field-worker as doing "vanity ethnography," blurring what happened, and may be seen as self-indulgent writing. An impressionist account may focus too much on the exemplary and dramatic moments of fieldwork to the neglect of a site's mundane and patterned reality. (These are only sketchy summaries. We recommend John van Maanen's *Tales of the Field: On Writing Ethnography* to the reader seeking an articulate, experienced researcher's reflections on writing.)

Writing Example

Dana L. Miller, John W. Creswell, and Lisa S. Olander (1998) explored the writing of a fieldwork project in three different ways for their compelling article, "Writing and Retelling Multiple Ethnographic Tales of a Soup Kitchen for the Homeless." The coauthors employed the realist, confessional, and critical genres of van Maanen's tales outlined above to portray their research experiences. Extended excerpts are provided here to demonstrate an exemplar of qualitative research writing. The coauthors first share with readers the essential "front matter"—their modified conceptual framework, the purpose of the study, the fieldwork setting, and major research questions:

The soup kitchen becomes a microcosm for studying the homeless population . . . and we can learn much from an ethnographic study that explores alternative narratives about the culture of a soup kitchen.

The purpose of this ethnographic study was to describe and interpret the cultural setting of the St. Tabor Soup Kitchen, located in a small Midwestern city called Midtown. St. Tabor is housed in a multipurpose complex with Daily Refuge (a daytime shelter for the homeless and near-homeless) and Community Thrift Shop. Three research questions emerged during the study: How might the soup kitchen, as a cultural setting, be described? What are the cultural themes of the soup kitchen? How can we become advocates for the soup kitchen, day-shelter and the homeless population?

Other necessary elements for this ethnographic report are documentation of the data collection methods, selection of key "informants," and how the coresearchers' findings were verified. Notice how the amounts and forms of data and the explanation of triangulation procedures establish a sense of trustworthiness for the forthcoming account:

> We observed homeless guests for 4 months during the noon lunch hour at St. Tabor Soup Kitchen. Our methodology was qualitative, involving ethnographic procedures . . . , and an evolving design to best understand the culture of the soup kitchen and the needs of the low-income and homeless population in Midtown. The noon lunch at St. Tabor was provided by Daily Refuge. Gaining access through the director of Daily Refuge, we volunteered for 4 months, serving meals in the soup kitchen and helping with clean-up. Data collection consisted of 35 observations, and formal and informal interviews. In addition, we collected documents describing the low-income population in the city, sign-in sheets that provided census data about guests, written materials about Daily Refuge, daily food menus, and we took photographs of the facility, town and guests. Our personal fieldnotes included conversations with guests, volunteers, and staff; notes from our research team meetings; and our interpretations and personal reflections.
>
> Information-rich key informants were purposefully selected to participate in the study, including the director of Daily Refuge, the facility manager, and a homeless man who volunteered as a cook for many days during our visit. With these individuals, we periodically shared our emerging cultural description of St. Tabor. Throughout the study, we verified the accuracy of our account by taking our report back to key informants and by triangulating among multiple participants, investigators, and data collection methods. We use pseudonyms throughout this report to protect the anonymity of the site and participants. (p. 472)

The coresearchers do not label the above sections as ways of rendering van Maanen's *formal* genre of writing and tale-telling, but that is what they have done. The formal (or *analytic*) tale presents the researcher's systematic procedures and thinking of how the data come together to explain how things work. Descriptions and explanations of features such as research design and methods, including codes, patterns, categories, themes, concepts, assertions, and theories, are spelled out and sometimes self-critiqued for their effectiveness. For lack of a better term, this style is robust *technical* writing because it focuses on the techniques and outcomes of traditional qualitative data analysis (Saldaña, 2011b, p. 148).

The Realist Tale

The coresearchers first present their ethnographic fieldwork in van Maanen's realist genre. This approach is characterized by writing that is factual with "studied neutrality." Although free of bias, objective reportage is virtually impossible; descriptive and realistic accounts remain firmly rooted in the data themselves. No judgment or critique is proffered, only straightforward details of the field site. This style of writing may help the reader imagine the setting more vividly and lend a sense of credibility to the author's experiences—in other words, "I was there, and this is what I saw and heard" (Saldaña, 2011b, p. 147).

In this excerpt, Miller et al. (1998) provide visual elements of the setting and its participants through concrete imagery and through what Saldaña calls "significant trivia"—rich, telling details:

The Soup Kitchen, run by a Catholic church, provides dinner 7 days a week and lunch on weekends. Daily Refuge rents the kitchen on weekdays to serve free lunches. St. Tabor's dining area is one modest sized room, about 45 by 30 feet. Guests sit around three rows of tables (2 by 24 feet each) covered with green, plastic, flannel-backed tablecloths with tiny paw prints. When not in use, chairs line one of the walls of the room. The dining area is modern and clean, with sparse accessories—a couple of trash cans, a small cross hanging on the wall, a bulletin board advertising services available to the homeless, and a few community service awards. A long serving counter divides the dining area from the kitchen—a modern, clean cooking area with a stove; commercial size oven; microwave; stainless steel, locked refrigerator; dishwasher; and mops and buckets for clean-up.

The guests who come to this soup kitchen are homeless, sometimes homeless, and low-income individuals. One fourth to one half are homeless. Few children are among the guests, and there are four to five times as many men as women. The guests represent varied backgrounds with slightly more Hispanics than other ethnicities. They wear an assortment of clothes and their personal appearance varies from mangled, unbrushed hair, dirty faces, and sometimes obvious physical disabilities to clean and well kept. The majority, though, are unkempt and in torn clothing. (p. 474)

Chapter 7 profiles the analytic method of vignettes. Below is a vignette based on a brief observation of one of the homeless men's interactions with a staff member. Again, note its factual reporting tone as an approach to the realist tale:

Michael was tall, bearded, with medium long, dark matted hair twisted in every direction, greasy hands and a dirty face. While mopping the floor he began talking about a trip he took to Turkey after he graduated from college in the early seventies. Michael described a man in Turkey, "part of the FBI or CIA," who wanted him to loan him "a million dollars," and related how "pissed off" the agent was that Michael had refused. As he rolled the mop and bucket to the dining area, Michael continued and referenced the government and the Pentagon. Rich [the facilities manager with rehab training], who overheard the conversation, asked, "are you sure all those things are accurate?" Michael nodded confidently. "I just wondered," said Rich, "You are kind of getting 'out there' with your talk about the CIA and FBI—kind of loose, almost delusional," and asked, "Are you supposed to be on medication?" Michael looked Rich squarely in the eye and replied, "No, are you?" Rich reiterated his concern about Michael's grasp on reality while Michael, shaking his head, muttered that it was all true . . . that it was all in his books and papers and that he would bring them the next day so that Rich could read them. (p. 478)

The Confessional Tale

The coresearchers shift genres after their descriptive account to provide readers with confessional tales—"the backstage account of what happened during the study. Such matters as the investigator's personal biases, fieldwork problems, ethical dilemmas, and emotional responses are openly addressed alongside the participants' stories" (Saldaña, 2011b, p. 150). The poignant excerpt below openly shares the coresearchers' struggles as academics working in a socially harsh environment. Notice how the point of view shifts from the realist's third-person stance to the confessional's first-person perspective:

> We were constantly faced with situations that made us feel uncomfortable, even hypocritical. For example, on some days we rationed food, or served guests cold, leftover pizza for lunch, then retired to our comfortable, middle-class homes, and threw steaks on the grill for dinner. We were painfully aware of our "privilege." Pedro, one of our key informants who was homeless and helped cook and serve, always insisted that we (the volunteers) prepared our plates with the best food before the supply ran out. And by the end of some meals, the food we served guests was not as appealing. We also watched Pedro give extra food to friends, and steal food and trash bags from the kitchen, and struggled with whether we should report him. He was the primary informant with whom we had built a relationship, yet we were torn about our responsibility to the staff and kitchen, which was actually owned by another group. Then there was the advice we received from a staff member on how to treat an African American homeless woman who came in almost daily and was described as "extremely volatile" and "dangerous": "ignore her, treat her as though she doesn't exist, because you don't exist to her." But isn't that the problem: homeless individuals have been treated like they are invisible for far too long? (pp. 483–484)

Confessional tales can also serve as *cautionary* tales—words of advice from one researcher to another about the possible dilemmas and hazards to be aware of in certain types of fieldwork.

The Critical Tale

The coresearchers' third approach to their project is not only labeled a critical tale but also contains elements of van Maanen's *advocacy* tale. These combined genres of writing address the political and social ramifications of fieldwork, with a deliberate focus on the injustices and oppressions of the world, ranging from unfair practices at the local level to atrocities against life at the international level. The goals of both the research and the write-up are to expose inequities through factual information and testimony, to increase awareness among readers about the issues at hand, and to work toward emancipation, balances of power, and the dignity of human rights (Saldaña, 2011b, p. 157).

The coresearchers bravely and admirably respond to audiences of critics in this section through honest, retrospective, and reflective commentary about the larger issues at stake. One passage in particular from their critical tale captures the function and tone of the genre:

> The facility survived on grants and donations, but there had been months when the staff had come close to closing the doors because of insufficient resources. Although the number of meals served had increased, Mary [the Director] explained that donations had "decreased." If Daily Refuge closed, "where would guests go—would they take up residence on community streets, and in sheltered alleys and doorways?" asked one staff member. Each year the staff asked for funding from the city, and to date, the city had rejected every request. Other philanthropic organizations had provided modest increases, but they had

been reluctant to allocate substantial increases. We [attempted] to advocate for the soup kitchen and homeless population. Near the end of our fieldwork we attended a budget meeting with United Way to advocate for increased funding for the shelter. As we wrote our realist tale, we heard from the director of Daily Refuge that United Way had passed a preliminary review to double their gift to the shelter, only to be rescinded later. (p. 486)

Same Story, Different Genres

Miller et al. (1998) insightfully rendered their fieldwork account through three different genres. But other possibilities exist. Imagine if their fieldwork could also have been represented through poetry, as a documentary film, as a series of monologues and scenes for the stage, or as a photographic exhibit of images taken by the homeless participants themselves. The genre(s) you select for telling your research story should be the most effective one(s) for presenting an account that is persuasive yet provocative, emotionally rich yet factually grounded, and analytically rigorous yet elegantly presented.

Overall, what were the lessons learned by Miller et al. (1998) through this soup kitchen fieldwork and writing experience?

We learned that research is dynamic rather than static, causing ethnographers to reflect on how they write and present their studies to different audiences. This raises the question of whether the tale should change or should remain the same after retelling it to different audiences. Our retelling represents further data analysis, completed after we left the field. We believe our evolving tales provide a more richly textured portrait of the soup kitchen and guests, developed through multiple layers of analysis and perspectives. (p. 489)

We recommend that if you ever feel stuck with your writing, explore how the material at hand can be approached through a different genre. If your descriptive or realistic prose seems static, explore writing the passage confessionally and/or critically.

You have *choices* about the voice, genre, and stance of your report, and they need to be made purposefully and strategically. Sometimes, these issues become clear only after you have looked at some first-draft material. Get feedback and revision recommendations of your drafts from trusted colleagues with strong editorial skills and/ or from the intended recipients of the report. Bottom line: As much as possible, try not to be boring.

Formats and Structures

Careful description of the settings, people, and events is one of the main contributions of qualitative research. A good case history, by definition, must trace the flow of events over time. But such descriptions also have an *analytic* and *interpretive* purpose: to illuminate the constant, influential, and determining factors shaping the course of events and what it all means in the grander scheme of things.

Our main findings entail themes and constructs derived from the interactions between settings and people. In our own work, we've aimed to keep the chronology of events conceptually tied to variables emerging during interim analyses. For example, an emerging theme of "distrust of school officials by parents" may be derived from many episodes, public interactions, and private conversations—each with clear antecedents and consequences. The sense and coherence of these happenings, seen over time, is the grounding of the emerging theme. What it all means in the grander scheme of things is the irony of how our educational system may be failing to connect with the very people whom schools were created to serve.

Stories without variables do not tell us enough about the meaning and larger import of what we are seeing. Variables without stories are ultimately abstract and unconvincing—which may explain certain scrupulous rules for reporting quantitative studies, as well as the familiar comment "I couldn't really understand the numbers until I looked at the open-ended data."

Is there an optimum balance of stories and variables?

Traditional Presentation Modes

In this book, we stress two basic modes of presentation: text (with varying degrees of detail and organization), associated with organized displays in either matrix or network form. We think these modes are an enormous help in drawing coherent meaning from data and in confirming and deepening conclusions. By extension, they communicate clearly and well to readers.

But text does not have to be sterile. Qualitative researchers characteristically employ a range of literary devices. The description of the study's context is often rendered in quasi-pictorial form ("Yellow Falls lies at the end of a fertile valley, with small farms in its hollow and a creek meandering through the flood plain"). Important events or interactions may be reported in the form of vignettes ("This happened near the entrance to the outpatient clinic, when the cardiologist, two residents, and several patients were within earshot."). Many codes—especially pattern codes—are captured in the form of metaphors ("dwindling efforts" and "interactive glue"), where they can synthesize large blocks of data in a single trope. Metaphor, irony, and metonymy—even comedy, satire, tragedy, and farce—are seen as workable tools. But qualitative research reports are both something more and something less than traditional fictional literature. Our tropes are about something that we have realistic reasons for believing in. Warrants are behind our assertions and claims.

How are qualitative reports organized? Not surprisingly, there are no standard setups, except at a very general level. Each researcher must craft a report structure that fits the intellectual and local context of the particular study, combined with the in-house requirements of a journal editor or book publisher. A study's research questions, context, and audiences drive the design of reports more than any general canon could. Nevertheless, we humbly offer what we feel are minimum guidelines for a traditional qualitative report:

1. The report should tell us what the study was about or came to be about.

2. It should communicate a clear sense of the social and historical context of the setting(s) where the data were collected.

3. It should provide us with what Erickson (1986) calls the "natural history of the inquiry," so we see clearly what was done, by whom, and how. More deeply than

in a sheer "methods" account, we should see how key concepts emerged over time, which variables appeared and disappeared, and which categories led to important insights.

4. A good report should provide basic data, preferably in focused form (vignettes, organized narratives, or data displays), so that the reader can, in parallel with the researcher, draw warranted conclusions. (This is very different from what has been called the "sprinkling" function of anecdotes in text, where the researcher hunts for items that will entertain or convince the reader and then "sprinkles" them here and there as needed. Conclusions without data are a sort of oxymoron.)

5. Finally, researchers should address the conclusions' broader meaning in the worlds of ideas and action they affect. (This guideline brings us full circle to the "goodness" questions we explored in Chapter 11.)

Progressive Presentation Modes

Reports can go beyond words. We've restricted our analytic and presentation modes in this book, but many qualitative researchers use presentation display modes of drawings and digital photographs. Some have created studio art installations of their research, and others have posted online digital video recordings of their fieldwork and findings. There are other qualitative report possibilities such as poetry, ethnodramas, novels, and even musical compositions. Such accounts are typically "larger than life." Like all good fiction, they make these accounts compelling to the reader because they describe situations that are more extreme or archetypal than most instances of daily life. Yet coherence, plausibility, compellingness, and novelty are not enough to ensure the goodness of a progressive qualitative report. These progressive presentation modes must, first and foremost, be excellent artistic products; but they must also be based on excellent research. The trick is to find a proper balance between the aesthetic and the academic.

As an example of arts-based research, Saldaña (2008b) composed an *autoethnodrama*—a hybrid research genre with a blend of autobiography, ethnography, and dramatic playwriting. (Other terms and variants for this genre include "performance ethnography," "nonfiction playwriting," and "documentary theatre.") *Second Chair* is an extended monologue for the stage performed by Saldaña himself as a one-man show for audiences of qualitative researchers, music educators, and theatre practitioners. The piece takes the spectator back to his high school band days and his attempt to become a "first chair" musician—an honor designated to the best player of an instrumental section. The small cultural details of a specific time and a specific place are recollected to give the audience member a sense of—like a traditional ethnography—"being there." Notice how theatrical devices such as actor movements, props, sounds, and set pieces are notated in the italicized stage directions:

JOHNNY: In Austin, Texas, in the early 1970s, there were three things that ruled: cowboys, football, and marching band. Competition was drilled into our spirits:

(fist in the air, chanting loudly, as if at a pep rally)

We are great! Better than you! We are the class of seventy-two!

(cheers)

Texas was the biggest state in the union.

(aside)

Actually, Alaska was the biggest state in the union. But to Texans, Alaska didn't really count.

(picks up a baton, moves a music stand downstage center)

And with being the biggest came egos to match.

(he taps the music stand with his baton, raises it sharply and scans an imaginary band in front of him; he swings the baton to the downbeat and conducts; W. Francis McBeth's Battaglia music up)

Conducting us masterfully with his baton was Mr. Garcia—a great band director who knew his art, taught with passion, demanded nothing less than precision and perfection, and shaped us into the best musicians we could be. And yes, when he got pissed off at our sloppy playing, Mr. Garcia would throw his baton angrily to the floor!

(he throws baton down; music stops suddenly)

Then all of us would freeze and stare at him in frightened silence as he scowled.

(he scowls as Mr. Garcia, glaring at the band in front of him; gestures as if to say, 'What the hell's wrong with you?!'; picks up baton)

Well, there was no time to fool around. Sweepstakes, all-state, first ratings, blue ribbons, gold medals—that's what it was all about. In those days, we weren't told to "do your best," we were told to "be the best." And it was not only that way with the entire band, it was that way with me. Young men are taught to strive, to accomplish, to achieve success, to be number one, to be—first chair. (pp. 180–181)

Saldaña advocates that ethnographic-based stage performance is also a form of research display, for it exhibits through theatrical media the stories and insights of the researcher and research participants.

Though progressive forms of qualitative inquiry are not the primary focus of this book's purpose, we acknowledge that they can be just as revelatory and rigorous as more traditional approaches. See Knowles and Cole (2008), Leavy (2009), Norris (2009), and Saldaña (2011a) for more on these innovative arts-based genres.

On Theses and Dissertations

One of the primary readers of this book is the graduate student. So we offer a few recommendations for guidance through the qualitative thesis and dissertation document process and refer you to the Appendix for excellent titles on writing up qualitative research.

First, write at least one page a day, and in a year, you'll have a draft or two—if not the finished document itself. This sounds like a relatively simple and simplistic formula, but you'd be surprised how many do not follow it and end up spending 4 to 6 years writing (or mostly procrastinating) a work that could have been completed in 1 to 2 years. Granted, fieldwork has to be completed before your conclusions can be confidently asserted, but a good amount of the document can be drafted during the prospectus and fieldwork stages. One page a day may motivate you to continue and write two additional pages, or even five or more. But hold yourself to one page a day *minimum*.

Second, don't assume that you have to write chapter 1 first, then chapters 2, 3, 4, and so on. Write on whatever can be written about when you sit in front of a monitor, regardless of where it appears in the document. If you're in the middle of fieldwork and caught up on your transcription work, you can tighten up your literature review section. If you're tired and feel unmotivated to write, then start assembling or cleaning up your references or bibliography. Imagine yourself as a time traveler, who can jump back and forth from one portion of your document to another as the need arises. Each day, write on whatever can be written about.

Third, create the template or shell of the document itself in finished form, with strict adherence to the format manual guidelines prescribed by your college or university. Saldaña tells his students, "Make your draft *look* like a dissertation, and it'll start *feeling* like a dissertation." Creating the front matter, such as the cover page, abstract, table of contents/figures, and acknowledgments pages (even if there's nothing below the headings at these early stages) gets you prepared for what eventually needs to go in them. When you start separate files for your chapter drafts, set the page margins, spacing, fonts, page numbers (one of the most frequently missing items), and all other technical format matters from the very start. What you actually write on the pages can be in first draft or messy prose as a start, but it's the shell or template for the document that should always be in finished format.

Fourth, have a separate meeting and conversation with your mentor or supervisor after the prospectus has been approved on writing—not necessarily on your research topic or fieldwork matters, but on *writing* itself. It's assumed that the supervisor has written a comparable document of some type, plus other works such as articles, books, and so on. Discuss the writing process itself—personal ways of working, dilemmas, self-discipline, emotional roadblocks, problem solving, and so on. Sharing stories about the craft and art of writing with a mentor or peer group demystifies the process and creates a sense of community about what is primarily a solitary act.

Fifth, stick to deadlines. That may sound like obvious advice, but not everyone adheres to it. A recent televised news story reported that "personal drama" was the major reason for the loss of a worker's productivity. And as we reflect on that reason, it seems to apply to college and university students as well. Personal drama (e.g., extended illness, caretaking responsibilities, relationship difficulties, financial matters, and emotional upheaval) interferes with fieldwork, writing, and meeting deadlines. Certainly, each individual should decide what gets personal priority during those inconvenient and tumultuous periods of daily living. Sometimes, family needs to come first; and keeping a roof over your head is vital for other good things to happen. But if you want to meet thesis or dissertation deadlines, try as much as possible to eliminate the personal drama—yours or someone else's—from your life. Having a detailed, long-range calendar of due dates for tasks (e.g., prospectus approved, IRB [institutional review board] application submitted, fieldwork completed, first draft of chapter 1 completed) and fiercely sticking to it also helps.

This final piece of advice is directed toward thesis and dissertation supervisors: Conduct monthly reality checks with your students. Research suggests that students are more likely to "deliver" their work (even late work) when their teachers give the impression "I've got my eyes on you, and I'm watching you like a hawk." Sometimes, we assume that the master's or doctoral student is mature enough to work independently and responsibly without our intervention and to successfully complete major tasks such as a thesis or dissertation by an expected deadline. But some students need to be periodically reminded by a supervisor, "I've got my eyes on you, and I'm watching you like a hawk." It adds a little pressure and motivation to make progress and keeps lines of communication open. These reality checks can be as simple as a phone call (preferred), e-mail, or submission of a one-page summary progress report at the end of each month.

See the Appendix for recommended writing references, particularly Harry F. Wolcott's (2009) *Writing Up Qualitative Research* and Alison B. Miller's (2009) *Finish Your Dissertation Once and For All!: How to Overcome Psychological Barriers, Get Results, and Move On With Your Life.*

Closure and Transition

The vast majority of graduate students, scholars, and research practitioners can write *competently*. But only a few individuals from these groups write *well*. We advocate that if you want to become a better writer of qualitative research, then read a lot of it—with conscious attunement to the author's word choices, sentence structures, overall organization, report genre, and general style. The purpose is not to imitate other outstanding writers' ways of documenting social life but to acquaint yourself with a broad spectrum of possibilities for reporting qualitatively.

The final chapter now follows. It brings closure to the book by recapping the qualitative research process and offering final strands of advice.

Closure

Chapter Summary

This final chapter reviews the book's qualitative analytic methods through a network model, then offers closing reflections and advice for researchers.

Contents

Qualitative Analysis at a Glance
Reflections
Final Advice

Qualitative Analysis at a Glance

Display 13.1, adapted from training workshops we (Miles and Huberman) have led, pulls together all of the aspects of the approach to qualitative data analysis we have explored in this book. The purpose is to provide an integrated overview. As with causal networks, it helps to walk through the figure, piece by piece. The time dimension, for once, goes vertically.

Display 13.1

Overview of Qualitative Data Analysis Processes

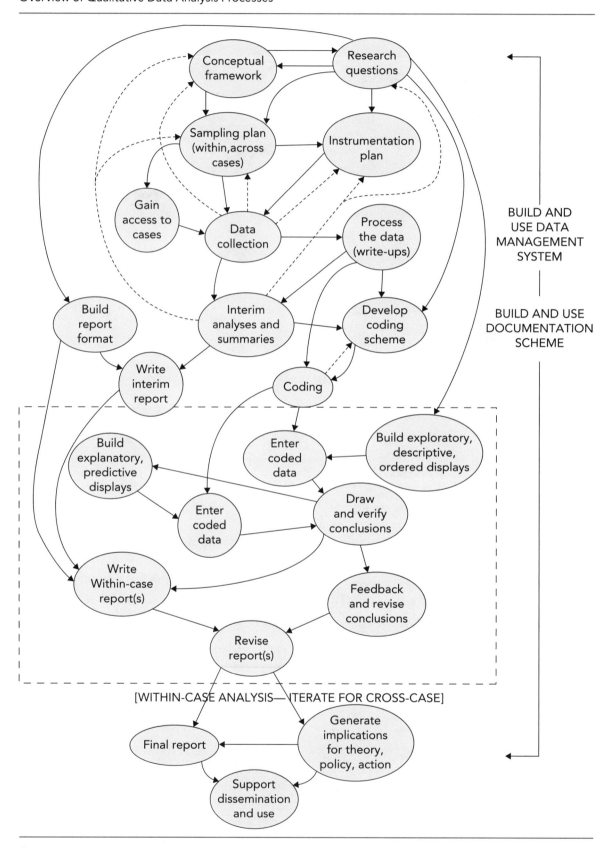

BUILD AND USE DATA MANAGEMENT SYSTEM

BUILD AND USE DOCUMENTATION SCHEME

[WITHIN-CASE ANALYSIS—ITERATE FOR CROSS-CASE]

Source: Miles, M. B., & Huberman, A. M. (1994). *Qualitative data analysis: An expanded sourcebook* (2nd ed.). Thousand Oaks, CA: Sage Publications.

Starting at the top, we see the early mutual influence of conceptual framework and research questions. Both lead to plans for sampling (within and across cases) and instrumentation. Once the sampling plan is clear, access to cases starts and data collection begins.

During this time, it's a good idea to build a well-defined data management system, which will be used—with evolutionary changes—throughout the project. We also advocate building a documentation scheme for regular tracking of project data analysis activities.

The first experiences of data collection nearly always have back effects (dashed lines), which induce reconsideration not only of sampling and instrumentation but also of the conceptual framework itself. Initial processing of the data often leads to interim summaries of various kinds, which also have effects back to the sampling and instrumentation approaches being taken as well as, more conceptually, to the framework and the research questions.

The initial coding scheme is usually influenced by the research questions, but it develops and iterates steadily as further coding is carried out. Interim analyses also make a clear contribution here. If interim reports are contemplated, a format is designed at this point, and the interim summaries are fed into it.

After assuming a body of coded data (not necessarily complete or full), the next move is into within-case analysis. The general strategy is to build, first, *exploratory*, *descriptive*, and *ordered* display formats designed to answer the research questions. Coded data are entered and, from them, conclusions of a descriptive sort are drawn and verified. With those conclusions in hand, *explanatory* (and, if needed, *predictive*) displays can be built, coded data can be entered, and explanatory conclusions can be drawn.

Both descriptive and explanatory conclusions can be fed back for verification and revision. By now, a format for within-site reporting, based as always on the research questions, as well as on the interim results, has been prepared. Within-case reports are written and then revised on the basis of respondent feedback.

If more than one case is included, this entire cycle of within-case analysis is repeated to draw cross-case conclusions. These conclusions and the within-case results go into the final report, which will include implications for theory, policy, and action. Depending on the study's audiences and intentions, some degree of support for dissemination and use of the findings will be provided.

Any particular project will always loop among the nodes of Display 13.1 in idiosyncratic ways. The issue is to be aware of where you are in the flow right now and where you want to be by a later date.

Reflections

Writing and revising this book has been a long, sometimes arduous, and always fascinating journey. We have encountered many new and thoughtful treatments of the core issues of qualitative data analysis. The experience has reconfirmed the old saying that trying to teach something deepens your understanding of it—as the folk saying goes, "To teach is to learn twice." The process of clarifying, reformulating, and synthesizing the ideas in this third edition has extended and enriched our thinking about qualitative data analysis methods.

Throughout the book, we have tried to stay practical, "talking aloud" as we went, offering both methods and advice. Some qualitative data analysis texts tend toward the abstract, with brief examples that always seem to work out clearly, even effortlessly. Yet when you actually come to grips with collecting and analyzing real-life data, things seldom work out that way. Research-in-use is almost always more messy, disjointed, and perverse than research-in-theory, and we have tried to take careful account of that fact. In short, *doing* qualitative analysis is the way you get better at it—and we believe that holds true not just for novices and new entrants to qualitative work but also for seasoned researchers.

We believe that methodological quagmires, mazes, and dead ends are not necessarily a product of researcher incapacity but of qualitative data themselves. Like the phenomena they mirror, they are usually complex, ambiguous, and sometimes downright contradictory. Doing qualitative analysis means living for as long as possible with that complexity and ambiguity, coming to terms with it, and passing on your conclusions to the reader in a form that clarifies and deepens understanding. It's not surprising that the mechanics of analysis seem formidable or elusive even to experienced analysts—and that researchers have often shied away from making them fully explicit.

It's right to say that qualitative data analysis is a craft—one that carries its own disciplines. There are many ways of getting analyses "right"—precise, trustworthy, compelling, and credible—and they cannot be wholly predicted in advance.

We've found that making the steps of analysis explicit makes them less formidable and uncertain and more manageable. The core requisites for qualitative analysis seem to be a little creativity, systematic doggedness, some good conceptual sensibilities, and cognitive flexibility—the capacity to rapidly undo your way of construing or transforming the data and to try another, more promising tack. In revising this book, we have continued our goal from the first and second editions: to create a self-help book for researchers, rather than coining a new, only remotely accessible set of methods.

We also don't think that good qualitative analysis necessarily calls for formal prerequisites (e.g., long ethnographic experience, knowledge of scientific logic, and a deep background in philosophy, ontology, and epistemology). Those are all useful tools and can empower the analyses you are interested in doing. But working without them, at least initially, is not fatal—and can help you see what else you need to know to do good analysis.

Qualitative researchers come in many varieties and flavors. The views we have expressed will almost certainly be seen by some of our colleagues as narrow-minded, perhaps even outdated. We don't want to be seen as pretending to be ideology-free, that our biases are the noblest, or that we are just being old-fashioned, plain folks—pragmatic and practical without understanding the issues.

To those who believe that analysis is an intuitive, nearly incommunicable act, we have insisted that analyses can be workably replicated and that to be taken seriously, you should be fully explicit about what is being done at each step of the way.

To those who believe that qualitative data analysis requires years of training and apprenticeship, we have offered an expanded set of working methods that can be tried on for size and adapted or modified for particular projects—all in the service of a stronger methodology.

To those enamored of long narrative accounts as the sole route to understanding, we have counterposed the idea of focused, organized displays that permit systematic analyses and enhance confidence in findings.

To those who believe that nowadays we can only put forth our ambiguities, uncertainties, and unanswered questions as conclusions, we acknowledge the social complexities of contemporary life, but we also emphasize that the purpose of research is ultimately to reveal, clarify, and construct significant awareness, understanding, and meaning.

To those colleagues who are pleased with what we have done in this third edition, we express our gratitude, along with our hope for continuous testing and revision of these methods, so that we all can advance our craft.

Final Advice

Throughout the book, we've provided detailed advice on a method-by-method basis. Here, we offer some generalized last words of encouragement to our colleagues, of whatever persuasion.

Think display. Given a research question or a puzzling issue in a qualitative database, consider what forms of display—matrices and networks or other forms—are most likely to bring together relevant, transformed data in a way that will permit good conclusion drawing—and strengthening of those conclusions.

Be open to invention. The wide range of methods we and many others have created reinforces our belief that the repertoire of useful displays is very large and, like other collections, constantly expanding. Don't shy away from more progressive forms of data display such as poetry, painting, and performance.

Expect iteration. The modes of analysis we've advocated throughout the book involve shuttling among data condensation, display, and preliminary and verified conclusions. New data enter the picture, new display forms evolve, and conclusions get reshaped and revised. All of these will have back effects on each other, effects that are crucial to the evolving analysis.

Seek formalization, and distrust it. We have steadily emphasized a structured approach to drawing meaning from qualitative data. Becoming more systematic, whatever your epistemological position, strikes us as a priority for those who wish to advance analysis methodology. Of course, increased formalization carries its own risks: narrowness, overconfidence, obsessiveness, and blindness to the emergent—and the risk of arrogant orthodoxy. Patience, trying to do things better, humility, sharing, and accepting multiple perspectives are more like it.

Entertain mixed models. We have sought to make a virtue of avoiding polarization, polemics, and life at the extremes. Quantitative and qualitative inquiry can support and inform each other. Narratives and variable-driven analyses need to interpenetrate and inform each other. Realists, idealists, and critical theorists can do better by incorporating other ideas than by remaining pure. Think of it as hybrid vigor, or eclectic rigor.

Stay self-aware. Our own experience showed us vividly how useful it is to maintain a part of your attention on the processes involved in analysis—from the selection of research questions through coding, the creation of displays, data entry, conclusion drawing, and verification. Only through such sustained awareness can regular self-correction occur—not just during specific analysis episodes but over time, as the methods themselves iterate and develop.

Share methodological learnings. The methodological sections of most reports of qualitative studies are still thin. Articles focusing directly on analysis issues and approaches are emerging but are still relatively few in number. We believe that anyone who wants to advance the craft of qualitative analysis owes it to colleagues to communicate what they have learned to others. We advise stronger methodological emphasis in articles and books drawn from qualitative data and encourage reports of training methods in courses and workshops that have successfully expanded analysis skills.

In sum, we hope that more and more qualitative researchers will tell each other, concretely and specifically, just how they went about it and what they learned. Perhaps, we can all be as vivid and rich in describing our own work as we are in describing the inner and outer lives of the people we study.

Appendix

An Annotated Bibliography of Qualitative Research Resources

This Appendix includes a selected listing of recommend titles for learning more about qualitative inquiry. It is limited to English-language works and primarily monographs. We cannot possibly include everything in print and online; we provide only a representative sample of resources.

Reference Texts for Qualitative Inquiry

Bothamley, J. (1993). *Dictionary of theories*. London, England: Gale Research International. Reference guide to theories from all disciplines, including the arts, sociology, psychology, history, and the natural sciences—useful for terminology reference, definitions, and associated names.

Given, L. M. (Ed.). (2008). *The SAGE encyclopedia of qualitative research methods*. Thousand Oaks, CA: Sage. Superior reference for summaries of philosophical and methodological principles of qualitative inquiry.

Schwandt, T. A. (2007). *Dictionary of qualitative inquiry* (3rd ed.). Thousand Oaks, CA: Sage. Extended dictionary of terms in the field; many entries include origins of the terms, applications across various social science fields, and references for additional investigation.

Quantitative and Qualitative Research Design (General Textbooks)

Creswell, J. W. (2014). *Research design: Qualitative, quantitative, and mixed methods approaches* (4th ed.). Thousand Oaks, CA: Sage. Excellent overview of all three paradigms for the beginning researcher.

Mertens, D. M. (2009). *Research and evaluation in education and psychology: Integrating diversity with quantitative, qualitative, and mixed methods* (3rd ed.). Thousand Oaks, CA: Sage. Introductory text that surveys various approaches to research but focuses more on the quantitative approach; compares various paradigms (emancipatory, feminist, etc.) and offers detailed guidelines for research design or evaluation of research.

Wilkinson, D., & Birmingham, P. (2003). *Using research instruments: A guide for researchers*. London: Routledge. User-friendly introduction to techniques such as survey construction, interview questions, focus group facilitation, participant observation, content analysis, and so on.

Qualitative Research (General Textbooks)

Creswell, J. W. (2013). *Qualitative inquiry and research design: Choosing among five approaches* (3rd ed.). Thousand Oaks, CA: Sage. Describes and compares the unique features of biography, phenomenology, grounded theory, ethnography, and case study research; includes article examples.

Glesne, C. (2011). *Becoming qualitative researchers: An introduction* (4th ed.). Boston: Pearson Education. Excellent overview and introductory text on the nature and process of qualitative research/ethnography.

Lofland, J., Snow, D. A., Anderson, L., & Lofland, L. H. (2006). *Analyzing social settings: A guide to qualitative observation and analysis* (4th ed.). Belmont: Wadsworth. Highly systematic techniques for qualitative studies; a dense but comprehensive "how to" text.

Marshall, C., & Rossman, G. B. (2011). *Designing qualitative research* (5th ed.). Thousand Oaks, CA: Sage. Overview of considerations for the preparatory phases of qualitative studies; written for doctoral students; provides numerous illustrative vignettes.

Mason, J. (2002). *Qualitative researching*. London: Sage. Overview of qualitative research based on ontological, epistemological, and methodological decision making; includes a series of questions to consider during all phases of research.

Maxwell, J. A. (2013). *Qualitative research design: An interactive approach* (3rd ed.). Thousand Oaks, CA: Sage. Particularly thorough book for preparing research proposals by considering how research design elements link together.

Richards, L., & Morse, J. M. (2013). *Readme first for a user's guide to qualitative methods* (3rd ed.). Thousand Oaks, CA: Sage. Introduction to principles of qualitative research for phenomenology, ethnography, and grounded theory; includes an accompanying CD-ROM demonstration disk and tutorial for the analytic software NVivo.

Saldaña, J. (2011). *Fundamentals of qualitative research*. New York: Oxford University Press. A survey of qualitative research methods with an emphasis on qualitative data analysis and writing styles for qualitative reports.

Stake, R. E. (2010). *Qualitative research: Studying how things work*. New York: Guilford Press. Introduces global principles of qualitative inquiry, with a focus on interpretation and assertion development.

Tracy, S. J. (2013). *Qualitative research methods: Collecting evidence, crafting analysis, communicating impact*. Oxford: Wiley-Blackwell. An excellent introductory methods text with multiple student exercises and ancillary materials.

Mixed-Methods Research

Creswell, J. W., & Plano Clark, V. L. (2011). *Designing and conducting mixed methods research* (2nd ed.). Thousand Oaks, CA: Sage. Primer on mixing quantitative and qualitative paradigms and data in research studies; includes sample articles.

Morrison, K. (2009). *Causation in educational research*. London: Routledge. Superior overview of the intricacies and nuances of causation in both quantitative and qualitative research; recommended for researchers from all fields of study.

Tashakkori, A., & Teddlie, C. (1998). *Mixed methodology: Combining qualitative and quantitative approaches*. Thousand Oaks, CA: Sage. Examines both approaches through systematic profiles; includes theory and examples of how qualitative and quantitative data can be used in the same study to strengthen answers to research questions.

Tashakkori, A., & Teddlie, C. (Eds.). (2010). *The SAGE handbook of mixed methods in social and behavioral research* (2nd ed.). Thousand Oaks, CA: Sage. Extensive chapters on the current trend in mixing the quantitative and qualitative paradigms for research.

Thomas, R. M. (2003). *Blending qualitative and quantitative research methods in theses and dissertations.* Thousand Oaks, CA: Corwin Press. Overview of methods from both paradigms, but primarily a collection of brief prospectus examples from 20 student works that illustrate the blending of data forms.

Methodological Foundations/Handbooks of Qualitative Research

Denzin, N. K., & Lincoln, Y. S. (Eds.). (2011). *The SAGE handbook of qualitative research* (4th ed.). Thousand Oaks, CA: Sage. A collection of chapters on various topics of qualitative research by selected experts in the field.

Ellingson, L. L. (2009). *Engaging crystallization in qualitative research: An introduction.* Thousand Oaks, CA: Sage. Strategies for blending two or more approaches to qualitative inquiry, ranging from arts-based approaches to traditional constructivist methodologies (e.g., grounded theory).

Hesse-Biber, S. N., & Leavy, P. (2008). *Handbook of emergent methods.* New York: Guilford Press. Chapters on new methods of qualitative and selected quantitative inquiry at the beginning of the 21st century, including research with media, mixed methods, documents, and so on.

Lincoln, Y. S., & Denzin, N. K. (2003). *Turning points in qualitative research: Tying knots in a handkerchief.* Walnut Creek, CA: AltaMira Press. Collection of seminal essays and articles in the field of qualitative research by writers such as Clifford Geertz, Margaret Mead, Dwight Conquergood, and others.

Lincoln, Y. S., & Guba, E. G. (1985). *Naturalistic inquiry.* Beverley Hills, CA: Sage. Detailed argument on the naturalistic paradigm as a valid framework for analysis; includes methods for establishing trustworthiness and audits.

Packer, M. J. (2011). *The science of qualitative research.* New York: Cambridge University Press. A title on the ontologies and epistemologies of qualitative inquiry; extensive scholarship and overview of knowledge construction.

Pascale, C.-M. (2011). *Cartographies of knowledge: Exploring qualitative epistemologies.* Thousand Oaks, CA: Sage. Overview of theoretical and historical foundations that shape current practices of qualitative research; focuses on analytic induction, symbolic interaction, and ethnomethodology.

Symbolic Interactionism

Blumer, H. (1969). *Symbolic interactionism: Perspective and method.* Englewood Cliffs, NJ: Prentice Hall. Collection of essays by Blumer detailing the interpretive process of human and group action, labeled "symbolic interactionism"; a seminal method for later research methodologists.

Denzin, N. K. (1992). *Symbolic interactionism and cultural studies*. Cambridge, MA: Blackwell. Commentary and critique on proponents and opponents of symbolic interactionism; chapter 6, "Interactionist Cultural Criticism," has applicability to arts and multicultural researchers.

Prus, R. C. (1996). *Symbolic interaction and ethnographic research: Intersubjectivity and the study of human lived experience*. New York: SUNY Press. Detailed explanations and approach to symbolic interactionism and its function in ethnography; excellent discussion and outline of social processes and studying emotions in sociological research.

Ethnography/Anthropology

Angrosino, M. V. (2002). *Doing cultural anthropology: Projects for ethnographic data collection*. Prospect Heights, IL: Waveland Press. Excellent primer on ethnographic data collection, with various projects for individuals and groups.

Bernard, H. R. (2011). *Research methods in anthropology: Qualitative and quantitative approaches* (5th ed.). Walnut Creek, CA: AltaMira Press. Reader-friendly and exhaustive overview of research methods in both paradigms; more for advanced researchers with a focus on traditional anthropological fieldwork.

Brown, I. C. (1963). *Understanding other cultures*. Englewood Cliffs: Prentice Hall. A layperson's introduction to anthropology; despite the early publication date, the book has a remarkable timelessness; surveys basic human constructs such as religion, arts, kinship, values, work, and so on.

Fetterman, D. M. (2010). *Ethnography: Step by step* (3rd ed.). Thousand Oaks, CA: Sage. Excellent overview of methods and techniques involved with field research from an ethnographic approach; includes information on computer utilization, websites, and data management.

Galman, S. C. (2007). *Shane, the lone ethnographer: A beginner's guide to ethnography*. Thousand Oaks, CA: AltaMira Press. Humorous cartoon drawing overview of a graduate student learning how to conduct an ethnography.

Geertz, C. (1973). *The interpretation of cultures*. New York: Basic Books. Seminal essays on ethnographic writing in anthropology, including "Thick Description: Toward an Interpretive Theory of Culture," and "Deep Play: Notes on a Balinese Cockfight."

Geertz, C. (1983). *Local knowledge: Further essays in interpretive anthropology*. New York: Basic Books. Chapters 1 to 7 present intriguing essays on topics such as "blurred genres," "common sense," and "art" as culturally constructed systems.

Hammersley, M. (1992). *What's wrong with ethnography?* New York: Routledge. Essays on methodological questions and issues about validity, generalizability, quantitative vs. qualitative, and so on, in ethnographic practice; requires reader background experience in ethnography.

Hammersley, M., & Atkinson, P. (2007). *Ethnography: Principles in practice* (3rd ed.). London: Routledge. A distinctively U.K. approach to the research genre; rigorous and rooted in traditional approaches.

Handwerker, W. P. (2001). *Quick ethnography*. Walnut Creek, CA: AltaMira Press. Qualitative and quantitative methods for short-term ethnographic work; systematic procedures for extracting variability of cultural variables.

Madden, R. (2010). *Being ethnographic: A guide to the theory and practice of ethnography*. London: Sage. Excellent conceptual and practical overview of foundations for ethnographic fieldwork; not many examples of "how to" but a solid narrative overview of "how" and "why."

McCurdy, D. W., Spradley, J. P., & Shandy, D. J. (2005). *The cultural experience: Ethnography in complex society* (2nd ed.). Long Grove, IL: Waveland Press. For undergraduate ethnography courses, provides an overview of ethnographic interviewing and taxonomic domain development; includes students' sample reports.

Norris, J., Sawyer, R. D., & Lund, D. (Eds.). (2012). *Duoethnography: Dialogic methods for social, health, and educational research.* Walnut Creek, CA: Left Coast Press. A collaborative methodology in which two or more researchers exchange perceptions of personal life histories to better understand a social phenomenon.

Pink, S. (2007). *Doing visual ethnography* (2nd ed.). London: Sage. An overview of the use of photography, video, and hypermedia in ethnographic fieldwork for representation and presentation.

Sunstein, B. S., & Chiseri-Strater, E. (2012). *FieldWorking: Reading and writing research* (4th ed.). Boston: Bedford/St. Martin's. User-friendly introduction to ethnographic fieldwork; includes numerous student samples of writing.

Thomas, J. (1993). *Doing critical ethnography.* Newbury Park, CA: Sage. Monograph on critical approaches to qualitative research to examine power structures, race relationships, and so on, for social change.

Wiseman, B., & Groves, J. (1997). *Lévi-Strauss for beginners.* London: Icon Books. An introduction to the major cultural theories by one of the 20th century's most noted structural anthropologists.

Wolcott, H. F. (2005). *The art of fieldwork* (2nd ed.). Walnut Creek: AltaMira Press. An overview of fundamental principles and sage advice on educational anthropology from one of the leaders in the field.

Wolcott, H. F. (2008). *Ethnography: A way of seeing* (2nd ed.). Walnut Creek, CA: AltaMira Press. For those with some ethnographic background, a foundational text on the purposes and charges of ethnography; superior chapter (chapter 11) on the concept of culture.

Grounded Theory

Birks, M., & Mills, J. (2011). *Grounded theory: A practical guide.* London: Sage. General descriptive overview of the method; includes a few examples for guidance.

Bryant, A., & Charmaz, K. (2007). *The SAGE handbook of grounded theory.* London: Sage. Chapters on the nuances of grounded theory methodology; not for beginners of the method.

Charmaz, K. (2006). *Constructing grounded theory: A practical guide through qualitative analysis.* London: Sage. A clear and concise overview of grounded theory method; provides an excellent theoretical and explanatory overview of the classic procedures developed by Strauss, Glaser, and Corbin.

Clarke, A. E. (2005). *Situational analysis: Grounded theory after the postmodern turn.* Thousand Oaks, CA: Sage. Adaptation of grounded theory, which acknowledges the complexity and context of social process through the development of situational maps, charts, and graphics; extensive background on epistemological foundations for the method.

Corbin, J., & Strauss, A. L. (2007). *Basics of qualitative research: Techniques and procedures for developing grounded theory* (3rd ed.). Thousand Oaks, CA: Sage. The third edition does not systematically focus on techniques; it does, however, profile analytic memo writing extensively.

Glaser, B. G., & Strauss, A. L. (1967). *The discovery of grounded theory: Strategies for qualitative research*. Hawthorne, CA: Aldine de Gruyter. Premiere work on the constant-comparative method of data analysis to generate grounded theory.

Stern, P. N., & Porr, C. J. (2011). *Essentials of accessible grounded theory*. Walnut Creek, CA: Left Coast Press. An elegant summary and synthesis of "classic" Glaserian grounded theory.

Phenomenology

Brinkmann, S. (2012). *Qualitative inquiry in everyday life: Working with everyday life materials*. London: Sage. Fascinating self-exploration of and research about everyday experiences, including our interactions with humans, media, fiction, and artifacts.

Smith, J. A., Flowers, P., & Larkin, M. (2009). *Interpretative phenomenological analysis: Theory, method and research*. London: Sage. Interpretative phenomenological analysis from a psychological perspective; clear description of the origins and processes; includes sample studies that use interpretative phenomenological analysis.

van Manen, M. (1990). *Researching lived experience*. New York: SUNY Press. A classic of the field; focus is on phenomenology and its reporting, plus the purposes of this type of research, primarily in education.

Case Study Research

Denzin, N. K. (2001). *Interpretive interactionism* (2nd ed.). Thousand Oaks, CA: Sage. Methodology and methods for biographical research of an individual's epiphanies.

Stake, R. E. (1995). *The art of case study research*. Thousand Oaks, CA: Sage. "Artistic" approach to profiling the case study; a good introduction to the method.

Yin, R. K. (2014). *Case study research: Design and methods* (5th ed.). Thousand Oaks, CA: Sage. Overview of research design principles for case studies of individuals, organizations, and so on; somewhat positivist in its approach, but a good overview of the fundamentals of design and analysis.

Evaluation Research

Patton, M. Q. (2002). *Qualitative research and evaluation methods* (3rd ed.). Thousand Oaks, CA: Sage. Designed for evaluation research initially, now an excellent overview of paradigms, methods, and techniques for observation and interviews.

Patton, M. Q. (2008). *Utilization-focused evaluation* (4th ed.). Thousand Oaks, CA: Sage. Exhaustive resource for evaluation methods, especially for programs and organizations.

Wadsworth, Y. (2011). *Everyday evaluation on the run: The user-friendly introductory guide to effective evaluation* (3rd ed.). Walnut Creek, CA: Left Coast Press. A layperson's guide, but includes a broad overview of basics and models.

Autoethnography

Chang, H. (2008). *Autoethnography as method*. Walnut Creek, CA: Left Coast Press. Systematic approach to autoethnographic research; includes an excellent overview of cultural concepts.

Ellis, C., & Bochner, A. P. (Eds.). (1996). *Composing ethnography: Alternative forms of qualitative writing*. Walnut Creek, CA: AltaMira Press. Collection of autoethographies focusing on social issues such as domestic violence, bulemia, detoxification, and discrimination.

Poulos, C. N. (2009). *Accidental ethnography: An inquiry into family secrecy*. Walnut Creek, CA: Left Coast Press. Autoethnographic stories and writing prompts for personal and family history.

Spry, T. (2011). *Body, paper, stage: Writing and performing autoethnography*. Walnut Creek, CA: Left Coast Press. Selected works from Spry, plus theoretical and practical approaches to performance studies.

Narrative Inquiry

Clandinin, D. J., & Connelly, F. M. (2000). *Narrative inquiry: Experience and story in qualitative research*. San Francisco: Jossey-Bass. Methods of three-dimensional renderings of participants in narrative inquiry.

Gubrium, J. F., & Holstein, J. A. (2009). *Analyzing narrative reality*. Thousand Oaks, CA: Sage. Not a "how to" book, but an excellent overview of what to be aware of and look for when analyzing narrative texts from fieldwork.

Holstein, J. A., & Gubrium, J. F. (2012). *Varieties of narrative analysis*. Thousand Oaks, CA: Sage. Chapter collection of varied approaches to the analysis of narrative texts, ranging from mixed methods to psychological interpretations.

Riessman, C. K. (2008). *Narrative methods for the human sciences*. Thousand Oaks, CA: Sage. Not necessarily a "how to" text, but surveys with examples four major approaches to narrative analysis; contains representative examples about children and adolescents.

Discourse Analysis

Gee, J. P. (2011). *How to do discourse analysis: A toolkit*. New York: Routledge. A series of questions and perspectives to consider when analyzing language in documented data and narratives; considers aspects such as grammar, vocabulary, intertextuality, identity, politics, and so on.

Arts-Based Research

Ackroyd, J., & O'Toole, J. (2010). *Performing research: Tensions, triumphs and trade-offs of ethnodrama*. Stoke on Trent, England: Trentham Books. Treatise on the genre (terminology, ethics, representation, etc.) and six case studies of ethnodrama projects in Australia and Hong Kong.

Barone, T., & Eisner, E. W. (2012). *Arts based research*. Thousand Oaks, CA: Sage. Two pioneers in the genre offer methodological and aesthetic perspectives and criteria for this approach to qualitative inquiry.

Butler-Kisber, L. (2010). *Qualitative inquiry: Thematic, narrative and arts-informed perspectives*. London: Sage. Overview of various modalities of qualitative inquiry, including approaches such as narrative, phenomenology, collage, poetry, photography, and performance.

Denzin, N. K. (1997). *Interpretive ethnography: Ethnographic practices for the 21st century*. Thousand Oaks, CA: Sage. Inspirational reading about new, progressive forms of ethnography including performance texts, journalism, and poetics.

Eisner, E. W. (1993). *The enlightened eye: Qualitative inquiry and the enhancement of educational practice*. New York: Macmillan. An "artistic" approach to qualitative inquiry. Does not profile methods but provides an intriguing, commonsense approach to knowledge construction by the researcher.

Gergen, M. M., & Gergen, K. J. (2012). *Playing with purpose: Adventures in performative social science*. Walnut Creek, CA: Left Coast Press. Overview of arts-based modalities in qualitative inquiry—narrative, drama, visual art—and their theoretical groundings.

Janesick, V. J. (2011). *"Stretching" exercises for qualitative researchers* (3rd ed.). Thousand Oaks, CA: Sage. A series of arts-based exercises for honing observation, interview, and conceptualization skills of researchers.

Knowles, J. G., & Cole, A. L. (2008). *Handbook of the arts in qualitative research: Perspectives, methodologies, examples, and issues*. Thousand Oaks, CA: Sage. Collection of essays on arts-based research, including theatre.

Leavy, P. (2009). *Method meets art: Arts-based research practice*. New York: Guilford Press. Chapter overview of arts-based research techniques, with representative samples of the genre.

Madison, D. S., & Hamera, J. (2006). *The SAGE handbook of performance studies*. Thousand Oaks, CA: Sage. Collection of essays on the field of performance studies; includes a few good selections.

Nisbet, R. (1976). *Sociology as an art form*. New York: Oxford University Press. Comparison of how the fine arts, humanities, and sociology have historic parallels in paradigm development and conceptual approaches; also addresses modern parallels in the goals and functions of both disciplines.

Norris, J. (2010). *Playbuilding as qualitative research: A participatory arts-based approach*. Walnut Creek, CA: Left Coast Press. Norris examines how playbuilding original devised work both employs and serves as a qualitative research modality/genre.

Saldaña, J. (2005). *Ethnodrama: An anthology of reality theatre*. Walnut Creek, CA: AltaMira Press. Collection of nine examples of play scripts developed from qualitative and ethnographic research (interviews, participant observation).

Saldaña, J. (2011). *Ethnotheatre: Research from page to stage*. Walnut Creek, CA: Left Coast Press. A playwriting textbook for ethnodramatic forms of research representation and presentation; includes extensive bibliographies of plays, articles, media, and texts.

Action/Participatory Action Research

Altrichter, H., Posch, P., & Somekh, B. (1993). *Teachers investigate their work: An introduction to the methods of action research*. New York: Routledge. Superior text on action research; includes practical examples and techniques for generating a focal point and analyzing data.

Coghlan, D., & Brannick, T. (2010). *Doing action research in your own organization* (3rd ed.). London: Sage. Dense, but practical, manual on the logistics of action research in business and education; not much on data analysis, but superior foregrounding, especially on the human aspects of change.

Fox, M., Martin, P., & Green, G. (2007). *Doing practitioner research*. London: Sage. Superior overview of practitioner research for those in the service and helping professions; provides excellent foundations for clinical and educational research.

Hitchcock, G., & Hughes, D. (1995). *Research and the teacher: A qualitative introduction to school-based research* (2nd ed.). London: Routledge. General survey of how the teacher can also play the role of researcher in the classroom; examples tailored to the British school system, but the methods are universal.

Schön, D. A. (1983). *The reflective practitioner: How professionals think in action*. New York: Basic Books. Methodological basis of "reflection-in-action" in selected professions; describes the cognitive and communicative processes of problem solving; a foundational book for action researchers.

Stringer, E. T. (2007). *Action research* (3rd ed.). Thousand Oaks, CA: Sage. Detailed methods for community and collaborative research projects to improve or change existing social practices.

Thomas, R. M. (2005). *Teachers doing research: An introductory guidebook*. Boston: Pearson Education. General overview of teacher-as-researcher models in quantitative and qualitative studies; provides brush-stroke description and examples.

Wadsworth, Y. (2011). *Do it yourself social research* (3rd ed.). Walnut Creek, CA: Left Coast Press. An introductory overview of basic social research principles for community program evaluation.

Longitudinal/Life Course Research

Giele, J. Z., & Elder, G. H., Jr., (Eds.). (1998). *Methods of life course research: Qualitative and quantitative approaches*. Thousand Oaks, CA: Sage. Collection of essays on longitudinal (retrospective and prospective) research with individuals and populations; exceptional chapter by John Clausen, "Life Reviews and Life Stories."

Holstein, J. A., & Gubrium, J. F. (2000). *Constructing the life course* (2nd ed.). Dix Hills, NY: General Hall. Reconceptualizes for the reader how traditional life course constructs (cycles, development, stages, etc.) have been socially constructed and potentially misused for assessment in education and therapy.

McLeod, J., & Thomson, R. (2009). *Researching social change*. London: Sage. Complex but rich ways of researching change through ethnographic, longitudinal, oral history, and other methods.

Saldaña, J. (2003). *Longitudinal qualitative research: Analyzing change through time*. Walnut Creek, CA: AltaMira Press. Methods book on long-term fieldwork and data analysis; uses three education studies as examples throughout the text.

Sociology (General Textbooks)

Charon, J. M. (2001). *Ten questions: A sociological perspective* (4th ed.). Belmont, CA: Wadsworth Thomson Learning. Superior overview of basic sociological principles and theories, such as social reality, inequality, ethnocentrism, social change, and so on.

Churton, M., & Brown, A. (2010). *Theory and method* (2nd ed.). New York: Palgrave Macmillan. From sociology, an excellent overview of traditional, modern, and postmodern theories of the field.

Cuzzort, R. P., & King, E. W. (2002). *Social thought into the twenty-first century* (6th ed.). Orlando, FL: Harcourt. An overview of the major works of 17 prominent social thinkers, such as Marx, Goffman, Freud, and Mead; each chapter profiles the writer's prominent theories through everyday examples.

Gabler, J. (2010). *Sociology for dummies*. Hoboken, NJ: Wiley. A thorough yet readable overview of sociological principles, writers, and concepts.

Psychology and Qualitative Research

Camic, P. M., Rhodes, J. E., & Yardley, L. (Eds.). (2003). *Qualitative research in psychology: Expanding perspectives in methodology and design*. Washington, DC: American Psychological Association. Chapter collection of qualitative methods for psychological research, therapy, and so on; good overview of some approaches commonly referenced in the area.

Forrester, M. A. (Ed.). (2010). *Doing qualitative research in psychology: A practical guide*. London: Sage. A handbook of the methodology; includes pragmatic sections on discourse analysis, grounded theory, phenomenology, and conversation analysis.

Smith, J. A. (2008). *Qualitative psychology: A practical guide to research methods* (2nd ed.). London: Sage. Not just for psychology but for all social science fields; excellent chapter overviews of methods such as grounded theory, plus narrative, discourse, conversation analysis, and so on.

Human Communication and Qualitative Research

Lindlof, T. R., & Taylor, B. C. (2011). *Qualitative communication research methods* (3rd ed.). Thousand Oaks, CA: Sage. General textbook overview of qualitative research in human communication.

Qualitative Research in Education (General Textbooks)

Bogdan, R. C., & Biklen, S. K. (2007). *Qualitative research for education: An introduction to theory and methods* (5th ed.). Boston: Allyn & Bacon. Excellent overview of the method, with an emphasis on fieldwork; includes good sections on development of qualitative research, photograph analysis, and the novice researcher.

Eisner, E. W. (1998). *The kind of schools we need: Personal essays*. Portsmouth, NH: Heinemann. Several essays provide foundations for research in the arts and arts-based approaches to research; sections include "The Arts and Their Role in Education," "Cognition and Representation," and "Rethinking Educational Research."

Lancy, D. F. (1993). *Qualitative research in education: An introduction to the major traditions.* New York: Longman. A survey of types of qualitative research, with examples in fields such as anthropology, sociology, and education.

LeCompte, M. D., & Preissle, J. (1993). *Ethnography and qualitative design in educational research* (2nd ed.). San Diego: Academic Press. Detailed methods for the design and execution of qualitative studies in the classroom.

Wolcott, H. F. (2003). *Teachers vs. technocrats: An educational innovation in anthropological perspective* (Updated ed.). Walnut Creek, CA: AltaMira Press. A case study that illustrates the concept of "moieties" (dual/opposing cultures) in education between teachers and administrators.

Researching Children

Christensen, P., & James, A. (2008). *Research with children: Perspectives and practices* (2nd ed.). New York: Routledge. Collection of essays about theoretical and social dimensions of researching children; includes chapters on working with children in war-affected areas, street children, and the disabled.

Clark, C. D. (2011). *In a younger voice: Doing child-centered qualitative research.* New York: Oxford University Press. Wonderful insider knowledge and nuances on researching children; excellent coverage of interpersonal dynamics between adults and youth.

Corsaro, W. A. (2011). *The sociology of childhood* (3rd ed.). Thousand Oaks, CA: Pine Forge Press. Outstanding resource on sociological dimensions of children and youth; cross-national comparisons and current U.S. statistics and trends presented.

Fine, G. A., & Sandstrom, K. L. (1988). *Knowing children: Participant observation with minors.* Newbury Park, CA: Sage. Monograph on the techniques and ethical issues of research with preschoolers through adolescents.

Freeman, M., & Mathison, S. (2009). *Researching children's experiences.* New York: Guilford Press. Superior, straightforward survey of researching children from a constructivist perspective.

Graue, M. E., & Walsh, D. J. (1998). *Studying children in context: Theories, methods, and ethics.* Thousand Oaks, CA: Sage. Overview of methods of social science research with children; includes sample studies and excellent advice through all stages of the research process.

Greene, S., & Hogan, D. (2005). *Researching children's experience: Approaches and methods.* London: Sage. Excellent chapters on qualitative research with children, from interviews to participant observation to arts-based methods.

Greig, A. D., Taylor, J., & MacKay, T. (2007). *Doing research with children* (2nd ed.). London: Sage. Overview of classic/traditional and contemporary methods of data gathering from children; focuses primarily on preschool and younger children; excellent theoretical overview.

Hatch, J. A. (Ed.). (2007). *Early childhood qualitative research.* New York: Routledge. Collection of essays, including digital video, action research, focus groups, and so on, on research with young children.

Heiligman, D. (1998). *The New York Public Library kid's guide to research.* New York: Scholastic. Designed for upper elementary grades, an overview of basic research strategies and tools, including the Internet, conducting interviews and surveys, and fieldwork.

Holmes, R. M. (1998). *Fieldwork with children*. Thousand Oaks, CA: Sage. Practical advice on interviewing and observing children and gaining entry to their world; focuses on how gender interplays with rapport.

Lancy, D. F., Bock, J., & Gaskins, S. (Eds.). (2010). *The anthropology of learning in childhood*. Walnut Creek, CA: AltaMira Press. Outstanding chapters on how children from various cultures "learn," in its broadest sense; rich concepts, yet written in accessible language; not a "how to" book but an exceptional model for documenting participant observation.

Mukherji, P., & Albon, D. (2010). *Research methods in early childhood: An introductory guide*. London: Sage. Readable overview of quantitative and qualitative research design approaches to research with young children; emphasizes British perspectives but applicable to U.S. youth.

Pellegrini, A. D. (2013). *Observing children in their natural worlds: A methodological primer* (3rd ed.). New York: Psychology Press. A primarily quantitative and systematic approach to observing young people's behaviors; includes a chapter by John Hoch and Frank J. Symons on new technology methods for data collection and analysis.

Thomson, P. (Ed.). (2008). *Doing visual research with children and young people*. London: Routledge. Excellent collection of chapters on using photography, video, scrapbooks, drawings, and other visual materials as data when researching children.

Tisdall, E. K., Davis, J. M., & Gallagher, M. (2009). *Researching with children and young people: Research design, methods and analysis*. London: Sage. Superior collection of methods and case study profiles for designing and conducting research with children; geared toward U.K. programs but still has relevance for U.S. readers.

Qualitative Data Collection (General)

Guest, G., Namey, E. E., & Mitchell, M. L. (2013). *Collecting qualitative data: A field manual for applied research*. Thousand Oaks, CA: Sage. Detailed methods for sampling, participant observation, interviews, focus groups, and data management.

Interviewing

Gubrium, J. F., Holstein, J. A., Marvasti, A. B., & McKinney, K. D. (Eds.). (2012). *The SAGE handbook of interview research: The complexity of the craft* (2nd ed.). Thousand Oaks, CA: Sage. Superior collection of chapters on all aspects of interviewing, including methods, analysis, and ethics.

Janesick, V. J. (2010). *Oral history for the qualitative researcher: Choreographing the story*. New York: Guilford Press. Includes an overview of oral history documentation with multiple examples; includes references to many resources for learning more about the genre.

Krueger, R. A., & Casey, M. A. (2009). *Focus groups: A practical guide for applied research* (4th ed.). Thousand Oaks, CA: Sage. Detailed manual on techniques for planning and moderating focus groups for corporate and nonprofit research.

Kvale, S., & Brinkmann, S. (2009). *Interviews: Learning the craft of qualitative research interviewing* (2nd ed.). Thousand Oaks, CA: Sage. Overview of interview methods for qualitative inquiry.

Mears, C. L. (2009). *Interviewing for education and social science research: The gateway approach*. New York: Palgrave Macmillan. Outstanding resource on interviewing participants, with transformation of transcripts into poetic mosaics.

Morgan, D. L. (1997). *Focus groups as qualitative research* (2nd ed.). Thousand Oaks, CA: Sage. The design, dynamics, and analysis of group interviews.

Roulston, K. (2010). *Reflective interviewing: A guide to theory and practice*. London: Sage. Superior treatise on interviewing participants, ranging from theory to technique.

Rubin, H. J., & Rubin, I. S. (2012). *Qualitative interviewing: The art of hearing data* (3rd ed.). Thousand Oaks, CA: Sage. Excellently detailed overview of designing and conducting interviews, with numerous examples from the authors' studies.

Seidman, I. (2006). *Interviewing as qualitative research: A guide for researchers in education and the social sciences* (3rd ed.). New York: Teachers College Press. Specific techniques and methods for conducting three-series, in-depth interviews with adult participants.

Spradley, J. P. (1979). *The ethnographic interview*. New York: Holt, Rinehart & Winston. Essential reading for interviewing techniques; analytic methods are exclusively Spradley's, but they have become "standard" to some methodologists.

Participant Observation

Adler, P. A., & Adler, P. (1987). *Membership roles in field research*. Newbury Park, CA: Sage. Describes three types of participant observation for researchers in field settings.

Angrosino, M. V. (2007). *Naturalistic observation*. Walnut Creek, CA: Left Coast Press. Not a "how to" book but an excellent primer on all facets of ethnographic participant observation.

DeWalt, K. M., & DeWalt, B. R. (2011). *Participant observation: A guide for fieldworkers* (2nd ed.). Lanham, MD: AltaMira Press. Geared toward anthropological studies, the text reviews methods of taking field notes and interviewing participants.

Emerson, R. M., Fretz, R. I., & Shaw, L. L. (2011). *Writing ethnographic fieldnotes* (2nd ed.). Chicago: University of Chicago Press. Superior overview of the field note–taking process and how it springboards to analysis and write-up.

Spradley, J. P. (1980). *Participant observation*. New York: Holt, Rinehart & Winston. Companion volume to Spradley's *The Ethnographic Interview*; much is reiterated in this text, but the focus is on observation techniques.

Artifacts/Visual and Material Culture

Berger, A. A. (2009). *What objects mean: An introduction to material culture*. Walnut Creek, CA: Left Coast Press. Elegant and clearly explained approaches to the critical and cultural analysis of artifacts.

Margolis, E., & Pauwels, L. (Eds.). (2011). *The SAGE handbook of visual research methods*. London: Sage. An exhaustive collection of chapters devoted to visual analysis of photographs, film, digital work, material culture, and so on.

Qualitative Data Analysis

Abbott, A. (2004). *Methods of discovery: Heuristics for the social sciences*. New York: W. W. Norton. Excellent overview of current methodological debates in social science research and examples of problem-solving strategies used in landmark studies; provides guidance for seeing data and their analyses in new ways.

Auerbach, C. F., & Silverstein, L. B. (2003). *Qualitative data: An introduction to coding and analysis.* New York: New York University Press. Systematic procedures for finding "relevant text" in transcripts for pattern and thematic development; very readable, with good examples of procedures.

Bernard, H. R., & Ryan, G. W. (2010). *Analyzing qualitative data: Systematic approaches.* Thousand Oaks, CA: Sage. The emphasis is on systematic rather than interpretive approaches, meaning forms of content analysis, discourse analysis, and so on.

Boeije, H. (2010). *Analysis in qualitative research.* London: Sage. Primarily explicates the grounded theory model of qualitative research and data analysis, yet does a good job of explaining its procedures.

Bryman, A., & Burgess, R. G. (Eds.). (1994). *Analyzing qualitative data.* London: Routledge. Series of chapters describing the behind-the-scenes coding and analytic work of researchers.

Dey, I. (1993). *Qualitative data analysis: A user-friendly guide for social scientists.* London: Routledge. An excellent overview of specific techniques such as creating categories and splitting, splicing, linking, and connecting data.

Erickson, F. (1986). Qualitative methods in research on teaching. In M. C. Wittrock (Ed.), *Handbook of research on teaching* (3rd ed., pp. 119–161). New York: Macmillan. Classic chapter on an intuitive approach to qualitative inquiry through heuristics of assertion development.

Ezzy, D. (2002). *Qualitative analysis: Practice and innovation.* London: Routledge. Readable introduction to and overview of qualitative inquiry; explains conceptual ideas clearly.

Fielding, N. G., & Fielding, J. L. (1986). *Linking data.* Beverley Hills, CA: Sage. Monograph on the technique of triangulation with multiple methods of data gathering.

Gibbs, G. R. (2007). *Analysing qualitative data.* London: Sage. Monograph with an overview of fundamental data-analytic techniques, with excellent content on narrative analysis and comparative analysis.

Grbich, C. (2013). *Qualitative data analysis: An introduction* (2nd ed.). London: Sage. Not a "how to" guide but an introductory overview of the types of analysis (e.g., grounded theory, narrative analysis, content analysis, etc.) available to qualitative researchers.

Guest, G., & MacQueen, K. M. (2008). *Handbook for team-based qualitative research.* Lanham, MD: AltaMira Press. Chapters on team research, including ethics, politics, coding, and data management.

Guest, G., MacQueen, K. M., & Namey, E. E. (2012). *Applied thematic analysis.* Thousand Oaks, CA: Sage. Systematic qualitative and quantitative procedures for segmenting and analyzing themes (in their broadest sense) for research reports; emphasizes team research collaboration.

Knowlton, L. W., & Phillips, C. C. (2013). *The logic model guidebook: Better strategies for great results* (2nd ed.). Thousand Oaks, CA: Sage. Graphic displays for program and theory of change models; illustrates possible complex interconnections.

LeCompte, M. D., & Schensul, J. J. (2012). *Analysis and interpretation of ethnographic data: A mixed methods approach* (2nd ed.; Ethnographer's Toolkit Series, Book 5). Lanham, MD: AltaMira Press. Overview of primarily qualitative analytic strategies for traditional ethnographies; provides a systematic approach to data management, analysis, and integration with quantitative data.

Lyons, E., & Coyle, C. (2007). *Analysing qualitative data in psychology.* London: Sage. Overview of four approaches to data analysis in psychology: interpretative phenomenological analysis, grounded theory, discourse analysis, and narrative analysis—the latter includes a superior interview protocol for autobiographical/biographical work.

Northcutt, N., & McCoy, D. (2004). *Interactive qualitative analysis: A systems method for qualitative research*. Thousand Oaks, CA: Sage. For focus group synthesis—the development of flow charts for process through systematic qualitative analytic procedures.

Richards, L. (2009). *Handling qualitative data: A practical guide* (2nd ed.). London: Sage. An overview of data management principles before and during analysis; excellent content on category construction.

Saldaña, J. (2013). *The coding manual for qualitative researchers* (2nd ed.). London: Sage. Profiles 32 different methods for coding qualitative data; includes examples, along with ways to develop analytic memos.

Schreier, M. (2012). *Qualitative content analysis in practice*. London: Sage. Systematic procedures for qualitative content analysis; a hybrid blend of qualitative and quantitative approaches.

Sullivan, P. (2012). *Qualitative data analysis using a dialogical approach*. London: Sage. Intriguing methods for qualitative data analysis, particularly for thematic and discourse analysis; first three chapters are heavy on theory but lay the foundation for Sullivan's analytic methods in the remaining chapters.

Wertz, F. J., Charmaz, K., McMullen, L. M., Josselson, R., Anderson, R., & McSpadden, E. (2011). *Five ways of doing qualitative analysis: Phenomenological psychology, grounded theory, discourse analysis, narrative research, and intuitive inquiry*. New York: Guilford Press. A detailed examination of an interview transcript through five methods of data analysis: phenomenological psychology, grounded theory, discourse analysis, narrative research, and intuitive inquiry; includes reflexive statements by the analysts and the interview participant herself.

Wheeldon, J., & Ahlberg, M. A. (2012). *Visualizing social science research: Maps, methods, and meaning*. Thousand Oaks, CA: Sage. Overview of quantitative, qualitative, and mixed-methods research and how diagrams (e.g., concept maps and mind maps) can be employed during all phases of the research project.

Wolcott, H. F. (1994). *Transforming qualitative data: Description, analysis, and interpretation*. Thousand Oaks, CA: Sage. Anthology of Wolcott's work, with accompanying narrative on three levels of qualitative data analysis.

Technology and CAQDAS (Computer Assisted Qualitative Data Analysis Software)

Altheide, D. L., & Schneider, C. J. (2013). *Qualitative media analysis* (2nd ed.). Thousand Oaks, CA: Sage. Reviews search, collection, and analysis strategies for media documents from television broadcasts, the Internet, social media, and other sources.

Bazeley, P. (2007). *Qualitative data analysis with NVivo*. London: Sage. Reference guide to computer-assisted qualitative data analysis with the program software NVivo.

Berger, A. A. (2012). *Media analysis techniques* (4th ed.). Thousand Oaks, CA: Sage. Paradigms for media analysis of television programs, films, print advertisements, popular technology (e.g., cell phones, the Internet).

Edhlund, B. M. (2011). *NVivo 9 essentials*. Stallarholmen, Sweden: Form & Kunskap AB. Technical manual for the functions of NVivo 9 software; no guidance on analysis, just the program features.

Friese, S. (2012). *Qualitative data analysis with ATLAS.ti*. London: Sage. Detailed technical manual for the functions of ATLAS.ti software; focuses primarily on program features.

Gaiser, T. J., & Schreiner, A. E. (2009). *A guide to conducting online research*. London: Sage. Overview of electronic methods of data gathering through e-mail, websites, social networking sites, and so on.

Gibbs, G. R. (2002). *Qualitative data analysis: Explorations with NVivo*. Berkshire: Open University Press. The software version of NVivo demonstrated in this book is outdated, but there is still an excellent overview of data-analytic strategies.

Hahn, C. (2008). *Doing qualitative research using your computer: A practical guide*. London: Sage. Step-by-step instructions for using Microsoft Word, Excel, and Access for qualitative data management and coding.

Haw, K., & Hadfield, M. (2011). *Video in social science research: Functions and forms*. London, England: Routledge. Reference for theoretical applications of video; contains excellent guidelines for video production by young people as a form of participatory research.

Heath, C., Hindmarsh, J., & Luff, P. (2010). *Video in qualitative research: Analysing social interaction in everyday life*. London: Sage. Focuses on microanalysis of video data fragments; shows transcription models for talk and action; excellent guidelines for working with video cameras in the field.

Kozinets, R. V. (2010). *Netnography: Doing ethnographic research online*. London: Sage. Exceptionally well-detailed guide to online ethnographic research; includes excellent considerations for entrée, data collection, and ethical/legal matters.

Lewins, A., & Silver, C. (2007). *Using software in qualitative research: A step-by-step guide*. London: Sage. Critically compares and illustrates the basic procedures for three CAQDAS programs: ATLAS.ti, MAXQDA, and NVivo; excellent introductory survey and accompanying reference manual.

Makagon, D., & Neumann, M. (2009). *Recording culture: Audio documentary and the ethnographic experience*. Thousand Oaks, CA: Sage. Methods for creating audio documentation of fieldwork, including soundscapes, interviews, citizen journals, and so on.

Theory Development and Applications

Alvesson, M., & Kärreman, D. (2011). *Qualitative research and theory development: Mystery as method*. London: Sage. Approach to theory development through problematizing the data and resolving "breakdowns" in patterns and fieldwork observations.

Jackson, A. Y., & Mazzei, L. A. (2012). *Thinking with theory in qualitative research: Viewing data across multiple perspectives*. New York: Routledge. Approaches data analysis through theoretical lenses rather than codification; applies the principles of theorists such as Derrida, Foucault, and Butler to an interview data set from female professors.

Ravitch, S. M., & Riggan, M. (2012). *Reason and rigor: How conceptual frameworks guide research*. Thousand Oaks, CA: Sage. Explanation with examples of how a conceptual framework functions as a through-line during all phases and stages of the research process, from design to data analysis and from fieldwork to write-up.

Qualitative Metasynthesis

Major, C. H., & Savin-Baden, M. (2010). *An introduction to qualitative research synthesis: Managing the information explosion in social science research*. London: Routledge. Excellent theoretical and practical overview of qualitative research synthesis; includes extended examples.

Sandelowski, M., & Barroso, J. (2007). *Handbook for synthesizing qualitative research*. New York: Springer. Detailed methods book on metasummary and metasynthesis of related qualitative studies; for advanced researchers.

Writing Qualitative Research

Belcher, W. L. (2009). *Writing your journal article in 12 weeks: A guide to academic publishing success*. Thousand Oaks, CA: Sage. Step-by-step and detailed procedures for revising drafts of papers for publication submission.

Booth, W. C., Colomb, G. G., & Williams, J. M. (2008). *The craft of research* (3rd ed.). Chicago: University of Chicago Press. A handbook of basics in logic, argumentation, writing, outlining, revising, and crafting the research report.

Goodall, H. L., Jr. (2008). *Writing qualitative inquiry: Self, stories, and academic life*. Walnut Creek, CA: Left Coast Press. Overview of writing and writing for the profession (journals, books, in the academy, etc.).

Higgs, J., Horsfall, D., & Grace, S. (Eds.). (2009). *Writing qualitative research on practice*. Rotterdam: Sense. Chapter collection of writing up research; includes excellent chapters on question development, argument construction, and genres (narrative inquiry, arts-based research, etc.).

Miller, A. B. (2009). *Finish your dissertation once and for all! How to overcome psychological barriers, get results, and move on with your life*. Washington, DC: American Psychological Association. Focuses on the cognitive/emotional barriers of progress and completion, plus the practical matters of timelines, project management, and writing.

van Maanen, J. (2011). *Tales of the field* (2nd ed.). Chicago: University of Chicago Press. Contemporary classic on structuring and writing ethnography in various story forms (realistic, confessional, etc.).

Wolcott, H. F. (2009). *Writing up qualitative research* (3rd ed.). Thousand Oaks, CA: Sage. Excellent monograph on writing reports clearly and briefly from the first draft to publication.

Woods, P. (2006). *Successful writing for qualitative researchers* (2nd ed.). London: Routledge. Offers specific strategies for writing up final reports; especially good with transitioning from data analysis to reporting; includes numerous examples.

Online Resources

Forum: Qualitative Social Research. The multilingual (English, German, Spanish) peer-reviewed e-journal includes articles, interviews with leading figures in the field, commentary, and book reviews: http://www.qualitative-research.net/index.php/fqs/index

Methodspace. Hosted by Sage Publications; a community networking site for researchers from various social science disciplines; members can join interest groups such as Qualitative Inquiry, Narrative Research, and Performative Social Science: http://www.methodspace.com

Pacific Standard. A print and online publication of the Miller-McCune Center for Research, Media and Public Policy; includes articles ranging from health to culture, bringing research to a general readership: http://www.psmag.com

The Qualitative Report: Hosted by Nova Southeastern University; an online journal with a weekly newsletter featuring recent publication links; the site also includes an extensive list of Internet addresses of other organizations devoted to qualitative research: http://www.nova.edu/ssss/QR/index.html

References

Adler, T. (1991, December). Outright fraud rare, but not poor science. *Monitor on Psychology,* 11.

Bazeley, P. (2007). *Qualitative data analysis with NVivo.* London: Sage.

Belli, R. F., Stafford, F. P., & Alwin, D. F. (Eds.). (2009). *Calendar and time diary methods in life course research.* Thousand Oaks, CA: Sage.

Bernard, H. R. (2011). *Research methods in anthropology: Qualitative and quantitative approaches* (5th ed.). Walnut Creek, CA: AltaMira Press.

Bernard, H. R., & Ryan, G. W. (2010). *Analyzing qualitative data: Systematic approaches.* Thousand Oaks, CA: Sage.

Bogdan, R. C., & Biklen, S. K. (2007). *Qualitative research for education: An introduction to theories and methods* (5th ed.). Boston: Pearson Education.

Charmaz, K. (2001). Grounded theory. In R. M. Emerson (Ed.), *Contemporary field research: Perspectives and formulations* (2nd ed., pp. 335–352). Prospect Heights, IL: Waveland Press.

Charmaz, K. (2006). *Constructing grounded theory: A practical guide through qualitative analysis.* Thousand Oaks, CA: Sage.

Clarke, A. E. (2005). *Situational analysis: Grounded theory after the postmodern turn.* Thousand Oaks, CA: Sage.

Cochran-Smith, M., McQullian, P., Mitchell, K., Terrell, D. G., Barnatt, J., D'Souza, L., . . . Gleeson, A. M. (2012). A longitudinal study of teaching practice and early career decisions: A cautionary tale. *American Educational Research Journal, 49*(5), 844–880.

Cressey, D. R. (1953). *Other people's money: A study in the social psychology of embezzlement.* New York: Free Press.

Creswell, J. W. (2009). *Research design: Qualitative, quantitative, and mixed methods approaches* (3rd ed.). Thousand Oaks, CA: Sage.

Creswell, J. W. (2013). *Qualitative inquiry and research design: Choosing among five approaches* (3rd ed.). Thousand Oaks, CA: Sage.

Creswell, J. W., & Plano Clark, V. L. (2011). *Designing and conducting mixed methods research* (2nd ed.). Thousand Oaks, CA: Sage.

Denzin, N. K. (1993). *The alcoholic society: Addiction and recovery of the self.* Piscataway, NJ: Transaction.

Denzin, N. K. (2001). *Interpretive interactionism* (2nd ed.). Thousand Oaks, CA: Sage.

Denzin, N. K., & Lincoln, Y. S. (2012). *The SAGE handbook of qualitative research* (4th ed.). Thousand Oaks, CA: Sage.

Douglas, J. (1976). *Investigative social research.* Beverly Hills, CA: Sage.

Duhigg, C. (2012). *The power of habit: How we do what we do in life and business.* New York: Random House.

Ehrenreich, B. (2001). *Nickel and dimed: On (not) getting by in America.* New York: Henry Holt.

Eisner, E. W. (1991). *The enlightened eye: Qualitative inquiry and the enhancement of educational practice.* New York: Macmillan.

Emerson, R. M., Fretz, R. I., & Shaw, L. L. (2011). *Writing ethnographic fieldnotes* (2nd ed.). Chicago, IL: University of Chicago Press.

Erickson, F. (1986). Qualitative methods in research on teaching. In M. C. Wittrock (Ed.), *Handbook of research on teaching* (3rd ed., pp. 119–161). New York: Macmillan.

Festinger, L. (1957). *A theory of cognitive dissonance.* Evanston, IL: Row, Peterson.

Friese, S. (2012). *Qualitative data analysis with ATLAS.ti.* London: Sage.

Geertz, C. (1973). Thick description: Toward an interpretive theory of culture. In *The interpretation of cultures* (pp. 3–30). New York: Basic Books.

Gibbs, G. R. (2007). *Analysing qualitative data.* London: Sage.

Glaser, B. G. (2005). *The grounded theory perspective III: Theoretical coding.* Mill Valley, CA: Sociology Press.

Gobo, G. (2008). Re-conceptualizing generalization: Old issues in a new frame. In P. Alasuutari, L. Bickman, & J. Brannen (Eds.), *The SAGE handbook of social research methods* (pp. 193–213). London: Sage.

Goetz, J. P., & LeCompte, M. D. (1984). *Ethnography and qualitative design in educational research.* New York: Academic Press.

Goffman, E. (1959). *The presentation of self in everyday life.* Garden City, NY: Doubleday.

Goleman, D. (1995). *Emotional intelligence.* New York: Bantam Books.

Goleman, D. (2007). *Social intelligence: The new science of human relationships.* New York: Bantam Books.

Gubrium, J. F., Holstein, J. A., Marvasti, A. B., & McKinney, K. D. (2012). *The SAGE handbook of interview research: The complexity of the craft* (2nd ed.). Thousand Oaks, CA: Sage.

Hager, L., Maier, B. J., O'Hara, E., Ott, D., & Saldaña, J. (2000). Theatre teachers' perceptions of Arizona state standards. *Youth Theatre Journal, 14,* 64–77.

Hahn, C. (2008). *Doing qualitative research using your computer: A practical guide.* London: Sage.

Huberman, A. M. (1989). The professional life cycle of teachers. *Teachers College Record, 97*(1), 31–57.

Huberman, A. M. (1993). *The lives of teachers.* London: Cassell.

Huberman, A. M., & Miles, M. B. (1983). *Innovation up close: A field study in 12 school settings.* Andover, MA: Network.

Huberman, A. M., & Miles, M. B. (1984). *Innovation up close: How school improvement works.* New York: Plenum Press.

Huberman, M., & Miles, M. (1989). Some procedures for causal analysis of multiple-case data. *Qualitative Studies in Education, 2*(1), 55–68.

Humphreys, L. (1970). *Tearoom trade: Impersonal sex in public places.* Chicago: Aldine.

Kell, D. G. (1990). *Multimethod approach to analyzing effects of computers on classroom teaching and learning.* Andover, MA: Author.

Knowles, J. G., & Cole, A. L. (2008). *Handbook of the arts in qualitative research: Perspectives, methodologies, examples, and issues.* Thousand Oaks, CA: Sage.

Knowlton, L. W., & Phillips, C. C. (2013). *The logic model guidebook: Better strategies for great results* (2nd ed.). Thousand Oaks, CA: Sage.

Kozol, J. (1991). *Savage inequalities: Children in America's schools.* New York: Crown.

Kvale, S., & Brinkmann, S. (2009). *Interviews: Learning the craft of qualitative research interviewing* (2nd ed.). Thousand Oaks, CA: Sage.

Lakoff, G., & Johnson, M. (1980). *Metaphors we live by.* Chicago: University of Chicago Press.

Lancy, D. F., Bock, J., & Gaskins, S. (Eds.). (2010). *The anthropology of learning in childhood.* Walnut Creek, CA: AltaMira Press.

Leavy, P. (2009). *Method meets art: Arts-based research practice.* New York: Guilford Press.

Lewins, A., & Silver, C. (2007). *Using software in qualitative research: A step-by-step guide.* London: Sage.

Lincoln, Y. S., & Guba, E. G. (1985). *Naturalistic inquiry.* Beverly Hills, CA: Sage.

Lofland, J., Snow, D., Anderson, L., & Lofland, L. H. (2006). *Analyzing social settings: A guide to qualitative observation and analysis* (4th ed.). Belmont, CA: Thomson/ Wadsworth.

Louis, K. S., & Miles, M. B. (1990). *Improving the urban high school: What works and why.* New York: Teachers College Press.

Major, C. H., & Savin-Baden, M. (2010). *An introduction to qualitative research synthesis: Managing the information explosion in social science research.* London: Routledge.

Maxwell, J. A. (1992, December). *A synthesis of similarity/continuity distinctions.* Poster presented at the annual meeting of the American Anthropological Association, San Francisco, CA.

McCammon, L. A., & Saldaña, J. (2011). *Lifelong impact: Adult perceptions of their high school speech and/or theatre participation.* Unpublished manuscript, School of Theatre and Film, Arizona State University, Tempe.

McCammon, L., Saldaña, J., Hines, A., & Omasta, M. (2012). Lifelong impact: Adult perceptions of their high school speech and/or theatre participation. *Youth Theatre Journal, 26*(1), 2–25.

McCurdy, D. W., Spradley, J. P., & Shandy, D. J. (2005). *The cultural experience: Ethnography in complex society* (2nd ed.). Long Grove, IL: Waveland Press.

McVea, K. (2001, April). *Collaborative qualitative research: Reflections for a quantitative researcher.* Paper presented at the annual conference of the American Educational Research Association, Seattle, WA.

Mears, C. L. (2009). *Interviewing for education and social science research: The gateway approach.* New York: Palgrave Macmillan.

Melnick, C. R., & Beaudry, J. S. (1990, April). *A qualitative research perspective: Theory, practice, essence.* Paper presented at the annual meeting of the American Educational Research Association, Boston, MA.

Miles, M. B. (1986, April). *Improving the urban high school: Some preliminary news from five cases.* Paper presented at the annual meeting of the American Educational Research Association, San Francisco, CA.

Miles, M. B. (1990). New methods for qualitative data collection and analysis: Vignettes and pre-structured cases. *Qualitative Studies in Education, 5*(1), 37–51.

Miles, M. B., & Huberman, A. M. (1994). *Qualitative data analysis: An expanded sourcebook* (2nd ed.). Thousand Oaks, CA: Sage.

Miller, A. B. (2009). *Finish your dissertation once and for all! How to overcome psychological barriers, get results, and move on with your life*. Washington, DC: American Psychological Association.

Miller, D. L., Creswell, J. W., & Olander, L. S. (1998). Writing and retelling multiple ethnographic tales of a soup kitchen for the homeless. *Qualitative Inquiry, 4*(4), 469–491.

Miller, S. I. (n.d.). *Qualitative research methods: A philosophical and practical inquiry* [Prospectus for a monograph]. Chicago: Loyola University.

Mishler, E. G. (1979). Meaning in context: Is there any other kind? *Harvard Educational Review, 49*(1), 1–19.

Morgan, G. (1980). Paradigms, metaphors, and puzzle solving in organizational theory. *Administrative Science Quarterly, 25*(4), 605–622.

Morine-Dershimer, G. (1991, April). *Tracing conceptual change in pre-service teachers*. Paper presented at the annual meeting of the American Educational Research Association, Chicago, IL.

Morrison, K. (2009). *Causation in educational research*. London: Routledge.

Morse, J. M., & Bottorff, J. L. (1992). The emotional experience of breast expression. In J. M. Morse (Ed.), *Qualitative health research* (pp. 319–332). Newbury Park, CA: Sage.

Munton, A. G., Silvester, J., Stratton, P., & Hanks, H. (1999). *Attributions in action: A practical approach to coding qualitative data*. Chichester, England: Wiley.

Noblit, G. W., & Hare, R. D. (1988). *Meta-ethnography: Synthesizing qualitative studies* (Qualitative Research Methods Series, Vol. 11). Newbury Park, CA: Sage.

Norris, J. (2009). *Playbuilding as qualitative research: A participatory arts-based approach*. Walnut Creek, CA: Left Coast Press.

Patton, M. Q. (2002). *Qualitative research and evaluation methods* (3rd ed.). Thousand Oaks, CA: Sage.

Patton, M. Q. (2008). *Utilization-focused evaluation* (4th ed.). Thousand Oaks, CA: Sage.

Pearsol, J. A. (1985, April). *Controlling qualitative data: Understanding teachers' value perspectives on a sex equity education project*. Paper presented at the annual meeting of the American Educational Research Association, Chicago, IL.

Prendergast, M., Leggo, C., & Sameshima, P. (Eds.). (2009). *Poetic inquiry: Vibrant voices in the social sciences*. Rotterdam, Netherlands: Sense.

Ragin, C. C. (1987). *The comparative method: Moving beyond qualitative and quantitative strategies*. Berkeley: University of California Press.

Ravitch, S. M., & Riggan, M. (2012). *Reason and rigor: How conceptual frameworks guide research*. Thousand Oaks, CA: Sage.

Richards, L. (2009). *Handling qualitative data: A practical guide* (2nd ed.). London: Sage.

Rosenthal, R. (1976). *Experimenter effects in behavioral research*. New York: Irvington.

Saldaña, J. (1995). "Is theatre necessary?": Final exit interviews with sixth grade participants from the ASU longitudinal study. *Youth Theatre Journal, 9,* 14–30.

Saldaña, J. (1997). "Survival": A white teacher's conception of drama with inner city Hispanic youth. *Youth Theatre Journal, 11,* 25–46.

Saldaña, J. (1998). "Maybe someday, if I'm famous . . .": An ethnographic performance text. In J. Saxton & C. Miller (Eds.), *Drama and theatre in education: The research of practice, the practice of research* (pp. 89–109). Brisbane, Queensland, Australia: IDEA.

Saldaña, J. (1999). Social class and social consciousness: Adolescent perceptions of oppression in forum theatre workshops. *Multicultural Perspectives, 1*(3), 14–18.

Saldaña, J. (2003). *Longitudinal qualitative research: Analyzing change through time*. Walnut Creek, CA: AltaMira Press.

Saldaña, J. (2005). Theatre of the oppressed with children: A field experiment. *Youth Theatre Journal, 19,* 117–133.

Saldaña, J. (2008a). Analyzing longitudinal qualitative observational data. In S. Menard (Ed.), *Handbook of longitudinal research: Design, measurement, and analysis* (pp. 297–311). Burlington, MA: Academic Press.

Saldaña, J. (2008b). Second chair: An autoethnodrama. *Research Studies in Music Education, 30*(2), 177–191.

Saldaña, J. (2011a). *Ethnotheatre: Research from page to stage*. Walnut Creek, CA: Left Coast Press.

Saldaña, J. (2011b). *Fundamentals of qualitative research*. New York: Oxford University Press.

Saldaña, J. (2013). *The coding manual for qualitative researchers* (2nd ed.). London: Sage.

Sandelowski, M., & Barroso, J. (2007). *Handbook for synthesizing qualitative research*. New York: Springer.

Schillemans, L., et al. (n.d.). *Treating victims of incest*. Antwerp, Belgium: Flemish Institute for General Practice/University of Antwerp, Department of Family Medicine.

Schreier, M. (2012). *Qualitative content analysis in practice*. London: Sage.

Seidman, I. (2006). *Interviewing as qualitative research: A guide for researchers in education and the social sciences*. New York: Teachers College Press.

Sieber, J. E. (1992). *Planning ethically responsible research: A guide for students and internal review boards* (Applied Social Research Methods Series, Vol. 31). Newbury Park, CA: Sage.

Spradley, J. P. (1979). *The ethnographic interview*. Fort Worth, TX: Harcourt Brace Jovanovich.

Spradley, J. P. (1980). *Participant observation*. Fort Worth, TX: Harcourt Brace Jovanovich.

Stake, R. E. (1995). *The art of case study research*. Thousand Oaks, CA: Sage.

Stiegelbauer, S., Goldstein, M., & Huling, L. L. (1982). *Through the eye of the beholder: On the use of qualitative methods in data analysis* (R & D Report 3137). Austin: University of Texas, R&D Center for Teacher Education.

Tashakkori, A., & Teddlie, C. (Eds.). (2003). *Handbook of mixed methods in social and behavioral research*. Thousand Oaks, CA: Sage.

Tufte, E. R. (1986). Designing statistical presentations. *Social Science, 7*(1), 75–80.

van Maanen, J. (1979). The fact of fiction in organizational ethnography. *Administrative Science Quarterly, 24,* 539–611.

van Maanen, J. (1983). The moral fix: On the ethics of fieldwork. In R. M. Emerson (Ed.), *Contemporary field research* (pp. 269–287). Prospect Heights, IL: Waveland.

van Maanen, J. (2011). *Tales of the field: On writing ethnography* (2nd ed.). Chicago: University of Chicago Press.

Wallis, W. A., & Roberts, H. V. (1956). *Statistics: A new approach*. New York: Free Press.

Warner, W. (1991, February). *Improving interpretive validity of camera-based qualitative research*. Paper presented at the Qualitative Health Research Conference, Edmonton, Alberta, Canada.

Wolcott, H. F. (1990). On seeking—and rejecting—validity in qualitative research. In E. W. Eisner & A. Peshkin (Eds.), *Qualitative inquiry in education: The continuing debate* (pp. 121–152). New York: Teachers College Press.

Wolcott, H. F. (1992). Posturing in qualitative inquiry. In M. D. LeCompte, W. L. Millroy, & J. Preissle (Eds.), *The handbook of qualitative research in education* (pp. 3–52). New York: Academic Press.

Wolcott, H. F. (1994). *Transforming qualitative data: Description, analysis, and interpretation.* Thousand Oaks, CA: Sage.

Wolcott, H. F. (2009). *Writing up qualitative research* (3rd ed.). Thousand Oaks, CA: Sage.

Yin, R. K. (2009). *Case study research: Design and methods* (4th ed.). Thousand Oaks, CA: Sage.

Zeller, N. (1991, April). *A new use for new journalism: Humanizing the case report.* Paper presented at the annual meeting of the American Educational Research Association, Chicago, IL.

Author Index

Abbott, A., 357
Ackroyd, J., 351
Adler, P., 357
Adler, P. A., 357
Adler, T., 64
Ahlberg, M. A., 359
Albon, D., 356
Altheide, D. L., 359
Altrichter, H., 352
Alvesson, M., 360
Alwin, D. F., 201
Anderson, L., 115, 346
Anderson, R., 359
Angrosino, M. V., 348, 357
Atkinson, P., 348
Auerbach, C. F., 358

Barone, T., 352
Barroso, J., 103, 361
Bazeley, P., 50, 359
Beaudry, J. S., 309
Belcher, W. L., 361
Belli, R. F., 201
Berger, A. A., 357, 359
Bernard, H. R., 181, 208, 348, 358
Biklen, S. K., 95, 115, 354
Birks, M., 349
Birmingham, P., 345
Blumer, H., 347
Bochner, A. P., 351
Bock, J., 98
Boeije, H., 358
Bogdan, R. S., 95, 115, 354
Bonaparte, N., 256
Booth, W. C., 361
Bothamley, J., 345
Bottorff, J. L., 103
Brannick, T., 353
Brinkmann, S., 37, 46, 350, 356
Brown, A., 354
Brown, I. C., 348
Bryant, A., 349
Bryman, A., 358
Burgess, R. G., 358
Burt, C., 64–65
Butler-Kisber, L., 352

Camic, P. M., 354
Casey, M. A., 356
Chang, H., 351
Charmaz, K., 4, 72, 313, 349, 359
Charon, J. M., 353
Chiseri-Strater, E., 349
Christensen, P., 355
Churton, M., 354

Clandinin, D. J., 351
Clark, C. D., 355
Clarke, A. E., 314, 349
Cochran-Smith, M., 214
Cole, A. L., 335, 352
Colomb, G. G., 361
Connelly, F. M., 351
Corbin, J., 99, 350
Corsaro, W. A., 355
Coughlan, D., 353
Coyle, C., 358
Cressey, D. R., 304
Creswell, J. W., 4, 101, 328, 345, 346
Cuzzort, R. P., 354

Davis, J. M., 356
Denzin, N. K., 4, 101, 103, 299,
    347, 348, 350, 352
DeWalt, B. R., 357
DeWalt, K. M., 357
Dey, I., 358
Douglas, J., 301
Duhigg, C., 189, 279

Edhlund, B. M., 360
Einstein, A., 304
Eisner, E. W., 313, 352, 354
Elder, G. H., Jr., 353
Ellingson, L. L., 347
Ellis, C., 351
Emerson, R. M., 93, 357
Erickson, F., 32, 185, 314, 325, 333, 358
Ezzy, D., 358

Festinger, L., 293
Fetterman, D. M., 348
Fielding, J. L., 358
Fielding, N. G., 358
Fine, G. A., 355
Flowers, P., 350
Forrester, M. A., 354
Fox, M., 353
Freeman, M., 355
Fretz, R. I., 93, 357
Friese, S., 50, 360

Gabler, J., 354
Gaiser, T. J., 360
Gallagher, M., 356
Galman, S. C., 348
Gaskins, S., 98, 356
Gee, J. P., 351
Geertz, C., 313, 348
Gergen, K. J., 352
Gergen, M. M., 352

Gibbs, G. R., 282, 358, 360
Giele, J. Z., 353
Given, L. M., 345
Glaser, B. G., 99, 314, 350
Glesne, C., 346
Gobo, G., 115
Goetz, J. P., 32
Goffman, E., 297
Goldberg, J. A., 53
Goldstein, M., 134
Goleman, D., 308
Goodall, H. L., Jr., 361
Grace, S., 361
Graue, M. E., 355
Grbich, C., 358
Green, G., 353
Greene, S., 355
Greig, A. D., 355
Groves, J., 349
Guba, E. G., 311, 312, 315, 317, 347
Gubrium, J. F., 4, 351, 353, 356
Guest, G., 356, 358

Hadfield, M., 360
Hager, L., 286
Hahn, C., 50, 360
Hamera, J., 352
Hammersley, M., 348
Handwerker, W. P., 348
Hanks, H., 222
Hare, R. D., 103, 314
Hatch, J. A., 355
Haw, K., 360
Heath, C., 360
Heiligman, D., 355
Hesse-Biber, S. N., 347
Higgs, J., 361
Hindmarsh, J., 360
Hines, A., 45, 308
Hitchcock, G., 353
Hogan, D., 355
Holmes, R. M., 356
Holstein, J. A., 4, 351, 353, 356
Horsfall, D., 361
Huberman, A. M., 9, 23, 53, 211
Hughes, D., 353
Huling, L. L., 134
Humphreys, L., 62

Jackson, A. Y., 360
James, A., 355
Janesick, V. J., 352, 356
Johnson, M., 281
Josselson, R., 359

Karreman, D., 360
Kell, D. G., 45, 100
King, E. W., 354
Knowles, J. G., 335, 352
Knowlton, L. W., 112, 358
Kozinets, R. V., 360

Krueger, R. A., 356
Kvale, S., 37, 46, 356

Lakoff, G., 281
Lancy, D. F., 98, 355, 356
Larkin, M., 350
Leavy, P., 335, 347, 352
LeCompte, M. D., 32, 355, 358
Leggo, C., 187
Lewins, A., 50, 360
Lincoln, Y. S., 4, 311, 312, 315, 317, 347
Lindlof, T. R., 354
Lofland, J., 115, 346
Lofland, L. H., 115, 346
Louis, K. S., 155, 226
Luff, P., 360
Lund, D., 349
Lyons, E., 358

MacKay, T., 355
MacQueen, K. M., 358
Madden, R., 348
Madison, D. S., 352
Maier, B. J., 286
Major, C. H., 103, 361
Makagon, D., 360
Margolis, E., 357
Marshall, C., 346
Martin, P., 353
Marvasti, A. B., 4, 356
Mason, J., 346
Mathison, S., 355
Maxwell, J. A., 313, 315, 346
Mazzei, L. A., 360
McCammon, L., 45, 96, 111, 172, 173, 278, 283, 297, 308
McCoy, D., 359
McCurdy, D. W., 179, 349
McKinney, K. D., 4, 356
McLeod, J., 353
McMullen, L. M., 359
McSpadden, E., 359
McVea, K., 158
Mears, C. L., 187, 356
Melnick, C. R., 309
Mertens, D. M., 345
Miles, M. B., 9, 23, 53, 155, 226
Miller, A. B., 337, 361
Miller, D. L., 328, 330, 332
Miller, S. I., 304
Mills, J., 349
Mishler, E. G., 167
Mitchell, M. L., 356
Morgan, D. L., 357
Morgan, G., 281
Morine-Dershimer, G., 191
Morrison, K., 222, 288, 346
Morse, J. M., 103, 346
Mukherji, P., 356
Munton, A. G., 222

Namey, E. E., 356, 358
Neumann, M., 360
Nisbet, R., 352
Noblit, G. W., 103, 314
Norris, J., 335, 349, 352
Northcutt, N., 359

O'Hara, E., 286
Olander, L. S., 328
Omasta, M., 45, 308
O'Toole, J., 351
Ott, D., 286

Packer, M. J., 347
Pascale, C.-M., 347
Patton, M. Q., 32, 350
Pauwels, L., 357
Pearsol, J. A., 103
Pellegrini, A. D., 356
Phillips, C. C., 112, 358
Pink, S., 349
Plano-Clark, V. L., 101, 346
Porr, C. J., 350
Posch, P., 352
Poulos, C. N., 351
Preissle, J., 355
Prendergast, M., 187
Prus, R. C., 348

Ragin, C. C., 102
Ravitch, S. M., 25, 360
Rhodes, J. E., 354
Richards, L., 50, 280, 346, 359
Riessman, C. K., 351
Riggan, M., 25, 360
Roberts, H. V., 305–306
Robinson, K., 276
Rosenthal, R., 297
Rossman, G. B., 346
Roulston, K., 357
Rubin, H. J., 357
Rubin, I. S., 357
Ryan, G. W., 208, 358

Saldaña, J., 8, 9, 45, 51, 72, 73–74, 96, 99,
    159, 173, 180, 181, 182, 183, 198, 211,
    222, 236, 239, 278, 280, 283, 286, 299,
    302, 303, 305, 308, 313, 329, 334–335,
    346, 352, 353, 359
Sameshina, P., 187
Sandelowski, M., 103, 361
Sandstrom, K. L., 355
Savin-Baden, M., 103, 361
Sawyer, R. D., 349
Schensul, J. J., 358
Schillemans, L., 158
Schneider, C. J., 359
Schön, D. A., 353

Schreier, M., 280, 359
Schreiner, A. E., 360
Schwandt, T. A., 345
Seidman, I., 185, 357
Shandy, D. J., 179, 349
Shaw, L. L., 93, 357
Sieber, J. E., 61, 62–63
Silver, C., 50, 360
Silverstein, L. B., 358
Silvester, J., 222
Smith, A. D., 186
Smith, J. A., 350, 354
Snow, D. A., 115, 346
Somekh, B., 352
Spradley, J. P., 179, 181, 314, 349, 357
Spry, T., 351
Stafford, F. P., 201
Stake, R. E., 104, 346, 350
Stern, P. N., 350
Stiegelbauer, S., 134
Stratton, P., 222
Strauss, A. L., 99, 350
Stringer, E. T., 353
Sullivan, P., 359
Sunstein, B. S., 349

Tashakkori, A., 45, 346–347
Taylor, B. C., 354
Taylor, B. L., 53
Taylor, J., 355
Teddlie, C., 45, 346–347
Thomas, J., 349
Thomas, R. M., 347, 353
Thomson, P., 356
Thomson, R., 353
Tisdall, E. K., 356
Tracy, S. J., 346
Tufte, E. R., 118

van Maanen, J., 26, 62, 64, 327, 328, 361
van Manen, M., 350

Wadsworth, Y., 350, 353
Wallis, W. A., 305–306
Walsh, D. J., 355
Warner, W., 309
Wertz, F. J., 359
Wheeldon, J., 359
Williams, J. M., 361
Wiseman, B., 349
Wolcott, H. F., 122, 162, 311, 313, 337, 349,
    355, 359, 361
Woods, P., 361

Yardley, L., 354
Yin, R. K., 30, 33, 103, 350

Zeller, N., 324

Subject Index

Action orientation of findings, 314–315
Action research, 8
    resources, 352–353
Advocacy issues, 64
Advocacy tale, 328, 331
Affective coding methods, 75–76
    emotion, 75
    evaluation, 76
    values, 75–76
Agreements with study participants, 56–58
    updating, 68
Analytic induction, 292
Analytic memoing, 95–99, 242, 321
Analytic terms, 179
Anonymity, 57, 63
AnSWR, 47, 48
Anticipatory data condensation, 18
Application of research findings, 314–315
Artifacts, 357
Arts-based research, 8, 334–335
    privacy issues, 63
    resources, 351–352
Assertions, 99–100
ATLAS.ti, 47, 182
Attitudes, 76
Attribute coding, 79
Audiences, 5, 315–316, 325–327
Audio recordings, 11
Auditing, 317
Authenticity of conclusions, 312–313
Autoethnodrama, 334–335
Autoethnography, 8, 351

Beliefs, 76
Belmont Report, 67
Benefits of research, 60–61, 315
Bias, 294
    checking for researcher effects, 296–299
    effects of site on researcher, 298–299
    elite, 294, 298
    feedback, 309
    researcher effects on site, 297–298
Bibliography of qualitative research resources.
    See Qualitative research resources
Building a logical chain of evidence,
    231, 242, 290–292

Case analysis meeting, 122, 128–131
Case-based ordering. See Ordering methods,
    ordering by cases
Case dynamics matrix, 228, 231–234
Case-ordered descriptive meta-matrix,
    214–220
Case-ordered predictor-outcome
    meta-matrix, 268

Case-oriented approaches, 102–103
    construct tables, 172
    mixed strategies, 103
    network displays and, 111
    pre-structured case, 154–157
Case studies
    case definition, 28–30
    resources, 350
    subcases, 29
Case summary, 131–134
CAT (Coding Analysis Toolkit), 47
Categories or themes, pattern codes, 87
Causal chains, 234–236, 265
Causal network, cross-case analysis, 235,
    247–253
    assembling the networks, 248
    isolating causal streams, 248–250
    pattern matching, 250
    variable lists, 253
Causal network, within-case analysis, 235,
    236–247
    causal fragments, 238–239
    codes, analytic memos, and summaries, 242
    event-state networks and, 239
    inductive and deductive approaches to
        building, 237–238
    narrative, 245–246
    recommendations, 245, 247
    variable list generation, 241–242
Causal-prediction models, 256, 266–271
Causal streams, 243, 245, 248–250, 259
Causation, qualitative analysis and assessing,
    222–223. See also Explanatory methods,
    explaining causation
Causation coding, 79, 242
Cause and effect, 222
    causal chains, 235–236
    influences and affects, 222, 236
Causes/explanations, pattern codes, 88
Censorship rights, 58
Chain of evidence, building,
    231, 242, 290–292
Checklist matrix, 142–148
Children, research with, 60
    resources, 355–356
Clustering, 117, 138–140, 174,
    204, 213, 234, 279–280
Codes and coding, 14, 71–72, 341
    advice, 93
    applications, 73
    assertions and propositions, 99–100
    causal networks and, 242
    contact summary forms, 127
    creating codes, 81
    data condensation, 73

deductive and inductive, 81
definition, 72
definitions of codes, 84–85
documentation, 319–320
First Cycle to Second Cycle transformation, 89–91
intracoder and intercoder agreement, 85
jottings, 93–95
levels of coding detail, 85–86
revising codes, 82
simultaneous coding, 81
software tools, 81, 82, 84, 88
start lists, 81
structure and unity in code lists, 82–84
subcoding, 76, 80
team coding, 84
Codes and coding, First Cycle examples
affective methods, 75–76
elemental methods, 74–75
exploratory methods, 76–77
grammatical methods, 79–81
literary and language method, 76–77
procedural methods, 78–79
See also specific methods
Codes and coding, Second Cycle, 72, 86–93, 242. See also Pattern coding
Codes of ethics, 58
Cognitive dissonance, 293
Cognitive maps, 182, 187–191
Collaborative research model, 56, 58
Color coding, 219
Community-based research, 315
Comparable case selection, 32
Comparison/contrast tactics, 117, 142, 146, 150, 163, 166, 178, 218, 234, 266, 268, 284
Competence of researchers, 59
Composite sequence analysis, 206, 211–214
Comprehensive sampling, 32
Computer assisted qualitative data analysis software (CAQDAS), 47–50, 108
checklist matrix formatting, 144
coding tools, 81, 82, 84, 88
"comments" capability, 93
data entry for display formats, 116
data reformatting capability, 114
documentation capabilities, 321
drawing causal streams, 247
drawing cognitive maps, 190
drawing taxonomies, 182
event-state networks, 209
matrix display capability, 228
meta-matrix generation, 140
network displays and, 112
resources, 359–360
Conceptual framework, 20–25
advice, 25
example, 21–24
research questions and, 26–27
Conceptually clustered matrix, 170–171, 173–178

Conceptual/theoretical coherence, 230, 292–293
Conclusion drawing and verification, 13–14, 275–276
from matrix and network displays, 117–118
generating meaning. See Meaning, tactics for generating
qualitative metasynthesis resources, 361
See also Findings, tactics for testing or confirming
Conclusions, standards for the quality of, 310–311
external validity/transferability/fittingness, 314
internal validity/credibility/authenticity, 312–313
objectivity/confirmability, 311–312
reliability/dependability/auditability, 312
utilization/application/action orientation, 314–315
Confessional tale, 327, 328, 330–331
Confidentiality, 57, 63, 67, 317
Confirmability of research conclusions, 311–312
Confirmatory research, instrumentation considerations, 39
Confirming and disconfirming cases, 32
Confirming findings. See Findings, tactics for testing or confirming
Consent issues, 59–60
Constant comparison method, 285, 292
Construct table, 170, 171–173
Contact summary form, 122, 124–128
Content analysis, 8
Content-analytic summary table, 142, 148–150
Context chart, 162, 167–170
Contrast/comparison tactics, 117, 142, 146, 150, 163, 166, 178, 218, 234, 266, 268, 284
Contrast table, 142, 150–152, 284
Convenience sampling, 32
Conversation analysis, 8
Costs of research, 60–61
Counting, 117, 140, 150, 152, 163, 234, 282–284
Craft of research, 7
Credibility of research conclusions, 312–313
documentation and, 315
See also Conclusions, standards for the quality of
Critical case, 32
Critical ethnography, 315
Critical voice, 327, 331–332
Cross-case analysis, 101
causal network, 235, 247–253
conceptual framework and, 20
content-analytic summary table, 148–150
interim summaries, 133
meta-matrix displays, 136

predictor-outcome-consequences matrix, 263
  strategies for, 102–103
  variables versus cases, 101–102

Data accounting log, 122–124
Data collection, 11, 341
  agreements with participants, 57
  concurrent data analysis, 70
  display design and, 112–113
  instrumentation, 37–42
  research questions and, 26
  resources, 356
  selective process, 73
  sequential analyses, 157–159
  staffing issues, 52
Data condensation, 12
  anticipatory research design decisions, 18
  clustering and, 279
  coding as, 73
  metaphors and, 281
  See also Codes and coding;
    Display methods
Data display methods. *See* Display methods
Data entry, for display formats, 115–116
Data management, 50–52, 341
Data overload, 4, 20, 73, 155, 278
Data processing and preparation, 71
Data quality issues, weighting the
  evidence, 301
Decision modeling, 206–208
Dedoose, 47
Deductive approach, building causal networks,
  237–238
Deductive coding, 81
Delusional error, 304
Dependent variables, effects matrix, 231
Descriptive coding, 74
Descriptive methods, 161–162, 341
Descriptive methods, describing action,
  162, 182
  cognitive maps, 182, 187–191
  poetic display, 182, 185–187
  vignettes, 182–185
Descriptive methods, describing
  participants, 162
  context chart, 162, 167–170
  role-ordered matrix, 162–167
Descriptive methods, describing variability,
  162, 170–171
  conceptually clustered matrix, 170–171,
    173–178
  construct table, 170, 171–173
  folk taxonomy, 171, 179–182
Deviant cases, 32
Dimensions, construct tables and, 172
Discourse analysis, 8, 351
DiscoverText, 47
Display methods, 5, 12–13, 107–109, 341, 343
  accompanying text, 117
  conceptual framework, 21–24

cross-case analysis and, 102–103
  data entry, 115–116
  descriptive uses. *See* Descriptive methods
  documentation and, 319, 321
  explanatory uses. *See* Explanatory methods
  exploratory uses. *See* Exploratory methods
  extended text, 13
  format options, 109–112
  getting feedback from participants and, 310
  making inferences and drawing conclusions,
    117–118
  ordering uses. *See* Ordering methods
  predictive uses. *See* Predictive methods
  progressive presentation modes, 334–335
  reporting format and, 118
  reports as displays, 325
  software tools, 48, 108
  timing of display design, 112–113
  "you know what you display," 13, 108
  See also Matrix display methods; Network
    display methods
Documentation, 315–321
  code lists, 319–320
  displays and, 319, 321
  form for, 317–321
  recommendations, 321
  software tools, 321
Dramaturgical coding, 76–77
Duoethnography, 8

Education-oriented qualitative research
  resources, 354–355
Effects matrix, 228–231, 239
Elemental coding methods, 74–75
  descriptive, 74
  in vivo, 74
  process, 75
Eliminative induction, 292
Elite bias, 294, 298
Emotion coding, 75
Enumerative induction, 292
Ethical issues, 55–56
  advice, 67–68
  agreements with participants, 56–58
  benefits, costs, and reciprocity, 60–61
  codes of ethics, 58
  competence, 59
  dilemmas, 67
  documentation and, 317
  harm and risk, 61–62
  honesty issues, 62
  informed consent, 59–60
  intervention and advocacy, 64
  ownership of data and conclusions,
    65–66
  predictions, 260
  privacy, confidentiality, and anonymity,
    57, 62–63
  research integrity and quality, 64–65
  scientific understanding versus individual
    rights, 66–67

study applications, 315
   use and misuse of results, 66
   worthiness of project, 59
Ethnodrama, 8
Ethnographic methods, 8
   progressive presentation modes, 334–335
   resources, 348–349
   writing example, 328–329
Evaluation coding, 76
Evaluation research, 315
   resources, 350
Evaluative validity, 315
Event-listing matrix, 194–198
Event-state network, 206, 209–211, 239
"Experimenter" effect, 297
Explanatory effects matrix, 122, 140–142
Explanatory methods, 221–223, 341
   assessing causation, 222–223
   variables and processes, 223
Explanatory methods, explaining causation,
   223, 234–235
   causal chains, 234–236
   causal network, cross-case analysis, 235,
     247–253
   causal network, within-case analysis, 235,
     236–247
Explanatory methods, explaining change,
   223, 228
   case dynamics matrix, 228, 231–234
   effects matrix, 228–231
Explanatory methods, explaining
   interrelationship, 223
   variable-by-variable matrix, 223–228
Exploratory methods, 121–122, 341
Exploratory methods, exploring fieldwork in
   progress, 122
   case analysis meeting, 122, 128–131
   contact summary form, 122, 124–128
   data accounting log, 122–124
   explanatory effects matrix, 122, 140–142
   interim case summary, 122, 131–134
   partially-ordered meta-matrix,
     122, 135–140
Exploratory methods, exploring reports in
   progress, 154
   pre-structured case, 154–157
   sequential analyses, 154, 157–159
Exploratory methods, exploring variables, 142
   checklist matrix, 142–148
   content-analytic summary table, 142,
     148–150
   contrast table, 142, 150–152
   two-variable case-ordered matrix, 142,
     152–154
Exploratory methods of coding, 77–78
   holistic, 77
   hypothesis, 78
   provisional, 77–78
Exploratory research, instrumentation
   considerations, 39

Extended text, 13, 108
External reliability, 311
External validity/transferability/fittingness of
   conclusions, 314
Extreme cases, 32, 154, 218, 271, 302–303.
   See also Outliers

Factor analysis, 286
Factoring, 154, 286–287
Feedback from participants, 239, 258,
   309–310
Field notes, data processing and
   preparation, 71
Findings, quality of. *See* Conclusions,
   standards for the quality of
Findings, tactics for testing or confirming,
   293–295
   checking for representativeness, 295–296
   checking for researcher effects, 296–299
   checking out rival explanations, 89, 117,
     231, 271, 308–309
   checking the meaning of outliers, 268, 271,
     301–302
   following up surprises, 117, 166, 234,
     303–304
   getting feedback from participants, 239,
     258, 309–310
   looking for negative evidence, 231,
     259–260, 304
   making if-then tests, 117, 139, 166, 257,
     291, 304–305
   replicating a finding, 307–308. *See also*
     Replication
   ruling out spurious relations, 305–307
   sources of analytic bias, 294
   triangulation, 117, 157, 299–300, 307
   using extreme cases, 32, 154, 218, 271,
     302–303
   weighting the evidence, 300–301
Folk taxonomy, 171, 179–182
Following up surprises, 117, 166, 234,
   303–304
Formalization, 7, 343
Formal voice, 328
Freedom of Information Act, 65

Generalizability, multiple-case research
   and, 34, 101
Generalization, 282, 295
   checking for representativeness, 295–296
   external validity/transferability/fittingness, 314
   pitfalls, 295
   subsuming particulars into the general, 170,
     285–286
Genres of qualitative research, 8–9
Going native, 294, 296, 298
Goodness of research findings and conclusions.
   See Conclusions, standards for the quality
   of; Findings, tactics for testing
   or confirming

Grammatical methods of coding, 79–81
  attribute, 79
  magnitude, 80
  subcoding, 80
Grounded theory, 8, 31
  causation coding, 79
  constant comparison methods, 285
  construct tables, 171
  process coding, 75
  resources, 349–350
Growth gradient, 194, 198–201, 284

Handbooks of qualitative research, 4, 347
Harm to participants, 61–62
Holistic coding, 77
Holistic fallacy, 134, 294, 307
Homogeneous sampling, 32
Honesty and trust issues, 62
Human communication resources, 354
HyperRESEARCH, 47
Hypothesis development, 12
Hypothesis testing, 12
  counting and, 283–284

If-then tests, 89, 117, 139, 166, 257, 291,
    304–305
Impressionist voice, 327, 328
Individual-level cases, 28–29
Induction, 292
Inductive approach, building causal networks,
    237–238
Inductive coding, 81
Influences and affects, 222, 236
Informed consent, 59–60
Institutional review board (IRB), 317
Instrumentation, 37–42
  advice, 42
  example, 40–41
  preplanning and structuring, 38–40
  research questions and, 26
Interim case summary, 122, 131–134
Internal validity/credibility/authenticity of
    conclusions, 312–313
Interpretation. *See* Conclusion drawing and
    verification
Interpretive synthesis, 103
Intervening variables, 178, 228, 243, 268,
    271, 289–290
Intervention issues, 64
Interview guide, 40–41
Interviewing, 37
  instrumentation considerations, 40–41
  resources, 356–357
Intracoder and intercoder agreement, 85
In vivo coding, 74
Irony, 282
Iteration, 14, 343

Jointly told voice, 328
Jottings, 93–95

Kitchen Stories, 191

Links, 111
Literary and language methods of coding,
    76–77
Literary voice, 328
Logical chain of evidence, building, 231, 242,
    290–292
Longitudinal research, 211
  resources, 353

Magnitude coding, 79
Magnitudes, 44
Matrix display methods, 14, 109–111
  case dynamics matrix, 228, 231–234
  case-ordered predictor-outcome meta-
      matrix, 268
  checklist matrix, 142–148
  conceptually clustered matrix,
      170–171, 173–178
  content-analytic summary table,
      148–150
  data entry, 115–116
  effects matrix, 228–231, 239
  event-listing matrix, 194–198
  explanatory effects matrix, 122, 140–142
  making inferences and drawing conclusions,
      117–118
  meta-matrices, 111, 114, 122, 135–140,
      214–220
  partially-ordered meta-matrix,
      122, 135–140
  pattern coding, 91
  predictor-outcome-consequences matrix,
      256, 262–266, 284
  role-ordered matrix, 162–167
  template formatting, 113–115
  time-ordered matrix, 194, 202–206
  two-variable case-ordered matrix, 142,
      152–154
  variable-by-variable matrix, 223–228
  variable partitioning, 285
Maximum variation sampling, 32
MAXQDA, 47
Meaning, tactics for generating, 277
  building a logical chain of evidence, 231,
      242, 290–292
  clustering, 117, 138–140, 174, 204, 213,
      234, 279–280
  counting, 117, 140, 150, 152, 163, 234,
      282–284
  factoring, 154, 286–287
  finding intervening variables, 178, 228, 243,
      268, 289–290
  making conceptual/theoretical coherence,
      230, 292–293
  making contrasts/comparisons, 117, 142,
      146, 150, 163, 166, 178, 218, 234,
      266, 268, 284
  making metaphors, 204, 280–282, 286

noting patterns, themes, 117, 140, 145, 170, 202, 218, 227, 233, 266, 277–278
noting relations between variables, 152, 154, 163, 178, 204, 218, 287–289
partitioning variables, 138–139, 285
seeing plausibility, 278–279
subsuming particulars into the general, 170, 285–286
Member checking, 58, 63
Memoing, 71
Memoing, analytic, 95–99
Meta-matrices, 111, 114
case-ordered descriptive meta-matrix, 214–220
case-ordered predictor-outcome meta-matrix, 268
partially-ordered meta-matrix, 122, 135–140
Metaphors, 204, 280–282, 333
Metasummary, metasynthesis, and meta-ethnography, 103
Methodological foundations resources, 347
Methods section, 311, 316–317, 344
Metonymy, 282
Microsoft Excel, 47, 108, 144, 218, 219
Microsoft Word, 47, 108, 109, 144, 219
Missing data, 116
Mixed-methods research, 4, 8, 43–45, 343
linking data types, 45
multimethod designs, 45
quantizing level, 44
reporting statistical data, 316
resources, 346–347
Modus operandi logic, 292, 299
Monetary compensation, 61
Multimethod designs, 45
Multiple-case research, 30
case analysis meeting, 128
design considerations, 20
generalizability issues, 34
generating explanations, 223
instrumentation considerations, 39
sampling considerations, 30–31, 33–34
time planning, 52
See also Cross-case analysis

Narrative inquiry, 8
pattern coding, 91
resources, 351
Negative evidence, looking for, 231, 259–260, 304
Nested sampling, 33
Network display methods, 111–112
causal network, cross-case analysis, 235, 247–253
causal network, within-case analysis, 235, 236–247
causal-prediction models, 266–271
composite sequence analysis, 211–214
context chart, 167–170

data entry, 115–116
event-state network, 206, 209–211, 239
folk taxonomy, 179–182
growth gradient, 198–202
making inferences and drawing conclusions, 117–118
noting relations between variables, 287–289
pattern coding, 91–93
software tools, 48, 112
subnetwork, 249
use of bidirectional arrows, 239
Nodes, 111
Nonrepresentative events or activities, generalizing from, 295
Nonrepresentative participants, sampling from, 295
Nonrepresentative processes, drawing inferences from, 295
NVivo, 47, 48, 209

Objectivity/confirmability of conclusions, 311–312
Observation, 37
Online resources, 361–362
Open-ended interviewing, 37
Opportunistic sampling, 32
Oral history, 8
Ordering methods, 193–194, 341
Ordering methods, ordering by cases, 194, 214–220
Ordering methods, ordering by time
event-listing matrix, 194–198
growth gradient, 194, 198–201
time-ordered matrix, 194, 202–206
Ordering methods, ordering processes, 194, 206
composite sequence analysis, 206, 211–214
decision modeling, 206–208
event-state network, 206, 209–211
Outcomes
cross-case causal network analysis, 247
effects matrix, 231–234
predictor-outcome-consequences matrix, 256, 262–266, 284
Outliers, 268, 271, 301–302
maximum variation sampling, 32
Ownership of data and conclusions, 65–66

Paradigmatic corroboration, 45
Partially-ordered meta-matrix, 122, 135–140
Participant benefits from research, 60–61, 315
Participant feedback, 239, 258, 309–310
Participant observation resources, 357
Participatory action research, 56, 58, 352–353
Partitioning, 138–139, 285
Pattern coding, 86
applications, 86
categories or themes, 87
causal networks and, 242
causes/explanations, 88

First Cycle to Second Cycle transformation, 89–91
  generating codes, 86–87
  matrix display, 91
  narrative display, 91
  network display, 91–93
  relationships among people, 88
  theoretical constructs, 88
  using, 88–89
Pattern matching, cross-case causal network analysis, 250
Patterns or themes in data, 117, 140, 145, 170, 202, 218, 227, 233, 266, 277–278
Phenomenology, 8
  construct tables, 171
  resources, 350
Photographs, 71
Photovoice, 8
Plausibility, 278–279
Poetic display, 182, 185–187
Poetic inquiry, 8
Polio patient mortality study, 305–306
Politically important cases, 32
Poststructural voice, 328
Pragmatic realists, 7
Predictive methods, 255–256, 341
  applications, 256–258
  assessing predictions, 262
  causal-prediction models, 256, 266–271
  ethical review, 260
  example, making and justifying a prediction, 258–259
  looking for contrary data, 259–260
  predictor-outcome-consequences matrix, 256, 262–266
  selecting participants to confirm/disconfirm predictions, 260
Predictor-outcome-consequences matrix, 256, 262–266, 284
Presentation modes for research reports, 333–335
Pre-structured case, 154–157
Privacy, 62–63
Procedural methods of coding, 78–79
  causation, 79
  protocol, 78
Process-based ordering. See Ordering methods, ordering processes
Process coding, 74
Processes
  clustering, 280
  nonrepresentative, drawing inferences from, 295
  variables and, 223
Progressive focusing, 292
Progressive presentation modes, 334–335
Propositions, 99–100
Protocol coding, 78
Psychology and qualitative researchx resources, 354
Purposive sampling, 31, 32

QDA Miner, 47, 112
Qualitative data, 4, 10–11, 342
  data overload, 4, 20, 73, 155, 278
  linking qualitative and quantitative data, 42–45
  ownership of, 65–66
  reporting formats and, 324
  strengths of, 11–12
  visual data, 98–99
  words, 10–11, 71
Qualitative data analysis
  as craft, 7, 342
  assessing causation, 222
  audiences for this book, 5
  authors' approach and orientation, 6–7, 9–10
  common features, 10
  concurrent data collection, 70
  core requisites for, 342
  data processing and preparation, 71
  final advice, 343–344
  iteration, 14, 343
  overview of processes, 339–341
  purpose of this book, 4–5
  resources, 357–359
  See also Codes and coding
Qualitative data analysis software. See Computer assisted qualitative data analysis software
Qualitative metasynthesis resources, 361
Qualitative research design. See Research design
Qualitative research genres, 8–9
Qualitative research resources, 4, 344
  action/participatory action research, 352–353
  artifacts/visual and material culture, 357
  arts-based research, 351–352
  autoethnography, 351
  case study research, 350
  data collection, 356
  discourse analysis, 351
  ethnography/anthropology, 348–349
  evaluation research, 350
  general textbooks, 346
  grounded theory, 349–350
  handbooks, 4, 347
  human communication and qualitative research, 354
  interviewing, 356–357
  longitudinal/life course research, 353
  methodological foundations/handbooks, 347
  mixed-methods, 346–347
  narrative inquiry, 351
  online resources, 361–362
  participant observation, 357
  phenomenology, 350
  psychology and qualitative research, 354
  qualitative data analysis, 357–359
  qualitative metasynthesis, 361

reference texts, 344
research design textbooks, 345
research in education, 354–355
researching children, 355–356
sociology, 353–354
symbolic interactionism, 347–348
technology and CAQDAS, 359–360
theory development and applications, 360
Quality of research, 64–65
Quality of research conclusions. *See*
    Conclusions, standards for the quality of
Qualrus, 47
Quantitative data, 42–43
mixed-methods designs, 43–45
See also Mixed-methods research
Quantizing level, mixed-methods designs, 44
Quota selection, 32

Random sampling, 32, 296
Rating scales, 44
Raw data, processing and preparation, 71
Realist approach, 7
Realist voice, 327, 328, 329–330
Record keeping, 122. *See also* Documentation
Reliability/dependability/auditability of
    conclusions, 312
Replication, 103, 227, 307–308
comparable case selection, 32
multiple-case sampling, 33–34
predictor-outcome-consequences
    matrix, 265
See also Triangulation
Reporting findings and conclusions, 324–325
analytic documentation, 315–321
audiences and effects, 325–327
display formats and, 118
methods sections, 311, 316–317
progressive presentation modes, 334–335
reports as displays, 325
strengths of qualitative data, 324
traditional presentation mode, 333–334
voices, 327–332
See also Writing
Representativeness, checking for, 295–296
Reputational case sampling, 32
Research design, 17–19
balance of stories and variables, 333
case definition, 28–30
conceptual framework, 20–25
instrumentation, 37–42
linking qualitative and quantitative data,
    42–45
mixed-methods, 43–45. *See also* Mixed-
    methods research
research questions, 25–28
resources (general textbooks), 345
tight versus loose designs, 19–20
See also Research questions; Sampling
Researcher-as-instrument, 42
Researcher competence, 59

Researcher's bias. *See* Bias
Research integrity and quality, 64–65
Research management issues, 45–46
computer and software use, 46–50
data management, 50–52
staffing, 52
time planning, 52
See also Exploratory methods, exploring
    fieldwork in progress
Research questions, 25–28
advice, 27–28
conceptual framework and, 26–27
conceptually clustered matrices, 174
data collection and, 26
example, 26–27
sampling and instrumentation choices
    and, 26
Rival explanations, 89, 117, 231, 271,
    308–309
Role-ordered matrix, 162–167
Ruling out spurious relations, 305–307

Sampling, 30–37
advice, 36–37
case definition, 29
checking for representativeness, 295–296
example, 34–36
features of qualitative sampling, 31–32
general strategies, 32
pitfalls of generalization, 295
practical guidelines, 35
research questions and, 26
within-case, 33
Second Chair (Saldaña), 334–335
Selective sampling, 295–296
Self-awareness, 344
Semantic relationships, 179
Sequential analyses, 154, 157–159
Settings, 31
Simultaneous coding, 81
Snowball sampling, 32
Sociology resources, 353–354
Software tools. *See* Computer assisted
    qualitative data analysis software
Soup kitchen report writing example, 328–332
Spurious relations, ruling out, 305–307
Stacking comparable cases, 103
Staffing, 52
Standards for the quality of conclusions. *See*
    Conclusions, standards for the quality of
Start lists of codes, 81, 82–84
Statistical data reporting, 316
Sticky notes, 93
Stratification, 296
Structural corroborations, 292
Structural voice, 328
Study findings, testing and confirming. *See*
    Findings, tactics for testing or confirming
Study findings, use and misuse of, 66
Subcoding, 76, 79

Subnetwork, 249
Subsuming particulars into the general, 170, 285–286
Surprises, following up, 117, 166, 234, 303–304
Symbolic interactionism, 347–348
Synecdoche, 282

Taxonomies, 179–182
Team coding, 84
Template formatting, 113–115
Themes, variable-oriented strategies, 103
Themes or patterns in data, 117, 140, 145, 170, 202, 218, 227, 233, 266, 277–278
Theoretical constructs, pattern coding, 88
Theory building, 20
    making conceptual/theoretical coherence, 230, 292–293
    resources, 360
Theory-driven sampling, 31, 33
Theses and dissertations, 335–337
Time-based ordering. *See* Ordering methods, ordering by time
Time-ordered matrix, 194, 202–206
Time planning for research, 52
Transana, 47
Transcription, 11, 71
Transferability of research results, 314
Triangulation, 117, 157, 299–300, 307, 313
Trust issues, 62
Tuskegee Institute syphilis studies, 66–67
Two-variable case-ordered matrix, 142, 152–154
Typical cases, 32

Utilization/application/action orientation of conclusions, 314–315

Validity, 14
    contested term, 313
    ethical dilemmas, 67
    external validity/transferability/ fittingness, 314
    instrumentation considerations, 42
    internal validity/credibility/authenticity, 312–313

sources of analytic bias, 294. *See also* Bias
See also Conclusion drawing and verification; Findings, tactics for testing or confirming
Values coding, 75–76
Variability, describing. *See* Descriptive methods, describing variability
Variable-by-variable matrix, 223–228
Variable exploration methods. *See* Exploratory methods, exploring variables
Variable interrelationships
    intervening variables, 178, 228, 243, 268, 271, 289–290
    noting relations between variables, 152, 154, 163, 178, 204, 218, 287–289
    partitioning, 138–139, 285
    ruling out spurious relations, 305–307
Variable list, causal network, 241–242, 253
Variable-oriented approaches, 102–103
Variable partitioning, 138–139, 285
Variables and processes, 223
Variables versus cases, 101–102
Verification, 13. *See also* Conclusion drawing and verification
Vignettes, 182–185, 330, 333
Visual and material culture, 357
Visual data analysis, 98–99
Voices for report writing, 327–332

Weft QDA, 47, 48
Weighting the evidence, 300–301
Within-case analysis, 100–101
    causal network, 235, 236–247
Within-case sampling, 33
Wordle, 48
Words, as qualitative data, 10–11, 71
Worthiness of research projects, 59
Writing, 321
    audiences and effects, 325–327
    examples, 328–332
    progressive presentation modes, 334–335
    resources, 361
    theses and dissertations, 335–337
    traditional presentation mode, 333–334
    voices, genres, and stances, 327–332
    See also Reporting findings and conclusions